India's Development Experience

*To Shanta Guhan
in the knowledge that it would
have been Guhan's fondest wish*

INDIA'S DEVELOPMENT EXPERIENCE

Selected Writings of S. Guhan

Edited by
S. SUBRAMANIAN

OXFORD
UNIVERSITY PRESS

OXFORD
UNIVERSITY PRESS

YMCA Library Building, Jai Singh Road, New Delhi 110001

Oxford University Press is a department of the University of Oxford. It furthers the
University's objective of excellence in research, scholarship, and education
by publishing worldwide in

Oxford New York

Athens Auckland Bangkok Bogota Buenos Aires Cape Town
Chennai Dar es Salaam Delhi Florence Hong Kong Istanbul Karachi
Kolkata Kuala Lumpur Madrid Melbourne Mexico City Mumbai Nairobi
Paris Sao Paulo Shanghai Singapore Taipei Tokyo Toronto Warsaw

with associated companies in Berlin Ibadan

Oxford is a registered trade mark of Oxford University Press
in the UK and in certain other countries

Published in India
By Oxford University Press, New Delhi

© Oxford University Press 2001
The moral rights of the author have been asserted
Database right Oxford University Press (maker)
First published by Oxford University Press, 2001

All rights reserved. No part of this publication may be reproduced,
stored in a retrieval system, or transmitted, in any form or by any means,
without the prior permission in writing of Oxford University Press,
or as expressly permitted by law, or under terms agreed with the appropriate
reprographics rights organization. Enquiries concerning reproduction
outside the scope of the above should be sent to the Rights Department,
Oxford University Press, at the address above
You must not circulate this book in any other binding or cover and you must
impose this same condition on any acquirer

ISBN 019 565523 0

Typeset in Garamond (TTF)
by Excellent Laser Typesetters, Pitampura, Delhi 110 034.
Printed in India at Saurabh Print-O-Pack, NOIDA, UP
Published by Manzar Khan, Oxford University Press
YMCA Library Building, Jai Singh Road, New Delhi 110 001

But from my first articles to my latest book I have written so much, and perhaps too much, only because I cannot keep from being drawn towards everyday life, towards those, whoever they may be, who are humiliated and debased. They need to hope, and if all keep silent or if they are given a choice between two kinds of humiliation, they will be forever deprived of hope and we with them. It seems to me impossible to endure that idea nor can he who cannot endure it lie down to sleep in his tower. Not through virtue, as you see, but through a sort of almost organic intolerance, which you feel or do not feel. Indeed, I see many who fail to feel it, but I cannot envy their sleep.

Albert Camus

Acknowledgements

In putting together this selection of Guhan's works and writing an introduction for it, I have contracted a number of debts. I am grateful to the editorial staff of Oxford University Press (OUP) for their support in seeing this volume through. I (alongwith OUP) would like to thank the original publishers of Guhan's writings for granting permission to reproduce the pieces in this volume. My colleague D. Jayaraj was unremittingly helpful in consolidating nearly all of Guhan's work for the purpose of selection. I thank him and S. Janakarajan, for their continual support, encouragement, and suggestions (both sought and, especially, unsought) for the book's (and my) improvement. R. Dharumaperumal was, as always, tolerantly and cheerfully prepared to guide me through the mysteries of word-processing. For their eager approval of this project, and their warm acceptance of the invitation to write their recollections of Guhan, I am deeply grateful to Granville Austin, Robert Cassen, Ashoke Chatterjee, Gopal Krishna Gandhi, Barbara Harriss-White, Jonathan Moore, B. K. Nehru, I. G. Patel and Manu Shroff. Whether she knows it or not, Barbara, from afar, was a persistently guiding spirit. Rajeswari Sunder Rajan helped with the introduction, by both offering substantively good counsel and taking a tough line on split infinitives and mixed metaphors. For useful comments on the introduction, I am indebted to Gita Gopalkrishnan and Pushpa Sundar. Gita also went through the entire manuscript and wielded a sharp editorial pencil. Quietly but firmly, my wife Prabha Appasamy both planted and erased doubts, as the situation demanded; and through the inevitable troughs of a project such as this, she has unwaveringly reminded me of the worthiness of the enterprise. Without her support and my daughter Daya's constant designs on my computer time, this book would not have been done.

S. SUBRAMANIAN

Contents

List of Tables	ix
INTRODUCTION	1

Economy, Society, and Polity

1. RURAL POVERTY ALLEVIATION IN INDIA	15
2. APPLES, ORANGES, AND THE MEASUREMENT OF POVERTY	47
3. SOCIAL SECURITY FOR THE POOR IN THE UNORGANIZED SECTOR	50
4. HEALTH IN INDIA DURING A PERIOD OF STRUCTURAL ADJUSTMENT	86
5. SOCIAL EXPENDITURES IN THE UNION BUDGET: 1991–6	103
6. CENTRE AND THE STATES IN THE REFORM PROCESS	125
7. ADJUSTMENT: TO WHAT END?	171
8. SOCIAL DISCRIMINATION AND CASTE RESERVATIONS	203
9. COMPREHENDING EQUALITIES	209
10. DARK FOREBODINGS	227
11. CORRUPTION IN INDIA	245
12. THINKING ABOUT GOVERNANCE	264

Outside the Curriculum

13. BALA'S SRINGARA — 282
14. EIGHT POEMS OF THAYUMANAVAR — 284
15. THE CAT AND THE MAHATMA — 289
16. POLICY, AS IT HAS BEEN LAID DOWN IN THE MUNDAKA UPANISHAD — 293
17. MEMORIES OF AN UNCLE — 295

RECOLLECTIONS OF GUHAN

I called him Guhan Sahib
Granville Austin — 327

S. Guhan: An Appreciation
Robert Cassen — 329

S. Guhan: In Memory
Ashoke Chatterjee — 332

Remembering Guhan
Gopal Krishna Gandhi — 337

The Ferryman
Barbara Harriss-White — 343

Recollections of Guhan
Jonathan Moore — 347

My Life and Crimes with Mr S. Guhan
B. K. Nehru — 351

Guhan: A Charmer and An Activist
I. G. Patel — 356

S. Guhan: A Memoir
Manu Shroff — 358

A Bibliography of Guhan's Works — 361

Tables

1.1	Health Indicators of Some Developing Countries	35
3.1	Protective Social Security Entitlements Available for the Organized Sector in India	53
3.2	Coverage of Social Assistance Schemes in Tamilnadu, 1989–90	62
3.3	Cost of Social Security Schemes in Tamilnadu, 1989–90	64
3.4	Proposed Benefits, Estimated Numbers, and Annual Cost of Protective Social Security for the Poor	69
3.5	Likely Yield from Proposed Social Security Surcharges	72
3.6	Estimated Growth in Coverage of Social Security Schemes	75
3.7	Projections of Eligible Population for Normal Old-age Pensions	76
5.1	Outlays on Rural Development and Social Services in the Central Budget	107
5.2	Outlays in States on Rural Development and Social Services	108
5.3	Integrated Outlays of Centre and States on Rural Development and Social Services	110
5.4	Outlays on Major Rural Development and Social Services Programmes in the Central Budget	113

x □ *Tables*

5.5	Functional Classification of Rural Development and Social Services Outlays in the Central Budget for 1995–6	116
5.6	Transfer Efficiency in the JRY	122
6.1	Tax Structure: Centre and States, 1989–90	129
6.2	Receipts, Transfers and Expenditure: Centre and States, 1989–90	130
6.3	Modalities of Central Transfers to States, 1989–90	131
6.4	Pattern of Expenditure, Centre and States, 1989–90	134
6.5	Eighth Plan Outlays, Centre and States	134
6.6	Eighth Plan Financing Pattern, Centre and States	135
6.7	Fiscal Deficits as a Proportion of GDP, Centre and States, 1980–1 to 1992–3	137
6.8	Imposition of President's Rule in the States	164
6.9	Tenure of Chief Ministers in Major States	165
6.10	Centre–State Nexus in Economic Reforms	169
7.1	GDP Growth Rates, 1960–84	173
7.2	Developing Countries: External Financing, 1980–4	175
7.3	Commodity Price Changes, 1973–4 to 1983–4	177
7.4	Terms of Trade: Annual Rates of Change	177
7.5	Debt Indicators for Developing Countries	179
7.6	Net Resource Receipts of Developing Countries from all Sources	181
7.7	Non-project Lending from the World Bank and IDA	187
7.A1	Imports and GDP: DAC Countries	196
7.A2	ODA Target Performance 1982: DAC Countries	199
7.A3	Incremental Proportions of Government Expenditure Required to Reach ODA Target by 1990: DAC Countries	200
7.A4	Distribution of Multilateral and Bilateral Aid: DAC Countries, 1982	202

Introduction

In this brief introduction, I shall attempt to do three things: provide a capsule account of Guhan's career; introduce the essays in this volume; and offer a somewhat personalized view of what Guhan's work adds up to.

☆

Guhan was born in 1933, the oldest of three children. His father, K. S. Sanjivi, was a distinguished physician, and founder of the Voluntary Health Services, which is now one of the most reputed medical institutions in the city of Chennai. Dr Sanjivi had two older brothers, who both achieved distinction in their respective, chosen fields. The oldest brother, K. Swaminathan, was a well-known professor of English literature at Madras University, but is perhaps most widely recognized for his work as principal editor of *Collected Works of Mahatma Gandhi*. The other brother, K. Venkataraman, was an illustrious chemist, and his name is intimately associated with the National Chemical Laboratory, Pune. He was also the father of Dharma Kumar, the economic historian. All three brothers—Swaminathan, Venkataraman, and Sanjivi—were recipients of the Padma Bhushan. It is unquestionably true that his family background conferred certain distinct advantages on Guhan, in terms of providing an atmosphere and an ambience most pronouncedly conducive to intellectual development as well as to those material comforts which promote the flourishing of the mind and the spirit. Having said this, it must also be said to Guhan's credit that he was never other than soberly sensible of, and grateful for, these advantages.

Guhan had his schooling in Mylapore, the heartland of the Tamil brahmin community in Madras. During his school years, he received a solid foundation in both Tamil and Sanskrit, and these links with early learning were never severed in later life. While Guhan himself grew up in a familial atmosphere of liberalism and emancipation, the larger environment of Mylapore was one of a crabbed, narrow orthodoxy of brahminical outlook and prejudice. To put it neutrally, he must have got to know some interesting people in Mylapore. Towards the end of his life, he once told me (with the sort of delicious cruelty one might expect from a 'Saki' protagonist) that, in a reversal of the Dravidian movement's formal line on caste, brahminism was fine with him; it was brahmins he couldn't stand.

In 1953, Guhan graduated with Honours in Statistics from Presidency College, where he also taught for some time before joining the Indian Administrative Service in 1955, having been ranked first in the all-India competitive examination. In 1956, he married Shanta Krishnaswamy (despite, apparently, having proposed to her and furnished her with eight sound reasons why it might not be such a good idea for her to say yes). In 1979, he took voluntary retirement from the Government of India. In the course of his career as a bureaucrat, he held the positions of Indian Alternate Director of the World Bank (1964–8), Finance Secretary, Government of Tamilnadu (1974–8), and Senior Economist in the Brandt Commission Secretariat (1978–9). During this period, he acquired extensive practical experience in dealing with issues of fiscal economics and international development, which stood him in good stead in his subsequent research endeavours in these fields. After retiring from the government, Guhan embarked upon his career in academics when he joined the Madras Institute of Development Studies (MIDS) in 1979 as a Senior Fellow. Upon retirement from the MIDS in 1993, he was invited to continue as a Professor Emeritus of the Institute. In the course of his career, he served as a consultant to many UN and Bretton Woods agencies, and as adviser to the Chief Minister of Tamilnadu (1989–90). In 1996, Guhan was diagnosed as having oesophageal cancer. The unequal battle was terminated in February of 1998.

✩

Considering that Guhan entered academics only in middle age, his output has been remarkably prolific. Apart from the energy and intellectual stamina which this displays, what is also noteworthy is his versatility of interest as evidenced in the wide compass of subjects he has dealt with. A catalogue—which is very probably incomplete—of Guhan's writings is furnished at the end of this book. Guhan's *curriculum vitae* offers a helpful classification (due to himself) of his work, into the following categories of research interest: international economic relations; Tamilnadu issues; village studies; poverty and poverty alleviation; social security; public finance; centre–state relations; reservations; book reviews; and other.

This volume has been divided into three sections. The first section offers, in so far as it has proved possible, a representative sample of Guhan's academic work, collected under the broad heading of 'Economy, Society and Polity': this constitutes that aspect of his output which (following the BBC) one might call 'hardtalk'. The second section features writings under the heading 'Outside the Curriculum': this consists of non-academic pieces, written in a spirit of both seriousness and levity, but essentially reflective of the relaxedness one associates with a busman's holiday. This section clearly requires no exegesis, and I shall, accordingly, refrain from offering any editorial commentary on it. The third section consists of reminiscences of Guhan written by a small number of persons of whom it can be said that the relationship between Guhan and them was a matter of some significance in the lives of both parties. Again I shall, rightly, have nothing whatever to say by way of introduction or comment on these recollections, which speak for themselves. In what follows, I shall try and briefly introduce the articles figuring in the first section of this volume.

Taking his work as a whole, it is easy to discern that Guhan's most systematic and recurring engagement has been with deprivation and its redressal. This concern has been at the centre of his work, and stands in sharp distinction to his own criticism of policy effort in India: '...whatever might have been the rhetoric of planning or politics, poverty alleviation has been an *adjunct* to India's development plans and policies rather than the *core* of their purpose...'. The first five essays in this volume, allowing for some overlap with his other fields of research interest, represent the core of Guhan's perceptions about, and involvement with, India's social sector.

The first paper, 'Rural Poverty Alleviation in India: Policy, Performance, and Possibilities' offers a comprehensive review of the literature on rural poverty in India. The outcome is a thoroughgoing, systematic, and aggregative synopsis of the prior works of several hands and, as such, provides a detailed and informative account of the subject all in one place. Apart from providing descriptions of trends and magnitudes, a distinctive feature of the paper is its concern with policy questions. A critical appraisal which focuses on the deficiencies of overall state intervention is followed by a responsible set of prescriptions designed to improve, reorient, and supplement existing measures of policy within a framework of reform which abjures a posture of nihilism and hopelessness. The paper's chief merit lies in its usefulness rather than in any startlingly original revelations: it is useful alike for the professional who tends to get lost in the minutiae of his specialization, for the concerned bureaucrat or politician entrusted with policy making, and for the interested and involved lay reader.

The second piece is one for which I have taken the liberty of supplying a title: 'Apples, Oranges, and the Measurement of Poverty'. It is actually a note of dissent addressed to the chairman of an Expert Group (of which Guhan was a member) set up by the Planning Commission to determine norms for assessing the numbers and proportions of persons in poverty. Guhan's concerns, at one level, are methodological; while at another, they attend also to the practical implications of getting methodology right, so that the issue is not reduced to the obdurate fussiness of a pettifogging grammarian. What Guhan is essentially doing is to advance the cause of adopting a relative view of absolute poverty, whereby state-specific particularities are reflected in state-specific poverty lines, which is a matter of some distinctive importance in a federal setting such as India's.

The third piece ('Social Security for the Poor in the Unorganized Sector: A Feasible Blueprint for India') belongs to a province of expertise which Guhan made his especial forte. In this paper (as well as in a number of related works, the details of which are available in the Bibliography), Guhan takes on the hard challenge of actually coming up with a package of practical social assistance measures, complete with estimates of coverage, cost, and feasibility, such as would be required in order to ensure that the policy-maker has to bridge the least possible distance between conceptualization and implementation. Indeed, it is well known that he played a major part in devising the National Assistance Scheme credited to the P. V. Narasimha Rao Government. Apart from demonstrating both the affordability and sustainability of a minimum social security package, covering the requirements of old-age pensions, survivor benefits, maternity assistance, and accident relief for the poorer among the poor, he points out that such a package has something to commend it in terms of cost-effectiveness inasmuch as the problems of adverse selection and moral hazard which bedevil means-tested assistance might be expected to be relatively muted in the present context: old age, death, maternity, and disability are difficult to either simulate or provoke.

In the next paper ('Health in India During a Period of Structural Adjustment'), Guhan considers a crucial aspect of well-being: the health of the population. This invited lecture serves as an occasion for Guhan to again present a lucid account of problems and issues based on a useful survey of the literature. He undertakes three tasks: (i) to review the health status of the population in terms of both input and output related indicators; (ii) to assess the likely impact of structural adjustment on state assistance to the social sector in general, and the health sector in particular; and (iii) to offer policy prescriptions in the light of the findings under (i) and (ii) respectively. The indications with respect to both (i) and (ii) are discouraging, which leads Guhan, in respect of (iii), to assume an explicit stance of advocacy in which he invites the voluntary health sector to engage in mutual networking and liaising, to share a common platform, and to present a united stand against a negligent and irresponsible state.

In 'Social Expenditures in the Union Budget: 1991–6', Guhan combines his concern for the social sector with that specialized public finance expertise which is needed to unravel the mysteries of budgetary documents and make sense of them. This is a task which requires much first-hand familiarity with the rituals and rigours of budgetary exercises, considerable skill in unscrambling accounting eggs, a great deal of patience in keeping track of concepts and definitions, and finally, an ability and willingness to engage in the messy task of taking things apart and putting them together again. Social-sector spending is found to be not only abysmally low but also deficient in respect of an appreciation of priorities. The way is pointed to the benefits that may be had from a reconfiguration of the jurisdiction over specific schemes, and from enhancing their cost-effectiveness through rationalization and streamlining, both on the ground and in the presentation of accounts.

A major strand of Guhan's work has been in the area of centre-state relations, with particular emphasis on problems of federal finance. In 'Centre and States in the Reform Process', he addresses a question which would appear to have been largely neglected both by politicians and academics, namely the role, during a period of macroeconomic stabilization and structural adjustment, of the centre and the state *vis-à-vis* each other within a federal setting. Given the jurisdictional guidelines on the allocation of taxes between the centre and the states and the transfer of resources from the former to the latter, as these are ordained by the Constitution, the quinquennial Finance Commissions, and the Planning Commission, Guhan presents a set of detailed recommendations for a possible division of responsibilities between the centre and the states in relation to various components of the reform package. Guhan is deeply sensible of the fact that federal finance is not just a matter of getting the solution to a programming exercise right: rather, it has to be located squarely within the context of the sort of federal politics which obtains. Here, he points to the disappointing nature of post-1967 centre–state politics, in which the repeated misuse of Article 356 of the Constitution has had such a devastating role to play.

While the preceding paper was concerned with one dimension of how best a country undergoing 'reform' might adapt itself to that process, the next one 'Adjustment: To What End?' deals with the central issue of the adequacy and appropriateness of the 'macroeconomic-stabilization-cum-structural-adjustment' package as a response to a crisis in the economic affairs of a developing country. This paper is representative of one significant set of Guhan's research interests—that constituted by the subjects of international development, economic relations and global finance. Written in the mid-eighties, the paper first undertakes a useful review of the factors underlying and associated with the economic debacles experienced by a number of African, Latin American, and Asian countries. An appendix to the paper highlights a set of concrete and practical measures by which 'automatic resource transfers' could be effected from the developed world and multilateral lending agencies to the developing world. These recommendations of Guhan's, however, would appear to be a counsel of perfection in the face of what is actually available, namely, the Bank–Fund's standard package of macroeconomic stabilization and structural adjustment. Appraising the package as a whole, Guhan refers to the 'harsh and perverse logic of the prescription', one which is inspired not by a model of misfortune and amelioration but by one of crime and punishment.

Guhan's versatility has proved to be deeply antagonistic to an even modest representation of the range of his research: constraints on space have precluded the possibility of featuring, in this collection, two vitally important aspects of his work. The first of these pertains to the area of village studies, and the second to that of riparian dispute settlement. By way of anaemic compensation, the least one can do is to point the interested reader in the direction of the missing pieces.

In this spirit, I would first draw attention to a paper co-authored with Joan Mencher and titled 'Iruvelpattu Revisited', which appeared in the *Economic and Political Weekly* (vol. XVII, nos 23 and 24, June 4 and 11, 1983). In this report of a resurvey of a village in South Arcot district of Tamilnadu, we have a shift in focus from the macro to the micro; from the 'global village' to the local one; from the general to the particular. This work is an example of Guhan's catholic and eclectic approach to the apprehension of social and economic reality. Indeed, Guhan was an enthusiastic sponsor of the view that what he called 'elementary, systematic village studies' should be promoted, to the point where these would become part of collegiate curricula in the social sciences. Apart from constructing a painstaking descriptive mosaic of a set of Tamilnadu villages based on the 1961 Census Village Monographs, Guhan also participated in a resurvey, during the early 1980s, of a group of villages which had originally been surveyed by Gilbert Slater in 1918 and were subsequently resurveyed by other sets of researchers in 1937 and 1961. In approaching village studies through field research, Guhan was inclined to adopt a middle path between quick, touristy, impressionistic appraisals, on the one hand, and endlessly time-consuming 'art for art's sake' varieties of miniaturisation, on the other. 'Iruvelpattu Revisited' represents an attempt at constructing an intertemporal picture of comparison and contrast in the destiny of a single village. The reader will note that while the authors discern considerable changes in the technology and productivity of cultivation, they also find a depressing stagnancy in poverty, inequality and caste discrimination, despite legislation on land reform, minimum wages and the abolition of untouchability. In another three years' time, it will have been two full decades since the Guhan–Mencher study was undertaken: Iruvelpattu is due for yet another resurvey.

A second regretted omission is Guhan's work on the Cauvery river dispute. The most comprehensive treatment of this important subject is to be found in his monograph 'The Cauvery River Dispute: Towards Conciliation' (Frontline Publishers, Madras, 1993). Even a set of excerpts from this book, for them to cohere meaningfully in an integrated whole, would take up far more space than the prescribed length of this collection will permit. All one can do here is to share with the reader the view that the work under review is an excellent example of Guhan's proclivity for engaging squarely with the 'knots and muddles' of contemporaneous problems which have wound their tangled way through the thickets of history to a seemingly intractable impasse. The response, typically, is a mixture of patient scholarship, a cogent and sequential presentation of the contours of the problem, and a commonsensical application of mind to the possibilities of a solution. This work of Guhan's is a particularly impressive illustration of his ability to straddle various disciplines in working his way around a concrete problem—in the present instance, history, geography, hydrology, jurisprudence, politics, diplomacy, and arithmetic.

I return now, from the preceding digression on absences, to a consideration of the writings represented in this volume. The first seven papers in the collection all fall predominantly in the domain of 'economy' while the remaining five essays are more proximately concerned with aspects of 'society and polity'. Three of these five papers deal with two momentous phenomena which have occurred in the final decade of the millenium—those of 'Mandal' and 'Mandir'. Of these, two papers address the questions raised by the decision of the V. P. Singh Government to implement (however thinly) the recommendations of the so-called Mandal Commission Report', relating to reservations for the 'Other Backward Classes' (OBCs) in employment and education. The first, 'Social Discrimination and Caste Reservations' is a compact and clearly argued case for 'reverse discrimination' in favour of groups that have been historically disadvantaged by the accumulated burdens of the caste system; the second, 'Comprehending Equalities' is an extended review article inspired by Mark Gallanter's far-reaching book *Competing Equalities: Law and the Backward Classes in India*. Both pieces are best read together. The third paper, 'Dark Forebodings', is the text of an invited talk on 'Ayodhya and the Future India'. Delivered shortly after the destruction of the Babri Masjid in Ayodhya, this lecture reviews the claims, before rejecting them wholesale, of the Hindu fundamentalists at two levels: those of fact and faith. In all three pieces, it is hard to resist admiration for the way in which evidence is marshalled, in which the argument is structured and unfolded, and in which a certain strategic canniness is deployed to advantage through a cumulation of orchestrated body-blows dealt to the opposition. Above all, one is moved by the strength of feeling and uncompromising courage of conviction that come through.

The last two papers in this collection deal with the themes of, respectively, corruption and governance. The first of these is an editorial introduction to a book on corruption in India. The essay again is characteristic of the way in which Guhan deals with large themes: systematically, cogently, and in such a way that the bits-and-pieces which the typical reader is already familiar with are presented in one orderly and comprehensive whole. While Guhan is clear-eyed about the immensely large obstacle to the developmental process posed by corruption, he steers clear of both 'helplessness' and 'apathy': instead, he advocates concerted public action, not from any presumed facility of this option but from the consideration that if this problem (like that of chronic poverty) must be overcome, it can be overcome.

The final paper in the first part of this volume is the one on 'Thinking About Governance'. It is also the final piece of work which Guhan undertook. It is, in a way, tragically appropriate that Guhan should have signed off with a treatise on governance, explicitly so addressed, since the end to which much of his professional work has been directed is that of appropriate government policy in diverse areas of development activity. Governance, for Guhan, is most fruitfully conceived of as the interplay between a state committed to the Aristotelian goal of human good and the Rawlsian notion of a well-ordered society underpinned by the purposive functioning of institutions. From these foundational issues, he turns to those practical questions which he has always regarded as the appropriate end of academic enquiry, namely, questions relating to the nature and content of good governance. In this connection he presents a large checklist of operational queries, which could serve as a useful spot reference for assessing the quality of governance in specific developing countries. There is no doubt that he would have gone on to address these issues himself had he been permitted the time and the health. But in general terms he does lay down an agenda for academic research. This agenda, as expressed in his own words, is a faithful characterization of the motivation underlying not only the essays collected in this volume but his life's work:

...academic analysis can be important and useful in two main respects: (a) to help in envisioning the principles of good governance steadily and as a whole; and (b) thereby to provide the framework for understanding, interpretation, evaluation and appropriate prescription that might be relevant for the political process whether in constructive or critical ways as circumstances might call for.

☆

I should now like to wind up this introduction with a few observations on what appear to me to be certain salient features of Guhan's work, viewed as a whole.

I shall first consider some possibly problematic aspects of his work. It has to be acknowledged that a career made in equal parts of bureaucracy and academe does not lend itself to uncomplicated appraisal. For one thing, Guhan presents a 'fish or fowl?' kind of problem: even at a gross level of identification, it is difficult to tell whether he was primarily a bureaucrat or an academic. This difficulty is compounded by his own native contrariness. He quite liked to play the role of the academic among bureaucrats, and that of the bureaucrat among academics. The community of civil servants was often a target of his attack for its failure to display imaginativeness or scholarship or the perspective which is afforded by seeing things from afar. The community of professional scholars was equally often a target of his attack for its failure to display social responsibility or a concern with reality or the perspective which is afforded by seeing things from close to. The tension, as far as I can tell, was not ever, even internally, wholly resolved.

Then there is the problem, given the enormous range of subjects Guhan has addressed, of finding a suitable descriptive tag with which to classify him. If one has to fix a label, there may be a case for employing that of 'policy analyst'. A good part of the responsibility for such a label would have to be borne by Guhan who, most especially in the early years of his entry into academics, did much to propagate such an image of himself. In those early years he pushed his own distinctive competence, born of his background and his experience, rather to the hilt; partly, I suspect, in order to underline what he fancied he was best at, and partly for reasons of 'product differentiation', to set himself apart from the imagined preciosity and affectations of the professional scholar: 'Yes, but what's the policy implication of what you say?' was a frequent refrain of his, by way of critical comment on his colleagues' work. The fervour espousing such a reductionist nuts-and-bolts approach did, however, gradually become less conspicuous with time.

So, while 'policy analyst' may justifiably constitute one part of a complicated truth, it is unlikely to add up to anything like the whole truth. It is just too restricted an appellation for Guhan, for it fails to take account of the fact that Guhan evolved. If he taught academics a great deal, he also learnt much from them (although the closest he came to a gracious acknowledgement of this, and that too only when confronted, was by way of flashing a quick and criminal grin). I believe he came to accept that scholarship could not always be expected to yield immediate implications for policy, any more than scholars could always be expected to forsake either their academic predilections or their academic pleasures. Further, Guhan came to see 'policy' less and less in 'managerial' terms and more and more in terms of its implications for the responsibility of the state: to deny, or even to neglect, the question of agency for the state was also to relieve it of accountability, to let it off the hook.

This transformation in orientation was not a product of being 'co-opted': that would have been wholly unacceptable to a proud spirit. But it certainly was a product of allowing oneself to be persuaded by what made sense. The transition is reflected in Guhan's work as it evolved over the years. For instance, one can see that in an early paper, such as the first one included in this collection, the work of other scholar in the measurement of poverty is employed largely as a means to an end, as material that will facilitate policy analysis. In a later paper, 'Apples, Oranges and the Measurement of Poverty', there is direct engagement with a more fundamentally methodological concern. Likewise, the preoccupation with 'policy' can be seen to gradually flower, over time, into involvement with the more ambitious theme of 'governance'. 'Foundational' concerns are less and less treated with suspicion: they are, rather, seen to have both intrinsic usefulness and the value of a certain intellectual enjoyment for the person entertaining them. None of this is to suggest that there were any dramatic breaks and discontinuities. Thankfully not! If the seeds of academic virtue were always present in the early bureaucrat, so too were the fruits of bureaucratic antagonism always present in the later academic. Intolerance did mellow, but never beyond the point of healthy scepticism; and the quest for abstract formulations intensified, without ever breaking free of its pragmatic moorings. As a result, the world of academics has gained immeasurably from the work of Guhan.

The gain is best comprehended by recognizing that, judged according to conventional academic standards, Guhan's work is *different*. To understand and appreciate that work, it is certainly instructive to remember that Guhan turned to academics only after over a half of his entire career had already been spent in the civil services. He did not have a Ph.D. In short, at the time of his entry into academics he was not equipped (nor burdened) with any of the formal trappings of the institutionalized academic scholar. But even when he came to acquire these trappings, even after there had occurred a measure of fusion between the man of the world and the man of letters, he continued to remain sceptical of the wisdom of what he called 'higher minds'. He reverted at will to the status of a remarkably gifted amateur. He firmly refused to leave it up to the professional expert to pronounce magisterially on matters which he believed should be everyman's concern.

It is perhaps in the light of this orientation that one should view the great diversity of themes which he has addressed. Virtually all of these themes are the stuff of which everyday life is made. Guhan's work in its entirety is characterized by a persistent preoccupation with those events and phenomena which have a bearing on economy, polity, and society. What is on display is a sustained, intimate, and critical involvement with the affairs of the world. This involvement is manifested both as an obligation and as a prerogative to intervene. It is Guhan's singular achievement that he succeeded in conferring academic respectability on such an orientation. Indeed, he went further: he often thoroughly shamed the professional specialist, not just in terms of the breadth of his interests but in terms of the depth of his knowledge, acquired through a quite enormous erudition and scholarship.

This does not, of course, mean that Guhan drew distinctions between 'highbrow' and 'lowbrow', still less between 'theory' and 'applied work'. (In passing, one may note that the notion of 'theory' as sin and 'applied research' as a self-conscious virtue is very much the prickly protective suit of the failed theorist.) Guhan could be as abstract or as grassroots as his mood dictated. Here, indeed, he could be, and often was, capricious: if you had your head in the clouds, then that was all right as long as you also had your feet firmly planted on earth; and if you claimed to have your feet firmly planted on the ground, such philistinism would be forgiven only if you also had the ability to occasionally lose your head in the clouds. But these games apart, Guhan's firm commitment was to research which aimed at presenting implementable solutions to real problems.

One outcome of such a commitment is manifested in the language which Guhan employed. He never stumbled into the vices of jargon, obfuscation, or academespeak. To the contrary, his written work is characterized by a clear, elegant, spare, and easily accessed prose. An uncommon feature of his writing is that it is addressed at one and the same time to the professional, the bureaucrat, the politician, and the lay person.

Consistent with this overall approach was Guhan's implicit faith in the persuasive powers of logic and facts. (He owned a well-thumbed paperback book carrying the title *Straight and Crooked Thinking*—a sort of Emily Post's guide to the protocols of rational thought.) Like Sherlock Holmes, he believed it to be a cardinal error to theorize without data. Much of his work was thus inspired by a positivist-empiricist orientation, which I suppose makes him something of a dinosaur in a post-modern world. To make matters worse, there were elements of both essentialism and absolutism in his thought. This, combined with his epistemological predilections and practical concerns invariably led him to take clear and unambiguous positions on issues: things were right or wrong, acceptable or not. In this he was guided by Camus' assessment: 'The tyrannies of today are improved; they no longer admit of silence or neutrality. One has to take a stand, be either for or against.'

To take positions was also to refuse to confine dialogue to one's professional colleagues. In this matter, Guhan had a pronounced desire to speak intelligibly to as many people as possible. As his involvement in politics became deeper and more explicit with time, so too did the perceived need to educate, challenge, and engage with large numbers of people become more and more urgent. He wrote extensively for the newspapers and periodicals, he accepted invitations for lectures at a large number of non-academic fora. But, whether he was writing a newspaper article or addressing undergraduates at a city college, he took the same amount of trouble and expended the same degree of scholarship as he would have done in the cause of a purely academic enterprise. He strongly believed in the importance of being what he called a 'publicist', and deliberately ordained some part of his work so as to be able to realize this end.

There are other ways in which Guhan was a bit *passé*. He was naturally and intensely patriotic, at a time when the nation's fragments have been announced. India could and did enrage him, but he never despaired of the prospects of his country coming good in the end. Somewhere he has written that pessimism, like optimism, should be sober. Likewise, he persistently believed in the improvability of policy, the redeemability of governance, and the reform of the law. The Constitution of India was a sacred text for him—not, of course, in terms of its infallibility, but in terms of its being an important locus of corrective change. Here, again, one comes up against an old-fashioned position which seems to be rather oblivious of a certain revolution in the social sciences wrought by a movement which one might, in an unlettered sort of way, call post-modernism. Guhan, of course, was not oblivious: he had read, with great delight, Malcolm Bradbury on Mensonge.

This book is a record, and therefore a testament. It bears witness to a certain stance, a certain temper, a certain quiddity, a certain veritable 'spirit of the age' which seized and sustained a certain type of Indian intellectual at a certain period in India's history. The value of this record does not depend on its being able to elicit some sort of consensus as to the 'rightness' of its contents. That value, rather, resides in its ability to provoke engagement with a view of the world that reflects its author's lucid intelligence, steadfast honesty, and unsentimental passion.

Economy, Society, and Polity

1

Rural Poverty Alleviation in India
Policy, Performance, and Possibilities*

BACKGROUND

The distributional aspects of India's development experience, in the nearly four decades since she gained freedom from colonial rule (1947–85), are of importance and interest for two broad reasons. First, because of India's size: with about 733 million people (1983), India constitutes 16 per cent of global population and more than a third of the combined population of all low-income countries. The 'absolute poor' in India, of the order of 300 million, are nearly two-fifths of the world's poor.[1] India's efforts to alleviate poverty, and the extent to which they succeed, will therefore be of decisive importance in any global assault on poverty. Secondly, there is the fact that India has not experienced the initial conditions or (at least as yet) the historical conjunctures for a thoroughgoing social and economic revolution such as those witnessed in the USSR, China, and Cuba. Instead, she has pursued a reformist path towards social justice under continued conditions of parliamentary democracy, a federal polity, and a mixed system comprising elements of public ownership and private enterprise in economic activity. Since Independence, political leadership in India has shown remarkable resilience, stability, and continuity. These features have not been common in most Third World countries; while, to that extent, the Indian experience is somewhat unique,

---

* Paper presented in the Franco–Indian Colloquium on Technological Choices for Rural Development, Montpellier, France, 18–20 March 1986.

[1] The World Bank (1980) estimates the 'absolutely poor' in 1980 in the world at 780 million.

it might, at the same time, illustrate the limitations and possibilities for poverty alleviation within the framework of a liberal democracy and an open economy.

The study of the Indian experience is facilitated by the fact that an extensive body of data, analysis, and debate is available on issues related to rural poverty, a field in which Indian academics have been particularly active. It is however possible within the compass of this paper only to give a broad picture at an all-India level which might mask important variations inevitable in a country of continental dimensions that is diverse in numerous ways. This paper begins in section II with a brief account of the evolution of policy towards social justice in India. Section III explains the characteristics of mass poverty in rural India. Section IV attempts an evaluation of the three main pillars on which policy has rested, namely, (a) economic growth, (b) direct anti-poverty programmes, and (c) programmes for the satisfaction of basic needs of social consumption. In the final section, we shall venture to discuss possibilities for a more effective effort for rural poverty reduction within an essentially social democratic framework.

Evolution of Policy

Social justice has featured as a primary objective of the Indian Constitution and in the country's development plans. The First Five-year Plan (1951–6) recognized that 'the urge to economic and social change under present conditions comes from the fact of poverty and of inequalities in income, wealth, and opportunity'. The Second Plan (1956–61) pointed out that 'the benefits of economic development must accrue more and more to the relatively less privileged classes of society.' Towards the end of this plan period, the government explicitly took note of distributional issues by setting up a high-level Committee on Distribution of Income and Levels of Living (1960). In the early years of the Third Plan, the problem of 'absolute poverty' and the need to eradicate it was recognized in an influential paper on 'Implications of Planning for a Minimum Level of Living' prepared in the Perspective Planning Division (PPD) of the Planning Commission (Planning Commission 1962).

The paper pointed out that 'the stage has now come when we should sharply focus our efforts on providing an assured minimum income to every citizen of the country within a reasonable time.

Progressively this minimum itself would be raised as development goes apace.' It then argued that 'the minimum which can be guaranteed is limited by the size of the total product and the extent of redistribution which is feasible' and proceeded to point out that 'output would have to be increased very considerably' to raise the standard of living of the vast masses of the people since large-scale redistribution of a low aggregate output would (a) entail 'revolutionary changes in property rights and in the scale and structure of wages and compensations', (b) leave the average standard of the poorest at a 'pitifully low' level despite a material improvement from their current standards, and (c) make the mobilization of savings for investment and future growth 'far more difficult'. For these reasons, the paper concluded that the appropriate strategy would be to attempt the highest feasible rate of overall economic growth, combining it with an increase in the public ownership of the means of production and redistributive taxation which can finance social consumption needs such as health and education for the poor and which could reduce, in the long run, inequalities in wealth, income, and opportunity. The PPD paper projected that an overall growth of 7 per cent per annum in 1966–76 would be able to assure a minimum consumption of Rs 20 per capita per month for the third poorest decile at the end of the period. It left the poorest two deciles to be taken care of by 'specific steps to deal with their problems' but did not discuss what these steps might be. Another element of this broad strategy, which was reflected in the Second Plan model, was encouragement, through regulatory and promotional policies, for labour-intensive cottage, village, and small-scale industries as a means of generating employment as well as expanding the supply of mass consumption goods.

The Fourth Plan (1969–74) continued the growth-oriented approach to poverty alleviation and began also to include direct programmes to benefit poverty groups and backward regions such as programmes for rural employment, the development of dry-farming areas, and for the benefit of small farmers, marginal farmers, and agricultural labour. The major programmes were the Drought Prone Areas Programmes (DPAP), the programme for the development of small and marginal farmers and agricultural labour (SMAL), and employment programmes dating from the early sixties such as the Rural Manpower Programme (RMP), the Crash Scheme for Rural Employment (CSRE), and the Pilot Intensive Rural Employment Programme (PIREP). A preparatory document for the Fifth Plan

(Planning Commission 1972) went a step further in calling for 'a direct attack on unemployment, under-employment, and poverty' with 'adequate growth' and argued that the economy 'has now reached a stage where a larger availability of resources makes it possible' to launch such a direct attack. The elements of the direct attack were basically employment generation in rural areas through public works programmes and the provision of 'basic minimum needs' to the poor such as health, education, drinking water supply, and housing. The Fifth Plan (1974–9) continued and enlarged some of the special programmes begun in earlier plans and included a National Minimum Needs Programme comprising elementary education, rural health, rural water supply, rural roads, rural electrification, housing for rural landless labourers, environmental improvement of urban slums, and nutrition for pregnant and nursing mothers and pre-school children and school meals for primary school children in the age group 6 to 11. The Sixth Plan (1980–5) took a distinct step further by including two types of programmes for the 'direct' alleviation of poverty: (a) rural public works programmes such as the National Rural Employment Programme (NREP) and the Rural Labour Employment Guarantee Programme (RLEGP) and (b) a set of programmes, with the Integrated Rural Development Programme (IRDP) as the core, which seek to assist 'target group' households below the poverty line through 'an appropriate package of technologies, services, and asset transfers' so as to lift such households on a sustained basis above the poverty level. The Seventh Plan (1985–90), which has been recently published (November 1985), continues with basically the same set of schemes for direct poverty alleviation.

Policy in India toward poverty alleviation has thus evolved in a gradualist fashion over some four decades spanned in the seven Plan periods (1951–90). It has not undergone any radical transformation although mutations can be discerned. Throughout, far-reaching structural changes in asset ownership, property rights, and in processes of production and distribution have been ruled out; or, they have been allowed to remain at the level of non-operationalized objectives.[2] The pursuit of growth, supplemented with fiscal redistribution, better regional balance, and encouragement to small-scale manufactures,

[2] The replacement of individual landownership with cooperative farming was, for instance, publicly favoured by Prime Minister Jawaharlal Nehru in the early fifties.

has been the main plank of policy. Since about the mid-sixties, the growth-oriented approach has been combined with increased resource allocations for the provision of minimum needs and a set of programmes for improving employment and incomes for poor households conceived of as a 'target group'. 'Growth and social justice' in the earlier phase—in the fifties and early sixties—coincided with a period of sustained improvements in GNP. The mutation to 'growth with social justice' since the mid-sixties could be traced to a variety of factors such as a deceleration in the growth rate, widening regional and inter-class disparities consequent on the 'Green Revolution',[3] internal dissensions in the ruling Congress party',[4] and the confidence that a higher base of development might permit larger resources being devoted to welfare and poverty alleviation. Policies of international agencies which began emphasizing basic needs and direct anti-poverty programmes in the late sixties have also played a not insignificant role.[5]

CHARACTERISTICS OF MASS POVERTY IN INDIA

Mass poverty can be understood as a condition in which very large numbers and a sizable proportion of the population persistently suffer from the lack of adequate food and other basic needs of personal and social consumption. Inequality and poverty were not unknown in India in pre-British times but it is perhaps the colonial period which was responsible for the emergence and accentuation of mass poverty on the scale in which we know it (Raychaudhuri 1985). Among the causal factors for this were wars, famines, and economic dislocation; the colonial land settlement systems, high land taxes, and commercialization of agriculture; the continuous 'drain' of surpluses from

---

[3] 'Green Revolution' has come to mean the new technology in agriculture introduced in India in the mid-sixties based on high-yielding seeds for wheat and rice, developed respectively in Mexico and the Philippines, with complementary inputs of irrigation and chemical inputs such as fertilizers and pesticides.

[4] There was a major split in the Congress party in 1969, initiated by Prime Minister Indira Gandhi, on the basis of a 'socialist' platform, which included the nationalization of major commercial banks and the introduction of a few direct programmes for poverty alleviation.

[5] For these developments, mainly in the International Labour Organization and in the World Bank under the presidency of Robert McNamara, see ILO 1976, van de Laar 1980, and Ayres 1983.

India to the metropolitan power; stagnant, if not declining, agricultural productivity; the neglect of industrialization; and population increase.[6]

Poverty as an interlocking condition of assetlessness, underemployment, low wages and incomes, proneness to disease, illiteracy, economic vulnerability, social disadvantage, and political powerlessness is well understood. But, its measurement needs concepts and yardsticks. In the early sixties, when the problem of 'absolute poverty' began to be discussed in India, a distinguished group of economists and public personalities proposed a 'poverty line' equivalent to a per capita monthly consumption of Rs 15 in rural areas and Rs 20 in urban areas in 1960–1 prices (Planning Commission 1962). This normative level or 'poverty line', consumption below which is taken as 'absolute poverty' has come to be widely used in India for poverty estimates. More recently, the Planning Commission has been using a norm related to a per capita daily calorie consumption of 2400 calories in rural areas and 2100 calories in urban areas (Planning Commission 1981). These two norms yield a range, in terms of the monthly per capita consumption level, of Rs 78.5 to 101.8 in rural areas and Rs 117.5 to 129.2 in urban areas in 1983–4 prices.

In current exchange rates, the rural poverty line is in the range US $ 78–102 per capita per annum and the urban poverty line in the range of US $ 118–130. In terms of international purchasing power parities, the equivalences can be estimated to be in the range of US $ 250–330 for rural poverty (per capita per annum) and US $ 380–420 for urban poverty.[7] The Indian rural poverty line is thus about one-sixth to one-third of US $ 1000–1500 per capita per annum which is considered as poverty in the United States. While what might be considered as the bare necessities of life differ from country to country on account of a variety of factors (Townsend 1970), it will be clear even so that the official as well as the academic notions of poverty in India tend to be conservative, closely related as they are to simple subsistence. In this context, a great deal of discussion that has taken place among Indian academics that poverty defined in this way does not necessarily entail 'malnourishment' in

---

[6] See in this connection Naoroji 1876, Dutt 1940, George Blyn 1966, and Dantwala 1973.

[7] The equivalences are based on those worked out for 1975 in Kravis *et al.* 1975.

all cases of the poor at all times would seem to be largely beside the point.[8]

A systematic analysis of trends in rural poverty indicates that the proportion of the population in rural India below the poverty line has fluctuated from year to year over the period 1957-8 to 1973-4 but there is no evidence for any significant trend of increase or decrease (Ahluwalia 1978). The proportion declined from about 50 per cent in 1957-8 to about 40 per cent in the early sixties, peaked at nearly 57 per cent in 1966-7 (a year of serious and widespread drought), and declined to 46 per cent in 1973-4.[9] The pattern has been for the proportion to fall in years of good agricultural output and to rise in years in which crop production is affected on account of adverse weather conditions. The level and trends in the rural poverty proportion show broad variations amongst the states in India. Punjab and Haryana have shown a relatively low incidence (20 to 30 per cent), the eastern states of Bihar, Orissa and West Bengal have had a relatively high ratio (55 per cent or more in most years) with the other states being closer to the all-India average. At the all-India level, there is strong support for the hypothesis that the trends in rural poverty are inversely related to agricultural performance but the evidence at the level of individual states is much less clear. In quite a few of the states, notably Punjab and Haryana who have had an excellent agricultural performance, this relationship did not hold, leading to the conclusion that there may be 'processes at work in the rural economy' which offset the poverty-reducing effects of any increase in per capita agricultural output.

Given the increase in aggregate population, the absolute numbers of the rural poor have gone up from about 170 million in 1957-8 to

[8] The controversy has been around Sukhatme 1977. He pointed out that not all those who may fall below a uniform subsistence-related poverty line could be taken to be 'malnourished' because there are important intra- and inter-individual variances in calorie requirements and intakes. See also Srinivasan 1979.

[9] Ahluwalia's analysis extends only to 1973-4. Based on a two-point comparison between 1977-8 and 1983-4, the Planning Commission (Planning Commission 1985b) has recently claimed that there has been a rather rapid decline in the poverty ratio from 48.3 to 37.4 per cent in this short period. The claim can be questioned on the ground that a two-point comparison over six years cannot indicate a long-term trend, or in fact any trend at all. The methodology followed by the Planning Commission is also materially different from that in the long-term analysis of Ahluwalia.

about 200 million in 1983–4. About 70 per cent of the 'absolutely poor' in India live in its rural areas. In so far as urban poverty is a spill-over of rural distress via migration, rural poverty forms not only the bulk but also the core of the Indian poverty problem.

There are no definitive estimates of the composition of the poor in relation to landholding or in terms of occupational groups. Indicative calculations show that about a half to two-thirds of households belonging to small farmers (operating two hectares of land or less), about three-fourths or more of agricultural labour households and about two-thirds to three-fourths of non-agricultural labour households (artisans, weavers, casual labour, fishermen, etc.) may fall within the poverty line (Minhas 1974; Kurien 1977). Probably more than half of the poor are small farmers, about a third are agricultural labour with the rest being non-agricultural workers and others like the old, handicapped and destitute who are outside the pale of economic activity (Guhan 1981). The incidence of poverty is also particularly high (and has remained so) among socially disadvantaged sections of the population such as the Scheduled Castes and the Scheduled Tribes (Hanumantha Rao 1985). Demographic factors are an important factor in poverty: the poor are characterized by larger households, with a higher proportion of children aged less than 15 years and therefore higher dependence ratios (Vaidyanathan 1974; Visaria 1980). Another dimension is vulnerability to seasonal fluctuations within and between years. In the off-season, there is little employment and wages are low for the farm worker. The small peasant has to sell his grain at low post-harvest prices to meet various commitments and buy in the market later in the year when prices are high. Poverty is also accentuated during the wet season when food shortages, increased morbidity and agricultural work coincide, and becomes acute during periods of severe and prolonged drought (Chambers et al. 1981).

Poverty and Employment

The nexus between rural poverty on the one hand and employment and unemployment in rural areas on the other requires some discussion. The share in aggregate employment attributable to rural areas is 80 per cent and to agriculture and allied activities about 70 per cent. In the two decades 1961–81, the share of agriculture in NDP fell from 49 to 36 per cent but the share of agriculture in employment has declined only slightly, from about 70 to 67 per cent (Rao 1983). In fact, despite growth in industry and tertiary economic activities, the share of agriculture in employment has been consistently above 70 per cent over six decades (1911–71). This is on account of factors related to capital intensity, the product mix, and technological choices in industrial production which have resulted in employment in industry not keeping up with growth in its output.[10] Consequentially, agriculture and other rural activities have had to absorb, as well as they might, the very large bulk of the increase to the work force.

On the structure of employment, estimates relating to the early seventies showed that about 58 per cent of the rural workforce were self-employed, about 10 per cent were regular wage earners and about 30 per cent were casual workers (GOI, Planning Commission 1977). The 'totally' or 'chronically' unemployed were less than two per cent which may seem a low proportion but in absolute numbers as high as four million, by no means insignificant in a very poor country with no employment relief benefits. Under-employment is much the more serious problem. The most comprehensive available measure of it indicates that lack of work for those willing to work and seeking it was about four times as high as unemployment *per se* and equivalent at the end of the seventies to over 19 million person years, of which nearly two-thirds was to be located in rural areas.[11] 'The enormous problem,' as Raj Krishna (1984b) points out, is 'the discontinuous underemployment of a section of the labour force whose composition changes from day to day'. This section consists for the most part of small and marginal farmers and landless agricultural and non-agricultural workers, including women. The pressure on the market for wage labour, on the supply side, has intensified on account of a number of factors: demographic pressure, the marginalization of landholdings in successive generations, dispossession of tenants, and decline in rural household industries. There has been a marked increase in rural labour households as a percentage of all rural households from around 25 per cent in 1964–5 to nearly 40 per cent in 1983–4 with a steep rise within such households of those who depend on casual as distinct from regular wage or salaried employment

---

[10] Raj Krishna (1984b) estimates that the increase in capital intensity in the economy offset more than half of the employment effect of growth in investment.

[11] The best available comprehensive measure of unemployment including underemployment is the 'daily status' estimate. See Raj Krishna 1984b.

(Vaidyanathan 1986). Besides, self-employed cultivators and wage workers do not represent mutually exclusive categories: many of those, whose primary occupation may be the cultivation of owned or rented land, are also in the market for casual labour from time to time.

Rural poverty in India is a much more massive problem than rural unemployment because 'employment' *per se*, whether self-employment on small holdings or intermittent work for low wages, does not yield adequate incomes. In this connection, the distribution of landholdings and the low level of available wage employment become relevant. Landownership in India is highly concentrated: less than 10 per cent of cultivators own more than 10 acres of land but together account for over 50 per cent of land owned, while 40 per cent of cultivators with less than one acre of land claim hardly two per cent in land ownership. Estimates relating to the mid-seventies indicate that wage employment was available on an average for about only 200 days for male rural labourers and for about 140 days for female workers.

The picture of rural poverty in India can be summed up. Rural poverty accounts for the bulk and is at the root of the poverty problem in India. The incidence of rural poverty has been persistently high over a quarter of a century of planned development, namely, between 40 and 60 per cent, and the rural poor have increased in absolute numbers to the order of 200 million in the early eighties. The incidence has varied from year to year, depending on agricultural performance, but there is as yet no established trend of decline nor a definite association with long-term increases in agricultural output. Regional variations indicate that the north-western states of Punjab, Haryana and possibly western Uttar Pradesh have had a consistently lower incidence while the eastern states of Bihar, Orissa and West Bengal have had consistently high poverty levels.

The rural poor are mainly households belonging to (a) small farmers, owner-cultivators or tenants, operating two hectares or less of land; (b) agricultural labourers, with little or no land, mainly dependent on casual wage labour; (c) artisans, craftsmen, weavers and other non-agricultural workers engaged in petty production, trade, services etc.; and (d) the old, handicapped and destitute with no regular incomes. The poor tend to be in larger households with relatively larger numbers of non-earning dependents. The principal factors for the poor being poor and remaining so are the inadequate quantum and quality of assets—land and mainly cattle—they hold; the low volume and intermittent nature of employment for wage labour; the low real earnings resultant from employment and wages, given the prices of foodgrains and other essential necessities; and low incomes from household industries and other non-agricultural occupations. Social and locational factors compound these problems for disadvantaged sections such as the Scheduled Castes and Tribes. It is against this picture that we shall turn in the subsequent sections to an examination of the extent to which growth, direct programmes and minimum needs programmes have helped in alleviating rural poverty.

THE IMPACT OF GROWTH

India can be proud that its overall rate of economic growth since Independence has been in dramatic contrast to the long period of stagnation under British rule. Over the past three decades and a half, GDP in real terms has grown at an annual rate of 3.8 per cent, agriculture at 2.2 per cent and industrial output at 5.5 per cent while corresponding growth rates in the previous half century under colonial rule (1900–46) were 1.2 per cent (national income), 0.3 per cent (agriculture) and 2 per cent (industrial output) (Planning Commission 1981). Per capita growth in the post-Independence period at 1.1 per cent has however been only slightly more than twice its estimated growth in the last century of British rule, namely, 0.5 per cent, because annual population growth in 1951–81 has been of the order of 2.2 per cent, sharply higher than 0.9 per cent in 1900–51. The long-term per capita growth of 1.1 per cent is also significantly less than that experienced by low-income developing countries in the fifteen years, 1965–80, which has been of the order of 3 per cent per annum.[12]

Slow growth in per capita income has been compounded by an uneven growth profile over time and across different regions. Between 1950 and the mid-sixties, the annul growth rate in manufacturing industry was 6.6 per cent while it declined to 4.3 per cent during the subsequent two decades. Among the reasons for the decline was the slow growth in agricultural output which remained at 2.7 per cent

[12] Raj Krishna (1984a) points out that 'this rate keeps India as low as 71st in the list of 104 countries ordered according to the rate of growth of income per capita'.

per annum, despite the 'green revolution', largely because of a considerable reduction in cropped area and the fact that the impact of the new technology was mainly confined to wheat and rice and hardly made any difference to farming in the unirrigated areas which comprise about three-fourths of the cropped area in the country. Inter-state disparities in growth have also been significant: long-term per capita income growth in eight out of fifteen major states in India, accounting for about 65 per cent of the country's population, was less than the national average of 1.1 per cent and, over time, interstate disparities in per capita incomes have widened (Rao 1983).

It was noted earlier that agricultural performance was particularly relevant for rural poverty alleviation and also that there were 'processes at work in the rural economy' which offset the impact of agricultural growth on poverty reduction. Both of these themes require to be discussed together. The main characteristics of agricultural growth in India have been a near constancy of the trend growth rate in crop production, significant weather-induced variations from year to year, and a concentration of growth in terms of regions and crops. First, the constancy of growth coupled with an acceleration in population growth has meant a slowing down in the rate of growth of per capita agricultural output, from 0.7 per cent in 1950–64 to 0.5 per cent in 1967–77, with the result that in a long span of three decades the net availability of foodgrains per capita per day has remained at around 450 grams.[13] Secondly, while the highly irrigated states of Punjab and Haryana recorded annual output growth of 5 per cent, significantly higher than the national trend of about 3 per cent, output grew at less than 2 per cent per annum in as many as seven states and lagged behind growth in rural population in four of them. Thirdly, yield improvements among crops have been highly disparate: while notably wheat and to a lesser extent rice have recorded tangible productivity growth, other crops such as coarse grains (widely consumed by the poor), pulses (the main sources of protein) and major oil seeds have not. Fourthly, the new technology appears to have accentuated year-to-year and peak-to-trough instabilities in output caused by fluctuations of rainfall and weather.

[13] A dramatic illustration of mass hunger in India is provided by the fact that despite this low average per capita availability, public stocks of foodgrains had accumulated to 22.5 million tons at the end of 1984 consequent on two successive years of good agricultural output.

Given this pace and pattern of growth, public policy, market power and technology in combination have fuelled rather than mitigated unequal gains to the more prosperous farmers. Owing to legislative loopholes, widespread evasion and ambivalent implementation, the government's programmes for land reform based on land ceilings have failed to produce any worthwhile results. Surplus land available for redistribution was estimated at 8.6 million hectares in the late seventies, as against which the area actually declared surplus is 1.8 million hectares, area taken possession of is 1.2 million hectares, and the area finally distributed is 0.9 million hectares, that is, about one-tenth of the potential surplus (Bandyopadhyay 1985). Similarly, tenancy reform, intended to provide greater tenurial security to tenants, has had the perverse effect of resumption of rented land by landlords and concealed informal tenancies, particularly in areas of rapid agricultural growth. It is not surprising therefore that landholding surveys show that there has been no marked change in 1961–71 in the degree of inequality in distribution of land (owned and operated) in most parts of India, while in Punjab and Haryana the inequality in operational holdings has increased. Taking land and other assets together, the distribution of wealth in rural India has become more unequal in the same period: the top 10 per cent of rural households commanded more than half and the bottom 10 per cent only 0.1 per cent of the total stock of rural assets, both at the beginning and end of the 1960s.[14]

The new technology based on the complementary use of high-yielding seed varieties, irrigation, and chemical inputs such as fertilizers and pesticides has tended, given asset concentration and government policies, to favour large farmers.[15] The technology may be technically scale-neutral but it has not been so in socio-economic terms because it is the large farmers, typically owning ten acres or more, who are best placed in terms of land and resources to exploit its full potential; and, it is they again who have benefited most from state policies, projects and programmes. The rate of increase in irrigation, for instance, has been greater for the bigger holdings, a trend particularly pronounced in the exploitation of ground water

[14] The (Gini) coefficient of the distribution of assets in rural India increased from 0.56 in 1961–2 to 0.66 in 1971–2.
[15] For early assessments of the distributional effects of the green revolution see Frankel 1971 and Griffin 1974.

with the aid of electric pumpsets, which requires land and resource endowments generally beyond the reach of small farmers. Similarly, government's tax and subsidy policies, credit policies, and institutional infrastructures, have enabled large farmers to consolidate and extend their 'naturally' easier and larger access to extension services, fertilizers, pesticides, and credit and to farm equipment such as tractors and pumpsets while gaining most from remunerative prices available for the marketed surpluses sold by them.[16] For the small farmer, especially in dry areas, the new technology entails higher risk and uncertainty; his poor resource base, lack of effective access to inputs, and the absence of adequate arrangements for risk insurance for crop and cattle make the small farmer 'structurally unable to innovate'.

It is also significant that at an all-India level, growth in agricultural output has not resulted in a corresponding growth in labour absorption, that is, more employment and/or higher wages for the mass of agricultural labourers. Demographic pressure, the proliferation of small holdings resulting in a replacement of hired by family labour, mechanization, and technological factors have been responsible for dampening the impact of output on employment. Rural labour enquiries in 1964–5 and 1974–5 actually show a decline in the average per worker availability of wage employment for rural labour (male and female). At the same time, inflation in foodgrain prices has more than offset increases to nominal wages so that *real earnings* of male agricultural labourers in 1974–5 were estimated to be no more than 88 per cent of what they were a decade earlier. Minimum wage legislation for agricultural workers exists in India but governments have not been willing and/or able to enforce them given the large excess of supply over demand, the absence of any significant unionization of farm labour, and pressures from the landlord lobby.

We may sum up. The long-term growth rate, overall and in agriculture, has not been impressive. Population growth has resulted in very low growth in per capita incomes. Public policies have failed to reduce structural inequalities; in fact, they would appear to have widened them. It is not surprising therefore that the 'trickle-down'

[16] Fertilizer prices are subsidized in India and the subsidy relatively benefits large farmers rather than small farmers. On differential access to credit see Tendulkar 1983. Public credit is available on soft terms for the acquisition of tractors and pumpsets. Direct taxation of agricultural wealth and incomes in India is insignificant (GOI 1972).

or 'pull-up' effects of growth have been too feeble to have had any noteworthy effect in reducing the incidence of rural poverty which has remained more or less stationary for more than three decades. The consolation however could be that growth has served to contain poverty and to arrest its spread, besides averting its worst manifestations such as famine.

Direct Programmes for Rural Poverty Alleviation

The genesis of what have come to be known as 'direct' anti-poverty programmes can be traced to the perception from about the late sixties that the benefits of growth had insufficiently percolated to the rural poor. There were other factors as well. Growth itself had slackened from the mid-sixties and the Green Revolution was seen to have widened disparities, regionally and between large and small farmers. An influential study in the early seventies had made out a forceful case for massive public works programmes as the key for ameliorating rural poverty (Dandekar and Rath 1971). There was unwillingness or inability to redistribute land and in the face of it, a recognition that incomes and employment for the poor could be increased, if at all, only through the creation of incremental assets and by means of work generation. Asset creation and employment programmes had been initiated on an experimental scale in the Third Plan (1961-6) and progressively enlarged during the seventies in the Fourth and Fifth Plans; these provided the base of experience for a consolidated and comprehensive approach in this direction from the Sixth Plan (1980-5). Output increases in foodgrains, coupled with under-consumption on account of mass poverty, had led to the emergence of large food stocks in the mid-seventies, inducing a nationwide Food-for-Work programme, to be initiated with effect from 1977-8.[17]

The set of direct programmes, now in operation and relevant for our discussion, are the principal asset creation programme, namely, the Integrated Rural Development Programme (IRDP), and the two major employment generation programmes which consist of the National Rural Employment Programme (NREP) and the

---

[17] Public foodgrain stocks had accumulated by 16 million tons in 1975 and 1976. It is also relevant that the Food-for-Work programme was introduced at the end of 1976-7 on the eve of general elections to Parliament.

Rural Landless Employment Guarantee Programme (RLEGP). IRDP was initiated in 1978-9 and has been extended throughout the country since October 1980 when NREP was also initiated in replacement of the earlier Food-for-Work Programme. RLEGP is essentially a supplement to NREP introduced in September 1983.

The 'target group' for IRDP are those under the poverty line and its units of concern are households who fall within this target group. Under IRDP, 600 selected households under the poverty line are assisted each year in each of the 5000 development blocks in rural India, that is, about three million households annually, with subsidies and loans which finance a variety of income-earning assets such as irrigation wells, milch cattle, plough bullocks, other livestock like goats, sheep, and pigs, poultry, carts, and facilities for self-employment in small-scale production, services (for example, tailoring), and trade. The element of subsidy in the subsidy-cum-loan amount is 25 per cent for small farmers (operating two hectares or less of unirrigated land or its equivalent), one-third for marginal farmers (operating one hectare or less of unirrigated land or equivalent), agricultural labour and rural artisans, and one-half for Scheduled Caste and Tribe households. The subsidy is financed on a matching basis by the centre and state governments while the credit component comes from commercial banks. The ceiling for the subsidy, which is normally Rs 3000 per household, has recently been increased to Rs 6000. In actual fact, average per capita subsidy was Rs 1190 in 1984-5; and, with an average credit amount of Rs 2154, the total per capita investment assistance was Rs 3344 on an average (GOI 1985a).

In the last five years in which it has been operating countrywide, there have been a number of evaluations of IRDP made by official, banking and academic sources[18] which include two major official evaluations recently completed by the National Bank for Agriculture and Rural Development (NABARD 1984) and the Programme Evaluation Organization (PEO) of the Planning Commission (Planning Commission 1985a). These evaluations, undertaken by different agencies, in different parts of the country, and at different points of time agree to a remarkable degree in indicating certain

---

[18] Examples of independent evaluations are Guhan 1980, IFMR 1984, Jain 1985, MIDS 1980, and Rath 1985. A thoroughly objective evaluation by an official is Bandhyopadhyay 1985.

serious drawbacks in the programme. They can be summarized as follows:[19]

1. A not insignificant proportion of 'beneficiaries' are households who, being already above the poverty line, are not eligible for IRDP coverage but have infiltrated into the 'target group' because of wilful or faulty identification by the official machinery. The NABARD and PEO evaluations place the extent of such infiltration at 15 to 26 per cent of beneficiaries on an average, going up to between 40 and 50 per cent in certain areas.

2. While IRDP guidelines require that benefits should be concentrated on the poorest within the target group, the 'poorest-first' principle has not operated in practice. The PEO evaluation, for instance, shows that 40 per cent of the beneficiaries were located in the top 30 per cent of the income range for poverty (namely, Rs 2500–3500 per annum of household income).

3. Assets financed under IRDP have failed to generate incomes to the expected levels for a number of reasons. IRDP assistance has not been able in many cases to cover the full cost of the asset-entailing beneficiaries to supplement them with high-interest private borrowing; in many cases, assets financed (for example, milch cattle) have been of poor quality; support services for veterinary care, fodder and pasturage, and for marketing of milk and other products have been inadequate; and the distribution of benefits, in many areas, has been much in excess of local demand so that incomes to beneficiaries and non-beneficiaries alike have been reduced.

4. The subsidy-cum-loan approach suffers from an internal contradiction because the poor, who are the target group for subsidies, are also the least credit-worthy. It is not surprising therefore that they should divert asset-finance or income-earnings from assets to relieve earlier indebtedness or to meet contingencies or for subsistence requirements rather than for IRDP repayments or future asset-accumulation. These situations get exacerbated in periods of adverse seasonal conditions, such as droughts, when cattle get sold off in large numbers.

5. In the absence of adequate and strong arrangements for supportive links, such as veterinary and marketing services, assets distributed

---

[19] This summary is mainly based on Guhan 1985.

at the household level are weakly integrated with the externalities required for generating sustained incomes from them.

6. Populist political considerations require that benefits should get spread widely and thin so as to cover the largest number within given financial allocations. In such a process, optimal impact especially on the poorest is not achieved.

7. IRDP relies overwhelmingly on the government and commercial bank bureaucracies for its delivery system. For a large part, they are ill-motivated, inadequately trained, corruption-prone, and vulnerable to pressure from a variety of local elites.

Accordingly, most of the evaluations have been doubtful whether IRDP has been successful to any significant degree in reducing rural poverty and whether those 'lifted above' the poverty line through IRDP assistance have been able to sustain themselves above it. A recent assessment (Rath 1985) concludes that if inflation and the burden of loan repayments are allowed for 'at the end of seven years of the operation of the IRDP, about three per cent of the poor households in rural India would have been helped to live above poverty, even if for a while only.' It is also relevant that most of those 'uplifted' above the poverty line by IRDP are those who were already close to it and not the poorest who were supposed to constitute the prime target beneficiaries under the programme.

With all this, it needs to be recognized that IRDP has channelled funds on a hitherto unprecedented scale for creating supplementary incomes amongst the relatively poor in rural areas all over India. In the Sixth Plan period, assets have been created to the tune of some Rs 50 billion benefiting about 17 million families. Support facilities have not been able to keep pace with this order of investment; but, in the longer run, the latter itself might be able to give a strong impetus to the development of infrastructure services and facilities for a variety of rural economic activities which cater for increasing and diversified demand arising from growth in population and incomes. The basic validity of the IRDP approach and its potential should not therefore be dismissed. Within the known structural constraints, a number of improvements to the design and implementation of IRDP would appear to be possible. There is also some indication that such reforms are being considered.

The second plank of the direct programmes are NREP and RLEGP. They have so far generated 300 to 400 million mandays of employment per annum in rural areas on public works connected with small irrigation sources, land reclamation and conservation, afforestation, roads and construction of buildings. Here again evaluations have drawn attention to limitations and problems in the employment generation schemes (GOI, Planning Commission 1980). Despite an expenditure of over Rs 22 billion on these programmes during the Sixth Plan, employment generated has been to able to meet no more than about 9 per cent of the demand for it in rural areas. Secondly, it has not been possible to locate and organize sufficient useful, wage-intensive works at places and in the times of the year where and when they are needed most by the unemployed and underemployed. The discontinuous nature of rural under-employment and the changing composition of those subject to it are themselves major constraints in tackling the problem. Thirdly, while benefits to the poor have been short-term and seasonal, long-term benefits accruing from the formation of irrigation works, roads, etc. would accrue mostly to upper-income groups best placed to benefit from them. Finally, employment programmes have shown themselves to be prone to leakages in the form of excessive overheads, contractors' profits, corruption and waste.

To sum up, three broad sets of issues can be identified in relation to the direct programmes. They are structural, financial, and institutional. Given the systemic inequalities of land and asset ownership, benefits from these programmes have tended to be appropriated in the first instance by, or have tended in the second round to 'trickle-up' to, the rural non-poor.[20] Second, in relation to the magnitude of the rural poverty problem, the scale of resources allocated for these programmes—although not insignificant—has not been clearly anywhere near adequate. Thirdly, the programmes depend overwhelmingly on the bureaucratic apparatus for their implementation; and are, as such, vulnerable to inefficiency, waste and corruption inherent in such reliance. In most states, local-level institutions have not been given an effective role in these programmes. Without a greater degree of active people's involvement, it would be clearly not possible to significantly improve the cost-effectiveness of IRDP and NREP/RLEGP.

[20] On the latter point see Sinha *et al.* 1979.

Minimum Needs

Much before the phrase 'basic minimum needs' entered the international vocabulary of development, planners in India have been aware that the provision, largely through public expenditure, of social consumption needs such as education, health, water supply, and sanitation had high priority in development strategy. These were considered important not only for supplementing the consumption of the poor but also because employment and income opportunities could be expected to improve with better health and education. The Fifth Plan (1974-9) articulated the minimum needs approach by pointing out:

Even with expanded employment opportunities, the poor will not be able, with their level of earnings, to buy for themselves all the essential goods and services which should figure in any reasonable concept of a minimum standard of living. The measures for providing larger employment and incomes to the poorer sections will, therefore, have to be supplemented up to at least certain minimum standards by social consumption and investment in the form of education, health, nutrition, drinking water, housing, communications and electricity.

Since Independence, there has been notable progress in India in key indicators of social development. The literacy rate has more than doubled from about 17 per cent in 1951 to over 36 per cent in 1981; in the same period, female literacy has increased three-fold from about 8 to 25 per cent. The crude death rate has been brought down from 30 to 13 (per 1000 of population) and life expectancy at birth has improved from 41 to 55 years of age. However, Indian performance in these respects is less impressive when comparisons of it are made with low-income developing countries as a group and particularly when compared with the best performers amongst them. Moreover, there are significant differences in levels of achievement within the states in India, between rural and urban areas, and between the sexes, with the Scheduled Castes and Tribes in rural areas showing the lowest levels and rates of progress.

The percentage of literacy in India at 36.2 (1981) is less than the average for low-income countries (50 per cent in the late seventies) and considerably behind the performance of Vietnam (87 per cent), Sri Lanka (85 per cent), Tanzania (66 per cent) and China (66 per cent) (World Bank 1983). The rural literacy rate at 29.6 per cent is about half the urban rate (57.2 per cent); so is the female literacy rate (24.8 per cent) in relation to male literacy (46.9 per cent), with rural female literacy being as low as 18 per cent. Variations among states are also wide. As many as seven states, accounting for nearly 55 per cent of the country's population, have literacy levels below the national average. The outstanding performance of Kerala, with male and female literacy rates of 75.3 and 65.7 is far ahead of that of Rajasthan at the other end of the spectrum with 36.3 (male) and 11.4 (female). India's education policy has tended to emphasize higher education, which is highly subsidized and caters mostly for urban and upper-income groups, to the relative neglect of primary education. The constitutional directive that the state shall endeavour to provide free and compulsory education to all children under 14 years of age within ten years has not been fulfilled in the thirty five years since the Constitution came into force while, in this span of time, there has been a significant increase in facilities for graduate, postgraduate and professional education (Sen 1971).

The picture in regard to health indicators is not far different. India's achievements in key parameters do not compare favourably with what some low-income countries and its peer group as a whole have been able to achieve by the early eighties (World Bank 1985; see Table 1.1).

TABLE 1.1: Health Indicators of Some Developing Countries

	Overall for low-income countries	India	China	Sri Lanka	Vietnam
Crude death rate (per 1000 of population)	11	13	7	6	8
Infant mortality rate (per 1000 live births)	75	93	38	37	53
Life expectancy (at birth)	59	55	67	69	64

Once again, interstate and rural–urban differentials are large. While Kerala can boast of a death rate as low as 7, Uttar Pradesh has a rate of 20. Infant mortality accounts for some 20 per cent of all deaths and the reduction in the infant mortality rate (IMR) has been quite slow, particularly in rural India. In 1980, the rural IMR (124 per 1000 live births) was nearly twice the urban rate (65). Here again, Kerala is outstanding with an IMR of 40, which is about a third of the all-India rate of 114. Rural–urban disparities in the availability of health facilities are dramatically brought out by the fact that one hospital bed serves a population of 400 in urban areas while the corresponding ratio in rural India is one for over 10,000 of population. The availability of adequate and safe drinking water and sanitation are of crucial importance for health. Urban India has a high access to safe drinking water in statistical terms (covering 83 per cent of urban population) although the quantum is not adequate in many cities and the coverage is much lower in the slums which contain large numbers of the urban poor. Access to safe drinking water extends however only to 20 per cent of the rural population. Sanitary facilities for excreta disposal are almost non-existent in rural areas and cover barely one per cent of the population.

Estimates relating to nutrition levels show a daily per capita calorie availability of 2047 for India as compared to 2408 for low-income countries, 2562 in China and 2393 in Sri Lanka (World Bank 1985). Within the average, availabilities for the poor can significantly vary, especially between seasons and years. Food management in India operating through the public distribution system (PDS), based on imports and domestic procurement, has played a useful role in distributing basic cereals, namely, wheat and rice, at subsidized prices which could be 25 to 33⅓ per cent less than prices in the open market. The scope of PDS is however limited. In 1975–9, it covered less than 11 per cent of net availability of foodgrains; in terms of quantity supplied, its operations are concentrated in the cities and larger towns and are thinly extended to rural areas where the mass of low-income consumers such as landless rural labourers need it most; besides, the PDS does not include coarse grains such as millets, which are widely consumed by the poor. PDS has however served to even out price fluctuations for foodgrains in different parts of India, although mainly in urban centres.

Malnutrition is a particularly serious problem for vulnerable groups among the poor. In the case of pregnant women, it is a cause of low birth weight of children, a key factor in infant mortality; among young children, it could retard bodily and brain growth causing permanent damage. Studies across India indicate that between 15 and 20 per cent of schoolchildren may be suffering from severe malnutrition, that is, a weight deficit for age of 40 per cent or more (Gopalan 1984). Nutrition programmes for pregnant and nursing mothers and for pre-school and schoolchildren have been initiated in a number of states in India. They are undoubtedly desirable because they intervene at a crucial level to benefit poor families with a large number of dependent children. But, questions have been raised about their cost-effectiveness and in regard to leakages and inefficiencies in the delivery systems (Harriss 1985). Moreover, too-broadly targeted schoolmeal schemes, while politically popular, involve a significant opportunity cost by diverting limited financial resources away from health, water supply and sanitation without which nutrition by itself may not succeed in reducing morbidity or mortality.

Social insurance in India, especially for the rural poor who are almost entirely engaged in 'unorganized' farm or household occupations, is quite rudimentary and inadequate (GOI 1984) although a constitutional directive calls upon the state to extend, within its means, public assistance in cases of 'unemployment, old age, sickness and disablement, and to other cases of undeserved want'. Given the nature and magnitude of unemployment (including underemployment) in rural India, welfare payments to meet this contingency would be infeasible, financially as well as administratively. However, cash payments may be the only way to provide effective relief during times of prolonged or recurring droughts, which affect one part or other of India in most years, resulting in extreme distress to small peasants and rural labour from the loss of incomes, employment, and means of production such as cattle and seeds. Relief measures to meet such contingencies rely entirely on short-duration, dispersed works programmes which meet no more than a fraction of the real need. The approach to sickness and disablement has been largely through amelioration rather than insurance. Old-age pension schemes for the poor are however available in most states in India but on average their coverage is perhaps no more than a fifth of the need; the pension payments are also meagre. Some states have introduced pension schemes for widowed women but their coverage is grossly inadequate in relation to the magnitude of widowhood in rural India which has been estimated to be as much as 55 per cent among women of age 45 and above (GOI 1963).

There are a variety of interrelated reasons which might explain why India has not made more progress in the fulfillment of minimum needs despite official commitment and more than three decades of effort. First, policy has not been directed, specifically or in a sustained fashion, towards meeting these needs in rural areas (for example, in education and health), or with respect to disadvantaged sections (for example, women and Scheduled Castes and Tribes), or at primary levels of deprivation (for example, elementary vs. higher levels of education, preventive vs curative health, infant survival vs expensive urban hospitals). Secondly, in the Indian federal system, it is the state governments who have responsibility for education, health, nutrition, water supply and sanitation. Amongst them, administrative capabilities as well as resources allocated and effectively expended for these purposes have varied widely. Thirdly, the critical minimum effort for tackling interrelated problems such as disease, illiteracy, malnutrition and poor access to safe water and sanitation has been lacking, that is, intersectoral coordination has been inadequate. Fourthly, given their low level of incomes, the ability of the poor to gain, or benefit from, access to nutrition, health or education is restricted: school meals are a small proportion of the unmet needs of the household for food; children are not sent to school because they could otherwise earn, or relieve the working mother from childcare; and recourse to medical care has costs in travel, drugs, and forgone earnings which the poor are not able to afford.

Most important, there has been no real commitment or encouragement in India—in fact there is in many states an attitude of hostility—to decentralized local-level institutions which are responsible in most other countries for the establishment, operation and maintenance of basic facilities for health, education, water supply and sanitation. This is most unfortunate since decentralized participatory arrangements can be particularly useful in raising local resources for capital and running costs, for monitoring efficiency in delivery systems, securing coordination, and ensuring accountability. As Srinivasan (1977) points out: 'the socio-political institutional framework in which the basic needs programmes are to be implemented may be the overwhelming determinant of their feasibility and effectiveness.'

Looking Ahead

Our assessment of rural poverty alleviation in India in the last four decades or so has been largely negative in terms of actual policy and performance. This bleak picture could be legitimately qualified by drawing attention to the many achievements that India can claim, the enormous problems the country has had to face, and those, such as the entrenched social problem of caste, which she continues to confront. In the initial years of freedom, India successfully overcame the problems of partition and a massive transfer of population, welded a mosaic of states into a functioning polity, and laid the firm foundations for a federal democracy. It is a matter of pride that this basic structure has continued, with eight general elections being held to the national Parliament based on universal adult franchise. The federal system has worked well in reconciling diverse regional interests within a national framework. In terms of economic growth, India has broken through the long period of stagnation imposed on her by colonial domination; the growth process has been initiated and pursued under successive development plans; agricultural output has grown to a point where large-scale food imports have become unnecessary even in years of serious drought; a diversified industrial structure has been built reducing import dependence and underpinned by a pool of skilled manpower. There could, therefore, be much valid argument on whether 'the bottle is half-full or half-empty' and, indeed on which 'bottle' should be discussed.

The essential criticism remains that, whatever might have been the rhetoric of planning or politics, poverty alleviation has been an *adjunct* to India's development plans and policies rather than the *core* of their purpose, with other elements being integrated to the principal aim of poverty reduction. Arising from this critique two questions could be asked: on what lines should development policy evolve if the alleviation of rural poverty is to be the central concern? And, could such an evolution take place in a reformist process within the framework of a liberal democracy and a mixed economy? Some attempt seems necessary to answer these questions.

Most simply, development policy as a whole and in each of its aspects, that is, in a systemic manner, will have to be directed towards increasing entitlements to the rural poor from ownership and exchange. This will entail redistribution and transfer of assets in their favour, improving returns from assets and enterprise, increasing real earnings for wage labour, and the provision of social consumption and the safety net of social security. In all this, the same set of policies and programmes we have reviewed namely, growth, direct programmes, and minimum needs will be the most relevant.

The long-term trend of growth in India, overall and per capita, has been low but if recent experience since 1980 should continue, growth could well be on an upward course of 4 to 5 per cent per annum as compared to the long-term rate of under 4 per cent. Population control is of crucial importance for improving growth in per capita incomes and should be pursued as vigorously as possible within a promotional and persuasive framework. But it will still be a matter of decades before a demographic transition towards a low, stable population growth can be achieved, with such a transition itself depending on accelerated social and economic development. It has been pointed out that an appreciable dent could be made on unemployment and poverty if growth could be pushed up to 6 to 7 per cent per annum.[21] There are serious constraints in aiming at any such figure in terms of possibilities in agricultural or industrial growth and in the context of structural and functional factors in the domestic economy and in the international environment.[22] Whatever be the maximum feasible rate of growth, in the range of 4 to 6 per cent per annum, it is also clear that it is not so much the precise quantum of it but its sources, pattern and spread that will be crucial for rural poverty alleviation. This means that a wide array of social and macro-economic policies relating to production and consumption, fiscal policies in regard to taxes, subsidies and expenditure priorities, policies relating to employment, mechanization and technology, policies for the development of backward regions, and for redressing the condition of socially disadvantaged groups will all have to be reviewed and reoriented towards poverty alleviation, making it the prime purpose of development. Resource mobilization and efficiency in its use, employment promotion, and better regional balance will be of central importance. Along with such a reorientation, in fact as a part of it, a set of direct measures will also be necessary given the nature, magnitude and persistence of the rural poverty problem.

Land is the most important income-earning asset base for the rural poor. Large-scale land redistribution has not been found possible in India, given the nature of its political development; and there has been some debate whether, even if undertaken on a large scale, the redistribution of land can sufficiently benefit all classes of the rural poor because of the low land-man ratio.[23] Land reform, however, continues to be of primary importance for two reasons, one economic and the other political. The Planning Commission has estimated that 'if an additional 10 per cent of the operated area is transferred to small farmers either through proprietary rights or through secure tenurial arrangements and if adequate production support is provided to such farmers' a great deal of progress could be achieved

---

[21] cf. GOI, Planning Commission 1962 and Raj Krishna 1984b.
[22] These constraints are discussed in Vaidyanathan 1974b.
[23] cf. Dandekar and Rath 1971, Dantwala 1973, and Minhas 1974.

in increasing employment and incomes for the rural poor (GOI, Planning Commission 1978). An equally important argument for land reform is that the landlord's economic power is the means by which he acquires and retains social and political power to hold sway over land, labour, credit and produce markets and in relation to common property and village-level institutions. Unless this hegemony is broken at its root, the rural poor will not be able to come into their own in any real sense.

Adequate minimum wages for landless agricultural labour also belongs to the top of the agenda. It will need a combination of political activity for unionizing agricultural labour and committed legal enforcement through judicial and administrative processes. Female wages for non-harvest operations are typically one-half to three-fourths of male wages. Harvest earnings generally amount to a third of annual earnings of agricultural workers. The equalization of female wages, and support for collective bargaining at harvest (which is when labour is most advantageously placed to exercise it) could be the starting points for upgrading wages.

Rural non-agricultural employment in small-scale manufactures, crafts, dairying, livestock and so on has expanded in India but there is a hierarchy of middlemen, between the producer and consumer, who are involved in the supply of raw material and credit, and in selling the output. Interventions, through cooperatives or otherwise, whereby markets for rural household and small-scale manufactures could be enlarged and earnings from them safeguarded for producers can make an important contribution.

The Public Distribution System is the link to assure purchasing power in real terms from incomes and wages. Its operations would have to considerably expand in rural areas. Some successful experiments have been made by voluntary agencies in establishing 'grain banks' at local levels in order to contain seasonal increases in grain prices. Ways could be found to integrate such systems into the PDS network.

Alcohol is a real problem. It erodes the essential consumption of the poor and reduces the share for women and children in the household, besides the other deprivations it involves. There are arguments on the desirability, and more importantly on the feasibility, of total prohibition but serious effort seems necessary to tackle this problem if poverty is to be alleviated.

A number of reforms could be envisaged to IRDP and the NREP/

RLEGP. Identification of beneficiaries can be made more objective with reference to household landholdings data, with a programme for the compilation of such data being given high priority. The IRDP framework could be extended to include long-term, low-interest loans for the acquisition of land. Dairy programmes in India have provided successful models of integrated projects in which producers have been linked with arrangements for input supply, veterinary services, credit and marketing; such models could be extended to other agro-based, income-earning activities related to sheep, piggery, poultry, sericulture, and the growing of vegetables, fruits and flowers. There is need for a massive expansion in low-cost, customer-oriented, rural banking to extend small loans for trade, business and services; such a network can also help to mobilize rural savings. Micro-level planning and decentralized implementation can greatly improve benefits from the employment programmes both to the community and for rural labour, especially if works programmes are undertaken within the framework of land consolidation for which a forceful case has been made by B. S. Minhas (1970).

Resources for the minimum needs programme should be increased and its cost-effectiveness greatly improved. The concentration will have to be on (a) elementary education and adult literacy with special attention to women and Scheduled Castes and Tribes; (b) nutrition, maternity and child health services directed towards a reduction in infant mortality; (c) primary health care with the accent on prevention of disease; and (d) safe drinking water and sanitation. Social security for the old, handicapped, and fatherless families, and for prolonged unemployment during drought should be included as a minimum need recognizing the role of social insurance in alleviating the worst forms of low-end poverty. Most importantly, female literacy, infant survival, and old-age security can provide the framework within which family planning services could make significant headway.

The institutional structures for all these programmes are of fundamental importance. It is only on the basis of responsible and responsive participation by people, and particularly the poor, that this cluster of programmes can make any real progress—whether land reform, wage improvement, public distribution, temperance, direct programmes for asset creation and employment, or minimum needs. Land reform is the precondition for an egalitarian system of local participation. Along with it, resources, powers and responsibilities for poverty alleviation will have to be transferred as much as possible to a hierarchy of appropriate local levels; districts, development blocks, and villages. Decentralization on these lines could also draw in a variety of voluntary grassroots organizations which are yet to be integrated into the mainstream of development agents in India.

Many in India will argue that the kind of reforms sketched above (and similar ones) would make little difference to the rural poor in the absence of radical changes in asset distribution and in the processes of production, exchange and accumulation. There are also those who would be sceptical whether dominant 'distributional coalitions' such as the rural rich, the industrial elite, and the bureaucracy will permit such reforms to be effectively pursued.

No definitive answers to these questions are possible. One can only point out that reform need not prejudice more radical changes, might even stimulate them, and in the meanwhile do a great deal of good. It could also be pointed out that the poor in India if mobilized, could be, by far, the strongest 'distributional coalition' in a democracy. Political skill and will may be the crucial determinants in giving the rural poor their rightful place in a country in which they have continued to constitute such a large proportion.

REFERENCES

Ahluwalia, M. S. (1978), *Rural Poverty in India: 1957-58 to 1973-74*, Washington, DC: World Bank.

Ayres, R. L. (1983), *Banking on the Poor*, Cambridge, Mass.: MIT Press.

Bandyopadhyay, D. (1985), 'An Evaluation of Policies and Programmes for the Alleviation of Rural Poverty in India', in Rizwanul Islam (ed.), *Strategies for Alleviating Poverty in Rural Asia*, Bangkok: ILO (ARTEP).

Blyn, G. (1966), *Agricultural Trends in India 1891-1947: Output, Availability and Productivity*, University of Pennsylvania Press.

Bardhan, P. K. (1984), *The Political Economy of Development in India*, New Delhi: Oxford University Press.

Chambers, R. et al. (eds) (1981), *Seasonal Dimensions to Rural Poverty*, London: Frances Pinter.

Dandekar, V. M. and N. Rath (1971), *Poverty in India*, Pune: Indian School of Political Economy.

Dantwala, M. L. (1973), *Poverty in India: Then and Now, 1870-1970*, Macmillan.

Dutt, R. P. (1940), *India Today*, London: Victor Gollancz.

Frankel, F. R. (1971), *India's Green Revolution: Economic Gains and Political Costs*, Princeton: Princeton University Press.

GOI (Government of India), Cabinet Secretariat (1963), *Report of the National Sample Survey No. 76*, New Delhi.

GOI (Government of India), Ministry of Finance (1972), *Report of the Committee on Taxation of Agricultural Wealth and Income*, New Delhi.

GOI (Government of India), Economic Administration, Reforms Commission (1984), *Against Undeserved Want, Report of the Working Group on Social Security* (restricted), New Delhi.

GOI (Government of India), Department of Rural Development (1985a), *Poverty Alleviation: Sixth Plan*, New Delhi.

———, (1985b), *Thoughts on Rural Development*, Vols. I and II, New Delhi.

GOI, Planning Commission, Perspective Planning Division (1962), *Perspective of Development: India—1960-61 to 1975-76: Implications of Planning for a Minimum Level of Living*, New Delhi: Government of India.

———, (1972), *Towards an Approach to the Fifth Plan*, New Delhi: Government of India.

———, (1977), *Studies on the Structure of the Indian Economy and Planning for Development*, New Delhi: Government of India.

———, (1978), *Draft Five Year Plan 1978-83*, New Delhi: Government of India.

———, Project Evaluation Organization (1980), *Evaluation of the Food for Work Programme: Final Report*, New Delhi: Government of India.

———, (1981), *Sixth Five Year Plan 1980-85*, New Delhi: Government of India.

———, (1982), *Report of the Expert Group on Programmes for Alleviation of Poverty*, New Delhi: Government of India.

———, (1985a), *Evaluation Report on IRDP*, New Delhi: Government of India.

———, (1985b), *Seventh Five Year Plan 1985-90*, New Delhi: Government of India.

Gopalan, C. (1984), *Nutrition and Health Care: Problems and Policies*, New Delhi.

Griffin, K. (1974), *The Political Economy of Agrarian Change: An Essay on the Green Revolution*, Macmillan.

Guhan, S. (1980), 'Rural Poverty: Policy and Play Acting', *Economic and Political Weekly*, 22 November.

———, (1981), *A Primer on Poverty: India and Tamil Nadu*, Madras: Madras Institute of Development Studies.

———, (1985), 'Poverty Alleviation: Policy Options', in GOI 1985b.

Hanumantha Rao, C. H. (1975), *Technological Change and Distribution of Gains in Indian Agriculture*, New Delhi: Institute of Economic Growth.

———, (1985), *Changes in Rural Poverty in India: Implications for Agricultural Growth*, Dr Rajendra Prasad Memorial Lecture, Indian Society of Agricultural Statistics, Akola.

Harriss, B. (1985), 'Meals and Noon Meals in Tamil Nadu', London: London School of Hygiene and Tropical Medicine.

IFMR (Institute for Financial Management and Research) (1984), *An Economic Assessment of Poverty Eradication and Unemployment Alleviation Programmes and Their Prospects*, Madras.

ILO (International Labour Organization) (1976), *Employment, Growth and Basic Needs: A One-World Problem*, Geneva.

Jain, L. C. (1985), *Grass Without Roots*, New Delhi: Sage Publications.

Kravis, I. B. et al. (1975), *A System of International Comparisons of Gross Product and Purchasing Power*, Baltimore: Johns Hopkins University Press.

Kurien, C. T. (1977), 'Rural Poverty in Tamil Nadu', in *Poverty and Landlessness in Rural Asia*, Geneva: ILO.

———, (1981), *Dynamics of Rural Transformation: A Study of Tamil Nadu 1950–75*, Madras: Orient Longman.

———, (1985), 'Paradoxes of Planned Development: The Indian Experience', (mimeo), Madras: Madras Institute of Development Studies.

MIDS (Madras Institute of Development Studies) (1980), *Structure and Intervention: An Evaluation of IRDP, DPAP and Related Programmes in Ramanathapuram and Dharmapuri Districts of Tamil Nadu*, Madras.

Minhas, B. S. (1970), *Rural Poverty, Employment and Growth: An Agenda for Action*, New Delhi: Indian Statistical Institute.

———, (1974), 'Rural Poverty, Land Distribution and Development Strategy: Facts and Issues', in Srinivasan and Bardhan.

Naoroji, Dadabhai (1876), *Poverty and Un-British Rule in India*.

NABARD (National Bank for Agriculture and Rural Development) (1984), 'Study of Implementation of IRDP'. (mimeo), Bombay.

Raj Krishna (1973), 'Unemployment in India', *Economic and Political Weekly*, 3 March.

———, (1984a), 'Stagnant Parameters', *Seminar*, New Delhi, January.

———, (1984b), *The Growth of Aggregate Unemployment in India: Trends, Sources, and Macro-economic Policy Options*, Washington, DC: World Bank.

Rao, V. K. R. V. (1983), *India's National Income 1950–80: An Analysis of Economic Growth and Change*, New Delhi: Sage Publications.

Rath, N. (1985), 'Garibi Hatao' Can IRDP Do It?', *Economic and Political Weekly*, 9 February.

Raychaudhuri, T. (1985), 'Historical Roots of Mass Poverty in South Asia: A Hypothesis', *Economic and Political Weekly*, 4 May.

Rudra, A. (1978), *The Basic Needs Concept and its Implementation in Indian Development Planning*, Bangkok: ILO (ARTEP).

Sen, A. K. (1971), *Crisis in Indian Education*, Hyderabad: Institute of Public Enterprises.

———, (1981), *Poverty and Famines: An Essay on Entitlement and Deprivation*, Oxford: Clarendon Press.

Sinha, R. et al. (1979), *Income Distribution, Growth and Basic Needs in India*, London: Croom Helm.
Srinivasan, T. N. (1974), 'Income Distribution: A Survey of Policy Aspects', in Srinivasan and Bardhan.
———, (1977), *Development, Poverty and Basic Human Needs: Some Issues*, Washington, DC: World Bank.
———, (1979), *Malnutrition: Some Measurement and Policy Issues*, Washington, DC: World Bank.
Srinivasan, T. N. and P. K. Bardhan (eds) (1974), *Poverty and Income Distribution in India*, Calcutta: Statistical Publishing Society.
Sukhatme, P. V. (1977), *Nutrition and Poverty*, Lal Bahadur Shastri Memorial Lecture, New Delhi: Indian Agricultural Institute.
Tendulkar, S. D. (1981), 'Indian Development Strategy: Compulsions and Constraints'. (mimeo), Delhi: Delhi School of Economies.
———, (1983), 'Rural Institutional Credit and Rural Development: A Review Article', *Indian Economic Review*, January–June.
Townsend, P. (ed.) (1970), *The Concept of Poverty*, London: Heinemann.
van de Laar, A. J. (1980), *The World Bank and the Poor*, The Hague: Martinus Nijhoff.
Vaidyanathan, A. (1974a), 'Some Aspects of Inequalities in Living Standards in Rural India', in Srinivasan and Bardhan.
———, (1974b), 'On the New Economics of Poverty', in Mitra (ed.), *Economic Theory and Planning: Essays in Honour of Das Gupta*, Calcutta: Oxford University Press.
———, (1986), 'Aspects of Structure and Change in India's Rural Economy', (mimeo), New Delhi: Jawaharlal Nehru University.
Vaidyanathan, A. and G. Sen (1984), 'Growth and Social Justice: India's Experience and Prospects' (mimeo), New Delhi: Institute of Economic Growth.
Visaria, P. (1980), 'Poverty and Living Standards in Asia', *Population and Development Review*, June.
World Bank (1980), *World Development Report, 1980*, Washington, DC: World Bank.
———, (1983), *World Development Report, 1983*, Washington, DC: World Bank.
———, (1985), *World Development Report, 1985*, Washington, DC: World Bank.

2

Apples, Oranges, and the Measurement of Poverty*

The methodology recommended by the Expert Group for making poverty estimates represents a distinct improvement over the one adopted in the official estimates currently available. Three important improvements are: (a) the abandonment of the NSS-NAS adjustment procedure; (b) initial estimation of poverty state-wise and its aggregation for deriving all-India estimates; and (c) adoption of price indices and deflators that are related to consumption around the poverty line. The Group has recommended that the all-India calorie norms and the relevant consumption baskets at the all-India level may both be uniformly adopted for all states. Standardization of calorie norms and the consumption basket have been found to be necessary to enable aggregation of state-wise estimates and comparisons across states at each point of estimation.

While I recognize that the devices adopted by the Group are necessary for the stated purposes, I believe that the estimates recommended do not give a full and true picture of poverty at state levels because the standardization procedure necessarily ignores state-wise differences in normative calorie requirements and in consumption baskets. In a country as large and diverse as India, these parameters vary considerably across states because of differences in climate and terrain, levels of urbanization, average incomes, income distribution,

* This essay (title supplied by Subramanian) appeared as 'Annexure II: Supplementary Note from Shri S. Guhan' in *Report of the Expert Group on Estimation of Proportion and Number of Poor*, New Delhi: Planning Commission, Government of India, 1993, pp. 50–2.

local availability of cereals and other food items, consumer preferences, cultural patterns, and so on. These variations have been discussed in the report itself while dealing with the calorie intake criterion and with variations in the consumption pattern across states and over time.

In view of these state-wise differences, the Group could have recommended a *separate* set of state- level estimates *in addition to* the series recommended by it in order to approximate more closely to poverty at the state level. This will involve taking account of state-level normative calorie requirements and state-level differences in consumption baskets. The former cannot be done at present for want of technically determined normative calorie requirements at the state level. State-level consumption baskets are, however, available and it is possible to adopt them for deriving state-level poverty estimates. On this basis, the *separate* set of state-level estimates could be based on all-India calorie norms (for want of anything better), state-level consumption baskets in the base year, and state-level price indices and deflators relatable to the respective base year consumption baskets at the state level. There is no reason not to provide such estimates.

I realize that such state-level estimates cannot be aggregated for all-India. For that, we have to depend per force on the methodology recommended by the Group. But aggregation and stylized comparisons are not all. Differences too are important given the diversity of India which is only a 'Union of States', a fact recognized by the Group itself while basing its all-India poverty estimates on primary estimates at state levels.[1] The *separate* set of state-level estimates I recommend will give us better insight into two important dimensions of poverty in India. First, they will enable state governments and their citizens to follow the levels and trends of poverty in their state as closely as the available data will permit. This is, or ought to be, a matter of

---

[1] For loading oranges and apples as cargo, only their weight and volume are relevant. For invoicing them, only prices are relevant. That one has to engage in these activities need not rule out paying heed to the distinctiveness and varieties of oranges and apples in terms of other characteristics such as size, colour, flavour, taste, etc. More philosophically: measurements are based on conventions; conventions are use-related; different uses require appropriately different conventions and hence measures; if different measures are viewed as being conflictual and discarded in favour of a uniform standard measure, something may be gained but much is also needlessly lost in the process. The optimal course, therefore, will be to provide a plurality of measures.

concern and interest since in India's dual polity, politically and administratively, each state has a separate identity. Second, it is also a matter of interest to consider how state X stands in relation to state Y in terms of their *respective* poverty profiles defined on the basis of standards *appropriate to* each.[2]

For reasons that I have not been able to fully understand or appreciate, the Group could not be persuaded to accept my suggestion for providing a set of state-level estimates on the basis indicated by me *in addition to* the series which we have all recommended. Perhaps, the rest of the Group too did not fully understand or appreciate the value and validity of my arguments. I have reiterated my suggestion in this supplemental note in the hope that it will at least find favour with the Planning Commission and the state governments. In that case, the federal dimension of poverty will also get duly recognized and those interested in this topic need not rest content with abstractions such as an 'all-India' consumption pattern.

---

[2] In this connection, the following from Professor Amartya Sen should be persuasive (*Poverty and Famines*, Oxford University Press, 1981. p. 21).

There is, indeed, nothing contradictory in asserting both of the following pair of statements:

(1) There is less deprivation in community A than in community B in terms of some common standard, for example, the notions of minimum needs prevailing in community A.

(2) There is more deprivation in community A than in Community B in terms of their respective standards of minimum needs, which are a good deal higher in A than in B.

It is rather pointless to dispute which of these two senses is the 'correct' one, since it is quite clear that both types of questions are of interest. The important thing to note is that, the two questions are quite distinct from each other.

3

Social Security for the Poor in the Unorganized Sector
A Feasible Blueprint for India*

INTRODUCTION[1]

The relief of poverty has been, implicitly or explicitly, at the centre of the development objectives of the poor countries. It is, however, only since about the late sixties that it began to be widely recognized—among academics, national governments, international organizations and multilateral aid agencies—that the growth process by itself cannot be depended upon in terms of its pace or reach to alleviate poverty and that, therefore, *direct* measures were called for for making a sufficient and sufficiently early impact on poverty (ILO 1976; Singer 1979; van der Laar 1980; Streeten 1981; Ayres 1983). The concept of a direct attack on poverty, as a necessary complement to its gradual and progressive alleviation during the growth process, shares its lineage and logic with the concept of social security which originated in a formal sense[2] in the industrialized countries in the late nineteenth century.

Direct poverty alleviation measures can, therefore, be considered as social security in its widest sense. The essential elements of both

---

* Reprinted from Kirit S. Parikh and R. Sudarshan (eds), *Human Development and Structural Adjustment*, Chennai: Macmillan, 1993, pp. 203–37.

[1] I have drawn on my earlier papers on the subject in preparing this one.

[2] See Guhan 1988 for a brief account of informal social security traditions and practices in different religions and various parts of the world.

approaches are: (a) the recognition that poverty is a *social* condition, rather than a natural phenomenon, ordained by God or arising from the fecklessness of the poor, and that, therefore, society acting through the state has the responsibility to alleviate it (Himmelfarb 1984); (b) the acceptance of minimum norms, in regard to income, well-being, and capabilities, considered necessary for living without want and deprivation; and (c) formulation and implementation of operational measures to secure the realization of such norms. A variety of problems are involved in the coverage, identification, and valuation of the norms and their actual enforcement in different countries has been subject to political and financial exigencies from time to time. But, the acceptance, in principle, of norms and the effort to translate them into entitlements is basic to both social security in advanced countries and to direct anti-poverty measures in developing countries.[3]

Historically, however, there have been important differences between the advanced and the developing countries in regard to the developmental stage and the nature and dimensions of poverty which have defined the context for direct intervention in each case. When social security measures were first introduced in Germany (1883–9) and in Britain (1908), both countries were well advanced in their industrial revolutions.[4] Although the incidence of poverty was high and widespread, it was felt that normal processes of economic growth could be relied upon to reduce it except where potential participants were prevented from involvement in economic activity on account of biological circumstances (such as old age, sickness and disability, and maternity) or the failure in the functioning of the economic system itself (such as unemployment) and in cases where relief was needed because of large family sizes reflected in high dependency ratios.[5] Given this diagnosis of poverty, the concern of social security in the advanced countries was on *protective* rather than promotional

---

[3] For the problems involved in the concept and valuation of the norm, see Atkinson 1987 and Dreze and Sen 1989a.

[4] For an account of the German experience, see Stumpf 1979 and for the British, Barr 1987; Gilbert 1966; Rose 1972; Fraser 1984; and Himmelfarb 1984.

[5] Referring to social surveys of the condition of life conducted in the interwar years in a number of principal towns in Britain, Beveridge (1942) pointed out: 'Of all the want shown by the surveys, from three-quarters to five-sixths, according to the precise standard chosen for want, was due to interruption or loss of earning power. Practically the whole of the remaining one-quarter to one-sixth was due to failure to relate income during earning to the size of the family.'

measures. Continuing industrialization was expected to improve income levels and what was felt to be necessary was largely a safety net in the form of measures to protect incomes from falling below acceptable norms on account of contingencies that led to a transient interruption or a prolonged loss of earnings. Accordingly, social security mechanisms, as they have originated and evolved in advanced countries, aim at covering medical care and specific benefits related to unemployment, family size, maternity, sickness, employment injury, invalidity, old age, and death. These have come to be codified as standard social security benefits by the International Labour Organization (ILO 1984a).

PROMOTIONAL AND PROTECTIVE SOCIAL SECURITY

Faced with massive and persistent poverty and a large unorganized working population in the rural and urban areas, developing countries have adopted a basically dualistic approach to social security in the broad sense. Protective social security measures have been extended to public and quasi-public employees and to workers in the organized sector inspired partly by pressure from unionized labour, partly by western models, and partly by ILO conventions.[6] The covered categories of employees are benefited directly from budgetary funds (as in the case of public employees) or through insurance to which a sizable contribution is made from the exchequer to supplement employer and employee contributions. Formal protective social security of this kind available in India is shown in Table 3.1.

On the other hand, social assistance for the vast majority of workers in the unorganized sector and for the self-employed is very limited in India. Principally it consists of means–tested old-age pensions provided by state governments. Uttar Pradesh was the first to introduce such a general old-age pension scheme in 1957. This was followed in the sixties and seventies by similar schemes in other states and by now almost all states in India have provision for old-age pensions to the needy. Many states also have pensions schemes for destitute widows and the physically handicapped and some have arrangements to make survivor payments to families of those who

[6] For accounts of social security systems in developing countries, see US Department of Health and Human Services 1982 and Midgeley 1984 generally; Mesa-Lago 1978 for Latin America; Mouton 1976 for Africa; Dixon 1981 for pre-reform China; and GOI 1984 and Guhan 1988 for India.

TABLE 3.1: Protective Social Security Entitlements Available for the Organized Sector in India

Type of benefit	Government and quasi-government employees	Industrial workers in organized sector
Medical care	Free treatment in government hospitals Reimbursement of cost of drugs	Free treatment and reimbursement for drugs under Employees' State Insurance Scheme (ESI)
Sickness benefit	Medical leave on full pay	Sickness leave on pay under ESI
Maternity benefit	Maternity leave on full pay	Maternity benefits under the Maternity Relief Act
Unemployment benefit	Does not arise	Retrenchment benefits under labour laws
Employment injury benefit	Ex-gratia relief	Provided under Workmen's Compensation Act
Invalidity benefit	Ex-gratia relief	Provided under Workmen's Compensation Act
Old-age benefit	Pension or Contributory Provident Fund	Employees' Provident Fund (EPF)
Survivor benefit	Lump sum payments on death while in service financed with state subsidy; family pension on death of retired employees	Deposit–linked insurance under EPF

die in specified occupational hazards such as well-digging, sewer work, tree climbing, and fishing. In recent years, the central government has introduced an accident insurance scheme for those under the poverty line and group life insurance schemes for agricultural labourers and for beneficiaries under the IRDP.[7] Also relevant is

[7] The Personal Accident Insurance Social Security Scheme was introduced in the Central Budget for 1985–6. It provides for a lump-sum benefit of Rs 3000 in the case of death of an earning member in the age group 18 to 60 belonging to poor families (currently defined as falling within a household income limit of Rs 7200 per annum) among landless labourers, small and marginal farmers, traditional craftsmen, and others not covered by any insurance scheme or workmen's compensation. The premium is entirely borne by the central

compulsory third-party insurance under the Motor Vehicles Act which compensates road accident victims on a no-fault basis. Thus, a patchwork of social security arrangements has evolved in India over the years, in piecemeal fashion, comprising contractual benefits to public employees, standard social insurance schemes for workers in the organized industrial sector, and a modicum of social assistance for the poor mainly in the form of old-age pensions which are implemented according to diverse patterns in the states.

Promotional measures, which have constituted the main approach in regard to the unorganized poor, have aimed at averting or amelioriating conditions or contingencies such as low incomes (through growth-mediated as well as direct anti-poverty programmes), unemployment (through employment generation), and sickness and disability (through preventive, curative and rehabilitative facilities). Direct anti-poverty programmes in India, which constitute promotional social security of this kind, comprise, for instance, the wide gamut of (i) programmes for improving farm incomes through irrigation, credit, technical assistance, and subsidies; (ii) employment generation schemes such as the Jawahar Rozgar Yojana; (iii) asset distribution through the Integrated Rural Development Programme; (iv) backward area development programmes (such as the DPAP); (v) provision of basic needs such as subsidized housing for the poor, slum improvement, primary education, health care, child nutrition, water supply, sanitation; and (vi) the public distribution system. Such promotional measures are thinly spread and loosely targeted with their impact being in the long term and difficult to measure. Protective measures, on the other hand, seek to provide guarantees or enforceable entitlements to those affected by specific contingencies by compensating them for the loss of income and/or additional expenses arising thereby.

Protective Social Security Pessimism

The dominant reliance in India on promotional measures for the poor in the unorganized sector to the virtual neglect of protective

---

government. The central government has also introduced life insurance for earning members in agricultural labour households with a benefit of Rs 1000 and for IRDP beneficiaries with a benefit of Rs 3000. The premia in these cases are also entirely met by the government.

social security stems from several factors. Underlying them is the perception that in a country like India, with a massive population of the poor, it would not be feasible to think of protection against *contingent* poverty unless and until the level of *chronic* poverty gets reduced, much more than it has hitherto, in the process of normal growth. In particular, unemployment benefits, for instance, are sure to entail unsupportable expenditures in the Indian context. Besides, underemployment being the predominant feature of lack of work in India, targeting of unemployment benefits will be administratively intractable. Similarly, sickness insurance of the kind provided in advanced countries will be infeasible because of resource constraints and the thin spread of medical facilities, especially in the rural areas. Above all, wage employment is very largely in the unorganized sector, much of it being also casual employment; and the bulk of the self-employed are in petty production, trade and services. In these circumstances, social assistance funded by the state rather than social insurance financed by employers and beneficiaries would have to be the main mode of extending social security, and this again will make an unaffordable demand on the exchequer.

These fiscal and administrative constraints, valid as they are, have led to an unwillingness or inability to examine the need, scope, and feasibility of protective social security measures for the poor in the unorganized sector: the problem has been acknowledged, but has been consistently put aside in Indian Plan documents as well as in academic writings. As far back as the Second Plan, income maintenance was identified as the principal objective of development in the influential Planning Commission document (1961) on 'Implications for a Minimum Level of Living'. The document concluded that the growth process it envisaged, ambitious as it was with a target rate of 7 per cent per annum, was likely to remove poverty only up to the third decile from the bottom of the population and that 'specific steps' would have to be taken for the poorest fifth. Similarly, referring to the poorest decile, the Fourth Plan document stated:

This segment of the population consists mostly of the destitutes, disabled persons, pensioners and others who are not fully in the stream of economic activity. They constitute a special class whose income and living standards cannot be expected to rise with the growth of the economy in the absence of special assistance.

However, the recognition of the need for special measures for the poorest was not followed through with concerted attention to what forms such special assistance might take within the constraints and feasibilities of the Indian situation. Subsequent plans—the Fifth, Sixth and the Seventh—have confined themselves to proposing targets for an aggregate reduction in the head-count poverty ratio and have paid little or no attention to the role of social assistance for the poor. The Sixth Plan devoted half a page to this topic under the subject of labour welfare and the Seventh Plan was wholly silent on the subject. The most recent (June 1980) document on the 'Approach to the Eighth Plan' has, however, broken the silence, although in a noncommittal manner, with the statement:

A number of social security schemes—like old age and widows' pensions, accident insurance and the like—have been introduced by several states in a piecemeal and ad hoc fashion. The accumulated experience of schemes already introduced will need to be assessed critically. A number of ideas on the subject are available and provide a good basis for designing a better thought out, comprehensive, and affordable system.

Social security pessimism has also extended to Indian academics: while the literature on poverty and anti-poverty programmes is vast, various, and growing, very little attention has been paid to protective social security for the unorganized poor. Almost all of the Indian academic literature on the subject is on social security legislation and social insurance in the organized sector. A notable exception is Professor Amartya Sen who has done a great deal in his writings to draw attention to the role of social security entitlements as part of public action to combat both famines and 'persistent hunger'.

However, he too does not make a sufficiently sharp distinction between the protective and promotional roles of social security. Only the preventive aspect of the former, rather than its role in guaranteeing entitlements, is conceded and this too is confined to extraordinary situations such as famines (Drèze and Sen, 1989b):

It is useful to distinguish between two different aspects of social security, namely, *protection* and *promotion*. The former is concerned with the task of preventing a decline in living standards as might occur in, say, an economic recession or—more drastically—in a famine. The latter refers to the enhancement of general living standards and to the expansion of basic capabilities of the population, and will primarily have to be seen as a long-run challenge.

And, when it comes to ILO-type benefits for the poor in *the ordinary course of their lives*, Sen tends to be rather dismissive:

We should stress that 'social security' as we see it here is a much broader and far-reaching notion than the technical sense in which the term is sometimes used in the professional literature on social administration in the richer countries. Debates on social security issued in the more prosperous countries have tended, perhaps for good logistic reasons, to focus on a number of specific forms of intervention such as unemployment benefits, medical insurance or old-age pensions. Often the very definition of 'social security' is associated with these specific programmes (see, for example, the publications of the International Social Security Association). There is some debate as to the part that these programmes can play in removing deprivation in developing countries. But no matter what position we take on this issue, there is some obvious advantage in considering all the relevant forms of intervention in a common framework. (ibid.)

The only 'position' that the authors take on 'the part that these programmes (that is, ILO-type benefits) can play in removing deprivation in developing countries' is in the following footnote that is attached to this passage:

The social security measures that have been historically associated with the pursuit of social security objectives in the richer countries, and which are now formalized in the conventional usage of the term (for example, in ILO publications), are best seen as contingently relevant for social security in the broader sense.

This is inadequate and disappointing because, surely, social security, even in its 'much broader and far-reaching' sense, is only 'contingently relevant'. It would not be necessary if there were no poverty or deprivation!

The Case for Protective Social Security for the Poor

It is the argument of this paper that this pervasive pessimism deserves to be challenged and that it is necessary to explore the feasibility of protective social security measures that will cover contingencies to which and sections of the poor to whom promotional measures cannot reach out. Such measures should, in fact, be viewed as an integral, but now missing, element of the direct attack on poverty and as complementary to the promotional and targeted anti-poverty programmes. In principle, their justification rests on the following considerations:

• 'Promotional' measures have not so far been outstandingly successful in reducing poverty in India. There has been no significant or sustained decline in the proportion of the poor while their absolute numbers have increased. Millions of poor households who will be 'with us' for decades to come cannot be counselled to wait patiently for promotional measures to provide succour in a millennial perspective. In the meanwhile, appropriate protective measures are also necessary to save them from the worst forms of deprivation.

• 'Promotion' and 'protection' do not represent an 'either/or' dichotomy and in fact have a complementary role. It is not always the case that the need for 'protection' is diminished as 'promotion' proceeds to take effect. Notably, an increase in life expectancy—which is hailed as one of the key indicators of welfare—combined with persistent poverty provides little consolation unless the poor in their old age receive support for subsistence. Nor is 'promotion' capable of meeting all contingencies: families affected by the death of the bread-winner, which cannot be averted by 'promotional' measures, need, for instance, direct support.

• Under conditions of 'chronic' poverty, 'contingent' poverty significantly exacerbates the plight of the poor. It is the poor who can least afford loss of earnings arising from old age or widowhood or sickness or maternity. Nor are these contingencies of a transient nature from which the poor can 'bump back', if only, to their 'normal' condition of poverty. Old age and widowhood can last for a long while; the death of a bread-winner can have a ratchet effect in plunging a poor family into debt and destitution; and, lack of nutrition around maternity can cause permanent damage to both mother and child.

• ILO-type benefits are already available in large measure for employees of government and quasi-government undertakings and for industrial workers in the organized sector. They are also available to managerial cadres in the private sector qualifying for tax-eligible expenditures. Thus the exchequer already incurs, directly or indirectly, considerable cost on this score. It is not, therefore, as if the need for ILO-type benefits has not been recognized in principle; only that their extension has been skewed, regressive, and limited to the virtual neglect of the poor in the unorganized sector.

• Several studies have shown that direct anti-poverty measures, of which the IRDP is the principal one, are loosely targeted in the sense of missing out the eligible poor and including the ineligible non-poor. They also show that these programmes do not succeed in reaching out to the poorest deciles. On the other hand, protective social security benefits such as old-age pensions, death benefits, and maternity benefits can be quite precisely targeted to relieve the contingencies involved as there is little room for faking maternity, old-age, or death. Moreover, while expenditures on overheads, relatable to a given quantum of benefits to actual recipients, on the current anti-poverty programmes are quite high (such as on administrative supervision, lending and loan recovery cost in IRDP, and material and supervision costs in JRY), they can be much lower in the case of direct social security payments. Thus, protective social security can be more cost-effective in reaching those who are, or are on the way to becoming, the poorest as compared to promotional anti-poverty measures which typically reach only the upper crust of the poverty group.

The rationale for protective social security measures having been set out, the more difficult task would be to outline what a relevant package of measures might cover in the Indian context, the scales of benefits that could be considered reasonable, the affordability and sustainability of such a package, and the administrative aspects of the delivery system. In order to scope out these issues, we shall first describe, in the following section a social security package for the unorganized poor that has been implemented in Tamilnadu in recent years. Tamilnadu has been a pioneer state, along with Kerala, in welfare programmes with a high social security content and its recent measures could provide useful ideas for generalization at the all-India level.

PRE-1989 MEASURES IN TAMILNADU

Prior to 1989, social security in Tamilnadu for the unorganized poor consisted of old age, physically handicapped and widows' pensions, an accident relief scheme for workers engaged in hazardous occupations, and a contributory insurance scheme for weavers in the cooperative sector. The oldest and most significant of these was the Old-Age Pension (OAP) Scheme introduced in 1962. It provided monthly pensions to 'destitute' persons of age 65 and above, destitution being defined as the condition of those without an income of their own or means of support from others.[8] This basic scheme was

---

[8] For operational purposes, those who live in a house of value less than Rs 1000 or own only marginal extent of land are presumed not to have an income of their own. Those without an income of their own and without any relatives

extended to the physically handicapped in 1974 (with the age limit being lowered to 45), destitute widows in 1975 (age limit 40), agricultural labourers in 1981 (age limit 60), and deserted wives in 1986 (age limit 30). Availability of pensions was, however, subject to annual quantitative ceilings on the number in each category. Eligible persons who could not be sanctioned pensions, on account of the ceilings being exhausted, had to take their place in a waiting list. The amount of the cash benefit has been the same for all types of pensions.[9] Starting with Rs 20 per month, it had been progressively raised to Rs 35 per month by 1982. About 3.73 lakh persons were benefiting under all the five types of pensions in 1989 with the bulk of them coming under old-age (1.69 lakh) and widows' pensions (1.22 lakh). The Accident Relief Scheme, introduced in 1977, provided for a death benefit of Rs 5000 to families of certain categories of workers, who might die in hazardous occupations, such as fishermen, sewer workers, sprayers of pesticides and chemicals, persons engaged in the digging or deepening of wells, and palmyra and coconut tree climbers. The Savings and Security Scheme for weavers in the cooperative sector (1975) provided insurance coverage linked to deposits made by beneficiaries with a matching contribution from the government.

New Schemes of 1989

In 1989, the DMK government that came to power, introduced a much more comprehensive package of social security measures in fulfilment of its election manifesto. The elements of this package were:

- OAP and other pension schemes were liberalized in two ways. First, the practice of imposing annual ceilings on numbers for budgetary purpose was given up. Pensions were sanctioned to all on the waiting list as on 1 April 1989, and, for the future, eligible persons were to be sanctioned pensions within three months of application. Second, the amount of the monthly pension was increased to Rs 50.
- The Accident Relief Scheme was liberalized by extending its coverage to several additional categories of workers, notably

---

of age 20 and above in the form of son, daughter's son or spouse, are presumed to be destitutes.

[9] In addition to the monetary pension, OAP beneficiaries are now eligible to one free meal daily at the school meal centres and to two pairs of dhotis/saris in a year. The note under Table 3.6 gives the basis for estimation.

construction workers and drivers of vehicles; the amount of the benefit was raised to Rs 10,000 and disabilities were also covered (Rs 10,000 for serious disability and Rs 5000 for others); and the income limit for eligibility was removed.

Apart from these liberalizations in the two existing schemes, the following new social security schemes were introduced:

• Survivor Benefit Scheme providing a grant of Rs 3000 on the death of the bread-winner. The head of the family, male or female, is considered as the bread-winner, regardless of age, if he or she is an earning member. If the head of the family is not an earning member on account of old age, incapacity, or any other reason, the member of the family who is the prime earner is reckoned as the bread-winner. In this and other new schemes, the poverty criterion is the same as in IRDP.

• Maternity Assistance Scheme for working women belonging to poor households providing for a cash assistance of Rs 200 spread over four months, two months before and two months after delivery. The assistance covers only the first two children and is available only to mothers whose age at marriage was 18 or more.

• A Marriage Grant Scheme providing a cash benefit of Rs 5000 at the time of marriage to girls from poor households who have completed eighth standard of schooling and get married not below the age of 18. This unconventional form of social security attempted to combine three objectives: preventing poor families falling into debt on account of marriage expenses, inducement to female schooling, and enforcement of the legal age at marriage. It could also dilute discrimination against female children in the longer term.

Benefits and Coverage under the New Schemes

A detailed evaluation (Guhan 1990) has been undertaken of the reach-out of these schemes in 1989–90 in terms of the coverage of the target population relevant to each scheme. The methodology used for estimating the target population under each scheme has been explained in the evaluation. What is impressive is that in the first twelve months of its implementation, the package has been able to cover 7.32 lakh beneficiaries, 4.72 lakh under the pension schemes representing a 27 per cent increase over the previous year when ceilings were in force and 2.60 lakh beneficiaries under the new survivor benefit, maternity assistance, and marriage grant schemes (vide Table 3.2 for details). Individually, the contingencies covered, namely, old age, death, maternity and marriage, are mutually exclusive although the same household may benefit under more than one of these schemes. If it can be assumed that the extent of such overlap may not be significant, 7.32 lakh out of an estimated 44 lakh poor households in Tamilnadu, that is, about 17 per cent of them have been protected from contingencies which could have made them poorer. It is also significant that out of the total of 7.32 lakh beneficiaries at least 4.18 lakh or 57 per cent are women, namely, widows, deserted wives, working mothers, and brides belonging to poor households. Women would also have benefited in addition under the pension schemes.

TABLE 3.2: Coverage of Social Assistance Schemes in Tamilnadu, 1989–90

Item	No. of beneficiaries (as on 1.4.89)	No. of beneficiaries (1.4.90)	Ratio of beneficiaries to target population without adjustment for poverty ratio[b]
1. Total pensions	372,689	472,224	11.16[c]
• Old-age pensions	169,386	207,355	13.2
• Widows and deserted wives pensions	134,940	179,514	9.9
• Agricultural labourers pensions	47,665	60,835	14.7
• Physically handicapped pensions	20,698	24,520	5.7
2. Survivor benefit[a]	–	20,990	25.2
3. Maternity assistance[a]	–	218,680	36.0
4. Marriage grant[a]	–	19,687	25.0
5. Accident relief[a]	–	443	NA
	372,689	732,024	14.6[c]

[a] Numbers relate to first full year of implementation.
[b] Ratios relate to data as on 1.4.90.
[c] Weighted average.
Source: Guhan 1990.

Apart from the aggregate benefits, it is also important to examine what proportions of the estimated target population have been covered under each of these measures. The coverage ratios we have worked out (in Table 3.2) relate the number of beneficiaries to the relevant estimated target population (based on estimates of the old, widowed, physically handicapped, mortality of bread-winner, first two births, and marriage of girls with schooling up to eighth standard) in the *entire* population of the state and not just in the population of households under the poverty line. To arrive at the latter, the coverage ratios will have to be multiplied by a factor which might vary in each case. The overall poverty proportion in Tamilnadu in the late 1980s was around 40 per cent implying a factor of 2.5 by which the ratios could be blown up to estimate the coverage among eligible *poor* households. However, the factor might well be less in the case of the old among the poor owing to lower life expectancy at age 65-plus in their case and, more importantly, because eligibility for pensions is governed by the criterion of 'destitution' which is much stricter than 'poverty'. On the other hand, among marriages of girls with schooling only up to the eighth standard the proportion of girls belonging to poor households can be expected to be higher. A higher ratio may also apply to cases eligible for maternity assistance. In the absence of data for such fine-tuning, if the factor of 2.5 is applied across the board, the estimates suggest that pensions covered about 28 per cent of the poor, the survivor benefit and maternity assistance about 63 per cent, and the marriage grant a very high 90 per cent.

The coverage of target (poor) population achieved in the first year of implementation of the new measures can thus be considered to be quite encouraging. This will, of course, have to be qualified by the possibility that some of the non-poor might have infiltrated into the eligible group. Such infiltration is, however, not likely in the case of pension schemes because they are old, well-established schemes which in Tamilnadu are administered on the basis of fairly thorough local enquiries; besides, the destitution criterion will weed out the non-poor prima facie. Although it would be normally difficult to pretend death or maternity or to go through bogus marriages on a large scale, some infiltration might have taken place in the sense of the non-poor pretending to be poor in the case of the other schemes, especially the marriage grant. At the same time, it is important to note that these schemes are not subject to any ceilings on the number that can benefit since the Tamilnadu government has undertaken an open-ended commitment to meet the *entire* eligible demand under each scheme. In view of this, any intrusion of the non-poor, while it may lead to leakage of funds, will not entail denial of assistance to the eligible poor so long as the latter are able to establish their entitlements. This is an important difference between these schemes and anti-poverty programmes like the IRDP where, because of the budgetary constraint on total numbers, the non-poor benefit at the expense of the poor and not merely at the expense of the state.

Financial Implications

We shall now turn to the financial implication of the schemes. Table 3.3 gives the pre-liberalization cost on OAP and other pensions

TABLE 3.3: Cost of Social Security Schemes in Tamilnadu, 1989–90

(Rs crore)

Benefits	Pre-liberalization annual expenditure in 1989–90	Additional[a] expenditure for full year consequent on liberalization and new schemes	Total expenditure
OAP	13.89	8.09	21.98
DALP	3.91	2.54	6.45
DWP	10.02	7.05	17.07
DDWP	1.05	0.90	1.95
PHP	1.70	0.90	2.60
All pensions	30.57	19.48	50.05
Survivor benefit	–	6.30	6.30
Accident relief scheme	NA	NA	0.39
Maternity assistance	–	4.37	4.37
Marriage grant	–	9.84	9.84
	30.57	39.99	70.95

[a] Represents costs for a full year on number of pensions as on 1.4.1990 and the full year cost on other benefits.

Source: Guhan 1990.

as on 1 April 1989, the additional cost arising from the pension liberalization for a full year based on 1 April 1990, coverage and the full year cost involved in the new schemes based on coverage during the first twelve months of their operation. The pre-liberalization total cost was about Rs 30 crore per annum (entirely on pensions) and the cost, in the first full year, relatable to the new initiatives is about Rs 40 crore. The total outlay of Rs 70 crore is 1.5 per cent of the revenue expenditure of Rs 4563 crore (RE 1989-90) in the state budget, the additional expenditure of Rs 40 crore being 0.9 per cent. The NSDP of Tamilnadu in 1989-90 (at current prices) could be estimated at around Rs 19,000 crore. Of this, the total cost of Rs 70 crore is 0.4 per cent. The total cost per beneficiary works out to Rs 969 or about Rs 1000 heavily weighted as it is by old-age pensions which have a unit cost of Rs 1060 per annum (including the cost of benefits in kind).

The Tamilnadu schemes are being implemented, with some minimal augmentation, through the regular field-level staff of the Revenue, Social Welfare and Rural Development Departments. Certification and other procedures relating to applications, sanctions, and disbursements have been kept to the minimum and decentralized at the taluk and block levels. In the new schemes, the administrative overheads have been estimated at 4 per cent of the cost of benefits. This compares very favourably with overheads of insurance companies and with overheads in the traditional anti-poverty programmes (such as the IRDP) which are in the range of 12 to 15 per cent.

OUTLINE OF A BASIC MINIMUM SOCIAL ASSISTANCE PACKAGE FOR ALL INDIA

The value of the Tamilnadu experience, which we have reviewed, is threefold. It indicates the kinds and scales of protective social security it has been possible to provide within the confines and constraints of a state budget in India. It also shows that such measures can provide a significant measure of benefit, whether assessed quantitatively in terms of the coverage of poor households or qualitatively in terms of preventing them from regressing into debt and destitution on account of unavoidable contingencies. Third, and most important, the Tamilnadu experience might help to break the psychological barrier at a national level by demonstrating that it is possible to design and implement protective social security schemes for the unorganized poor.

General considerations, as well as the Tamilnadu pattern, would indicate that a basic minimum package of protective social security for the poor should include maternity, disability, old-age, survivor and employment injury benefits since the contingencies they seek to cover cannot be averted or ameliorated by promotional measures alone. Of these, old-age and widows' pensions will be the most significant in terms of both benefits and costs. Old-age pensions are, in fact, a necessary and logical corollary of promotional measures which seek to increase life expectancy. And, of the poor in India, widowed women are the most disadvantaged, socially and economically (Dreze 1990).

Under Indian conditions, this minimum package might also be the maximum feasible one. Of the nine ILO-type benefits we started with, resource constraints and administrative problems will make it impossible to provide medical care and sickness benefits by way of cash compensation. They can only be provided in kind for the poor-at-large through state-run facilities. These facilities will, of course, need to be massively expanded especially in rural areas, upgraded, and networked with referral systems to provide access to expensive diagnostic and curative facilities. Indirect costs of sickness need to be reduced through a wide dispersion of health-care facilities and adequate allocation for free supply of basic drugs. Similarly, a promotional approach will be all that will be possible in the matter of unemployment benefits. An expanded Jawahar Rozgar Yojana, employment guarantees in high-unemployment and high-poverty regions, and extensive and adequate relief works during droughts would appear to constitute the only feasible approach. In the matter of family benefits, the promotional approach will have to take the form of child nutrition, school meals, and free schooling. ICDS and programmes like the Tamilnadu Integrated Nutrition Programme specifically aimed at children in the most vulnerable age group of 6 to 36 months are models that could be followed.

Costing the Package

The basic minimum needs in the matter of protective social security for the poor having been outlined, the cost of the package can be worked out based on the benefits to be included and appropriate assumptions relating to eligibility and scales of benefits. We assume that the package will consist of (a) monthly pensions for the old, widowed and deserted women, and the physically handicapped; (b) a lump sum survivor benefit; and (c) maternity assistance, with these benefits being subjected to appropriate income criteria.

In regard to pensions, the minimum age limits for eligibility are assumed to be 65 for the general old-age pension, 60 for agricultural labourers, 40 for widowed and deserted wives, and 20 for the disabled. The income criterion in the case of pensions is assumed to be fixed at an appropriate level below the poverty norm, on the lines of the sub-poverty criteria (such as destitution) adopted by the states, so as to be able to cover 50 per cent of the eligible categories in the below poverty group. Using the Census age-distribution projections for 1991, the categories to be covered by pensions can be estimated to constitute 6.74 per cent of the 1991 population.[10] Assuming a 50 per cent coverage of the below-poverty population and a poverty ratio of 40 per cent, this will mean that 1.35 per cent (0.5 × 0.4 × 6.74) of total population will get covered by pensions. This would appear to be a robust estimate considering that in the late eighties, social security pensions covered 0.9 per cent and 1.2 per cent of the population respectively in Tamilnadu and Kerala, the two states with the best performance in this respect. For estimating total costs, the present population of India is taken as 850 million in round figures. Assuming the annual unit cost of the pension at Rs 900 (that is, Rs 75 per month), the outlay on pensions will come to Rs 1032.8 crore (85 × 0.0135 × 900) per annum.

The survivor benefit is assumed to be related to the death of the prime earner (or 'bread-winner'), in poor households on the basis of the standard poverty criterion. The number of deaths per annum in the earning age bracket of 20 to 59 years in a total population of 850 million can first be estimated using the 1991 projected age distribution and latest available (1984) age-specific mortality rates. The earning age bracket of 20–59 accounts for 47.10 of total population and the weighted average mortality rate in this age span is 5.9 per 1000. Deaths per annum in this age group will be 23.62 lakh for a universe of 850 million. Since survivor benefits are on a household basis, the number to be covered could be taken as 0.5 × 0.4, or 0.2 of this figure (assuming two earners in a household and a poverty proportion of

---

[10] The note to Table 3.6 gives the basis for estimation.

40 per cent). This will come to about 4.72 lakh cases per year and will entail an annual cost of Rs 141.6 crore based on a unit cost of Rs 3000.

For estimating the cost of maternity assistance, total annual births can be estimated as 235 lakh applying a CBR of 27.61 (1991-6 medium projection) to a population of 850 million. If the maternity assistance is confined to the first two births and to women in poor households, the number to be covered can be estimated at 0.16 (0.4 × 0.4) of 235 lakh or 37.6 lakh consistent with a total fertility rate of 5 and a 40 per cent poverty proportion. At a unit cost of Rs 200, the outlay on maternity assistance will come to Rs 75.2 crore per annum.

Applying accident mortality rates to the population and adjusting it for bread-winners in poor households as in the case of survivor benefits, the number to be covered will be 56,000 annually in a population of 850 million. An additional survivor benefit of Rs 3000 in these cases will entail an annual outlay of Rs 16.8 crore. It will actually be less if coverage is restricted to accidents in the course of occupation.

The total cost, in terms of orders of magnitude, of the minimum package will then be Rs 1266 crore per annum as follows:

Pensions	1032.8
Survivor benefit	141.6
Maternity assistance	75.2
Accident relief	16.8
Total	1266.4

Adding 10 per cent for overheads, the cost of the minimum package will be about Rs 1400 crore for entire eligible coverage in India. Table 3.4 gives the details.

While affordability and sustainability will be discussed in detail subsequently, it could be noted that the cost is not prima facie staggering considering that it will be about 0.3 of India's likely GDP and about 1 per cent of the combined current revenues of the central and state governments in 1991. Moreover, not all of this expenditure will be additional since old-age and other pensions are already being provided in the states with varying eligibility conditions, scales of benefits, and coverage. The Ninth Finance Commission (1989) had included a normative provision to the states for old-age pensions at 0.2 per cent of total population at a unit cost of Rs 1200 per annum.

This works out to about Rs 200 crore per annum. Actual expenditure being incurred by the states is, however, likely to be much more, indicating that the additional expenditure might turn out to be Rs 1200 crore per annum or less.

TABLE 3.4: Proposed Benefits, Estimated Numbers, and Annual Cost of Protective Social Security for the Poor

Benefits	Estimated number in population of 850 million (lakh)	Unit cost per annum (Rs million)	Total cost per annum (Rs crore)
1. Pensions	114.75	900	1032.8
• Old-age pensions	69.70		627.3
• Widows and deserted wives pensions	39.95		359.6
• Agricultural labourers pensions	3.40		30.6
• Physically handicapped pensions	1.70		15.3
2. Survivor benefit[a]	4.72	3000	141.6
3. Maternity assistance[a]	37.55	200	75.2
4. Accident relief[a]	0.56	3000	16.8
	157.63	803	1266.4[a]

[a] Weighted average.

Benefits

Turning, for a while, from costs to benefits, it might be pointed out that the proposed minimum package will not be an insignificant one. It will provide relief to about 16 million beneficiaries annually in an estimated 68 million poor households. Assuming non-overlap, a little less that about a quarter of poor households will be helped; even allowing for some overlap, it can be expected that perhaps about one-fifth of them will benefit from some measure of social security. At least nearly half of the beneficiaries will be women, namely, the proportion relatable to maternity assistance and widows pensions. The transfers will be directed to the relief of low-end poverty, current or prospective. Pensions will benefit the poorest of the poor (the old and the widowed without support) and the other benefits (survivor, accident relief, maternity assistance) will provide a safety net for the poor in times of dire need. Further, the availability of these benefits will put in place a framework to which promotional measures can be linked: for example, vocational training and IRDP loans to widows and deserted wives; antenatal and post-natal care for mothers; rehabilitation therapy for the handicapped; and geriatric care for the aged.

On Affordability

Issues relating to affordability to the exchequer on a sustainable basis are certainly important in the present context when India faces a very difficult process of fiscal adjustment on account of large and growing current account deficits in the Centre and in the states. In this situation, resources for additional expenditure can obviously be secured only by a combination of economies in currently incurred expenditures, reordering of priorities, and raising of additional resources. There is certainly need and scope for economy in public expenditure in India in terms of cutting down waste and leakage. Secondly, there is also a case for increasing the level of what the *Human Development Report (HDR) 1991* of the UNDP calls the 'human expenditure ratio' in public expenditure in India.[11] As the *HDR 1991* points out (Table 3.1 at p. 53), the human expenditure ratio in India (2.5 per cent of GNP) is below the average for a number of developing countries (2.9 per cent) and is only half of what the report considers to be necessary (5 per cent) 'if a country wishes to do well in human development'. This is so despite the public expenditure ratio in India (37 per cent) being above the average (28 per cent) because the social allocation ratio and the social priority ratios in India (20 per cent and 34 per cent respectively) are below the averages (28 per cent and 38 per cent respectively). In other words, within current overall levels of public expenditures in India, *prima facie* justification exists for improving the allocation for social services and within the latter for improving expenditures of 'human priority',

---

[11] According to the definition used by the *HDR 1991* (UNDP 1991), the human expenditure ratio is the percentage of national income devoted to human-priority concerns. It is the product of the percentage of public expenditure in national income (the public expenditure ratio), the percentage of expenditures earmarked for social services in public expenditure (the social allocation ratio) and the percentage of social expenditure devoted to human priority concerns (the social priority ratio).

a description that will certainly fit a basic minimum package of protective social security for the poor in the unorganized sector.

The third avenue, namely raising of additional revenues specifically for providing social assistance to the poor, should also be feasible. By way of background, it can be noted that percentage of tax revenues to GDP is typically between 30 and 35 in the industrialized countries while it is 10 to 15 in developing countries. Also, the proportion of direct taxes in industrialized countries is about 60 per cent while it is 10 per cent in developing countries. These large differences are mainly owing to social security payments in the advanced countries. Thus, there is clearly a case for mobilizing additional resources in the form of direct taxes for social assistance especially in India where the effective income-tax threshold is quite high in relation to per capita income and direct tax incidence has been progressively lowered at all income levels for the minority of the population liable to it. To illustrate possibilities, we have worked out the likely yield based on a graduated scale of social assistance surcharges on the incomes of the top 12 per cent of households with annual incomes of Rs 25,000 and above. The proposed surcharges are quite moderate being monthly amounts of Rs 25 in the Rs 25,000 to 40,000 annual income bracket, Rs 100 in the Rs 40,000 to 56,000 bracket, and Rs 200 in the above Rs 56,000 group, corresponding respectively to 1, 2.5, and 4 per cent of incomes. Table 3.5 gives the working sheet. It will show that moderate levies on about 20 million households which are in the country's top income-earning bracket can be expected to yield about Rs 1400 crore per annum which will fully meet the likely cost of the package.

Towards a More Liberal Package

The proposed package could also attract criticism on the ground of its being niggardly. It will be argued that even if the coverage of protective social security needs to be limited in India's circumstances, eligibility criteria are too restrictive and the scales of benefits are too low.

In response to such critics, a quick estimate can be made of what a more liberal package might cost. It will be reasonable to lower the minimum age limit for old-age pensions to 60 coinciding with the cut off limit for survivor benefits. The scales of benefits also deserve to be improved; a monthly sum of Rs 100, which is closer to the rural

TABLE 3.5: Likely Yield from Proposed Social Security Surcharges

Annual income range	No. of HHs 1989-90 (million)	Per cent to total HHs	Assumed mean income (Rs)	Rate of surcharge (per cent)	Amount of surcharge (Rs)	Rounded off amount (Rs)	Estimated yield per annum (Rs crore)
25,000-40,000	14.4	8.7	32,500	1.0	325	25 × 12 = 300	432
40,000-56,000	3.8	2.3	48,000	2.5	1200	100 × 12 = 1200	456
56,000<	2.1	1.2	60,000	4.0	2400	200 × 12 = 2400	504
	20.3	12.2					1392

Source: NCAER Household Consumption Survey (1989-90) for income distribution.

poverty line, will be a more reasonable scale of benefit. For survivor and accident relief benefits, amounts of Rs 5000 and Rs 10,000 respectively and Rs 300 for maternity assistance will certainly be more reasonable. Reworking the cost estimates on this basis—namely, lowering the age limit of old-age pensions to 60 and increasing the pension from Rs 75 to Rs 100 per month, improving the survivor/accident benefit from Rs 3000/6000 to Rs 5000/10,000, and the maternity assistance from Rs 200 to Rs 300—the cost of the package will increase from Rs 1400 crore to Rs 2285 crore (pensions: 1699; survivor benefit 237; maternity assistance: 113; accident relief: 28; and 10 per cent for overheads) or from 0.3 per cent of GDP to 0.5 per cent. This need not be back-breaking either. Moreover, the improvements can be made in phases. For instance, to start with, the survivor and maternity benefits can be enhanced; at the next stage, old-age pensions for women could be provided from age 60; thereafter, for men also from age 60; and the amount of the pensions can be increased in a phased manner.

The thrust of policy should also be to progressively upgrade the income criterion for pensions up to the poverty line so as to provide pensions to all old, widowed, and disabled who are part of, and depend on, poor households. As the poverty ratio declines, this should be progressively possible within the overall cost incidence. Our estimates assume a poverty proportion of 40 per cent and a sub-poverty criterion which will capture 50 per cent of the poor. If the poverty proportion declines to 20 per cent, it will be possible to upgrade the criterion up to the poverty line without breaching the budget constraint.

Whatever may be the degree of liberalization that may be introduced, it is important that the benefits should be indexed to take reasonable account of inflation. While ensuring equity, this will also avoid jerky and lumpy increases from time to time: in Tamilnadu, for instance, it took seventeen years for the amount of the monthly pension to be increased from Rs 20 to Rs 25 and another ten years for it to reach Rs 50.

Sustainability

Sustainability in the longer run will have to be examined in relation to changes in demographic parameters and GDP growth. Population growth and changes in age distribution, arising from fertility and mortality changes and increase in life expectancy, will lead to an increase in the size of the target population for various benefits. Offsetting factors will be a decline in the poverty proportion, lower mortality (relevant for survivor benefits and incidence of widowhood), and a decline in fertility (relevant for maternity assistance). Based on population and age structure projections for the year 2001, it can be estimated that the number of beneficiaries under pensions will increase by 37 per cent between 1991 and 2001, the number of survivor benefits by 27 per cent, the number for maternity assistance by 31 per cent and the number for accident relief by 9 per cent (Table 3.6 gives the details). The projection, however, is without taking into account any decline in the poverty proportion.

Table 3.7 gives estimates of the eligible population (namely, 0.2 of the population in the age group) for 65-plus (males and females), 65-plus males and 60-plus females, and 60-plus (males and females) between 1990 and 2020. It will show that decadal increases in the eligible population in the case of normal old-age pensions, whichever among the three alternatives are considered, continue to be within 40 per cent.

What is important to note is that the decadal increases, the highest in the case of pensions, will still be well within the likely increase in real GDP in the same decadal period—about 63 per cent—assuming a 5 per cent real growth per annum. Accordingly, expenditures on these benefits as a proportion of GDP (that is, after indexing both for inflation), will decline rather than increase in the coming decade. Normal old-age pensions being the critical component in the cost structure, sustainability of the package in terms of real GDP proportion should not be a matter for concern.

At a superficial level, sustainability concerns might be influenced by reports of the 'social security crisis' in the industrialized countries. It will be clear on further thought that no similar crisis need be anticipated from the kind of benefits that have been proposed. In the advanced countries, the share of the elderly in the population has risen sharply entailing large increases to the costs of benefits related to old age, medicare and disability. Concurrently, given high unemployment rates, the cost of unemployment benefits has also gone up. And, both these components have to be borne by a decreasing proportion of economically active earners.[12] These causal factors have no relevance to the content of the minimum package envisaged in this paper.

---

[12] For a discussion of the current debate on social security in the industrialized countries, see ILO 1984b.

TABLE 3.6: Estimated Growth in Coverage of Social Security Schemes 1991-2001

Benefit	Estimated eligible in 1991 population (%)	No. (million)	Estimated eligible in 2001 population (%)	No. (million)	Increase in numbers 1991-2001 (%)
1	2	3	4	5	6
1. Pensions	1.3465	11.262	1.5593	15.460	37.3
• Old-age (65+)	0.8212	6.868	0.9696	9.613	40.0
• Widows (40-64)	0.4693	3.925	0.5197	5.153	31.3
• Agricultural labourers (60-4)	0.0400	0.335	0.0500	0.496	48.1
• Physically handicapped (20-64)	0.0160	0.134	0.0200	0.198	47.8
2. Survivor benefit	0.0560	0.468	0.0600	0.595	27.1
3. Maternity Assistance	0.4418	3.695	0.4884	4.842	31.0
4. Accident relief	0.0066	0.055	0.0061	0.060	9.1
Total	1.8509	15.480	2.1138	20.957	35.4

Note: Eligible percent population in columns (2) and (4) has been worked out with reference to (a) medium age distribution projections of the Registrar General for 1991 and 2001, (b) incidence of widows and divorced or deserted women according to marital status tables of the Registrar General for 1991 and 2001, (c) incidence of agricultural labourers in population (1981), (d) incidence of disabled in population (1981), (e) CBR and CDR (1984), (c) incidence of agricultural labourers in population (1981). The total fertility rate is assumed roundly for 1991 and 2001 in medium projections (f) incidence of accident to total mortality (1981). The total fertility rate is assumed roundly as 5 in 1991 and 4 in 2001. Medium population projections for 1991 and 2001, used in columns (3) and (5), are 836.450 million and 991.479 million respectively.

TABLE 3.7: Projections of Eligible Population for Normal Old-age Pensions, 1990–2020

	65+males and females (million)	Decadal growth (%)	60+females and 65+males (million)	Decadal growth (%)	60+males and females (million)	Decadal growth (%)
1990	7.681		9.863		12.099	
2000	10.704	39.4	13.520	37.1	16.273	34.5
2010	14.340	34.0	17.862	32.1	21.403	31.3
2020	19.763	37.8	24.760	38.6	29.935	39.9

Source: Projections from Guha Roy 1989.

Cost control and prevention of leakages are other issues relevant to affordability and sustainability. Our estimates are based on a coverage under pensions, for instance, of 1.35 per cent of the population. What if, on account of misrepresentation of income and/or lax administrative scrutiny and/or political interference, the proportion turns out to be much higher in the course of actual implementation? One way to counteract such 'leakages', *if they were to prove otherwise intractable*, will be to decentralize the delivery system on a local area basis and preferably through local bodies indicating coverage ceilings. For example, a local area of 1000 population will be entitled to 14 pensions: pensions can be given to the poorest 14 among those eligible for them if their number were to exceed the normative ceiling. Based on experience, adjustments can be made in the coverage norm between richer and poorer local areas within the overall 1.35 per cent figure. A decentralized delivery system can also help in other ways such as better verification of claims and raising of voluntary local resources to supplement the benefits in cash or kind.

Some Other Concerns

Conventional discussions of social security also involve 'concerns' relating to moral hazards, disincentive effects on savings, and displacement of informal social security. Given the nature of the package that has been proposed, these issues are largely irrelevant. It is not possible to accelerate old age, and it is not likely that widowhood or disability or death will be invited in order to claim benefits. Maternity assistance, apart from being modest, is being restricted to the first two births and will have no pro-natal effect. The target population of the poor is not likely to have had any savings to speak of throughout their working life. The benefits are only likely to supplement rather than supplant informal security poor households might have from poor relatives; and even if they displace it, they will indirectly benefit 'the poor who help the poor', which is not a matter for regret.

The Centre's Role

Finally, the question could be raised why it is necessary to envisage a social assistance package on an all-India basis and whether it cannot be left to be evolved at the level of the states since they have already taken varying initiatives in this respect. Under the Constitution of India, social security, which features as entry 23 in the Concurrent

List (List III to the Seventh Schedule), is a *joint* responsibility of the Union and state governments. The Directive Principles under articles 41 and 42 of the Constitution, read along with article 12, prescribe that the state *at both levels* 'shall, within the limits of its economic capacity and development, make effective provision for the right to work, to education and to public assistance in cases of unemployment, old age, sickness and disablement, and in other cases of undeserved want' and for 'maternity relief'. It is, accordingly, necessary and appropriate that the Centre should stimulate, support and supplement the efforts of the states in the area of social security just as it has done in regard to other major anti-poverty programmes such as the IRDP and employment generation schemes. The rationale for a Central initiative for introducing a basic minimum programme recommends itself on two main grounds. It will bring about a common framework for the whole of India by enlarging existing benefits and by enforcing uniform eligibility criteria and scales of benefits for both existing and new measures. Second, while supplementing states' resources, the Centre could structure its contribution in such a way that lagging states are induced to do better and advanced states are able to sustain their measures. For instance, the estimate of Rs 1400 crore for the minimum package is equivalent to a per capita expenditure of about Rs 16.5 per annum. Of this, the Centre could come forward to meet in full any excess over a first slab of Rs 8 to be met by the states within a ceiling of Rs 16.5 for benefits in the package according to standardized scales and eligibility criteria. Central stimulus and assistance in this form will harmonize state-level schemes along the minimum package, induce lagging states to do more on this item of human priority expenditure, and enable the advanced states to improve benefits, utilizing funds released by the Centre's part contribution to their existing outlays.

Conclusion

This paper has attempted to establish a strong case for protective social security for the unorganized poor in India and to show that it is possible to implement a basic–minimum, affordable, and sustainable programme on which further refinements and improvements will be possible. But, then, in the words of the opening sentence of the *HDR 1991*: 'The lack of political commitment, not of financial resources, is the real cause of human neglect.'

REFERENCES

Atkinson, A. B. (1987), 'Income Maintenance and Social Insurance' in A. J. Auerbach and Martin Feldstein (ed.), *Handbook of Public Economics*, vol. II, Amsterdam: North-Holland.

Ayres, R. L. (1983), *Banking on the Poor*, Cambridge: MIT Press.

Barr, Nicholas (1987), *The Economics of the Welfare State*, London: Weidenfeld and Nicolson.

Beveridge, W. (1942), *Social Insurance and the Allied Services*, London: HMSO.

Dixon, J. (1981), *The Chinese Welfare State*, New York: Praeger.

Drèze, Jean (1990), *Widows in Rural India*, London: London School of Economics.

——————, and Amartya Sen (1989a), *Public Action for Social Security Foundations and Strategy*, London: London School of Economics.

——————, (1989b), *Hunger and Public Action*, Oxford: Clarendon Press.

Fraser, Derek (1984), *The Evolution of the British Welfare State*, London: Macmillan.

Gilbert, B. B. (1966), *The Evolution of National Insurance in Great Britain: The Origins of the Welfare State*, London: Michael Joseph.

GOI (Government of India), Economic Administration Reforms Commission (1984), *Against Undeserved Want: Report of the Working Group on Social Security*, New Delhi: Government of India.

Guha Roy, S. (1989), 'Perspectives on Population Ageing in India', in S. N. Singh *et al.* (ed.), *Population Transition in India*, vol. I, Delhi: B. R. Publishing Corporation.

Guhan, S. (1980), *Social Security: Lessons and Possibilities from the Tamil Nadu Experience*, Chennai: Madras Institute of Development Studies, *Bulletin*, XI (1).

—————— (1988), *Social Security in India: Looking One Step Ahead*, Chennai: Madras Institute of Development Studies, *Bulletin*, XVIII (9).

—————— (1990), *Social Security Initiatives in Tamil Nadu 1989*, Chennai: Madras Institute of Development Studies, Working Paper No. 96.

Himmelfarb, Gertrude (1984), *The Idea of Poverty: England in the Early Industrial Age*, London: Faber & Faber.

ILO (International Labour Organization) (1976), *Employment, Growth and Basic Needs: A One-World Problem*, Geneva: ILO.

—————— (1984), *Introduction to Social Security*, Geneva: ILO.

—————— (1984b), *World Labour Report*, Geneva: ILO.

Mesa-Lago, C. (1978), *Social Security in Latin America: Pressure Groups, Stratification and Inequality*, Pittsburgh: Pittsburgh University Press.

Midgeley, J. (1984), *Social Security, Inequality and the Third World*, New York: John Wiley.

Mouton (1976), *Social Security in Africa: Trends, Problems and Prospects*, Geneva: ILO.

Rose, Michael E. (1972), *The Relief of Poverty 1834–1914*, London: Macmillan.
Singer, H. W. (1979), 'Poverty, Income Distribution, and Levels of Living: Thirty Years of Changing Thought on Development Problems', in C. H. Hanumantha Rao and P. C. Joshi (eds), *Reflections on Economic Development and Social Change: Essays in Honour of Prof. V. K. R. V. Rao*, New Delhi: Allied Publishers.
Streeten, P. *et al*. (1981), *First Things First: Meeting Basic Human Needs in Developing Countries*, New York: Oxford University Press.
Stumpf, W. (1979), 'German Social Legislation under Otto Von Bismarck', in K. J. Rivinus (ed.), *The Social Movement in 19th Century Germany*, Inter Nationes, Bonn-Bad Godesbers.
UNDP (United Nations Development Programme) (1981), *Human Development Report 1991*, New York: Oxford University Press.
US Department of Health and Human Services (1982), *Social Security Programmes Throughout the World 1981*, Washington, DC.
van de Laar, A. J. (1980), *The World Bank and the Poor*, The Hague: Martinus Nijhoff.

DISCUSSION[13]

Arjun Sengupta: I think Guhan's paper can help us raise rather uncomfortable questions about the relationship between economic restructuring and possibilities for poverty alleviation.

In considering protective and promotional anti-poverty programmes, it seems that we must make a choice about what should be the logical priority in using scarce resources. If one frames the question in that way, it seems that those who argue for promotional anti-poverty programmes will have a stronger case, the argument being that the very scarce resources have to be used to help make people productive and to lift the burden from the shoulders of the government. So it is a question of placing promotional schemes before protective schemes.

T. R. Satish Chandran: The blueprint for a social security system is well presented, very persuasively argued. When we remember that for the government-employed and organized sector some benefits are already available, the case is strong for government intervention to provide some social security cover to the unorganized poor. It is also a fact, as evidenced by a number of studies, that what Guhan describes as promotional programmes for poverty alleviation do not always percolate to the poorest sections of society. It is clearly the responsibility of the government to take care of this section of the community.

---

[13] The seminar at which this paper was presented was followed by a discussion which is presented here.

While the case for social security is very strong, there is one statement which is perhaps arguable. Guhan has said that protective social security may be more cost-effective in reaching the poorest as compared with promotional anti-poverty measures. This statement is somewhat difficult to accept, since the two stand in very distinct categories and one cannot really compare the costs and effects of the two kinds of approaches. For instance, if you look at anti-poverty programmes, specially the wage employment programmes, and the minimum needs programmes which have been implemented in the Fifth Five-year Plan, there is ample documentation to show that these do touch the poorest sections of the community, and in the process also create productive assets. To my mind, therefore, the statement that protective social security can be more cost-effective may not be quite acceptable.

But the minimum protective package which he suggests is very reasonable. Since protection against sickness and unemployment are not amenable to any kind of manageable social security programme in India at the moment, he is suggesting a coverage for other kinds of contingencies, like maternity, disability, old age and so on. The numbers which he has worked out also appear very reasonable for the minimum package which he has presented. The expenditure estimated is around Rs 1300 crore. On the face of it, this looks very reasonable and acceptable.

If one looks at the present levels of expenditure on social security in the different states, the expenditure on social security amounts to 1.15 per cent of the total expenditure of the central and state governments. I tried to work out in a very approximate fashion what this means in terms of expenditure on social security only. My estimate, rough though it is, is that the current level is already about Rs 1000 crore, taking all the states together. The calculation is very simple. Rs 1520 crore was the money allocated in 1989-90 for social security and welfare, and probably for social security the percentage will be around 70 per cent. Therefore, the aggregate package suggested by Guhan seems very reasonable and affordable.

But when you disaggregate among the states you find that the problem is not that simple. There is a very large variation in the percentage of expenditure on social security from one state to another. The range varies from 0.35 per cent in Rajasthan to 2.1 per cent in Karnataka and Tamilnadu as a percentage of the total expenditure of the state government. Kindly remember that the bulk of the expenditure on social security is provided in the state budgets, and the central government really does not have much of a role.

Given this wide variation, the question arises whether the kind of lead which Tamilnadu or Kerala gave in establishing social security systems can really be matched by the other states. In Karnataka, which is one of the states spending quite a substantial amount on social security, in the 1990-1 budget, Rs 87 crore have been provided and the number of beneficiaries exceeds a million. But this is not typical of what you find in other states like Bihar or Orissa. Even Maharashtra is not spending very much on social security though it is a relatively rich state.

Basically, there are three kinds of requirements: physical resource development, which is very necessary for establishing the country on a sustained growth path, investment on human development, which is equally important, and investment in social security. What kind of balance can one expect when there is a severe constraint on resources? I may mention very briefly that government expenditure falls into three categories: general services, which essentially deals with regulatory organs of the state-police, judiciary, legislature, and so on; social and community service, which cover education, health, water supply, and so on; and economic services, which deals with agriculture, industry and other kinds of productive activities. Between 1974–5 and 1989–90, the rate of growth of expenditure on social and community services was higher than on general services in nine out of fourteen states. In all the states the proportion of expenditure on economic services registered a decline. What are the implications of this?

It is agreed that we must invest in human development, in social security, and we must also have growth, for one cannot sustain human development without growth, and vice versa. If you analyse the state expenditure from a slightly different, but related angle, that is, what has been the pattern of the division of expenditure as between revenue and capital outlay, taking Tamilnadu as an example, the share of revenue expenditure in 1961–2 was 65.3 per cent and capital outlay was 11.6 per cent. By 1989–90, the share of revenue expenditure in Tamilnadu had gone up to 84.3 per cent, the share of capital outlay had come down, to 3.4 per cent. The point I am submitting is that there are many states in India which face a rather difficult dilemma. Infrastructure development is still weak and has to be strengthened, and this has to go on simultaneously with investments on social security and human development. It is certainly not reasonable to expect all states to allocate as much for social security as Tamilnadu does. It is basically this interstate differential which is a major problem which will stand in the way of any kind of a uniform blueprint for social security systems all over the country.

Moving on to a slightly different point, Guhan in his paper has estimated that even with a more generous package of social security benefits, the cost will be only about Rs 2300 crore per year and that as the poverty ratio goes down, the requirement of funds for social security will diminish. I am not sure whether this will be the case.

If one goes by the experience in western countries, or even in Sri Lanka for that matter, one finds that as levels of income improve, expectations in terms of social security benefits also move up parallelly. It is very rarely that as income rises, the proportion of expenditure on social security comes down. To the best of my knowledge, this has not happened in any country in the world. I am not suggesting that for this reason India should not spend more on social security. I am only making the point that any kind of investment on social security, once made, will not diminish. Rather, the likelihood is it will increase in course of time. The question is whether in the next ten or twenty years, given the requirement of funds for sustaining growth, and for human development, the country can really think of a more generous social security package?

Guhan has suggested in his paper that social security payments can be quite readily met out of surcharge on personal income tax. Conceptually, certainly one can argue that those who can earn more, should pay for the relief of those who are less privileged. But there is one statement which may appear as a semantic point and maybe I have not understood it very clearly. Guhan makes the point that in western countries the percentage of income tax payers is much larger than in India, so also the proportion of tax revenues of the government much higher. He attributed this to social security payments. To my mind this logic is a little difficult to follow. I thought it was the reverse, or at least the two go in parallel. Social security payments in western countries are related to incomes earned. I do not see how social security leads to better tax revenue. I thought it was the other way about. This is a substantive point, although it is not germane to the main argument presented in the paper.

Lastly, I would say that the suggestion that the central government should intervene is not to my mind acceptable, partly from the fact that it raises a whole set of questions in regard to Centre–state relations which are already facing some kind of strain. Basically the concept in our Constitution is that the main interface with the ordinary citizens is of the state government and it is only the state government which can administer such a programme. In fact, if you really want to have a mass programme you will have to take it down to the lower levels also. I do not see any kind of justification for central intervention. Under the Constitution social security is a concurrent subject. But this provision was made only because insurance is a central government subject. Except for this limited role of the Centre, I do not think there is any need for the central government to get into the administration of social security.

To conclude, one still remains faced with this dilemma how to balance between requirements for physical resource development, human development, and social security. Undoubtedly there can be no clear-cut answers. It has to be a matter of judgement at a given point of time as to where that balance should be drawn. Personally, I would argue and take the position that of the three, social security would come last. I would place greater emphasis on both physical resource development and human development because in the long run it is these which will relieve poverty in the country. Certainly limited social security programmes of the type which are already operating in certain states can be continued. But enlarging them does not appear justified in the present context.

Giovanni Andrea Cornia: I like this paper which I think somewhat strangely shifts the emphasis in a country where the population structure is dominated by youth and children towards a group of the population which is perhaps less well represented both in numbers and in political power. Nevertheless, it does raise issues of overall similarity.

I do not know whether there are methods which can be efficiently used to compare benefits in different measures. In broader terms I found it a bit difficult to use a strict version of the human capital theory by which we invest only on those who are, or may become, productive. I think that it may not do much good to social values.

What are the criteria which can help us in assessing whether an employment guarantee scheme is more efficient *vis-à-vis* social security scheme? What is the political economy of the social security programme proposed by Guhan? What would be the institutions or who are the political parties, the social groups which would press for it? This is unclear to me.

Guhan suggests that about 16 million individuals living in 68 million poor households can be reached. Would that make a significant dent or would it be a drop in the sea? In terms of per capita, would the benefits proposed make up the income gap of the poor or at least 30 or 40 per cent of it? Are we sure that the four measures that Guhan has suggested are indeed the best ones? Where does one stand in terms of child benefits?

V. K. Ramachandran: I think the programme advocated by Guhan makes political sense. Tamilnadu has shown through its voting pattern that one of the factors in the repeated victory of the AIADMK has been the noon-meal scheme which was initially targeted to children in the age group 5 to 9 years. Once such a scheme is introduced, it cannot be withdrawn, unless there is a tangible trade-off. That is a very good aspect of the scheme.

Muchkund Dubey: I wish to raise two points of a general nature. Very few can question the desirability of the schemes. As regards interstate priority, there might be scope for different opinions. But the main point is, who is going to implement them and how? Another point is, the central government has already acquired too much power, particularly in the Concurrent List subjects, and there is not much justification for having such large central ministries for education, agriculture and industry. It would also be legitimate to take the view that this development is one of the reasons for the tensions in the country and the fissiparous tendencies. So, however desirable the schemes might be, one should not suggest that it should be taken up by the central government.

Regarding the universalization of the successful experiences in individual states, like land reforms in West Bengal, it would be too facile a solution to suggest that the Centre should intervene and force it upon the states. Basically the urge for it should arise from within the state itself. Bringing this about is the main problem that one should discuss.

Francine Frankel: One comment has been that Guhan's proposal is politically infeasible. I think it is particularly difficult. Clearly in the context of Tamilnadu, it has not been infeasible. We should try to learn why this is so.

With marketization, this type of scheme will become enormously important because the people left out of successful marketization will be the people who, for various reasons, cannot work. I think it is very important to introduce this scheme somewhere along the line before marketization.

S. Guhan: I had thought throughout that this seminar is related to human development and not to adjustment. Everything here has been discussed in the context of adjustment. I am not clear why humanity is out of court in a symposium devoted to human development. So, frankly I find some of the criticisms hard to take.

What are the logical or philosophical or economic criteria that can allow people to decide these issues? Anybody can erect a system of choices which will make sense. So long as there are old people who are destitute, I would assume, on an axiomatic basis, that they would have to be taken care of.

Someone has to do something for the silent poor. We are not talking of what the politicians are likely to do. It is obviously because they are not likely to do it that I thought it was the responsibility of academics to press for it.

Regarding differential expenditure in different states, I have gone into it quite carefully. I went into state-wise figures. The per capita expenditure is very low in UP, very high in Kerala. It is precisely because of this that I feel that the Centre should get a hand in promoting an all-India blueprint. I do not mean implementation by the Centre at all, but devising a scheme of transfers whereby, for instance, you say that the first slab of, say, Rs 5 or Rs 10 per capita is on account of the state and then the Centre matches whatever is done; so that progressive states like Kerala will get a little more money. But a state which is spending too low will be pulled up.

The point about the four specific measures is explained in my paper. If you want a more simple package, a one-point programme, it will be old-age pensions. For old-age pensions, I challenge any one of you to give me an alternative. Can we do without pensions? Can we prevent old age? This is something you have to decide, especially in a symposium devoted to human development.

4

Health in India During a Period of Structural Adjustment*

I am greatly honoured at being invited to deliver the fifth Father James S. Tong Memorial Oration. Father Tong practised the presence of God in a spirit of active humanism. Throughout his life, he continually enlarged and diversified the sphere of his activities. Most notably, his contribution to the creation of the voluntary Health Association of India reflected his belief that health cannot stop short of being a social concern. It is as a humble homage to this conviction that I would like to discuss the issues involved in the subject of this lecture.

In the terminology of plans and budgets, health is classified as one of the social services provided by the state and as one among basic minimum needs. Health is, in fact, the primary social welfare service and the most basic need in any society. It is the health status of the people, affecting as it does morbidity and mortality, that determines the quality and longevity of life itself. Health is, thus, not merely a need; it is an ingredient of the most fundamental of all rights, namely, the right to life. It is in this context that the Universal Declaration of Human Rights, adopted by the United Nations, states that everyone has the 'right to a standard of living adequate for the health and well-being of his family including medical care', and the World Health Assembly of WHO has resolved that 'the right to health is a fundamental right'.

---

* Text of the Father James Tong Memorial Oration delivered, under the auspices of the Voluntary Health Association of India, at New Delhi on 4 September, 1992.

shown significant increase. In the matter of curative services, the proportions of population to doctors and nurses have been brought down to 2500 and 1700 by the mid-eighties from levels of 6000 and 4300 that prevailed at the time of Independence.

These facts sufficiently indicate the striking progress that has been registered in India's health status compared to the very poor levels that the country inherited at the end of British rule. The legitimate satisfaction that one feels from these comparisons, however, gets diluted when we compare achievements in the health sector in India to those of some other developing countries or when achievements are compared to targets adopted within India itself. Comparisons apart, the objective facts relating to India's health scene can only be characterized as deeply disturbing.

Life expectancy in India in 1990 of 59 years was about ten years lower than in China or Sri Lanka and about three years less than for all low-income developing countries. In terms of the right to life, women and children are the most disadvantaged in our country. The infant mortality rate in India in 1990 (92 per 1000 live births) was about three times as much as in China (29) and only a little less than five times the IMR in Sri Lanka (19). The age-specific death rate for female children under age 5 (40.5) was about 25 per cent higher than for male children (31.9). The other vulnerable period for female mortality is the peak reproduction period. In this phase, the maternal mortality rate is an important indicator: India's MMR of 500 per 100,000 live births is many times that of 44 in China and 90 in Sri Lanka. Given also India's high fertility rates, Meera Chatterjee has pointed out that the lifetime mortality risk to the average Indian woman during reproduction is 300 times greater than that in many high-income countries. Higher female mortality at childhood and among young mothers largely explains the adverse sex ratio for women which in 1991 was 929 for 1000 males in the population. As Amartya Sen has graphically put it, what the adverse sex ratio means is that about 37 million women are 'missing' in India's population.

Maternal and child health are closely related. The proportion of low birth weight babies in India (180–8) is 30 per cent in all developing countries, and about 40 to 50 per cent of children are severely or moderately malnourished. Added to this is discrimination against girls in access to food and medical care which starts from infancy. Girls fail to reach their full growth potential, get married early, run considerable risk of obstetric complications, and give birth to low-weight babies, perpetuating the vicious circle.

Despite progress made since Independence, the situation in regard to public sanitation, preventive health care, control of communicable diseases, and health education are all far from satisfactory. Public sanitation is woefully inadequate where it is needed most, namely, in the poorer sections of large towns and in the smaller urban areas. Meanwhile, growing urbanization has considerably exacerbated the problem. As Sumit Guha has pointed out: 'The florid and lethal diseases—cholera and smallpox—have been controlled or eradicated, but the protean and familiar dysenteries seem unaffected... perhaps because contaminated soil, hands and flies still provide them with adequate means of propagation.' Equally disappointing is the continued prevalence of malaria: the original target was to eradicate it by the mid-sixties but during the whole of the last two decades about 2 to 3 lakh cases of malaria have been recorded every year. Episodes of cholera continue to recur and the incidence of leprosy, kala-azar and filariasis are not insignificant. In the allocation of resources, preventive health gets only a share of one-fourth to one-third.

Very little data is available on levels, trends, and on regional and case-wise patterns of morbidity in India. Official data on morbidity is seriously inadequate because it is confined to public facilities which are estimated to be used only for one-fourth of acute illnesses. The National Sample Survey (NSS) in 1974 reported a prevalence rate of about 2300 per 100,000 of population but this may be an underestimate considering that other surveys in India have estimated rates three to four times as much. We may get a firmer estimate when the results of the NSS 1987 survey are published. The interesting fact is that morbidity, as reported, in Kerala, is relatively high despite low levels of mortality. This is, no doubt, due in part to higher literacy and better availability and access to health services in Kerala. But it could also mean that high morbidity can coexist with low mortality and even get accentuated by it because of longer life expectancy and diseases of old age. In other words, life expectancy and death rates, which are the most commonly used indicators of health status, do not convey the full picture; and morbidity surveys, which have been relatively neglected in India, are of high priority.

Related to the subject of morbidity, we need to take note of the fact that India may be passing through an epidemiological transition. In addition to the diseases of poverty and undernutrition, those related to urbanization and affluence, such as cardio-vascular ailments and cancer, are becoming important. To these must be added environmental health hazards stemming from industrialization and transportation, behavioural health hazards related to smoking, alcoholism, and drug addiction, internationally high rates of road accidents, geriatric health problems and the looming spectre of AIDS. This is not a transition that uniformly affects all sections of the population all over the country at the same time. Differing epidemiological patterns between the rich and poor and between town and country coexist and continue to widen. In such a situation of polarization, the danger is that resources for diagnostic and curative services are likely to be shifted towards the needs of the urban and affluent, further worsening the already low level of preventive and curative services available to the rural and urban poor. We can all see evidence of this, particularly in the case of the commercialized medical market and, increasingly, in public hospitals as well.

Turning to curative services, India's ratio of population for doctors (2500) compares favourably with those for all low-income countries (5500) although it is less than half as good as the ratio in China (1000). There are, however, serious imbalances in respect of hospital beds and doctors between rural and urban areas, from state to state, and between the public and private sectors. In 1986, the rural share in hospital beds was less than 13 per cent compared to India's rural population share of more than 70 per cent. No all-India or systematic state-wise distribution of the rural–urban distribution of doctors is available but many studies have brought out the serious imbalance. Interstate differentials in this respect also continue to be very wide with the best-served state, which is Maharashtra, having a ratio three to four times as favourable as those for Uttar Pradesh, Rajasthan, Bihar or Madhya Pradesh. The public sector's share in doctors has steadily declined from about 40 per cent in the mid-sixties to about 25 per cent in the late eighties. While 75 per cent of hospital beds are in the public sector, about 75 per cent of doctors are in the private sector. Consequently, the bed-to-doctor ratio in public facilities in the mid-eighties was about nine times that in the private sector.

Of equal concern is the quality of medical care to which the rural, poor and the illiterate patient in India has access. The private sector in medical care includes not only qualified practitioners, but also large numbers and a wide variety of semiqualified and unqualified persons such as midwives, compounders and para-medical personnel, drug shop attendants, and so on, who practise any and all forms of treatment. One study (Viswanathan and Rhode 1990) found that among the practitioners surveyed who were commonly described in rural areas as 'doctors', only 3 per cent had an MBBS degree and only 38 per cent had any type of medical qualification at all. Studies of private medical practice also indicate the wide prevalence of dubious clinical methods. Ravi Duggal and Sucheta Amin, in their study of Jalgaon in Maharashtra, found that 70 per cent of all illnesses were treated with injections. Duggal and Amar Jessani have drawn attention to a number of facts to substantiate rampant commercialization and technical incompetence in the medical profession such as the reckless and irrational prescription of drugs and diagnostic procedures; the close nexus between doctors and drug stores, pathology laboratories, and diagnostic centres; and a variety of other unethical and commercial practices. Although it is impossible to precisely quantify the extent to which they prevail, we should not blind our eyes to the common knowledge that—apart from its adequacy, affordability, and spread—the quality of medical care available to the common man or woman in India is such as to cause serious concern. Nor are, by any means, unethical practices confined to the private sector. In fact, inasmuch as private practice is allowed to government doctors, the distinction between the public and private sectors in medical care is so blurred as to become notional. Many government doctors are also, in large measure, private doctors; if anything, they are worse because they utilize their public position to capture lucrative clientele for their private practice and devote the best part of their time and attention to such patients.

In regard to both preventive and curative health services, the outreach to rural areas is meant to be provided through the network of PHCs and sub-centres linked by referral to a network of taluk and district hospitals equipped with adequate facilities for diagnosis, treatment, nursing and specialist facilities. Successive plans have repeated coverage targets of one sub-centre for 5000 population and a PHC for 30,000 population. By the mid-eighties, actual coverage was one sub-centre for about 10,000 of population and a PHC for about 70,000 of population. In other words, as of now, we are only about halfway towards the achievement of the modest targets reiterated from time to time. This picture of inadequate coverage is vastly compounded by several shortcomings in the functioning of the primary health care network, which have been documented in a number of micro-level studies as well as in the more wide-ranging evaluations of the ICMR and the Operations Research Group (ORG), Baroda, both of which were published as recently as 1989. The position at the end of the eighties was that the full complement of staff had been posted only in 70 to 80 per cent of PHCs and sub-centres. About 15 to 20 per cent of the posts to which persons had been appointed were vacant at any given time. Transfers were frequent with doctors not remaining in any one PHC for more than about two years. Drugs, especially antibiotics, were almost always in short supply. In a majority of facilities, labour rooms and operation theatres were absent or inadequately equipped. Coverage of ante-natal care was low and attendance of trained health workers at deliveries was rare. Many ANMs were resident in nearby towns and only occasionally appeared at their places of duty. Their technical knowledge in regard to post-natal care was described as 'very poor'. To get the picture in all its dismal fullness, one must add corruption, private practice, and misuse of drugs and transport.

The critical importance of population control does not need much argument in the Indian context. In the demographic transition from high birth and death rates to low levels of both, India has covered only about half the distance. India's mortality decline has been under way for nearly six decades but fertility has begun to decline only in the last two decades or so. Between 1970 and 1987, India's total fertility rate is estimated to have declined from 6 to 4.1 and will need to reduce by another two points to reach the replacement level of 2.1. Sterilization still remains the main method of contraception, accounting for about three-fourths of all forms, but is beginning to yield diminishing returns because it has been mainly targeted at high-parity couples not interested in, or capable of, having any more children. Future reductions in fertility will have to involve not only the greater use of spacing methods but also a wide front of non-contraceptive measures, principally female literacy and reductions in the IMR through wider and better provision of maternity and child health services. Population control itself will also need to be closely targeted at the high-fertility states of Uttar Pradesh, Bihar, Madhya Pradesh and Rajasthan. Together these four states constitute 40 per cent of India's population and their fertility rates are around 5, about 25 per cent more than the national average and twice or more the levels in Kerala (2.2) and Tamilnadu (2.6).

There are immense problems in estimating the expenditure

on health in the economy as a whole including government, local body, private and household expenditures. We have to rely on the very broad magnitudes which emerge from various studies. Private expenditures on health care are probably of the order of 60 to 70 per cent of total expenditure. Budgetary figures for 1991-2 indicate that excluding family welfare, the combined expenditure of the central and state governments on medical care, medical education and public health was about Rs 5000 crore or 2.5 per cent of total expenditures of the Centre and the states. About 25 to 35 per cent was for preventive health and about 40 to 50 per cent was allocated to rural areas. There are considerable interstate differences in per capita government expenditure on health with backward-health status states such as Bihar, UP, Madhya Pradesh and Rajasthan having levels distinctly lower than the national average. Including family welfare, health expenditure in the public sector came to about one per cent of GDP and to about 4 per cent of government expenditure. These magnitudes are far below the WHO norm of 5 per cent of GDP and the targets of 3 per cent of GDP and 15 per cent of government expenditures recommended by the Bhore Committee, as far back as 1946. In fact, the Bhore Committee went so far as to recommend that 'it should be a statutory obligation on Governments to spend a minimum of 15 per cent of their revenues on health activities.'

I had begun this lecture by pointing out that health being of foundational value to individuals and society, it qualifies as a fundamental right. Our broad survey of India's current health status would amply show that the state in India, despite progress since Independence, has a long way to go in making the right to health a reality for its citizens. Resources of finance and manpower devoted to preventive health and for MCH have been neither adequate nor efficiently used. The states have chosen to remain minor partners in the provision of curative services, which are both inadequate and of poor quality for the bulk of the population. There are serious inequalities in respect of both inputs and output indicators between states, between rural and urban areas, between rich and poor, between male and female, and between children and adults. These inequalities are superimposed one upon another so that there is a yawning gap between the effective access to health of a poor woman or child, especially if Scheduled Caste or Tribal, in the rural areas of a backward state like Orissa and that of an affluent person in a metropolitan city like New Delhi or Mumbai. In these circumstances, 'Health for All' remains a distant dream.

☆

This has to be the background to our discussion of the economic adjustment process into which India has entered, its likely consequences for health, and how these consequences need to be responded to. The Finance Minister has succinctly summarized why adjustment has become necessary by saying that both the country and the government had been living beyond their means and cannot continue to do so any longer. The country had been living beyond its means in the sense that balance-of-payments deficits had become unsustainable at the beginning of the nineties. The Government has been living beyond its means since its large and growing fiscal deficits had become equally intolerable because of their implications for inflation, debt accumulation and the external payments gap. It is in these circumstances that adjustment has become inevitable and urgent.

Adjustment implies a process of moving to an equilibrium in our external and budgetary accounts through improving supplies and reducing demand in the economy and by increasing revenues and curtailing expenditure in the exchequer. Such an equilibrium can be attained at different levels and following different paths. At two ends of the range, adjustment can be accompanied by growth, equity, and price stability or it can involve stagnation, inequity and inflation. The real issue, therefore, is not whether adjustment is necessary but how it can be put through in a manner that reinforces, instead of undermining, our long-term objective of growth with social justice.

Various studies are now available on the impact of adjustment on social services generally and specifically on health, nutrition and child services in Latin American, African and Asian countries which have had to go through the adjustment process in the early eighties following the second oil shock, global recession and the debt crisis. In almost all cases, the impact of adjustment has been initially quite severe. Country responses to adjustment have, however, varied a great deal. While in some countries, government policies have not been able to overcome the impact or have even worsened it, a number of countries—notably Jamaica, Cuba, Costa Rica, Chile,

Botswana, China, Sri Lanka and South Korea—have been able to cope successfully with the crisis maintaining, and in some cases even improving their health performance. This should give us confidence that adjustment can provide the challenge and opportunity not only to safeguard health in the medium term but to promote longer-term objectives on a sustained basis.

Since India has embarked on adjustment only recently, the first task will be to anticipate the likely consequences of the adjustment process on the health sector. They will be direct and indirect, short term and long term, and will stem from budgetary constraints as well as more general policy perspectives. On the budgetary front, the sharp fiscal contraction that is being put through in the form of reductions to the fiscal deficit from 8.5 to 5 per cent of GDP in three years can have serious consequences for allocations available for health services which, for a variety of reasons, may be curtailed by much more than a pro-rata reduction. Given large requirements for capital outlays on sectors such as energy, transport, and irrigation, social services as a whole may be faced with a more than proportionate cut. Within broad health-related activities, there will be strong pressures favouring the claims of water supply and of family planning vis-à-vis resources for health services and particularly for preventive and rural health services. Within the health sector itself, increases to the costs of salaries and drugs and the prior claims of non-Plan maintenance expenditure will squeeze out resources available for incremental plan expenditures. Fiscal contraction, thus, will not only reduce aggregate levels of expenditure but can also be expected to result in sharp changes to previous patterns and purposes of public outlays. In this process, the devil will take the hindmost. Health is likely to be most affected since its visibility is low and its political constituency is weak compared, for instance, to the demands of defence, energy, salary increases to government employees, or subsidies to farmers.

In addition to reduced budgetary inputs for the health system, the possible indirect effects of the adjustment process on health status will be relevant. In the short to medium term, adjustment in many countries has been accompanied by low growth, inflation and higher levels of unemployment. In such a context, reductions in real terms in welfare subsidies, as part of fiscal contraction, especially in food subsidies, can considerably lower the standard of living of the poor with serious consequences to their health status. Such changes will work themselves over time and it will be possible to measure and analyse them only after several years. What is important, however, is to be aware that as far as health is concerned, adjustment has a scissors effect: on one hand, the resources available to the sector are reduced; concurrently, on the other, there is an increase in the needs to be met.

The third main consequence of adjustment is more intangible but none the less significant. Because adjustment causes governments to contract on their spending, it carries with it a tendency, if not a temptation, to argue for, or accept, a lesser role for public spending. Ideologically, the state begins to accept a posture of retreat and looks for all possible ways appropriate or inappropriate, 'to leave things to the market'. The concepts of liberalization and privatization—however valid they might be in certain spheres of governmental activity—take on the character of slogans. As applied to the health sector in a country like India this can prove to be utterly retrograde. According to the paradigm, the competitive market is characterized by numerous producers and consumers for homogeneous products. There are no barriers to information, and demand and supply are balanced at efficient levels of costs and prices. Without going into a detailed discussion of the market for medical care in India, it will be clear that this model is far from applicable to it either on the demand or the supply side. The ordinary person in need of medical care needs it soon and close to where he lives; he has no time, or money, or knowledge to explore the market or to assure himself of the quality of the product or to test out the market in a series of repeat transactions. In these circumstances, the seller is in a position to charge what the market will bear and is also under no compulsion to meet norms of quality. In medical care, as in other spheres, the market is highly dualistic. While the affluent are able to afford high-quality and adequate services, medical care for the poor is inadequate, substandard and expensive. This fundamental distortion can be corrected only if the state intervenes to provide adequate, effective and affordable medical care to the rural and urban poor.

☆

We have discussed symptoms and aetiology, and it is time to share some thoughts on how India might respond to the impact of adjustment on the health sector, assuming, of course, that the response will be positive and not one of passive drift. A minimal response would be to protect allocations to the health sector with such incremental outlays and improvements as are feasible in annual and five-year plans. A stronger response would be to use the opportunity of the present crisis to take a good hard look at policies, programmes, and implementation in a longer-term perspective—during and beyond adjustment—in order to achieve lasting improvements. If the impact of adjustment on the health sector can be likened to a bout of illness affecting an already malnourished patient, it is necessary not only to cure him but also to improve his general condition and stamina. My own proposals in this regard can be stated quite briefly: after all, when doctors start to write prescriptions they are swift even if they are not always sure!

To start with, the state must accept that it has to play the prime role in the health sector. The state alone can play a role in preventive health, in maternal and child services, and in family welfare. It has also to play a much larger role in curative health if existing gross injustices and inequalities are to be reduced instead of being aggravated.

Budgetary resources for the health sector should be increased to reach, within a period of about ten years, the norm of 15 per cent of total governmental expenditure. As a developing country, India urges industrialized nations to conform to targets for development assistance. It is equally, if not all the more, necessary for the government to accept an internal target for fulfilling obligations to its own people. Reaching this target in a decade will involve no more than a 15 per cent annual increase in real budgetary allocations from a low base. This should be entirely feasible. Additional resources for the health sector can be found in many ways such as reallocation of priorities, eliminating waste and leakage in government expenditure, and most importantly through better collection of taxes. Current efforts to reduce the fiscal deficit fall very heavily on expenditure reduction and quite lightly on revenue mobilization. There is no reason why this should be so in a country where black money is rampant and nearly 75 per cent of taxable income goes unreported.

Within the health sector itself, there is scope for cost recovery and for much more cost-effectiveness. Better cost recovery in curative services from those who can afford to pay, which is being strongly urged by agencies like the World Bank, is unexceptional in principle but for a variety of reasons too much should not be expected in practice from this avenue. In India, public hospital facilities are used mostly by the poor; the poor already have to incur considerable indirect costs for obtaining medical care on travel, waiting time, forgone earnings, and bribery; and income screening is generally a game that is not worth the candle under our conditions.

The brunt of the emphasis will, therefore, have to be on cost-effectiveness which should be understood as not cost reduction *per se* but maximizing value for unit of expenditure through improvements in the total factor productivity of all human, material and financial inputs. Specifically, this will involve much better motivation, management, supervision and discipline at all levels of the health administration. Private practice among government doctors will have to be effectively banned; moonlighting of para-medical personnel must be curbed; and corruption, waste and leakage at all levels and in all forms put down with an iron hand.

There has been a rapid increase in drug prices even in the last few months. India must firmly oppose changes in patent laws which might result in alarming increases to drug prices. Financial allocations for the free supply of drugs in PHCs must be increased so as to adequately meet demand. The use of only essential drugs should be enforced in public facilities and promoted in the private sector as well. The share of the public sector in their production must be increased. The subsidization of high-cost essential drugs may also become necessary.

Medical education in India is much sought after and is highly subsidized. There is need and scope for the state to impose societal obligations on medical graduates by requiring them to undergo a minimum period of public service in rural and semi-urban areas. The output of MBBS graduates has remained stagnant for many years despite increase in population and incomes. A good proportion of our doctors migrate, and the population-doctor ratio needs to be brought down. There is, therefore, a strong case for increasing output; also, a clear case for higher cost recovery in medical education.

The private sector in medical care and diagnostic services has mushroomed in large cities, giving rise to rank commercialization, unethical practices and negligence. However difficult it might be, it is necessary to formulate policies and procedures to regulate and monitor the private sector. They could include effective mechanisms for self-regulation, in consultation with responsible sections of the profession.

Given the episodic nature and lumpy cost of illness, insurance has a logical role to play in the financing of medical care. Government can promote poor-oriented medical insurance in three ways, learning from Latin American and Chinese experience. Compulsory social insurance can be promoted for occupational groups in the organized and unorganized sectors. Secondly, special incentives can be given to voluntary agencies who provide health care in their own institutions or through participating doctors on the basis of insurance. Thirdly, insurance can be linked to decentralized health services provided through local bodies.

Decentralization is of crucial importance for promoting accountability, for raising local resources for the health sector, and for giving content to the objective of participatory health care. The village health guides scheme introduced by the Janata Government in 1977 still covers only half the country. Learning from the experience of the last fifteen years, a new momentum can be given to this scheme in terms of both coverage and effectiveness. Panchayat Raj institutions must be given a clear mandate for monitoring primary health care, maternal, child and family welfare services, health education, and water supply and sanitation.

Finally, I come to the voluntary sector. Voluntary agencies are the most encouraging aspect of the health scene in India. They have grown in number and have shown a deep commitment to health care. They still, however, add up to a relatively small proportion of total facilities, and there are considerable variations among them in the magnitude and quality of coverage, financial viability, and sustainability of leadership. There is much scope for voluntary agencies to work together, under the leadership of VHAI and otherwise, on two main fronts. One would be for sharing experience and promoting replication, for the larger and established agencies to help upgrade the smaller and newer ones, and for organizing common services such as training, action research, documentation, and fund raising which can help the entire community of voluntary agencies. The second will be to create a common platform for lobbying and advocacy. Despite much rhetoric, the government's attitude to the voluntary sector remains one of benign neglect at its higher levels and often of indifference or hostility at the field level. Voluntary agencies have to work together to bring about an attitudinal change. Specifically, they must collectively demand a reform of the archaic grant-in-aid system. Net-deficit grants should be replaced with fair and flexible proportionate grants; grants must be indexed for inflation; the schedule of releases must be concurrent with expenditures; and audits and inspection should not be inquisitorial.

☆

The agenda I have outlined would naturally and logically follow from any review of the health situation in India. There is nothing startlingly novel about it and few are likely to dissent from it on a conceptual plane. Even so, as I see it, its acceptance will not be easy because of two main reasons. The first is that health does not enjoy what might be called a natural political constituency. It is difficult to mobilize opinion for the better provision of a collective good such as preventive health or sanitation because, being everybody's business, such things tend to be viewed as nobody's particular concern. When it comes to curative services, its clientele resort to them infrequently and episodically; they are not like the regular clientele of fair price shops or metropolitan transport services. On the other hand, the suppliers of medical services can be expected to resist any reform that is likely to affect their entrenched vested interests. They are mostly urban, well organized, and articulate, and have considerable political access and clout unlike the users who are mostly rural, poor, illiterate, and unorganized.

In these circumstances, generating the needed political and administrative will for reforming the health sector will not be easy. It will demand persistent and energetic advocacy, against the current and at different levels: with parliament and legislatures, through pamphleteering and the use of media; and most importantly at the local level in the form of exposing, and seeking redress for, corruption, maladministration, and commercialization. In recent years, environmentalists in India have shown the way along these lines. The voluntary sector in health has reached a size and standing where it can also provide a similar leadership in building a broad-based alliance for health. We must, however, recognize that it will not be possible for any such alliance to desist from politics and, when it becomes necessary, from confrontation.

Let me recall the words of Dr B. C. Roy in his Presidential address to the All India Medical Conference in Lahore in 1929. He said:

I have very definite views on whether this Association should take up matters which, in common parlance, are dubbed political. In India, we have never regarded the various affairs of life as being in watertight compartments: politics, technically so called, is intermixed with economic, social and medical problems. If politics means the science of organization for the purpose of securing the greatest good for the largest number, I declare, we members of the profession dare not keep away from politics.

If the politics of health in India today favours those who stand in the way of reform, by the same token, change cannot be brought about except through political activism. In the body politic, as in the human body, natural immunological factors have to be provoked into a course of conflictual correction.

5

Social Expenditures in the Union Budget: 1991–6*

Ever since the new economic policies were initiated in India in 1991 their possible impact on the poor has received sustained attention in academic writings as well as due recognition in official documents. It has been generally realized that economic adjustment could adversely affect the living standards of the poor in the medium term at least until the beneficial promises of the new policies materialize. This might happen in direct and indirect ways. This stabilization phase is likely to be accompanied by a decline in economic growth and employment. Alongside changes in aggregate levels of employment, significant shifts could occur in the labour market in terms of sectors, regions, gender, skill levels, wages and conditions of employment. These might worsen the position of some of the vulnerable sections of the labour force. Similarly, the real incomes of the poorer groups might be endangered through changes in earnings and prices affecting their incomes and consumption. Of particular concern is that fiscal contraction is likely to result in reductions to outlays on subsidies and on budgetary outlays which are intended to benefit the poor.[1]

In this context discussions of the new economic policies have focused on the central government's budgetary expenditures on what

---

* Reprinted from *Economic and Political Weekly*, XXX (18 and 19), 6–13 May 1995, pp. 1095–1101.

[1] See in this connection, ILO (ARTEP), *Social Dimensions of Structural Adjustment in India*, New Delhi, 1992; S. P. Gupta (ed.), *Liberalization: Its Impact on the Indian Economy*, Macmillan, 1993; S. Guhan and K. Nagaraj, *Adjustment, Employment and Equity in India*, ILO, 1995.

might be described as the 'social sectors'. The concentration on the central budget could be justified on more than one ground. It can be argued that inasmuch as it is the Centre that has initiated the new policies, the primary responsibility is also that of the Centre for cushioning their impact on the poor. Secondly, the food subsidy and central and centrally sponsored programmes for poverty alleviation, employment generation and basic needs are especially relevant because they are sizable and have a nation-wide impact. Thirdly, practical constraints have operated to confine most of the discussion to the central level although the states have a much larger share in social expenditures: data in regard to the latter are less accessible in a timely and sufficiently disaggregated form; besides, wide variations among the states make it difficult to arrive at conclusions of general interest.

On its part as well, the central government has recognized the importance of social expenditures in its budget. The need for 'social safety nets' has been repeatedly referred to in the finance minister's budget speeches and in the annual *Economic Surveys* with attention being drawn to increases to allocations for social expenditures, reforms being made to existing programmes and to the initiation of new ones in the relevant sectors.[2] Adjustment, it has been frequently claimed, is being put through with a 'human face'.

Given the emphasis from all sides to the Centre's social expenditures during the period of adjustment, an analysis of such expenditures in terms of dimensions, trends, composition and policy is of importance and interest. This paper attempts that based on material available from the last six central budgets (1990–1 to 1995–6). We begin with identifying the outlays on what might be grossly described as 'social expenditures'. The levels and trends in these outlays during 1990–6 are then analysed. Some idea is provided of the Centre's outlays in relation to that of the states in this period. Within the so-called 'social expenditures', the outlays on major programmes of particular salience for the poor are identified. The levels, trends and new initiatives in

[2] The discussion paper put out by the GOI Ministry of Finance (1993) on 'Economic Reforms: Two Years after and the Task Ahead', for instance, refers to the importance of ensuring that the social costs involved in structural reform 'do not fall heavily on those least able to bear them'. The 'social safety net' it envisages for this purpose includes the National Renewal Fund, the PDS and expenditures on employment generation, rural development, health and education.

these programmes are discussed. Finally, since the poor will be with us in the foreseeable future, the Centre's role is relevant not only in the context of adjustment but also in a longer-term perspective of poverty alleviation. It is, therefore, necessary to explore options for making its anti-poverty expenditures more purposeful and cost-effective. The paper concludes with some suggestions in this regard.

BROAD PICTURE

At the outset, it is necessary to broadly identify the outlays that belong to the domain of our discussion. The central budget documents classify its expenditures under interest payments, defence expenditures, subsidies, non-Plan grants and loans, other non-Plan expenditures (for general services, social services and economic services), Plan expenditures (which is mostly on social and economic services) and central grant and loan assistance to state and UT plans. As a first cut, it will be reasonable to confine the analysis to three heads: (i) food subsidies, (ii) rural development (the outlays on which are classified under economic services), and (iii) the outlays which come under 'social services'. The grants and loans extended to states and UTs for central and centrally sponsored schemes under these heads are part of the Plan expenditures in the central sector while normal central assistance for state and UT plans given in 'block' form constitutes a separate category. 'Social services' in the budget documents include general education, technical education, sports and youth services, art and culture; health and family welfare; water supply, sanitation, housing and urban development; information and broadcasting; welfare of SC/ST and other backward classes; labour welfare; and social security and welfare. It will be apparent from this list that not all outlays under 'social services' are meant exclusively or especially for the poor and some not even primarily for them. At a subsequent stage, we have sorted out this expenditures in some detail; initially, however, our account covers all that is grossly classified as 'social services' in the budget documents. Although food subsidies are, undoubtedly, social expenditures, this paper does not deal with them and is confined to outlays on rural development and social services. Apart from spatial and temporal constraints, there are other good reasons for leaving out food subsidies: they do not relate to 'programmes' unlike the outlays in the other two sectors; food subsidies raise issues of a different and complex character; and, most importantly, there is an extensive literature evaluating their impact on poverty alleviation.[3]

Table 5.1 presents the outlays on rural development and social services in the Union budgets from 1990-1 to 1995-6. Both non-Plan and Plan outlays are included. In nominal terms, total outlays under these two heads have more than doubled from Rs 8058 crore in 1990-1 to Rs 17,924 crore in the 1995-6 Budget. As a proportion of the Centre's aggregate budgetary expenditures, the increase has been from 7.7 to 10.4 per cent in the period. Plan outlays in the two sectors as a proportion of the Centre's overall budgetary Plan outlays have risen from 22.1 to 31.3 per cent. The increase in GDP terms has, however, been much less impressive. The GDP proportion has gone up only marginally from 1.5 per cent in 1990-1 to 1.7 per cent in 1995-6. Nevertheless, the Centre's outlays are quite significant considering that, in sectors which fall primarily within the responsibilities of the states, they currently amount to over 10 per cent of its aggregate expenditures and to over 30 per cent in the Plan. What is also noteworthy is that these outlays have been increased, in proportion to total budgetary and Plan expenditures, during the period of adjustment.

Table 5.2 shows the budgetary expenditures in the states on rural development and social services including outlays on programmes funded under central and centrally sponsored schemes. The data is for 1990-1 to 1994-5 since the figures for 1995-6 are not yet available in the annual RBI survey of state finances. In the case of the states, the budget classification 'social services' includes general and technical education, sports, art and culture; medical, public health and family welfare; water supply and sanitation; housing and urban development; welfare of SC/ST and other backward classes; labour welfare; social security, welfare and nutrition; and the relief of natural calamities. Table 5.2 will show that states' outlays on rural development and social services marginally declined between 1990-1 and 1994-5 as a proportion of their aggregate expenditures (from 38.7 to 38.1 per cent) while Plan outlays in these

---

[3] The *Economic and Political Weekly* itself has carried a number of articles on the subject. Most recently, a useful collection is the set of papers brought out by the UNDP Research Project on Strategies and Financing of Human Development in India for the Workshop on Food Security and the Public Distribution System sponsored by the Planning Commission (28-9 April, 1995).

TABLE 5.1: Outlays on Rural Development and Social Services in the Central Budget: 1990–1 to 1995–6

(Rs crore)

	1990–1 Actuals	1991–2 Actuals	1992–3 Actuals	1993–4 Actuals	1994–5 RE	1995–6 BE
1. Rural development	2678	2283	3211	4521	6427	7330
Plan[a]	2672	2279	3208	4517	6427[b]	7330[b]
Non-Plan	6	4	3	4	–	–
2. Social services	5380	5892	6397	7906	9420	10594
Plan[a]	3597	3947	4294	5349	6697	7845
Non-Plan	1783	1945	2103	2557	2723	2749
3. Total	8058	8175	9608	12427	15847	17924
Plan[a]	6269	6226	7502	9866	13124	15175
Non-Plan	1789	1949	2106	2561	2723	2749
Memo						
A Total as percentage of centre's aggregate expenditures	7.7	7.3	7.8	8.8	9.8	10.4
B Plan expenditures as percentage of centre's aggregate plan expenditures in the budget[a]	22.1	20.1	20.5	22.1	26.9	31.3
C Total as percentage of GDP[c]	1.5	1.3	1.4	1.5	1.6	1.7
(GDP estimates)	(535517)	(616061)	(702829)	(814284)	(1017250)	(1047891)

Notes: [a] Does not include plan expenditures financed from internal and extra-budgetary resources of public-sector enterprises.
[b] Includes Rs 790 crore for the MP local area development scheme.
[c] The GDP estimates are official estimates for 1990–1, 1991–2 and 1992–3. For the three subsequent years they are the implied GDP estimates related to official estimates of the fiscal deficit. These estimates have been used for Tables 5.2 and 5.3 also.

Source: GOI Expenditure Budget 1995–6, vol. I, Annexures 3, 3.2 and 3.3.

TABLE 5.2: Outlays in States on Rural Development and Social Services: 1990–1 to 1994–5

(Rs crore)

	1990–1 Actuals	1991–2 Actuals	1992–3 Actuals	1993–4 RE	1994–5 BE
1. Rural development	5337	6109	7190	8493	9545
Plan	4217	4641	5585	6672	7594
Non-Plan	1120	1468	1605	1821	1951
2. Social services	29960	33688	37332	42357	48705
Plan	7304	8568	8944	11221	14309
Non-Plan	22656	25120	28398	31136	34396
3. Total	35297	39797	44522	50850	58250
Plan	11521	13208	14519	17893	21903
Non-Plan	23776	26589	30003	32957	36347
Memo					
A Total as percentage of centre's aggregate expenditures	38.7	36.6	37.3	37.8	38.1
B Plan expenditures as percentage of states' aggregate plan outlays	42.0	42.5	43.5	47.6	47.6
C Non-plan expenditures as percentage of total	67.4	66.8	67.4	64.8	62.4
D Total as percentage of GDP	6.6	6.5	6.3	6.2	5.6

Source: RBI Annual Surveys of State Finances.

sectors as a ratio of overall Plan outlays distinctly went up (from 42 to 47.6 per cent). This has been accompanied by a decline in the proportion of non-Plan to total expenditures in these sectors (from 67.4 to 62.4 per cent). Most importantly, states' outlays in these sectors (including those funded by the Centre) have declined in GDP terms from 6.6 per cent in 1990–1 to 5.6 per cent in 1994–5.

Table 5.3 takes an integrated look at the budgetary outlays on rural development and social services both at the Centre and in the states after adjusting for the relevant transfers on central and centrally sponsored schemes so as to avoid double counting. The outlays at both levels taken together have declined in GDP terms from 7.3 per cent in 1990–1 to 6.7 per cent in 1994–5. Within overall outlays, the Centre's share has gone up (from 20.6 to 23.2 per cent) while that of the states has gone down *pari passu* (from 79.4 to 76.8 per cent).

In sum, the story that emerges from these three tables is broadly the following. During 1990–1 to 1995–6, the Centre has increased its budgetary outlays on rural development and social services in nominal terms, in relation to its aggregate expenditures and as part of its Plan outlays. It has also improved its share in the integrated outlays at the two levels. Considering that the Centre is a junior partner in these sectors, its current share of about 23 per cent in the total is not insignificant. On the side of the states, the picture is less encouraging. Their outlays in these two sectors as a ratio of their aggregate expenditures has marginally declined. The states have also tended to emphasize Plan outlays as the cost of non-Plan expenditures; in other words, new schemes have received priority at the cost of funds required for the maintenance of existing facilities and services. This should be a matter for serious concern since the latter constitute three-fifths to two-thirds of social expenditures in the states.

In GDP terms, there has been only a marginal increase in the Centre's outlays while there has been a distinct decline in that of the states' (by as much as one per cent point between 1990–1 and 1994–5). In effect, the growth in central outlays has tended to displace states' outlays, particularly on the non-Plan account which is relevant for the maintenance of existing facilities and services. Among the reasons for this are a decline in the Centre's aggregate transfer to states, a shift from developmental to non-developmental expenditures in the states, and a lower priority for maintenance *vis-à-vis* incremental Plan outlays within the developmental budget for these

TABLE 5.3: Integrated Outlays of Centre and States on Rural Development and Social Services: 1990-1 to 1994-5

(Rs crore)

	1990-1 Actuals	1991-2 Actuals	1992-3 Actuals	1993-4[a]	1994-5[b]
1 States' total outlays on rural development and social services	35297	39797	44522	50850	58250
2 Grants and loans for central and centrally-sponsored schemes in rural development and social services[c]	4303	4718	5684	6769	5744
3 States' own expenditures (1–2)	30994	35079	38838	44081	52506
4 Centre's outlays on rural development and social services	8058	8175	9605	12427	15847
5 Total centre and states (3+4)	39052	43254	48446	56508	68353
Memo					
A Centre's share in total (4/5)	20.6	18.9	19.8	22.0	23.2
B State's share in total (3/5)	79.4	81.1	80.2	78.0	76.8
C Per cent of total centre and states to GDP	7.3	7.0	6.9	6.9	6.7

Notes: [a] Actuals for centre, RE for states.
[b] RE for centre, BE for states.
[c] Revised estimates *vide* statement 17 in *GOI Expenditure Budget*, vol. I (annual issues).

Source: As in Tables 5.1 and 5.2.

two sectors.[4] In the final outcome, what is of concern is that the GDP ratio of outlays at both levels taken together has declined in the first four years of adjustment. Given the magnitudes of poverty and deprivation in India, their absolute level at less than 7 per cent of GDP is also grossly inadequate for rural development and the entire gamut of social services. This is only the aggregate picture. Important dimensions which we will not be able to probe in this exercise are interstate variations, intersectoral variations and shifts in the composition of expenditures between salary costs and essential non-salary expenditures.

Major Programmes

The next step in the analysis is to identify within the wide and heterogeneous budgetary classification of 'social services' the major programmes in the central budget which are of salience for the poor. For this purpose, we begin by excluding the following outlays:

• Non-Plan expenditures which were about 15 per cent of total allocations in BE 1995–6 for rural development and social services. They relate largely to administrative overheads and expenditures on central establishments.

• The outlays on technical education, sports and youth services, art and culture.

• Outlays on medical and public health and on family welfare. Central expenditures on medical and public health are largely on the control of communicable diseases. Family welfare is a 100 per cent centrally sponsored programme for the control of population growth. Their intrinsic importance notwithstanding, these outlays do not have a specific pro-poor orientation.

• Outlays on housing which are largely on HUDCO schemes (financed mostly from its internal resources and borrowings) and on schemes for central government employees.

[4] The Centre's net transfers to states under all accounts (Plan, non-Plan and revenue, capital) declined from 6.2 per cent of GDP in 1990–1 to 4.8 per cent in 1994–5. In the same period, the proportion of non-development expenditures to total expenditures in the states went up from about 25 per cent to over 30 per cent.

- The outlays on information and publicity and on broadcasting. There is clearly no justification for treating them as 'social services' except, perhaps, that Akashvani and Doordarshan are not 'economic' services either!

- Outlays on labour and employment which largely consist of the Centre's statutory contributions for benefits to industrial workers in the organized sector. They also include allocations for the 'National Renewal Fund' which, although advertised by the government as a 'safety net', only meets retrenchment payments for public sector employees.

An idea of the extent of these exclusions can be gained from the fact that in BE 1995-6 they add up to Rs 5855 crore or about 33 per cent of the total budgetary allocation of Rs 17,924 crore for rural development and social services. In other words, *prima facie*, only about two-thirds of the allocation in the central budget for rural development and social services can be construed as being oriented for the poor in a broad sense. Such outlays relate to rural development and employment, general education, water supply and sanitation, urban development, welfare of Scheduled Castes, Scheduled Tribes and other backward classes, social security, and welfare and nutrition. In the central budget for 1995-6, they add up to Rs 12,069 crore.

Table 5.4 identifies the major individual programmes included under the above heads. These programmes have been grouped into five categories: (i) employment generation, (ii) backward area development, (iii) asset creation for poor households, (iv) provision of basic needs, and (v) welfare of SC/ST and OBC. Under each category and programme, the table presents the outlays in the central budget for the six years from 1990-1 to 1995-6. It might be mentioned that in BE 1995-6, the total outlays on the major programmes comes to Rs 10,934 crore or over 90 per cent of the Rs 12,069 crore in the broadly comprised poor-oriented sectors.

Table 5.4 brings out the levels, trends, and schemewise composition of the outlays under each of the five categories. It shows that between 1990-1 and 1995-6 there has been a definite shift in favour of employment programmes which currently account for about 57 per cent of the allocations for the major programmes. Under rural development, the shares of programmes for asset creation and for area development have declined. Allocations for basic needs and for the

TABLE 5.4: Outlays on Major Rural Development and Social Services Programmes in the Central Budget: 1990-1 to 1995-6

(Rs crore)

	1990-1 RE	1991-2 RE	1992-3 RE	1993-4 RE	1994-5 RE	1995-6 BE
1. Employment generation	2001 (49.5)	1825 (42.5)	2546 (51.5)	3906 (53.1)	5465 (58.1)	6222 (56.9)
• Jawahar Rozgar Yojna (JRY)	2001	1825	2546	3306	3535	3862
• Employment Asurance Scheme (EAS)	–	–	–	600	1140	1570
• MP Scheme for local area development	–	–	–	–	790	790
2. Basic needs	1059 (26.3)	1345 (31.3)	1361 (27.5)	1934 (26.3)	2254 (23.9)	2727 (24.9)
• Elementary education	224	268	339	443	511	651
• Adult education	131	105	110	168	211	234
• ACC rural water supply	403	638	460	738	810	1110
• Rural sanitation	18	4	20	32	60	60
• Urban water supply and sanitation	25	33	23	41	106	65
• Child welfare	258	297	409	512	556	607
3. Asset creation	484 (12.0)	474 (11.0)	467 (9.5)	721 (9.8)	735 (7.8)	890 (8.1)
• IRDP	356	356	375	617	625	640
• DWCRA and TRYSEM	18	16	21	29	40	79

(Contd.)

Table 5.4 contd.

	1990–1 RE	1991–2 RE	1992–3 RE	1993–4 RE	1994–5 RE	1995–6 BE
• Nehru Rozgar Yojana	110	102	71	75	70	71
• PM's Razgar Yojana	–	–	–	–	–	100
4. Welfare of SC, ST and OBC	321 (8.0)	428 (10.0)	465 (9.4)	589 (8.0)	730 (7.8)	810 (7.4)
5. Backward area development	172 (4.2)	222 (5.2)	101 (2.1)	202 (2.8)	230 (2.4)	285 (2.7)
• DPAP	56	51	51	77	85	125
• DDP	50	50	50	75	85	100
• Wastelands development	76	121	–	50	60	60
	4037 (100)	4294 (100)	4940 (100)	7352 (100)	9414 (100)	10934 (100)

Notes: Figures in brackets are percentages to column totals.
Source: GOI *Expenditure Budget*, vol. II (annual issues).

welfare of SC/ST and OBC have remained at about 25 per cent and 8 per cent respectively in terms of their shares in the total.

It is necessary to further analysis the outlays on employment in terms of their final outcomes since employment generation is only an intermediate input and a by-product benefit in the process of creating communal assets or assets for individual households. For this we have relied on the annual report of the Ministry of Rural Development for 1993-4 which provides the data on the sectoral distribution of expenditures in JRY and information on the scheme details of JRY, EAS and the MP local area development scheme. For 1995-6 (BE), Table 5.5 regroups the outlays for these employment schemes under relevant functional categories. The broad picture that emerges is that the outlays on major programmes is distributed for the following purposes: 24 per cent each for the development of backward areas (drought prone, desert, wastelands, backward blocks) and for economic and social infrastructure in rural areas (such as roads, minor irrigation, social forestry, schools and other community buildings), 25 per cent for the provision of basic needs mainly in rural areas (elementary and adult education, drinking water and sanitation), 19 per cent for direct transfers for the welfare of SC/ST and OBC and 8 per cent for asset creation for the poor through loans and subsidies (under IRDP, NRY and the Prime Minister's Rozgar Yojana). This is the pattern in the central budget. The proportions will differ in the final outlays because of matching contributions—in varying scheme-wise proportions—from the states and the credit component in IRDP.

Programme Details

The dimensional analysis should be supplemented with an account of the schematic and administrative features of these programmes. The anti-poverty portfolio of central and centrally sponsored schemes is characterized by a fragmentation of schemes under the same or similar functional purposes; a variety of matching grants; diverse allocational criteria to states and sub-state levels; multiple earmarkings of allocations to different areas, levels and purposes; and earmarking to different target groups within them. Under employment generation, for instance, there are three different schemes, namely, JRY, EAS and the MP local area development scheme. JRY itself has been trifurcated into three streams. Under the first stream, which accounts

TABLE 5.5: Functional Classification of Rural Development and Social Services Outlays in the Central Budget for 1995-6

(Rs crore)

	BE 1995-6	Percentage to total
1. Rural economic and social infrastructure	2644	24.2
• Under JRY first stream[a]	1854	
• MP local area development scheme	790	
2. Backward area development	2627	24.1
• Under JRY second stream[b]	772	
• EAS	1570	
• DPAP	125	
• DDP	100	
• Wastelands development	60	
3. Basic needs	2727	24.9
• Electricity and adult education	885	
• Rural water supply and sanitation	1170	
• Urban water supply and sanitation	65	
• Child welfare	607	
4. Welfare of SC/ST and OBC	2046	18.7
• Under JRY first stream[c]	1236	
• Direct welfare programmes	810	
5. Asset creation	890	8.1
• IRDP and related	719	
• NRY and PMRY	171	
Total	10934	100.0

Notes: [a] 60 per cent in JRY first stream (3090) which is 80 per cent of total JRY (3862).
[b] 20 per cent of total JRY (3862).
[c] 40 per cent in JRY first stream (3090) earmarked for Million Wells Scheme and Indira Awas Yojana.
Source: Table 5.4 and assumptions stated above.

for about 75 per cent of the allocation, there is an earmarking at the state level of 30 per cent for the Million Wells Scheme (MWS) and 10 per cent for houses under the Indira Awas Yojana (IAY) both of which constituted direct transfers for individual SC/ST households. Of the balance, 20 per cent is earmarked for districts and 80 per cent for villages. At the district level, there are earmarkings for private assets

(35 per cent), social forestry (25 per cent), benefits for SC/ST (22.5 per cent) and other works (17.5 per cent). Further guidelines prescribe a wage-to-nonwage ratio of 60:40, preference for SC/ST in employment and an earmarking of 30 per cent in employment for women.

The allocation of funds to states is based on the proportion of the rural poor while from the states to their districts it is based on equal weights to the incidence of SC/ST population and the inverse of agricultural labour productivity. The second stream in JRY, accounting for about 20 per cent of the allocation, is confined to 120 backward districts and to economic and social infrastructure while the third stream is a tokenistic allocation of about 5 per cent for 'innovative' schemes to be taken up, where possible, in cooperation with NGOs. EAS is also a rural employment generation scheme but is confined to 1752 backward blocks (about a third of all blocks in the country) with allocations under it being earmarked for water and soil conservation (40 per cent), minor irrigation (20 per cent), link roads (20 per cent) and community buildings (20 per cent). The MP local area development scheme, introduced in 1993, provides a uniform allocation of Rs 1 crore annually to each of the 790 members of the two houses of Parliament for being spent on local schemes to be recommended by them so long as they are eligible under various guidelines.

Similar muddles and knots are to be found in the other central antipoverty schemes as well. In IRDP, there are two different cut-off levels for targeting beneficiaries (a household poverty line of Rs 11,000 in 1991–2 prices and a cut-off limit of Rs 8500); separate earmarkings for SC/ST (50 per cent), women (40 per cent) and the physically handicapped (5 per cent); differential subsidy rates for different target groups (small farmers, marginal farmers and agricultural labour, SC/ST and the physically handicapped); and differential subsidy ceilings for different areas (normal, drought prone and desert) and target groups (SC/ST and physically handicapped). By definition, DPAP and DDP are confined to listed blocks which are drought prone or desertified with the permissible expenditures under them being on land development, soil and water conservation and other forms of resource management while the development of wastelands in the extensive non-forest areas of the country gets a small and thinly spread allocation. The Accelerated Rural Water Supply Programme (ARWSP) is meant to meet the needs of 'no source' or problem villages. However, the allocation criteria to states in the ARWSP (namely, 35 per cent for rural population, 20 per cent each for rural area and rural poverty and 25 per cent for DPAP, DDP and hill areas) has no visible relation to the possible incidence of such villages. ARWSP also illustrates the problems in planning for village water supply from distant Delhi. At the beginning of 1993-4 it was declared that only 736 no-source villages remained to be covered while a later survey has revealed that as many as 40,000 villages (main habitations) are in this category. This has happened largely because the states have interpreted 'no source' according to local conditions while Delhi has tried to adopt a uniform all-India norm.

An examination of Table 5.4 will also show that in relation to patent needs, allocations for a number of schemes are far from adequate. For example, in the 1995-6 Budget DWCRA and TRYSEM get Rs 79 crore between them; rural sanitation is allotted Rs 60 crore and urban water supply and sewerage Rs 65 crore; asset creation schemes in urban areas get Rs 171 crore in all. In these activities, the Centre has been more interested in establishing its presence rather than in making a serious substantive contribution. The political motivation that underlies this approach is also reflected in higher allocations to existing schemes and in the introduction of new schemes since 1993-4. Table 5.4 brings this out clearly. No doubt, elections in as many as nine major states in 1993-4 and 1994-5 (Uttar Pradesh, Madhya Pradesh, Rajasthan, Karnataka, Andhra Pradesh, Orissa, Maharashtra, Gujarat and Bihar), the Congress party's debacle in five out of six state elections in 1994-5 and the fact that 1995-6 is the last full financial year before parliamentary elections in June 1996 have all lent a special poignancy to the central government's concern for the poor. However, the motivation in itself need not prejudice the merits of the new initiative for in a democracy all things, good or bad, are political. EAS, for instance, usefully concentrates additional allocations for employment generation in backward districts. The MP scheme, although pork barrel, sustains the links in the inter-election period between members of the Lok Sabha and the constituencies that they represent; and Rajya Sabha members (say, from the Punjab) will be able to help the states of their adoption (say, Assam). The Prime Minister's Rozgar Yojana extends the kind of programmes in the Nehru Rozgar Yojana (NRY) to small towns. It could very well have been consolidated with it: even the acronym lends itself to be expanded as Nehru Rao Yojana! The three new schemes included in the 1995-6 budget are entirely well conceived. In the National Social Assistance Scheme, the Centre has for the first time assumed a role in helping the states to provide a package of essential social protection to the poor—old-age pensions, survivor benefits and maternity relief—according to nationally uniform minimum standards. The group life insurance scheme to be implemented through panchayats has the potential to take life insurance to the rural poor in a massive way. The new rural infrastructure fund in NABARD will enable priority lending targets to be met, channel such lending into viable projects and assure repayments to banks. In this way, both lending and the use of loans will be made more viable.

In the final analysis, one cannot escape the conclusion that the Centre's anti-poverty portfolio is riddled with much needless confusion and complexity in its conceptualization, design and administration. Basically, this is to be attributed to the use of a limited set of instruments for promoting diverse multiple objectives: employment-in-itself, backward area development, rural infrastructure, basic needs, reservations for SC/ST and women, decentralization and, at the same time, some pocket money for members of Parliament. As a result, outlays addressed to the same or similar purposes are fragmented among a number of schemes; the activity-based classification of 'employment' fudges a number of functional ends; in many schemes allocations are no more than symbolic; and the overlap within the central portfolio is compounded by the overlap between central and states' schemes and within the latter.[5] Most important, there is no coherence between (a) criteria for allocation of funds to states and sub-state levels, (b) needs and potential at the local level for works and other expenditures, and (c) earmarking for various purposes and within them for target and sub-target groups. It is not clear how this over-determined approach can or does work. Evidence from evaluations suggests that the guidelines, criteria, norms and earmarkings may be parts of an elaborate bureaucratic charade with what happens in the field being quite different.[6]

---

[5] A SC/ST household can, for instance, hope to get a well financed under the state's minor irrigation or welfare schemes or under JRY (Million Wells Scheme) or under IRDP and a house under a state welfare or rural housing scheme or under JRY (Indira Awas Yojana).

[6] A detailed study of evaluations (official and non-official) will reveal considerable variations between the earmarkings on paper for different purposes, different target groups (poor, SC/ST, women) and for the wage component in JRY on one hand and what obtains in the field on the other. Interstate variations in these respects are also very wide.

Towards Reform and Restructuring

In this concluding section, we shall develop some ideas of a prescriptive character which can be seen as following logically from the foregoing account and analysis of the Centre's social expenditures. To begin with it will be useful to clarify the rationale for the Centre's involvement at all in social expenditures. Although the Constitution places the primary responsibility for such expenditures on the states, it does not preclude the Centre from playing a role. It can be granted that the Centre's involvement in the social sectors is not only permissible but also desirable. Indeed, it can be argued that the Centre's participation in these sectors is necessary and justified at least on six grounds: (i) to tackle nation-wide priorities to which not all states may be able or willing to devote adequate resources or emphasis (for example, family welfare), (ii) to deal with interstate externalities (for example, the control of communicable diseases), (iii) to set national standards (for example, in social assistance), (iv) to direct resources to areas or activities which are especially problematic (for example, low literacy blocks, girls' education, no-source villages in water supply), (v) to promote a standard set of anti-poverty schemes (for example, JRY, IRDP) and (vi) to extend technical assistance to the states (for example, in watershed development or through the drinking water supply missions).

In practice, as we have seen, other considerations, along with these objective ones, have also operated. The Centre has been anxious to demonstrate that the new economic policies have a 'human face'. Some of the new schemes introduced in the last few years have added rouge and lipstick to it; some have aimed at electoral gain while yet others, like the ones included in the 1995–6 budget, are well conceived initiatives. In addition, a couple of other factors can be discerned. One is the 'rut' syndrome which is most apparent in the employment generation schemes. They have been quantitatively expanded with progressively higher financial allocations without any attempt to reform or restructure them in the light of shortcomings evident from numerous evaluations. The same applies to IRDP and the area development schemes. There has been no systematic attempt to learn from experience in these longstanding schemes. The second is the bureaucratic tendency to extend and refine guidelines which have made the administration of these schemes increasingly cumbersome with little to show in terms of improvements at the cutting edge of ground-level implementation.

During and beyond economic adjustment, it is necessary to both increase the levels of social expenditures and to restructure the programmes so that whatever amounts are spent are cost-effective. This will entail (a) an optimal mix of the different approaches to poverty alleviation such as employment generation, basic needs provisions, welfare, asset creation, backward area developments, and social assistance, (b) reforms to individual programmes in the light of experience, (c) a clear delineation of the Centre's role, and (d) the involvement, to the fullest extent appropriate, of local bodies in the delivery of these programmes using the potential opened up in the 73rd and 74th Amendments to the Constitution.

The first of these issues relates to the *inter se* priority to be given to the different elements of the anti-poverty portfolio so as to arrive at the most cost-effective composition of the entire package. Currently, nearly 60 per cent of the outlays on major programmes goes to employment generation. It is necessary to be clear whether effecting wage transfers to the poor via special employment schemes is an end in itself. Or, whether employment generation is to be viewed as a by-product benefit in the process of creating durable communal assets or assets for individual poor households (such as wells and houses). In theory, the latter is the stated objective but there is enough evidence to show that in practice the thin spread of JRY, without being underpinned by local-level planning or consultation, results in a variety of distortions: non-durable rather than more permanent works are chosen; in many cases, works are abandoned incomplete and new ones started elsewhere; and maintenance is sorely neglected.[7] What needs to be appreciated is that to the extent that durable assets are not created, transfers via wage payments *per se* are a very expensive and inefficient approach to helping the poor. I have discussed this in some detail elsewhere[8] and shall confine myself in this paper to the illustrative exercise in Table 5.6. It will show that out of one rupee spent in JRY only 14 paise is likely to reach the

---

[7] One of the most revealing evaluations in regard to employment generation schemes is S. Mahendra Dev, *Poverty Alleviation Programmes: A Case Study of Maharashtra with Emphasis on the Employment Guarantee Scheme*, Discussion Paper No. 7, Indira Gandhi Institute of Development Research, Bombay, 1992.

[8] S. Guhan, 'Social Security Options for Developing Countries', *International Labour Review*, 133(1), 1994.

poor via effective net wage transfers. Three implications can be drawn from this: (i) if the objective is only to effect transfers for the poor, other modalities such as welfare programmes for SC/ST, basic needs provision and social assistance (such as the transfers envisaged in the new National Social Assistance Scheme) are likely to be more cost-effective than JRY; (ii) employment works should, therefore, be strictly confined to the creation or maintenance of rural economic and social infrastructure based on the needs and potential for such works at the local level; and (iii) from this standpoint, it will be desirable to abolish altogether 'employment generation' as a programme category replacing it with categories related to the purposes (rural infrastructure, welfare, basic needs, backward area development) that are the desired final outcomes from employment generation and with direct social assistance transfers.

TABLE 5.6: Transfer Efficiency in the JRY

1	Gross expenditures	100.0
2	Wage component[a]	53.0
3	Leakage[b]	5.3
4	Gross wage transfer (1–2–3)	47.7
5.	Participation cost[c]	19.1
6	Net benefit (4–5)	28.6
7	Coverage of poor[d] (targeting efficiency)	0.5
8	Transfer to poor (6 × 7) (transfer efficiency)	14.3

Notes: [a] As estimated in GOI Concurrent Evaluation of JRY (January–December 1992), July 1994.
[b] Underpayment of wages at 10 per cent of wage payment (assumed).
[c] 40 per cent of wage payment (47.7) representing forgone incomes based on estimate in Martin Ravallion, *Reaching the Poor through Rural Public Employment: A Survey of Theory and Evidence*, Discussion Paper No. 94, World Bank 1990.
[d] GOI Concurrent Evaluation of JRY (January–December 1992), July 1994 estimates this ratio at 0.43. We have improved it to 0.5.

The analysis in Table 5.5 can then suggest how the three other considerations we have outlined can be applied to the Centre's portfolio of major social sector programmes.

• Of the five functional categories in which the outlays have been grouped, the schemes relating to welfare and basic needs can be transferred to the states and made part of states' plans. Central schemes can be integrated with states' schemes in these sectors, extending or diversifying them. It could be suitably ensured that central assistance is additional to and does not displace normative levels of states' own expenditures. No earmarkings are necessary for it can be presumed that the states will be as interested as the Centre is in providing wells and houses to SC/ST, encouraging women's employment, eradicating illiteracy, and providing water supply to no-source villages.

- The allocations for area development (EAS, second stream of JRY, DPAP, DDP and wastelands development) can be transferred to NABARD's fund for rural infrastructure development. Financing can then be on an area-specific, project basis combined with technical assistance inputs from the IARI institutions, state agricultural universities, ICRISAT, CRIDA, and so on.

- Allocations for local economic and social infrastructure (roads, minor irrigation, social forestry, community buildings), currently available under JRY first stream and the MP local area development scheme, can be entirely made over to the district and intermediate levels of Panchayati Raj institutions. They can retain a part of such funds at their own levels and allocate a part, as may be appropriate, to village panchayats. In the longer term, these allocations, could be made statutory by including them in the terms of reference to Finance Commissions. This is provided for in article 280(3)(bb) of the Constitution introduced as part of the 73rd Amendment.[9]

- This leaves out IRDP. Numerous evaluations have established that IRDP has degenerated into a thinly spread, poorly targeted, political hand-out involving considerable leakages and corruption. Also, IRDP depends for about two-thirds of its funding on credit from commercial banks. In principle, financial sector reforms would call for the phasing out of this kind of administratively directed, high-default, subsidized lending. In these circumstances, there is a good case for winding up IRDP and for replacing it with alternative lending modalities. One could be for projects, through NABARD or otherwise, for such purposes as dairying, livestock, horticulture, poultry, fish farming, sericulture, small-scale production, and handicrafts.

---

[9] Article 280(3)(bb) states that 'it shall be the duty' of Finance Commissions to recommend 'measures needed to augment the Consolidated Fund of a State to supplement the resources of panchayats in the states on the basis of the recommendations made by the Finance Commission of the State'.

Such lending will be not to individual households but to groups of producers with special preference to the poor, SC/ST and women. Project lending of this kind can be complemented with technical assistance, input supply, disease control, quality upgrading, design inputs and marketing. The second modality will be small business loans in rural and urban areas for household or small-scale production, trade and services. The feasibility for such lending on a group guarantee basis has been demonstrated in the Bangladesh Grameen Bank and by NGOs in India such as SEWA in Ahmedabad and the Working Women's Forum in Madras. The time has come to institutionalize these experiments.

The third modality will be credit for land purchases by poor households. This could stimulate and facilitate natural market processes through which land tends to get transferred from the rich to the poor. With increasing urbanization and industrialization, such processes are visible in many parts of India. Landowning sections tend to move to towns and to non-agricultural vocations converting in the process landed assets into investments in urban property, financial assets, professional education, etc. At the same time, there is some increase in surpluses available with tenants, small farmers and rural craftsmen. It is necessary for credit to supplement their purchasing power so as to facilitate land transfers in their favour.

To conclude, the economic reforms have been content to treat social expenditures as a residual. They have been 'protected' in a minimal sense in the central budget. Although the states are, and will have to be, responsible for the bulk of social expenditures, on their own or as agents in the centrally sponsored programmes, no attempt has been made to evolve a national policy for social expenditures. This will require an agenda for the reform and restructuring of major programmes which is integrated between the Centre, the states and public financial institutions and is based on decentralized delivery, as far as feasible and appropriate, through Panchayati Raj institutions. The economic reforms will be seriously incomplete unless more funds are allocated at the centre and in the states for social expenditures and concurrently whatever funds that are available are put to the best use.

6

Centre and the States in the Reform Process*

The centre–state or federal dimension of the current economic reform process in India tends to be ignored or sidestepped in discussions of the reforms. The causes for this neglect are varied. External proponents of the reforms, the World Bank and the IMF, have had to address their policy dialogue to the national government leaving it to the latter to work out the implications for centre–state coordination.

In the two initial years of the reform process, the centre has concentrated on a heavy agenda of macroeconomic, trade and industrial policy reforms falling within its own jurisdiction and immediately relevant to the stabilization phase. These more urgent reforms have also been relatively feasible for the centre to put through, since it could do so on its own, compared with the more difficult and longer-term tasks of adjustment which entail complex and many-sided policy coordination with the states.

As far as the states are concerned, there seems to be a feeling that adjustment is largely the responsibility of the centre, involving fiscal and balance-of-payments corrections to its past profligate policies and, linked to them, trade and industrial policy changes. In consequence, the states' response so far to the reforms has been grudging at best and non-cooperative at worst.

The current Indian political context does not place the centre in a particularly strong position to embark upon a dialogue with as many as twenty-five states. The central government is formed by a party which does not have a majority in Parliament. Nearly a third—and

* Reprinted from R. H. Cassen and Vijay Joshi (eds), *India: The Future of Economic Reform*, New Delhi: Oxford University Press, 1995, pp. 73–111.

until recently nearly a half—of the governments of the major states are led by parties other than the one which governs at the centre. Altogether, therefore, not enough attention has been paid to co-opting the states in the reform process.[1]

This paper argues that the states have a crucial role in the reform process and the task of integrating them in it cannot be soft-pedalled or postponed. The argument proceeds by detailing the role of the states and the need for centre–state coordination in key sectors of the reforms, the importance and urgency of the issues involved, the opportunities available, and the constraints to be overcome. The next section sets out the main features of the Indian federal system of special relevance to fiscal reform. The third section details the role of the states in key sectors of adjustment. The concluding section discusses the political aspects of the economic reform process in India's federal context and the imperative need for cooperative federalism. It also outlines an agenda for a centre–state compact.

THE CENTRE–STATE NEXUS

It should be recognized that India consists of twenty-six governments, one at the centre and the rest in the states. At each of these levels of the dual polity, legislative, executive, and judicial arms are separately constituted. The relationship between the two levels is set out in detail in the Constitution of India. Its Seventh Schedule contains a demarcation of the legislative domains of the Union and the states in terms of three lists. List I (97 entries) pertains to the Union; list II (66 entries) to the states; and list III (47 entries) includes concurrent, that is, overlapping, items. These lists also determine the taxation and executive domains of the two levels. The centre has exclusive jurisdiction over residual matters, that is, those unspecified in any of the three lists.

DIVISION OF RESPONSIBILITIES

The wide-ranging responsibilities of the centre under List I extend far beyond the core functions of any central or national government,

[1] In the three post-reform budget speeches of the Union Finance Minister, there are no more than a couple of scattered reference to the states although large allocations have been included and strong concerns have been expressed in respect of sectors in which the states have responsibility.

such as defence, external political and economic relations, currency, central banking, and nation-wide transport and communications. They include control over the financial sector: public financing institutions; commercial banks, the major ones of which are nationalized; insurance, also nationalized; and regulation of the capital market. The centre is concerned with the conduct of elections and audit at both the central and state levels. It exercises control over the recruitment of all-India civil and police services. It is concerned with research, standards, basic labour laws, and institutions of national importance. It holds monopoly over radio and television. Legislation for the promotion and regulation of industries is a central responsibility and the centre exercises exclusive control over mines and oil development. The centre is also responsible, as it has to be, for coordination and umpiring in matters such as trade and commerce, migration, and river waters, in so far as they concern more than one state. Furthermore, the concurrent list (list III) enables the centre to extend itself to important areas in which the states have primary responsibilities, such as forests, higher education, power development, population control, labour welfare, and social security. Most importantly, the catch-all entry (no. 20 in list III), 'economic and social planning' has been very widely interpreted.

The states have large and important responsibilities as well. The basic responsibility for maintenance of law and order is with the states, although the centre can intervene to protect them from 'external aggression and internal disturbance', or to aid them at their request in maintaining civil peace. Primary judicial administration is with the states, while the Supreme Court is the highest appellate level and can also be directly approached when fundamental rights are violated. The responsibilities of the states for economic and social development are extensive. They include agriculture and allied sectors (fisheries, animal husbandry and dairying, forests), irrigation, power development, roads (other than national highways), education, health, water supply, and urban development.

As part of the field of legislation, the Seventh Schedule assigns individual taxes to the centre and the states. The major taxes allotted to the centre are: customs duties (import and export taxes), excise duties (other than those on liquor), and direct taxes on personal and corporate incomes. Major tax sources assigned to the states are sales taxes, liquor excise duties, land revenue and other taxes on agriculture, duties on property transactions, urban land taxes, and taxes on motor vehicles and entertainment. The concurrent list does not contain any entries relating to taxation; in other words, there is no overlap in the legal framework of tax jurisdiction between the Centre and the states. However, since various central and states taxes get superimposed on most goods, commodity taxation represents a major area in which these indirect taxes cascade. Similarly, there is overlap in the sphere of direct taxes, although to a lesser degree, between personal income-taxes (centre) and profession taxes (states) and between wealth taxes (centre) and taxes on urban land and property transactions (states).

Receipts and Transfers

Table 6.1 for 1989–90 shows the structure of taxation at the two levels.[2] The centre's tax receipts are nearly double that of the states. Both the centre and, more so, the states depend heavily on indirect taxes on commodities. In the case of the centre, a large part of commodity taxes comes from international trade. Domestic commodity taxation at the level of the states (sales taxes and the liquor excise) is not very much below that from excise duties in the centre, pointing to a considerable overlap in this area.

The Constitution implicitly recognizes that there can be a vertical imbalance between the centre and the states in the sense that resources available for exploitation by the states may not be commensurate with the expenditure responsibilities they are called upon to discharge. This structural imbalance is intended to be corrected by resource transfers from the centre to the states provided for in four ways:

(i) Revenues from personal income-taxes and Union excise duties, levied and collected by the centre, are shared with the states on the basis recommended by quinquennial Finance Commissions established under constitutional mandate. Currently, 85 per cent of income-taxes and 45 per cent of Union excise duties are shared.

(ii) Finance Commissions also recommend specific grants to states 'in need of assistance'.

[2] 1989–90 has been chosen as the reference year for the discussion of current dimensional magnitudes since it is the most recent year for which consistent data on budgetary transactions at both levels in terms of actuals have been published in the annual surveys of central and state finances by the Reserve Bank of India (RBI). It also supplies a pre-reform bench mark.

TABLE 6.1: Tax Structure: Centre and States, 1989–90

(Rs billion)

Item	Centre	States	Total
Taxes on Income	98.12	4.53	102.65
Income tax	50.04		50.04
Corporation tax	47.29		47.29
Other	0.79		0.79
Agricultural Income tax		0.93	0.93
Profession		3.60	.60
Taxes on Property and Capital Transactions	1.91	25.54	27.45
Estate duty, gift tax, wealth tax	1.91		1.91
Land revenue		6.90	6.90
Stamp duties and registration		18.45	18.45
Urban land taxes		0.19	0.19
Taxes on Commodities and Services	406.58	229.88	636.46
Customs duties	180.36		180.36
Union excise duties	224.06		224.06
Sales taxes		150.60	150.60
State excise duties		38.64	38.64
Other	2.16	40.64	42.80
Other taxes (including taxes in Union Territories)	7.85		7.85
Total	514.46	259.95	774.41

Source: RBI Annual Surveys of Centre and State Finances.

(iii) Apart from tax sharing and statutory grants recommended by Finance Commissions, the centre provides grants to states which it is free to do 'for any public purpose'.

(iv) In addition, the centre extends loans to the states and, in fact, it is the single most important source of borrowing for them. Market borrowings by the states are also regulated by the centre.

Table 6.2 for 1989–90 brings out the dimensional magnitudes of the vertical imbalance and the nature of the transfers used to bridge it. It will indicate the significant degree to which the finances of the centre and the states are integrated in both the revenue and capital accounts. The states' own overall receipts were only 31 per cent of the overall receipts of the centre and states taken together, while their share in aggregate expenditure at both levels was 48 per cent. To make good the imbalance, the centre had to transfer to the states 30 per cent of its overall receipts. The share of tax transfers in the centre's gross tax revenues was 25 per cent; the ratio of transfers in the centre's revenue account (tax shares and grants) to its gross revenue receipts (tax and non-tax) was 32 per cent and the share of net loans to states in the centre's own capital receipts was 26 per cent. Looked at from the receiving end, net transfers (that is, allowing for repayments of loans to the centre) accounted for 41 per cent of the states' aggregate receipts. Tax transfers came to 34 per cent of tax receipts; transfers in the form of tax shares and grants to 38 per cent of revenue receipts; and net loans from the centre for 49 per cent of net capital receipts.

TABLE 6.2: Receipts, Transfers and Expenditures: Centre and States, 1989–90

(Rs billion)

Item	Centre	States	Total
1. Own tax revenues	514.46	259.95	774.41
2. Own non-tax revenues	162.65	89.37	252.02
3. Total own revenues (1+2)	677.11	349.32	1026.43
4. Own capital receipts	300.18	83.95	384.13
5. Total own receipts (3+4)[a]	977.29	433.27	1410.56
6. Tax shares	–130.97	130.97	–
7. Grants	–85.05	85.05	–
8. Loans (net)	–79.17	79.17	–
9. Total transfers (net)(6+7+8)	–295.19	295.19	–
10. Total receipts (5+9)	682.10	728.46	1410.56
11. Revenue expenditures	580.21	602.17	1182.38
12. Capital expenditure	207.81	127.90	335.71
13. Total expenditure (11+12)	788.02	730.07	1518.09
14. Budget deficit (13–10)	105.92	1.61	107.53

[a] Includes additional excise duties in lieu of sales tax and excludes central sales tax.

Source: RBI Annual Surveys of Centre and State Finances.

The transfers from the centre to the states are channelled in three ways, as shown in Table 6.3. The first consists of tax shares and statutory grants recommended by the Finance Commissions. In 1989–90, they accounted for 44 per cent of gross transfers and 67 per cent of transfers in the revenue account. Transfers recommended by Finance Commissions are addressed principally to covering the non-Plan deficits in the revenue accounts of the states. They aim at not only bridging the vertical imbalance between the centre and the states (treated as a whole), but also at reducing horizontal disparities between economically advanced and economically or fiscally backward states. To the latter end, Finance Commissions, particularly since the Seventh Commission (1979–84), have tended to adopt increasingly redistributive criteria in their schemes for devolution based on such indicators as low per capita incomes, high poverty ratios, and revenue deficits.

TABLE 6.3: Modalities of Central Transfers to States, 1989–90

(Rs billion)

	Tax shares and Grants	Loans (Gross)	Total
Finance Commission	*144.92*		*144.92*
Tax shares	130.97		130.97
Grants	13.95		13.95
Planning Commission	*62.66*	*51.92*	*114.58*
Normal Plan assitance	34.05	50.14	84.19
Central and centrally sponsored schemes	28.61	1.78	30.39
Other	*8.44*	*60.67*	*69.11*
Total gross transfers	216.02	112.59	328.61
Repayments of loans		−33.42	−33.42
Total net transfers	216.02	79.17	295.19

Source: RBI Annual Surveys of Centre and State Finances.

The second channel, mediated by the Planning Commission, consists of grants and loans for Plan outlays in the states. Central transfers on the Plan account, which accounted for 35 per cent of gross transfers in 1989–90, consist of two main components: 'normal central assistance' for state plans and transfers for central and centrally sponsored schemes. In addition, there is a small component for area programmes in hill and tribal areas, the north-eastern states and border states. Except for a part related to externally aided projects (about 9 per cent in the Eighth Plan), the bulk of normal assistance for state plans is transferred according to a formula approved by the

National Development Council.[3] Such assistance financed about 37 per cent state plan outlays in 1989–90.

Central and centrally sponsored programmes are fully or partially funded by the centre, mainly through grants.[4] There are now more than two hundred individual schemes in the central and centrally sponsored portfolio. A large proportion of the outlays on them is accounted for by the family welfare programme, rural employment programmes, and the Integrated Rural Development Programme (IRDP). Other items include subsidies for backward regions, several small schemes in the agricultural sector, programmes for non-conventional energy, schemes for multi-state or interstate power development, and a variety of programmes in the social sectors such as health (communicable diseases), water supply (for rural areas), nutrition and child services (Integrated Child Development Services or ICDS), welfare (of Scheduled castes, tribes and other backward classes) and education (adult literacy, non-formal education, girls' education). Centrally sponsored schemes were originally included as a separate category in the Fourth Plan (1969–74). Until then, central Plan assistance to the states was scheme-wise, and when in the Fourth Plan it became related instead to overall Plan outlays in the states, it was felt necessary that scheme-wise transfers should be retained for a limited number of programmes of national priority. The National Development Council, while agreeing to the concept of centrally sponsored schemes, resolved that the outlays on them should be limited to one-sixth or one-seventh of the quantum of central assistance for state plans. Despite repeated requests since then to limit these schemes and to transfer some of them to the states, there has been a steady enlargement in the outlays for centrally sponsored schemes. In the 1993–4 central budget, such outlays came to as much as 48 per cent of normal central assistance for state plans and to 33 per cent of all central transfers on the Plan account. A combination of paternalistic, populist, and bureaucratic factors explains the proliferation of centrally sponsored schemes in numbers and amount.

---

[3] The current formula has a weightage of 60 per cent for population, 25 per cent for low per capita incomes, 7.5 per cent for fiscal and developmental performance and 7.5 per cent for special problems.

[4] At the instance of the National Development Council, three Working Groups in 1977, 1984 and 1987 have recommended discontinuance or transfer to the states of centrally sponsored schemes.

The centre would appear not to believe that the states, if left to themselves, would attend to priorities such as rural employment or family welfare. It stands to gain political mileage by increasing allocations in its own budget for welfare and social services, and central ministries have acquired a vested interest in tending their turf by these schemes.

The third channel consisting of non–Finance Commission, non-Plan transfers accounted in 1989–90 for 21 per cent of gross transfers. Non-Plan grants are mainly for the relief of natural calamities, such as droughts and floods, while non-Plan loans are mainly related to small savings mobilized by the states.

Overall, the influence that the centre is in a position to exercise through its transfers to the states operates only at a broad level. Finance Commission transfers constitute untied resource support and are determined quinquennially, mainly through tax shares recommended by the Commission. The quantum of normal Plan assistance, although subject to the centre's annual budgetary considerations, has to conform to parameters set out in the five-year plan and is shared according to a nationally approved formula. It is related to Plan outlays in the aggregate in the states, but beyond that there is no earmarking or tying to individual sectors or programmes. Assistance for central and centrally sponsored schemes, although purpose-tied, is subject to scheme-wise entitlement criteria. Non-Plan grants are mainly for emergency relief while non-Plan loans are mostly on account of small saving collections by the states themselves. Thus, although transfers from the centre account for about 40 per cent of states' receipts, the modalities of transfers do not have much cutting edge in influencing resource mobilization or economy and efficiency in resource use on the part of the states.

PATTERNS OF EXPENDITURE

The picture of receipts and intergovernmental transfers should be complemented with an indication of the pattern of expenditure at the two levels. Table 6.4 gives the break-up of central and state budgetary expenditure in 1989–90 between developmental and non-developmental categories under revenue and capital heads. Of total developmental outlays in budgets, 57 per cent is incurred by the states. A much higher proportion of states' expenditures (about 73 per cent) is for developmental purposes compared to the centre's (50 per cent). The developmental expenditure of the states is predominantly on the revenue account (about 77 per cent).

TABLE 6.4: Pattern of Expenditure, Centre and States, 1989-90

(Rs billion)

	Development expenditure	Non-development expenditure	Total
Centre	400.22	387.80	788.02
Revenue account	236.95	343.26	580.21
Capital account	163.27	44.54	207.81
States	531.51	198.56	730.07
Revenue account	407.81	194.36	602.17
Capital account	123.70	4.20	127.90
Centre and states	931.73	586.36	1518.09
Revenue account	644.76	537.62	1182.38
Capital account	286.97	48.74	335.71

Source: RBI Annual Surveys of Centre and State Finances.

Developmental outlays comprise expenditure on the maintenance of developmental facilities already established and incremental Plan outlays as part of five-year plans. The latter are incurred partly through the budget and partly through public sector enterprises (PSEs). Table 6.5 shows the Plan outlays by sector of the centre and

TABLE 6.5: Eighth Plan (1992-7) Outlays, Centre and States

(Rs billion)

Sector	Centre and UTs	States	Total
Agricultural and allied sectors	128.57	421.35	549.92
Rural development	242.12	102.13	344.25
Special area programme	–	67.50	67.50
Energy	682.70	472.92	1155.62
Industry and minerals	376.37	92.85	469.22
Transport and communications	672.36	137.99	810.35
Environment (including forestry)	12.56	36.54	49.10
Social services	374.23	415.89	790.12
Others	52.24	52.68	104.92
Total	2541.15	1799.85	4341.00

Source: Government of India, Eighth Five Year Plan (1992-7).

the states during the Eighth Plan (1992–7). The relative shares in the public sector Plan outlays are 58 per cent for the centre and 42 per cent for the states. However, a number of sectors involving outlays on the part of the centre relate to areas of responsibility assigned to the states under the Constitution: agriculture and allied sectors; rural development and social services; and the centrally sponsored programmes in these areas, although funded under the central plan, are implemented by the states. If this is taken into account, the relative proportions, are likely to be reversed with the states having the responsibility to implement 50–60 per cent of the Eighth Plan outlay in the public sector.

Table 6.6 on the financing pattern for the Eighth Plan will show that the states depend almost wholly (to the extent of 98 per cent) on budgetary resources for Plan financing, while in the case of the Centre PSEs contribute 57 per cent of Plan resources and budgetary support only to 43 per cent. Nearly 45 per cent of the states' budgetary contribution to the Plan comes from central assistance. In addition, outlays on centrally sponsored programmes support development in the states.

TABLE 6.6: Eighth Plan (1992–7) Financing Pattern, Centre and States
(Rs billion)

	Centre	States
1. Balance from current revenues	220.20	129.85
2. Domestic borrowings	1177.55	845.00
3. External borrowings	287.00	–
4. Deficit financing	200.00	–
5. Own budgetary resources (1+2+3+4)	1884.75	974.85
6. Central assistance to states	–785.00	785.00
7. Budget support for Plan (5+6)	1099.75	1759.85
8. Contribution (including borrowings) by PSEs	1441.40	40.00
9. Resources for Plan (7+8)	2541.15	1799.85

Source: Government of India, *Eighth Five Year Plan (1992–7)*.

The background furnished in this section shows that responsibilities and resources are highly integrated between the centre and the states in India's federal system. The centre is responsible for macroeconomic policies and the institutional instruments through which they are enforced. Industrial policies and legislation are its prerogative.

The planning mechanism and other concurrent power of the centre provide it with modalities for fiscal coordination and control over the states; for the promotion of policies and programmes of nation-wide priority; for the correction of regional disparities; and for broadly influencing developmental priorities in state Plans. Central transfers to the states amount to significant proportions of the gross receipts at the central (about 30 per cent) and the state (about 40 per cent) levels. Central Plan assistance amounts to very nearly half of the states' budgetary support to their Plan expenditures. The modes of transfer considerably respect the autonomy of the states. As a corollary, the effective use of resources transferred is very much a function of commitment and discipline on the part of state governments.

The states are major partners in development in overall as well as incremental terms. They are almost solely responsible for agriculture and allied sectors, irrigation, rural development and social services, and substantially responsible in the environmental sector. About three-fifths of the Plan outlay for power development, and close to a fifth of the Plan outlays in transport and communications, and in industry and minerals, falls to the states. Given the substantial role of the states in development, it is clear that policies and priorities, whether they relate to stabilization and structural adjustment or to longer-term development, will depend crucially for their realization on the political will and administrative competence of state governments.

KEY AREAS OF REFORM

This section discusses the specific policies and actions that will be required of the states in areas of the reform process in which their involvement will be crucial: fiscal adjustment; the industrial sector; power development; agricultural reforms; and social services. The discussion of fiscal adjustment has had to be elaborate since it is the area in which centre–state interaction is most explicit. Also, issues of fiscal reform include and illustrate reforms required in several sectors of the real economy.

Fiscal Adjustment

STATES' FISCAL DEFICITS

Targeted reduction of the fiscal deficit in the central budget has been viewed as the immediate priority of the stabilization phase. Steady progress in this direction has also been made with the fiscal deficit in the central budget being reduced from 8.4 per cent of GDP in 1990–1 (the pre-adjustment level) to 6.5 per cent in 1991–2 and to 5 per cent in 1992–3. No similar attention has been paid to the fiscal deficits of the states: aggregate fiscal deficits in state budgets which peaked at 3.6 per cent of GDP in 1990–1 are still likely to remain at 3.1 per cent in 1992–3. As the borrowings of the centre include the amounts which it lends to the states, these sums should be netted in order to arrive at the centres fiscal deficits *on its own account*. The figures arrived at can then be appropriately compared to the fiscal deficits of the states and combined with them, without double-counting, to obtain the aggregate fiscal deficits at the two levels. This is done in Table 6.7 which shows that while the centre's own fiscal deficit has been halved from 6.6. per cent of GDP in 1990–1 to 3.3 per cent in 1992–3, there has been only a marginal reduction from 3.6 per cent to 3.1 per cent in the GDP ratio of states' fiscal deficits over the three-year period.

TABLE 6.7: Fiscal Deficits as a Proportion of GDP, Centre and States, 1980–1 to 1992–3

Year	Centre's gross fiscal deficit	Centre's fiscal deficit on own account	States' fiscal deficits	Centre and states aggregate fiscal deficits	Proportion of states' fiscal deficits in aggregate fiscal deficits
	GDP ratio			(per cent)	
(1)	(2)	(3)	(4)	(5) = (3) + (4)	(6) = (4) ÷ 5
1980–1	6.10	4.95	2.73	7.68	35.5
1981–2	5.42	4.17	2.54	6.71	37.9
1982–3	5.97	4.43	2.80	7.23	38.7
1983–4	6.28	4.82	3.06	7.88	32.8
1984–5	7.53	5.98	3.54	9.52	37.2
1985–6	8.34	6.14	2.87	9.01	31.8
1986–7	9.02	7.38	3.17	10.55	30.1
1987–8	8.13	6.38	3.37	9.75	34.6
1988–9	7.83	6.14	2.96	9.10	32.5
1989–90	7.91	6.15	3.43	9.58	35.8
1990–1	8.43	6.55	3.55	10.10	35.2
1991–2 (RE)	6.50	4.83	3.48	8.31	41.9
1992–3 (BE)	5.00	3.25	3.05	6.30	48.4

Source: Derived from *RBI Annual Report 1992–3*.

In fact, in most years during the last decade, states' fiscal deficits have remained in the range of 3 to 3.5 per cent of GDP. The proportion of the states' fiscal deficits in the combined centre-and-states fiscal deficits, which was in the range of 30 to 40 per cent during 1980–91, has sharply increased from 35.2 per cent in 1990–1 to 48.4 per cent in 1992–3. With the states' fiscal deficits having by now become almost as large as that of the centre's own fiscal deficit, attention to reducing them can no longer be postponed, especially since the centre would appear to have reached a measure of fiscal consolidation that does not provide much further scope for reducing its own fiscal deficit.

Large and continuing fiscal deficits in the states have important implications for the centre. Since the states (unlike the centre) cannot resort to deficit financing through currency creation or directly to external loans, they depend heavily on loans from the centre and, next to that, on market borrowings. The combined contribution of these two sources to states' borrowings has risen from about 55 per cent in the early eighties to about 70 per cent in the second half of the decade. This implies that fiscal deficits of the states impact heavily both on the borrowings of the centre and on its access to borrowing: they increase the former because the centre has to lend to the states and they limit the latter because of the states' demand on the same pool of market savings.

Fiscal deficits at continuing high levels have naturally led to an increase in states' outstanding liabilities: from a total of about Rs 240 billion in 1980–1 to about Rs 1433 billion in 1992–3, that is, sixfold. Nearly two-thirds of these liabilities (about Rs 956 billion) represent borrowings from the centre. The large proportion of such borrowings have two important implications. Fist, the centre's lending to the states is at lower than market-related interest rates and entails an implicit subsidy. Secondly, while states are obligated to repay their market borrowings when due, they are in a position to negotiate debt accommodation on their intergovernmental borrowings from the centre.

In fact, as a measure of relief to the states on their mounting debt burden, successive Finance Commissions, at the request of the centre itself, have recommended the write-off, consolidation, and rescheduling of various components of states' debt to the centre. The impact of states' fiscal deficits on the centre is accordingly not only immediate in the year of occurrence, but is also prospective because of prepayments being reduced or postponed when they fall due.

The most serious concern in relation to the fiscal deficits of states is the sharp increase in their revenue deficits since the latter half of the eighties and particularly in the nineties. During 1980–5, the states registered a revenue surplus in most years, but in 1985–90, their revenue account went into the red. In this period, the average annual revenue deficit of states in the aggregate was Rs 11.5 billion. This has sharply escalated to an annual average revenue deficit of nearly Rs 47 billion in 1990–3. Consequently, borrowings have become necessary not only to cover capital outlays but also to bridge deficits in the revenue account: while about 10 per cent of borrowings during 1985–90 were applied to cover the gap in the revenue account, nearly 40 per cent was required for the purpose in 1990–3. The states as a group are thus getting sucked into the self-propelling spiral of revenue deficits leading to larger borrowings entailing higher outgoings on interest payments, which in turn lead to larger revenue deficits, and so on.

REDUCING FISCAL DEFICITS IN STATES:
CENTRE–STATE ASPECTS

The fiscal adjustment effort in the states will therefore need to concentrate on rolling back revenue deficits and in moving as soon as possible into generating revenue surpluses. This is necessary not just for reducing fiscal deficits at given levels but, in a dynamic framework, for increasing the capacity to finance useful current outlays. It will also be needed to generate surpluses to service the debt that will have to be incurred for financing capital outlays, such as on power development, irrigation, and infrastructure, in all of which large continuing needs have to be met primarily by the states. The fact that over 70 per cent of states' expenditure is on developmental purposes will indicate that the scope, *prima facie*, for expenditure reduction without affecting development will, in their case, be limited. The major thrust of the fiscal adjustment effort in the states will, therefore, need to be on improving revenue receipts. There is much scope in the states, as in the centre, for economy across the board, for eliminating wasteful spending, and curtailing non-Plan, non-developmental expenditures. The phasing out of surplus staff and of some of the perquisites of government employees is a priority. Without in any way underestimating the need for such expenditure reduction, its potential for yielding significant economies in the short term or in a sustained manner should not be exaggerated.

While the states themselves have the primary responsibility for reducing their revenue deficits, the centre too has an important role given that central transfers account for some 40 per cent of states' revenue receipts. Objectively, in fact, there is a strong case in favour of increasing central transfers to states through both the Finance Commission and the Planning Commission channels. Large and growing revenue deficits that have emerged in recent years in the states' accounts point to a structural inadequacy in meeting current account developmental outlays (on maintenance and incremental programmes) that the states have to incur. On the other hand, shares to states in the two shareable taxes have been more or less stagnant since 1979. That any increase in the immediate short term in central transfers to states can only be at the expense of worsening the centre's own fiscal deficit, should not dilute the importance of the centre having to augment its revenue receipts, particularly the taxes shareable with the states, in order to be able to effect larger transfers to them in the future.

Of available measures for revenue mobilization at the centre, the one that would appear to be most important—and also relatively neglected—is better tax enforcement, since the practical scope for enlarging the tax base or for enhancing tax rates would appear to be limited. The Tax Reforms Committee (Chelliah Committee) has pointed out that not more than 30 to 35 per cent of legally taxable incomes in India are being disclosed for personal income taxation.[5] It has estimated that if disclosure of 60 per cent can be induced and the average effective tax rate improved from the current 16 per cent to 20 per cent, the yield from income tax would go up to two-and-a-half times its present level. The committee has also made a number of specific recommendations for reaching these norms, such as widening the tax base, plugging loopholes, and more effective tax administration. If the reasonable targets set out by the committee are achieved, the resulting additional income tax transfers to the states could wipe out as much as 38 per cent of their fiscal deficits, assuming

---

[5] Government of India, Ministry of Finance, *Interim Report of the Tax Reforms Committee* (New Delhi, December 1991), p. 47.

the average ratio of income tax shares to states' fiscal deficits during 1989-93.[6]

Estimates of evasion in excise duties vary from commodity to commodity; overall, it appears to be reasonable to assume that evasion amounts to 30 per cent of duty actually paid.[7] If even half of this could be captured, the resulting increase in excise shares to states would be enough to wipe out another 9 per cent of their fiscal deficits, assuming 1989-93 proportions.[8]

Thus, a realistically reasonable measure of tax compliance in the shareable taxes, if brought about by the centre, will be adequate nearly to halve states' fiscal deficits at current levels. Earlier, attention was drawn to the burden thrown on the centre by states' fiscal deficits. These magnitudes relating to tax enforcement will show that the centre's responsibility for promoting fiscal adjustment in the states is equally significant.

In general, the centre's involvement in mobilizing revenues from the taxes shareable with the states (personal income tax and excises) has been noticeably less pronounced than its interest in raising revenues from non-shareable customs duties and corporate taxes. The centre, in fact, has been relatively forthcoming in reducing the tax base in personal income-taxes and the rates in both shareable taxes. Where possible, as in a high-yielding source like petroleum products, it has opted to increase administered prices rather than excise duties, thus denying shareable revenues to states; and, to repeat, not enough effort has been made to curb evasion in the shareable taxes. The Tax Reforms Committee has also referred to this aspect

---

[6] The annual average fiscal deficit of the states during 1989-93 was Rs 188.59 billion while average income-tax transfers in the period were Rs 48.02 billion or 25.5 per cent of it. An increase in income tax shares by a factor of 1.5 would be equivalent to 38.3 per cent of fiscal deficits.

[7] A NIPFP study, *Evasion of Excise Duties in India*, (1986), estimated that as a percentage of actual duty paid, evasion in excise duties accounted for about 20 per cent in copper and 47 per cent in cotton textile fabrics. Suraj B. Gupta, *Black Income in India* (Sage, 1992), estimates evasion in excise duties at 66.7 per cent of actual duty paid.

[8] Annual average excise transfers to states during 1989-93 were Rs 115.71 billion or 61.4 per cent of states' average fiscal deficit in the period (Rs 188.59 billion). A 15 per cent increase in this figure, representing a 50 per cent recapture of a possible evasion of 30 per cent of actual duty paid, would be equivalent to 9.2 per cent of fiscal deficits.

and has recommended that tax sharing, instead of being confined to the two shareable taxes, may be a proportion of the total gross tax revenues of the centre from all sources.[9] Such a reform will dissuade the centre from concentrating on non-shareable taxes and the states will benefit from greater buoyancy in tax transfers. In particular, the inclusion of the corporate tax in the divisible pool has been a long-standing demand of the states. It has not been acceded to despite its endorsement by the Commission on Centre–State Relations and by some of the Finance Commissions.

Centre–state cooperation will also be needed for structural tax reforms. The most important proposal in this regard is the one made by the Tax Reforms Committee for a value-added tax (VAT) up to the wholesale stage.[10] The proposal envisages that the VAT at this stage will be collected by the states with the amount of VAT relatable to the wholesale stage being retained by the state where it is collected. Thereafter, state sales taxes—confined to the retail level—can be considerably simplified reducing their distortionary effects. Besides rectifying cascading excise and sales taxes in large measure, a VAT of this kind could also secure a larger overall yield from both taxes because of the audit trail inherent in it. Another reform that has been on the anvil for some years is the consignment tax which can benefit the states by plugging evasion of sales taxes in interstate sales. Various

---

[9] *Interim Report of the Tax Reforms Committee*, p. 45. The committee's recommendation is,

> At present tax devolution to the States constitutes around 24 per cent of gross central government tax revenues. With the consent and cooperation of the States the relevant Constitutional provisions could be amended to the effect that 25 per cent of the aggregate tax revenues of the centre shall be shared with the States. There would be certainty then for the States and the Union regarding what revenues would accrue to their respective budgets and the centre would not have to distort its pattern of taxation by being virtually compelled to raise non-shareable taxes.

The states are not likely, however, to 'cooperate' in any constitutional amendment that freezes their share in tax devolution at any fixed figure, foregoing possibilities of quinquennial revisions by Finance Commissions. The formulation of the Committee is also unfortunate as it seems to suggest that the centre cannot be expected to have an enlightened interest in raising taxes shareable with the states.

[10] Government of India, Ministry of Finance, *Tax Reforms Committee: Final Report Part I* (New Delhi, August 1992), p. 45.

aspects of such a tax have been studied and discussed over a prolonged period, but the centre has consistently delayed introducing the necessary legislation.[11]

STATES' OWN RESPONSIBILITIES

Turning to the states' own tax revenues, agricultural taxation represents the main area of unexploited potential. Taxes on agriculture are only about 0.7 per cent of GDP in the sector; land revenue is not progressive or elastic; yields from agricultural income-taxes mainly arise from plantation crops and are subject to various loopholes and exemptions; costs of collection are very high. Moreover, on account of the very low tax incidence in the sector, agriculture provides a tax haven for converting black incomes into white. At the same time, quite apart from the strong political resistance to increasing agricultural taxation, there are equally daunting technical administrative problems in designing and implementing a system of progressive taxation in agriculture. The Committee on Agricultural Taxation (Raj Committee), which reported in 1974, outlined an elaborate agricultural holdings tax. It was, however, estimated to fetch only Rs 1.5 billion or 0.3 per cent of agricultural GDP in that year. Not surprisingly, these proposals failed to convince politicians and administrators that the game was worth the candle. The thrust of policy would, therefore, have to be on reducing agricultural subsidies rather than increasing agricultural taxes, although there is some scope for the latter as well through local cesses and surcharges on land revenue, levies on remunerative commercial crops or on irrigation charges related to them, and the aggregation of agricultural incomes above a certain level with incomes liable for income tax. The latter measure has been specifically recommended by the Tax Reforms Committee.[12] If the centre and the states cooperate to implement it, a serious loophole would get plugged.

[11] See *Interim Report of the Tax Reforms Committee*, pp. 124–5 for its recommendations on the consignment tax.

[12] The recommendation of the committee, *Final Report Part I*, p. 26, is that personal or corporate incomes from agricultural sources in excess of Rs 25,000 per annum should be aggregated with non-agricultural income, if the latter is not below the exemption level, and the tax levied on the aggregated income. The committee has recommended that the entire tax yield attributable to the agricultural component of the income should be distributed to the states on the basis of origin.

Evasion is a serious problem at the state level as well, particularly in sales taxes, stamp duties on sale transactions of immovable properties, municipal property taxes, and urban land taxes. In all these cases, centre–state coordination can benefit both parties. The VAT extending to the wholesale stage, as already discussed, can potentially increase revenues at both levels. Streamlining of the levy, assessment, and collection of taxes on property and property transactions can result in increasing collections from income, wealth, gifts, and capital gains taxes for the centre. Such opportunities largely remain to be exploited.

The excise duty on alcohol is next only in importance to sales taxes in the states. Technical approaches to optimal alcohol taxation have been discussed and have also emerged from trial and error with the following components: a state monopoly in manufacture, an auction system for licensing retail outlets, and reasonable levels of excise duties to discourage the shift to the illicit market.[13] Such a system, along with strict tax collection and strict measures against illicit production and consumption, can be expected to upgrade the yield from alcohol excise duties significantly. Severe political problems in the way must, however, be noted. The liquor lobby, consisting of manufacturers and traders in the commodity, is a powerful group in all states and an important source of political corruption. There are also in all states powerful 'liquor mafias' engaged in the manufacture and sale of illicit liquor that escapes the tax net. The overt lobby and the covert mafia overlap and link with each other and with politicians.

Having discussed central transfers and states' own taxes, we can turn to non-tax revenues of the states and subsidies in state budgets. Non-tax revenues comprise cost recoveries from various services provided by the state, administrative receipts, surpluses from departmental undertakings, dividends from public sector enterprises (PSEs), royalties and cesses on minerals, and interest receipts. The share of non-tax revenues in the states' own revenues is small (about 16 per cent in 1988–9) and has grown at a lower rate than tax revenues. There is also much variance between states and over time.

Subsidies, which are mostly implicit in the form of under-recovered costs on services provided by state governments, are

---

[13] See S. Musgrave and N. Stern, *Alcohol Demand and Taxation in South India in the 1970s*, (University of Warwick, 1985).

reflected in the level and growth of non-tax revenues; improving non-tax revenues is, therefore, linked to subsidy reduction through higher cost recovery. A study undertaken in the National Institute for Public Finance and Policy (NIPFP) estimated that—excluding expenditures on 'pure public goods', transfers and tax expenditures—directly unrecovered costs (DUC) in social and economic services in all states in 1987–8 amounted to about Rs 275 billion or 8.3 per cent of GDP and that they had increased at the rate of 18 per cent per annum between 1977–8 and 1987–8. The recovery rate in social and economic services was only about 14 per cent in 1987–8.[14]

DUCs are large—in quantum and as a proportion of total expenditures—in basic social services, a good proportion of which would qualify as merit goods: education, medical and health services, water supply and sanitation, urban services, and low-cost housing. The scope for reducing DUCs in this category consists mainly in cost-effective approaches to the provision of services, cost recovery by appropriate means, and selective targeting.[15]

The second category consists of outlays, mostly in the nature of outright transfers, for rural employment, subsidies for the rural poor, welfare expenditure on Scheduled castes, tribes and backward classes, child nutrition, support to handloom weavers, and so on. In this category, better targeting can ensure that benefits reach, and are confined to, the deserving, but the question of cost recovery does not arise since *ex definitio* welfare expenditures for the economically and/or socially disadvantaged are intended to be redistributive and free. The problem really is that such transfers have continually accumulated and have reached a significant proportion of current outlays. This has happened largely on account of electoral politics: every round of it has generated competitive populism with each major political party feeling called upon to promise welfare programmes, concessions, and subsidies to the population at large or to special groups bidding up the promises of other contestants. The winning party is, thereafter, held by the opposition to implement its manifesto promises in the state budget, even if it is not fully able or willing

---

[14] M. Govinda Rao and Sudipto Mundle, 'An Analysis of Changes in State Government Subsidies: 1977–87', in Amaresh Bagchi *et al.* (eds), *State Finances in India* (Vikas, 1992).

[15] There is also scope for privatization in segments of education and health care, but this subject has hardly been discussed in India, in contrast to extensive discussions of privatization of the public sector in industry.

to do so on its own. Once included, competitive politics renders it impossible to reduce or abandon transfers and subsidies. Competitive populism has not been confined to parties within individual states: it has extended across states and upstream to the centre. The loan write-off for farmers by the centre in 1990 is one example. Periodical increases to allocations for rural development and social services in the centrally sponsored schemes also indicate, at least in part, the ruling party's desire to gain political mileage.

The main items in the third category, which accounts for about a third of DUCs, are food subsidies, under-recovery of irrigation charges, and subsidized electricity tariffs. While the burden on account of the food subsidy is mainly borne by the centre, some of the states—particularly the rice-consuming ones in south India—provide additional food subsidies through their budgets. One reason for this is that the issue prices for rice fixed by the centre for sales to states is nearly 50 per cent higher compared to the sales price for wheat, because the centre subsidizes wheat to a much greater extent than rice: the ratio of the centre's subsidy to the economic cost is 41 per cent in the case of wheat and only 23 per cent for rice. It should also be pointed out that the distribution costs incurred by the centre's Food Corporation of India (FCI) are about 20 per cent of the economic cost and 57 per cent of the subsidy involved. Reduction of FCI's overheads and the narrowing or elimination of the disparity between wheat and rice will be a contribution to reducing the states' burden on food subsidies. The states themselves will, however, have the major responsibility for reducing them through curtailing leakages and better targeting.

The two other major subsidies in state budgets, which relate to underpriced water and electricity for irrigation, reflect the powerful influence of the farm lobby, particularly the large farmers. The pricing of irrigation water has been recently studied by a committee set up by the Planning Commission.[16] The committee has estimated that the unrecovered costs in major, medium, and multi-purpose surface irrigation projects in 1986–7 was of the order of Rs 15 billion. While working expenses alone came to Rs 4.9 billion, cost recovery was only Rs 1.7 billion. In other words, only about a third of basic operation and maintenance costs was recovered, leaving interest and

---

[16] Government of India, Planning Commission, *Report of the Committee on Pricing of Irrigation Water* (New Delhi, September 1992).

depreciation entirely unmet. In addition, irrigation is heavily subsidized through underpriced electricity for groundwater use. Pumpsets for well irrigation currently consume about 25 per cent of power sales in India. In 1989–90, while the average cost of supply of a unit of power was close to one rupee, the maximum agricultural tariff charged by any state electricity board (SEB) was 30 paise. The rate was much lower than this in most states; Tamilnadu is an extreme example where power for irrigation pumpsets is being supplied absolutely free. Average annual losses to SEBs on account of the agricultural subsidy have been estimated at Rs 46 billion during 1990–3. In 1992, state electricity ministers resolved in conference to adopt a minimum tariff for agriculture of 50 paisé, but hardly a handful of states have so far implemented the decision. If this floor tariff is introduced, SEBs will be able to mobilize additional resources of the order of Rs 21 billion. The consequent reduction that will be possible in the states' loans to SEBs will be equivalent to about 10 per cent of states' fiscal deficits.[17] (The overall financial performance of SEBs is discussed later.)

Outright losses and poor returns (implying subsidies) in state-level public enterprises (SLPEs) are another major drain on state finances. While the most important SLPEs are SEBs and state road transport corporations (SRTCs), numerous others are involved in a wide range of activities: industrial finance and promotion, manufacture, trading, infrastructure development, welfare, etc. In number, SLPEs are estimated to total about nine hundred, more than four times that of central PSEs, while aggregate investment in them is estimated to be three-fourths of that in central PSEs. In most states SRTCs provide bus services, although the share of the public sector in this activity varies among them. Data for 1987–8 show that SRTCs registered net profits only in six out of twenty-five states and aggregate losses in the rest came to about Rs 1.5 billion.[18] Among other SLPEs, manufacturing enterprises, which are the ones that can at all be expected to be profitable, yielded only a paltry average return (profits before interest and tax) of about 2 per cent on investment during 1982–7.[19]

[17] For a concise overview, see C. Rangarajan, 'Financial Performance of State Electricity Boards', *Reserve Bank of India Bulletin* (Bombay, February 1993).
[18] Government of India, Ministry of Finance, *Second Report of the Ninth Finance Commission (for 1990–95)*, (New Delhi, December, 1989), Ann. III. 6.
[19] T. L. Sankar *et al.*, 'Can State Level Public Enterprises in India Earn a Rate of Return?', *Economic and Political Weekly* (Bombay, 24 November 1990).

ADMINISTERED PRICES

Administered prices on commodities and services over which central PSEs have a monopoly—foodgrains for the PDS, coal, oil, diesel and railway freight—have a significant impact on the states and their enterprises, principally SEBs (which are dependent on coal and its transport) and SRTCs (which are large consumers of diesel). Administered prices have been frequently increased by the centre in recent years, at least once annually and sometimes more often. The level and growth of administered prices reflect not only justifiable economic costs and returns to central PSEs, but also inefficiencies in their working and indirect taxation (as in the case of petroleum products). Enjoying a monopolistic position in the provision of the concerned commodities and services and being distant from final consumers of food, electricity, and transport, it has been relatively easy for the centre periodically to increase administered prices. These increases cascade on costs and inefficiencies at the state level on one hand, while on the other, as the states are closer to final consumers, they face onerous economic burdens in meeting the cost of subsidies and political burdens involved in reducing them through increased cost recovery.[20]

To sum up broadly: fiscal consolidation in the centre has to be secured and followed by a similar process in the states. The states will not only have to eliminate revenue deficits, but generate revenue surpluses adequate to service borrowings for capital formation. This will mainly involve improving states' revenue receipts by actions on their part, actions by the centre, and on the basis of centre-state cooperation. The target areas will be: reduction of subsidies in state budgets, better tax enforcement at both levels, and tax reforms in indirect taxes which overlap in incidence and collection. There are strong reciprocities in responsibilities and benefits between the two levels in the area of fiscal reforms.

Industrial Restructuring

Although the prime instruments for industrial promotion and regulation fall within the jurisdiction of the centre, the role of the states is not insignificant in this area.

---

[20] On administered prices, see Malcolm S. Adiseshiah (ed.), *Price Policy* (Lancer International, New Delhi, 1987).

ENTRY AND EXIT

Policy changes at the central level have considerably eased entry restrictions for industrial investment. At the state level, agencies from which clearances are required for setting up and performing industrial activities include town planning authorities, authorities under the Factories and Electricity Acts, public health authorities, and pollution control boards. Most states have attempted to streamline these clearances and a number of them have 'single-window' procedures to expedite them.

However, the unwillingness of states to permit labour adjustment is a major inhibition to exit policies which have to be a corollary to the progressive relaxation of entry constraints that has taken place at the central level. As they are reluctant to accept any loss of employment in establishments located in their territories, state governments tend to delay or deny approvals required from them under the Industrial Disputes Act (as amended in 1984) for retrenchment, lay-off or closures in factories employing one hundred or more workers in industries other than those directly owned or controlled by the centre. Possible solutions to this problem have been studied by an official Working Group (1992) and an expert group, including trade union representatives (Ramanujam Committee). However, tripartite consensus between the centre, the states and labour is yet to be forged.

A second, although less important, constraint in the way of restructuring financially 'sick' units is that under Urban Land Ceiling Acts, such units require the permission of state governments to dispose of any part of their real estate which, especially in large metropolitan locations, is a valuable disposable asset. These permissions are hard to obtain because of competing claims on surplus land such as for public uses and low-cost housing.

INFRASTRUCTURE

The states are directly responsible for the provision of industrial infrastructure—developed land, power, water, roads, etc. In some cases, raw materials (for example, forest products, molasses, minor minerals like granite), are allotted at the state level. The training of skilled manpower and the maintenance of smooth industrial relations through the expeditious and effective settlement of industrial disputes are two of their basic responsibilities.

INCENTIVES

A virtue of India being a common market is that many of the instrumentalities available at the national level for inducing industrial promotion are not open to the states: they cannot, for instance, impose import tariffs, or provide export incentives, or extend corporate tax concessions, or adjust the exchange rate. They also have no voice in the operations of the major industrial financing institutions. In these circumstances, states have attempted to attract industries to their domains basically through two means: provision of infrastructure and financial incentives. Both these have involved implicit or direct subsidies. Given the keen competition among the states for attracting and retaining industries, subsidies of various kinds—concessional electricity tariffs, capital subsidies, subsidized provision of land and industrial sheds, soft loans to cover sales tax payments, sales tax holidays and so on—have proliferated. These are in addition to capital subsidies provided by the centre for industrial units in backward areas. With the pace set by two of the most industrialized states (Maharashtra and Gujarat), which have each been anxious to prevent the shift of capital to its contiguous neighbour, other states have willy-nilly followed suit.

One of the important objectives of the licensing system was to direct industrial investments to backward areas where possible. With its dismantling as part of the industrial reform process, incentives are likely to acquire added importance in the industrialization of backward regions. In this context, issues relating to the optimal forms, levels, and coverage of industrial incentives, and to the trade-off between incentives to individual units and infrastructure development in well-chosen growth centres, need to be focused upon. Centre–state and interstate cooperation will be desirable for evolving enforceable norms for industrial subsidies, so that competitive depreciation among the states is avoided, and resources saved by the better targeting of industrial incentives could be used for durable investments on industrial infrastructure.

RESTRUCTURING SLPEs

Attention was drawn earlier to state-level public enterprises (SLPEs). They are numerous, having proliferated for largely political reasons. Many are involved in activities in which there is no rationale or comparative advantage for the presence of the public sector. And, as a group, their financial performance has been dismal. There is, therefore a strong case for restructuring, privatization and closure of SLPEs. In most SLPEs, the process will also be less complex than in central PSEs because of the smaller sizes involved. The states can profit from all-India and interstate experience on revival, adaptation, privatization and retrenchment. An appropriate institutional forum for exchange of information, provision of technical assistance, and the evolution of replicable models could help the process.

SAFETY NET

The evolution of an exit policy as well as the restructuring of SLPEs will be facilitated if the scope of the recently established National Renewal Fund is widened to provide unemployment benefits to workers who might be retrenched from central or state PSEs. In the private sector, coverage of retrenchment compensation needs to extend not only to factory units but also to small-scale industrial units, since the burden of adjustment tends to get passed on to the latter; and disemployment in the small-scale sector is not less demanding of relief because it is less visible and dissipated. A wide and effective safety net can be created if retrenchment benefits are insured from appropriate premia levied on all industrial units or, alternatively, if the required resources are mobilized through surcharges on excise duties and sales taxes. Politically, the states are more vulnerable than the centre to the impact of disemployment on law and order, local politics, and industrial harmony. It will, therefore, make sense to involve them actively in the National Renewal Fund in all its aspects: funding, determination and disbursal of benefits, and provision of adjustment assistance for retention and relocation of labour.

Power Development

The Eighth Five Year Plan (1992-7) envisages an addition of about 28,000 MW of generation capacity in power in the public sector at an outlay of about Rs 796 billion. Of this, the states have the responsibility for about 15,000 MW in terms of capacity and Rs 470 billion in terms of outlay. Compared to past plans, the centre has assumed a larger role in this sector, but even so the states have very substantial responsibilities—financial and organizational—in ensuring that the Plan targets are met.

FINANCIAL PERFORMANCE OF SEBs

As the *Economic Survey, 1992–3* points out (p. 178), 'restoration of the financial health of SEBs and improvement in their operational performances are the most critical issues in the power sector.' The financial performance of SEBs is indeed a matter for critical concern. In some SEBs, gross revenues are not sufficient even for covering operating expenses, leaving a current account deficit; in most, operating expenses are not adequate to make full provision for depreciation and interest payments. The substantial subsidy to agriculture has been noted earlier. Without counting rural electricity subsidies from state governments, the average rate of return on net assets of SEBs during 1985–90 was *minus* 12 per cent and even after taking the subsidies into account it was *minus* 6 per cent.[21] This is a far cry from the minimum rate of return of 3 per cent prescribed for SEBs by statute.

EFFICIENCY IMPROVEMENTS

In absolute amount, the average annual loss in SEBs during 1985–90 was of the order of Rs 23 billion after allowing for depreciation and interest provisions in full. The loss would have been much higher but for cross-subsidization of agricultural and domestic consumers by industrial and commercial users of electricity. This loss could be covered only with rural electricity subsidies from state governments (about Rs 11 billion) and by substantially reneging on interest payments to state governments (interest due being about Rs 15 billion). In order to meet the 3 per cent statutory return in this period, SEBs would have had to show a surplus of about Rs 6 billion, that is, register an improvement of Rs 29 billion over their actual performance. The rural electricity subsidy of Rs 11 billion being only about 38 per cent of this gap, it is evident that a number of other factors relating to operational efficiency were also responsible for the SEBs being unable to fulfil the normative rate of return. Principal efficiency improvements required are well known: improvements to the plant load factor; reducing losses in transmission and distribution; reduction of over-manning; better inventory management; improvements to maintenance and upgrading the quality of supply;

---

[21] Government of India, Planning Commission, *Annual Reports on the Working of State Electricity Boards* (various issues).

curbing theft of electricity and corrupt practices; energy conservation; measures for evening out the demand. Better interstate coordination through regional grid operations can also make an important contribution to efficiency and economy. These essentially managerial tasks will have to go hand in hand with periodical tariff adjustments in order to legitimize them.

IMPLEMENTATION OF NEW PROJECTS

The implementation of new projects in the states has widely encountered interrelated time and cost overruns. These are the consequences not only of administrative delays in land acquisition, placement of contracts and the like, but of underfunding of investment in relation to absorptive capacity—a factor that is also responsible for a large pipeline of unutilized aid commitments. Typically, state governments, faced with a number of non-compressible current outlays such as on salaries, transfers, and other on-going committed expenditures, tend to phase out capital investments. Funds for power development, accounting for about a third of state Plan outlays, attract the axe because they are lumpy and also because the benefits postponed from long-gestation power projects tend to go unnoticed in populist political perceptions. Earmarking of Plan outlays in the power sector could be one approach to tackling this problem. It will, however, be only a partial solution unless the basic financial performance of SEBs is improved.

PRIVATE INVESTMENT

A beginning has been made in the Eighth Plan in allowing private investment in the power sector. The hope is that private sector plants would be able to contribute to 3000 to 5000 MW of new capacity. Private producers who are to sell power in bulk to SEBs have been guaranteed a 16 per cent rate of return on investment. While some private parties have expressed interest in investing in power projects, they are likely to go ahead only if they are confident that guarantees offered by SEBs will, or can, be enforced. As the *Economic Survey, 1992–3* points out (p. 178), 'absence of legally enforceable fuel linkages, lack of access to the final market for electricity, the poor finances of SEBs, their poor record in settling debts and hence poor credibility as buyers of power—these are the major obstacles to the attraction of private investment into the power sector.'

LEVERAGE

Part of the centre's reform strategy consists of seeking to influence improvements in SEBs while financing power development through central intermediaries such as the Power Finance Corporation (PFC) and the National Bank for Agricultural and Rural Development (NABARD). It will be legitimate for the centre to use financial mechanisms, both through its assistance for state Plans and through its intermediaries for power financing, for promoting efficiency and economy in investments and operations of the SEBs. However, it will take time for the share of central agencies to gain the critical proportion required in the overall funding for power to be able to influence system-wide reforms in SEBs. Moreover, as the experience of the World Bank has shown, project-related conditionalities have not been successful in promoting sectoral reforms. In particular, the need to meet Plan targets and political factors is likely to inhibit attempts to secure reforms through financial leverage. In the final analysis, there is, therefore, no substitute for a political consensus that will recognize that economic, technical, and administrative considerations alone should govern the functioning of SEBs.

Agriculture

The importance of reforms in the agricultural sector for sustained growth in production and productivity, price stability in wage goods, food security, and rural employment and poverty eradication, does not need to be argued. Agriculture is very much a state's responsibility.

REFORM AGENDA: INCENTIVES

Unlike the situation in trade and industrial policies, an agenda for reforms in the agricultural sector has yet to be crystallized. However, its elements have emerged in documents and discussions relating to the subject. Broadly, it is agreed that the reform package will have to include two major components. One will be incentives to promote investment and production. These are likely to involve international trade (consistent with India's opportunities and advantages), dismantling of restrictive domestic procurement practices, higher output prices along with the lowering of input subsidies, and a general realignment of relative prices to promote more efficient allocation of resources. The other relates to several largely non-price and institutional aspects such as land reform, irrigation, credit, research and extension, rural infrastructure, and sustainable resource management.

Concerns have been expressed that freer international trade and price reforms should not be at the expense of reasonable self-sufficiency in agricultural commodities or at the expense of food security to the poor.[22] It has been pointed out that freer trade will raise the average level of agricultural prices, especially prices of basic foodgrains like rice and wheat, and that these increases, compounded by the reduction of food and fertilizer subsidies in the central budget, will widen the gap between producer prices and prices to consumers, both under PDS and in the open market. The burden of any adjustment on these lines will in effect be passed on, in large measure, to the states since, being politically more proximate to final consumers, they will be forced to bear a larger burden on food subsidies. The feasibility of any reforms that the centre might seek to bring about in the incentive system will very much depend on the cushioning of the costs—economic and political—to the states.

STATES' RESPONSIBILITIES

It has also been pointed out that the administrative and institutional components of the reform process will be more important than price-related incentives for securing supply responses and will, in any case, have to complement them.[23] In all such components, the states are almost wholly responsible, as the following summary discussion will indicate.

IRRIGATION: The problems of the irrigation sector have been extensively studied and it is not necessary or possible to summarize them in any detail.[24] Some issues relate to the use of resources: choice of cost-effective investments, adequate funding for individual projects

---

[22] M. V. Nadkarni, *Agricultural Policy in India: Context, Issues and Instruments* (Reserve Bank of India, Bombay, 1993); Kirit S. Parikh, *Economic Reforms and Food and Agricultural Policy* (Indira Gandhi Institute of Development Research, Bombay, 1993).

[23] A. Vaidyanathan, 'Agricultural Policy', *Business India* (April 1993).

[24] World Bank, *India: Irrigation Sector Review*, No. 9518-IN (December 1991); Government of India, Planning Commission, *Report of the Committee on the Pricing of Irrigation Water* (1992).

instead of spreading resources thinly over a large pipeline of incomplete ones, and reasonable cost recovery. The second set of problems relates to implementation: technically sound designs, concern for environmental impacts, construction quality, and timely completion. The third set of issues involves operation and maintenance: avoiding waste, and adequate, timely, and equitable supplies to farmers. The fourth area is economic and efficient utilization of water in the field, involving on-farm development and management with the participation of users. This gamut of interrelated problems will for their solution demand much greater financial discipline and administrative competence than the states have displayed. They will also require considerable political commitment. As one review points out,

> most of the issues (in the irrigation sector) have political roots: poor quality control has direct links to corruption; the specialist skills needed for high-quality planning design, construction, and operation are inhibited by the perpetual merry-go-round of transfers; and new irrigation projects are often chosen for expediency rather than for returns.[25]

CREDIT: The rural credit system in India has been in crisis in the last few years on account of high overdues, poor loan appraisal and recovery, subsidies relating to the interest rate and those implicit in defaulted repayments, financially unviable intermediaries, and political interference. In several states, interest and/or repayments on agricultural loans have been waived for political reasons, and in 1990 a loan write-off scheme, entailing heavy burdens on the states, was implemented by the centre in fulfillment of an electoral promise. Wilful default has been encouraged in the process and the general experience is that larger farmers have a poorer repayment record compared to small farmers. As the adjustment process will involve the reduction of subsidies on fertilizers, irrigation, and electricity, it will be all the more necessary to rebuild the credit system and to maintain its viability so that equitable access to inputs for small and marginal farms is assured. In this area, as well, a high degree of political discipline will be required.

RESEARCH AND EXTENSION: The centre and states network in agricultural research. While, basically, genetic and commodity-related research is undertaken at all-India levels, state agricultural universities

---

[25] World Bank, *India–Agriculture: Challenges and Opportunities*, No. 9412-IN (April 1991), p. 82.

are involved in area-based, problem-oriented and adaptive research. A number of reports have drawn attention to the need for strengthening centre–state linkages, increasing funds for research, and for improving its quality and motivation.[26] The states are entirely responsible for agricultural extension. In most states, this is based on the training and visit (T&V) pattern involving a chain of interactions between research institutions, specialist agricultural staff, extension agents, and farmers. The continual maintenance and strengthening of this chain—which tends to become weak and wobbly—is a major responsibility of state agricultural administrations.[27]

OTHER STATE RESPONSIBILITIES: These include: rural infrastructure (especially roads and market development), forestry, including community woodlots for meeting fuel needs at local levels, land management (protection of common property resources, afforestation, soil conservation, desiltation, catchment treatment), and land reform (security of tenure, enforcement of land ceilings, land redistribution, and consolidation of fragmented holdings).

FUNDING FOR AGRICULTURE: During the eighties, public investment in agriculture has declined as a proportion of total investment in the sector, as well as in real absolute terms. The share in Plan outlays for agriculture which was at a high of 37 per cent in the First Plan (1951–6) has stagnated in the range of 20–5 per cent in subsequent Plan periods. Along with increased efficiency and economy in resource use, the states will be clearly called upon to devise larger allocations to the sector, especially for irrigation, rural infrastructure, resource management, and research. This calls for strengthening their financial capability and for better targeting and cost recovery within the sector. There is also much scope for encouraging the private sector in dairying, agri-business, horticulture, seeds, and even in research and extension.

In sum, the states are vitally involved in the agricultural reform process. Incentive reform at the national level is not likely to be feasible unless approached with due concern for the economic and political burdens that will get transmitted to the states. In the whole

[26] Government of India, Ministry of Agriculture, *The Report of the ICAR Review Committee* (New Delhi, 1988); World Bank, *Agricultural Research in India: Prologue, Performance and Prospects*, No. 8383-IN (1990).

[27] On problems relating to agricultural extension, see World Bank, *India: Agricultural Extension Review*, No. 6950-IN (1988).

gamut of institutional and administrative reforms which will have to accompany and reinforce price-related reforms, it is the response of the states that will be crucial.

Social Sectors and Safety Nets

The likely impact of the adjustment process on the poor is a theme on which the critics of economic reforms have concentrated. Nor have its protagonists been insensitive to it. On all sides, it is recognized that, in the short to medium term, adjustment could have direct and indirect effects on the standards of living of the poor and on their access to basic social services. These, it has been recognized, could be consequent on a fall in the growth rate, disemployment in the organized and unorganized sectors of industry, inflation, and reductions, in public expenditures, particularly on welfare subsidies and social services.[28] There has, however, been little quantification or desegregated (sector, region, occupational, gender) analysis of the impact of adjustment on the poor; part of the problem lies in the difficulties inherent in sorting out the specific impact of adjustment from longer-term factors contributing to the persistence of mass poverty in India.

COMPOSITION OF THE SAFETY NET AND MAKING IT MORE EFFECTIVE

The debate on the extent and ways in which the poor will be affected by the reforms has not prevented the emergence of a consensus on the kind of safety nets that will be needed to protect them during adjustment. There is general agreement that the safety net will have to include: (i) PDS; (ii) poor-oriented employment and income-generation programmes, such as JRY and IRDP; (iii) primary education; (iv) primary health care; (v) drinking water supply and sanitation in rural areas and urban slums; (vi) child nutrition, and (vii) maternal and child health services. The generic tasks involved in strengthening the various programmes in the safety net are also clear. They include: (i) protecting outlays for social services in real

---

[28] See Ch. 5 in 'Economic Reform and India's Poor', in World Bank, *India: Stabilizing and Reforming the Economy*, No. 10489-IN (May 1992); Martin Revallion and K. Subbarao, 'Adjustment and Human Development in India' (March 1992), mimeo.

terms in the first instance and increasing them where appropriate and to the extent feasible; (ii) reordering intra-sectoral priorities (for example, primary versus higher education, preventive versus curative health services); (iii) reduction in disparities in the provision of basic social services (rural–urban, regional, gender based and according to income classes); (iv) cost-effective implementation reducing waste and leakage; (v) better targeting towards the poor; and (vi) reasonable cost recovery.

Even the bare listing of this variety of tasks will bring out the wide-ranging implications for the states. Their ability to protect real outlays on safety net programmes will depend on improving revenues and curtailing dysfunctional subsidies and inessential current expenditures. It will also depend on the extent to which the centre is able to supplement outlays for important centrally supported programmes such as JRY, IRDP and ICDS and, more generally, the extent to which the centre is able to increase its revenue transfers to the states. These issues were discussed earlier in this chapter with reference to the states' fiscal adjustment.

There is considerable scope for prioritizing and restructuring safety-net programmes and for curbing waste, leakage and corruption. The discussion that follows is only indicative.

PDS

In PDS, the first priority could be to eliminate leakage from shops and through bogus ration cards. It has been estimated that more than a third of the quantity of subsidized wheat and rice gets sold in the market due to such leakages: this is much higher than any savings likely to be effected through better targeting.[29] Several other ideas for the reform of PDS are waiting to be evaluated and tried out. Targeting towards rural areas, the rural and urban poor, backward regions, and in terms of cereals consumed by the poor have all been proposed. The ideal solution, but a radical one, might be to replace PDS with a food stamps system targeted to the poor leaving them free to buy essential commodities of their choice in the market. The government's intervention can then be restricted to buffer stock operations in foodgrains based on purchases in domestic and international markets at relevant support or market prices. Given sufficient opinion building with the states, such a transition might be possible.

[29] World Bank, *India: Stabilizing and Reforming the Economy*, (May 1992), p. 83.

INTEGRATED RURAL DEVELOPMENT PROGRAMME (IRDP)

Numerous evaluations of IRDP have revealed that it has degenerated into a thinly spread, poorly targeted, political hand-out involving considerable leakage and corruption. Also, IRDP depends for about two-thirds of its funding on credit from commercial banks while reforms in the financial sector call for the phasing out of subsidized, high-default, administratively directed lending such as under IRDP. In these circumstances, there is a good case for winding up IRDP altogether and for diverting resources to other more cost-effective anti-poverty programmes.

JAWAHAR ROZGAR YOJANA (JRY)

JRY has generally come to be regarded as a useful programme, primarily because of its self-selecting characteristic. But the overheads in JRY, in terms of material and administrative cost, are high: currently Rs 30 is required to create one man-day of employment in order to effect a transfer via wages of Rs 15. The cent per cent overheads involved in this particular mode of transfers to the poor will be justified only to the extent that JRY results in durable local assets. Whether it does has been widely questioned. The need in this context is, on one hand, for improving communal asset formation through JRY and, on the other, when and where that is not possible, to attempt more cost-effective transfers. The former will need decentralized micro-level planning on an area basis for rural infrastructure of various kinds—roads, minor irrigation, land consolidation, soil conservation, afforestation, etc. The latter can take the form of protective social security measures for the poor—old-age pensions, maternity assistance, survivor benefits—for all of which there is a strong case.[30]

The restructuring of individual safety net programmes will have to go along with basic changes in the philosophy and practices of implementation. There is a growing recognition in India that poor-oriented programmes—employment programmes, basic social services, PDS, social security—are best implemented in a decentralized fashion by local bodies (Panchayati Raj institutions) with local participation and subject to local accountability. This is reflected in a recent Constitutional amendment which makes it mandatory

---

[30] S. Guhan, 'Social Security for the Unorganized Poor in India: A Feasible Blueprint', (January 1992), mimeo.

to hold regular elections to local bodies, and calls upon the states to endow them with adequate resources and responsibilities so that their role in welfare and development can be considerably enlarged. Much will, however, depend on the spirit in which the promotive provisions of the amendment are translated into substantive and sustained decentralization by the states.

The state's role in the social sectors is crucial in protecting the poor during adjustment. If it is adequately discharged, many longer-term improvements in anti-poverty programmes could turn challenge into opportunity. The debate in India on the social aspects of adjustment has, however, been confined so far to speculative concerns relating to the impact on the poor and to academic analysis of the scope of the safety net. Governments at the centre and in the states are yet to give systematic attention to the restructuring of social programmes as an integral part of reform policy and practice.

Conclusion: Cooperative Federalism

The earlier sections of the chapter brought out the nature and degree of centre–state interaction involved in the reform process. In fiscal reforms, there is a strong reflexive relationship between the two levels: fiscal adjustment in the centre depends upon, and can contribute to, fiscal adjustment in the states and vice-versa. The states have a predominant role in agriculture and the social sectors; they have more than equal responsibility for power development; and they are involved in important ways in both regulatory and promotional aspects of industrial development. Given this interface, the reforms cannot be approached in a dichotomous, segmented manner with the centre playing its own narrowly conceived part, leaving the states to play theirs at the pace and manner determined by each of them. Quite clearly, the reform process will have to be conceived and pursued in a framework of cooperative federalism that takes into account the distribution not only of economic burdens and benefits between the two levels, but also of the political constraints. Unless these constraints are explicitly recognized and overcome to the extent feasible, the reform process will fall far short of its objectives.

Politics in the States

In the alive-and-kicking Indian democracy, politics is in command at both levels, but more so in the states. This is because of two related factors: the states are much closer to the electorate and also much more vulnerable to instability in terms of the parties and person heading their governments. The states are responsible for much that affects the daily lives of people: law and order, land administration, power supply, irrigation, agricultural services, public road transport, education, health, urban development and water supply. By the same token, these several activities that lie at the cutting edge of administration expose state governments more intimately and continually to popular demands, conflicting pressures, and diverse local grievances. Pushing through reforms that are likely to affect one interest group or another and carry varying burdens and benefits to different groups will, in these circumstances, require considerable political education and commitment in the states, Without these, the administrative apparatus in the states cannot be expected, and will not be able, to discharge the complex and considerable tasks involved in the reform process; it will need not only non-interference, but positive direction and drive from the political echelon.

Endemic Instability

Political stability, quite clearly, is a necessary condition for the generation of political will. In the last quarter of a century, this condition has not obtained to any reasonable degree that might be expected at the state level. Endemic instability in the states has been induced basically by factors related to the Congress party which has held power at the centre all the time since Independence except during two intervals, adding up to four years in all. These are: the centralizing philosophy of the Congress in regard to its own party affairs and in relation to the states; the pronounced weakening of the Congress in several states since 1967; and the systematic abuse of constitutional provisions since then by the Congress party to undermine the autonomy of the states (practices that have been followed by non-Congress parties as well during their brief periods of power at the centre).

Some basic data will tellingly substantiate the syndrome. In the first three general elections held during 1952-63 (1952, 1957, 1962), the Congress party was able to win in all of them and form governments in the states except in a single election in Kerala. In the pre-1967 period, many of the states were led by Chief Ministers of stature, and the hegemony of the Congress throughout India, under

Prime Minister Nehru's enlightened leadership, enabled intra-party consensus on priorities, policies and processes of planned development.[31]

The post-1967 era has been dramatically different for the fortunes of the Congress in the states. In a total of ninety-eight elections held in fifteen major states since then, the Congress has been able to win only in forty-five with opposition parties taking the rest. In all major states, non-Congress parties have been in power for varying periods; in one state (Tamilnadu) the Congress has been out of power continuously since 1967, and in another (West Bengal) since 1977.

The response of the Congress party to its weakening in the states has been systematically to misuse article 356 of the Constitution which, under extraordinary conditions of Constitutional breakdown, empowers the central government to dismiss state governments and to impose President's rule (that is, direct central administration), dissolving or suspending state legislatures.[32] Prior to 1967, President's rule was imposed on eleven occasions (in the seventeen years since the Constitution came into effect in 1950). Its application was confined to five states with two of them (Kerala and Punjab) accounting for eight of these occasions. Between 1967 and 1991 (twenty-four years), this emergency provision has been used as many as seventy-eight times in the states and all but one of the twenty-five states now in existence have been brought under President's rule at some time or other. Table 6.8 gives the frequency distribution.[33]

---

[31] Almost all major states provide examples of such Congress Chief Ministers in the pre-1967 period: N. Sanjiva Reddy and K. Brahmananda Reddy (Andhra Pradesh); Bishnu Ram Medhi (Assam); Sri Krishna Sinha (Bihar); S. Nijalingappa (Karnataka); Morarji Desai, Y. B. Chavan and V. P. Naik (Maharashtra); H. K. Mahtab and Biju Patnaik (Orissa); Pratap Singh Kairon (Punjab); Mohan Lal Sukhadia (Rajasthan); C. Rajagopalachari and K. Kamaraj (Tamilnadu); Govind Ballabh Pant (Uttar Pradesh); and B. C. Roy (West Bengal).

[32] Article 356 empowers the President to assume 'all or any of the functions' of a state government if he is satisfied that a situation has arisen 'in which the government of the State cannot be carried on in accordance with provisions of the Constitution'.

[33] The data are from Lok Sabha Secretariat, *President's Rule in the States and Union Territories* (New Delhi, 1991). Meghalaya is the only state that has so far escaped President's Rule since coming into existence in 1971.

TABLE 6.8: Imposition of President's Rule in the States, 1950–91

Number of Occasions of President's Rule	Number of States			Total Number of Occasions
	1950–67	1967–91	1950–91	
(1)	(2)	(3)	(4)	(5) = (4) × (1)
1	3	4	3	3
2		6	6	12
3	1	3	4	12
4		6	5	20
5	1	2	1	5
6		2	2	12
7		1	1	7
8				
9			2	18
	5	24	24	89

Source: Compiled from Lok Sabha Secretariat: *President's Rule in the States and Union Territories 1991.*

The Commission on Centre–State Relations (1987),[34] after a detailed analysis of eighty-four cases of the use of Article 356 during 1950–87, came to the conclusion that in fifty-eight (or 70 per cent) of them the use of the provision was 'clearly unjustified' while it 'appeared to be inevitable' in the rest. The Commission's annotation of individual cases brought out that the 'clearly unjustified' category consisted mostly of dismissal of governments headed by non-Congress parties or dissolution of state legislatures in order to deny their claims for forming governments.[35] In some cases, the Congress at the centre has also used Article 356 to settle factional squabbles within its own ranks. Apart from the wide abuse of this provision, periods of President's rule—both in the unjustified and in the inevitable categories—have been in most cases prolonged much

---

[34] Government of India, *Report of the Commission on Centre–State Relations* (New Delhi, 1988), Part I, Ch. VI.

[35] The unjustified category includes the wholesale dismissal of nine Congress governments in the states by the Janata government at the Centre, and the dismissal of an equal number of non-Congress state governments when the Congress returned to power in 1980. The recent (end-1992) dismissal of three BJP governments also joins this class of cases.

beyond any objective requirement: in effect, as long as it has been considered necessary for the Congress to capture or retain power in the states.

In parallel to the systematic undermining of opposition parties and governments, the post-1967 period has also witnessed the destabilization of Congress governments themselves in the states. Factionalism in state Congress parties has taken advantage of, and reinforced, the centralizing tendencies, of the party's 'High Command' to nominate Chief Ministers of its liking and to displace ones who enjoy, or display a tendency to build, a strong base for themselves in their states.[36] This phenomenon is graphically brought out in Table 6.9. In the major states, the average tenure of individual Congress Chief Ministers (including more than one disjointed tenure in some cases) was 3.9 years in the pre-1967 period. This dropped to 2.6 years in the post-1967 period, slightly less than even the

TABLE 6.9: Tenure of Chief Ministers in Major States, 1950–92

Length of Period in Office (in years)[a]	No. of Chief Ministers			
	1950–66		1967–92	
	Congress	Non-Congress	Congress	Non-Congress
0–2	1		5	4
2–3	2	1	2	4
3–4	5		3	2
4–5	1		2	4
5–	5		2	1
	14	1	14	15
Average period in office (years)	3.9	2.0	2.6	2.7

[a] Relates to individuals including one or more spells in office.
Source: Compiled from data in David Butler et al., *India Decides*, Living Media (1991).

[36] As Paul Brass points out, there has been 'the unwillingness in the post-Nehru period of the ruling party or coalition at the Centre to permit strong Chief Ministers. Increasingly, therefore, many state legislatures have lost their powers to choose the Chief Ministers and cabinets, a function which has been taken up by the governing group at the Centre', Paul Brass, *The Politics of India Since Independence* (Cambridge University Press, 1992), p. 50.

average of 2.7 years for the frequently dismissed non-Congress Chief Ministers.[37]

In any democracy, changes in political parties are inevitable and could be healthy, but what is important to notice is that endemic instability has emerged in the Indian states as a result of intra-party factionalism in the Congress and its tendency, while in power at the centre, to destabilize non-Congress governments in the states. The implications for governance of this degree of instability are serious. State governments, or their Chief Ministers, with a time-horizon of two to three years cannot be expected to have any deep commitment to long-term development or even an involvement in medium-term issues during their uneasy and limited tenure; they will be forced to politicize and interfere with the administration in order to survive; and tempted to make hay while the sun shines. The kaleidoscopic changes in the parties and persons heading state governments also render impossible any durable or meaningful centre–state coordination. This problem may be outside the domain of economic reforms in a narrow definition, but it draws sharp attention to the need for the Congress, which has spearheaded the economic reforms, to reform its political practices as well.

Minimizing political instability in the state—exogenous or endogenous—is of fundamental importance. If this is recognized, the centre, as the prime agent in the reform process, will be in a position to build an alliance with the states based on three main elements.

First, the centre must seek to lessen the economic and political burdens of the reforms on the states rather than exacerbating them or only too readily passing them on. This point has been covered in a number of places in the earlier sections of the chapter.

Secondly, there is much scope for strengthening consultative mechanisms and practices between the centre and the states. Using

[37] The case of Maharashtra well illustrates the trend. Except for a brief spell (1978–80) when it came under a breakaway group of the Congress, the state has all along been under Congress rule. Even this paradigmatic Congress state has seen ten individual Chief Ministers in the thirty-seven years spanning 1956–1993. Only two of them had tenures extending for more than the normal five-year period and both came to office prior to 1967. The average Chief Ministerial tenure in other cases was 1.7 years. Three of the Chief Ministers have had two spells each, separated by gaps extending from five to eight years; the combined length of their tenures was 4.2 years on the average. Five other Chief Ministers continued in office only for 1.2 years on an average in each case.

them, the centre will have to convey its concerns to the states continuously *and* take into account *their* concerns while formulating its policies. Consultation must be adequately prepared for and structured so that they can result in national guidelines carrying operational content. Mechanisms are already available for consultation and coordination, such as the Planning Commission, the National Development Council, the Inter-State Council and Zonal Councils. The centre and the states also periodically come together at the political levels in conferences of Chief Ministers and of ministers concerned with individual sectors. These instrumentalities will need to be made much more systematic and purposeful in their operation.[38]

Thirdly, in order that the states become more responsible economic actors and agents, a better mix of autonomy and accountability in centre–state financial relationship must be sought. This will involve an integrated approach to central revenue transfers on the Plan and non-Plan accounts and a differentiated approach to transfers on the revenue and capital accounts. Ideally, all transfers on the revenue account (except those for emergency relief), whether by way of tax shares or grants, could be effected as a share in the centre's gross revenues.

The Finance Commission can advise on varying this vertical share and on its *inter se* distribution between the states. Financing of capital projects in the power, irrigation, infrastructure, and urban development sectors can be through development lending institutions which can seek to influence policy reforms in the states and in their entities through the exercise of financial leverage. In particular, the

---

[38] Recent experience illustrates how the centre tends to lose the initiative for consensus building. The National Development Council meeting in December 1991 decided to set up a Committee of Chief Ministers to recommend fiscal reforms in the states. The Committee, which included two Chief Ministers belonging to non-Congress parties (Biju Patnaik, Janata Dal, its Chairman and Kalyan Singh, BJP, the Chief Minister of Uttar Pradesh, India's largest state) submitted recommendations for improving revenue and reducing expenditure in the states. The report was originally scheduled for discussion in the NDC in September 1992, but this was postponed and the NDC discussion finally took place only in April 1993. At this meeting, an important recommendation to impound cost of living allowances (DA) for central and state employees was left for further consultations and the question of improving the financial performance of SEBs was remitted to yet another Committee.

financing of power development—whether through normal Plan assistance or financial intermediaries—lends itself to be related to better administrative, technical and financial performance on the part of the SEBs. It must be realized, however, that leverage cannot be the main or major instrument: and its application will essentially have to be confined to dealing with deviations from such consensus.

An approach of this kind—based on support, consultation, autonomy and discipline—can logically culminate in a centre–state compact for implementing the reforms. Based on the analysis in this paper, the ingredients around which such a compact can be formulated are indicated in Table 6.10. If the centre were to be forthcoming in supporting the states in matters that lie within its power (column 2 of table) and in coordinating with them in matters that impinge on the states (column 4), the states will have strong incentives for attending to the various tasks required of them by the reform process (column 3). The task of institutionalizing cooperative federalism on these lines cannot be avoided, for the simple reason that structural adjustments of any consequence cannot be put through in a multi-party federation on any other basis. It cannot be postponed either in a scenario in which centre–state politics is bound to become more rather than less pluralistic and stability at the centre itself is not assured.

TABLE 6.10: Centre–State Nexus in Economic Reforms

Area of Reform	Centre	States	Centre–State Coordination
Fiscal Reform	Tax sharing from all central taxes	Economy and expenditure control	VAT up to wholesale stage
	Better tax enforcement especially in shareable taxes	Improving tax revenue especially from agriculture and liquor excise and through better enforcement	Consignment tax
	Restraint in increasing administered prices	Reduction of subsidies and increased cost recovery, especially in power and irrigation	Integrating agricultural incomes in income-tax
		Improving returns from PSEs	Coordination of tax enforcement in taxes on property and property transactions
Industrial reforms	National Renewal Fund to become comprehensive safety net for industrial workers	Streamlining entry clearances	Safety net for industrial workers
		Industrial infrastructure	Exit policy
		Restructuring and privatization of PSEs	Industrial incentives
			Restructuring and privatization of PSEs

(Contd.)

Table 6.10 contd.

Area of Reform	Centre	States	Centre-State Coordination
Power Sector		Improving financial and technical performance of SEBs	National consensus on efficiency norms and tariff policy
			Mechanisms for enforcing above
			Improved grid operations
Agriculture	Incentive reform without exacerbating economic and political burdens to states	Reforms relating to irrigation sector	Increased funding
		Reforms in agricultural credit, especially political non-interference	Research network
		Improved agricultural administration especially in extension activities	Agricultural credit
		Rural infrastructure, resource management, land reform	
Social sectors and safety nets	Restructuring and resource support in national safety net programmes—PDS, JRY, IRDP, ICDS, etc.	Restructuring; privatization; curtailing waste, leakage and corruption; better targeting; appropriate cost recovery	National consensus on basic package of social services and safety nets to discourage populist proliferation
		Decentralization to local bodies.	

7

Adjustment: To What End?*

Growth, development and poverty alleviation were key words in the normative and evaluative literature of international development in the fifties, sixties and even until the late seventies. The striking change that has come about since the early eighties is the prominence that the word 'adjustment' has assumed in discussions of the performance, prospects, and problems of developing countries. The insistent advice to developing countries that they 'need to adjust' on the part of the World Establishment, represented by policy-makers and purse-wielders in the metropolitan capitals and in international financial institutions, makes it necessary that we should examine the notion of 'adjustment' in its concrete application.

One might begin by pointing out that adjustment refers to the culmination of a process in which one or more actors adjust to some state of affairs. As far as the world economy is concerned, its trade and payments flows are at any point of time in a state of adjustment since surpluses and deficits cancel each other out in a closed system. Defined exhaustively and mutually exclusively, the actors in the world economy have necessarily to adjust to one another. Antecedent causal factors influence the course of adjustment and its future dynamics. In each state of adjustment, relative burdens and opportunities differ for each actor vs. the others. The notion of adjustment

---

* Paper presented at the Second International Conference of the Research and Information System for the Non-Aligned and Other Developing Countries, New Delhi, 20–2 November 1985. The Appendix to this paper, originally titled 'Some Notes on Automatic Resources for Development', was presented at a seminar organized by the Swedish Ministry of Foreign Affairs at Stockholm in December 1984.

needs therefore to be explicated by spelling out its contextual content, namely, adjustment to what, whose adjustment vis-à-vis which others, and how the costs and benefits work out to various adjusters in any specific situation. Without such explication the repeated use of this term runs the danger of becoming a slogan. Faced with slogans, we have to be careful because they are essentially weapons rather than words. One has to find out not only what they mean but also why their users are using them against those at whom they are being used.

We shall first describe the current, that is, 1984–5, developments in the international economy which constitute the objective situation to which the developing countries are being advised, reprimanded or required to adjust, with particular reference to the groups of developing countries most affected in the current crisis.[1] We shall then discuss the process of adjustment that is being recommended to developing countries by the World Establishment and its implications. We shall conclude by sketching a possible Southern response to the present situation.

WORLD GROWTH: QUANTUM AND SPREAD

On past trends, aggregate growth in world output in 1984 has been impressive. From zero growth in 1982, the recovery to 2 per cent in 1983 accelerated to a growth rate of 4.3 per cent in 1984. World trade in volume rose by about 9 per cent in 1984. Table 7.1 will however show that the recovery has been extremely disparate as between industrialized countries (ICs) and developing countries (DCs) and within each of these groups. In contrast to the long-run trend in 1960–82, the market-oriented industrial countries as a group registered higher growth rates in 1983 and 1984 in comparison to the developing countries. For DCs as a whole, output increased by 3.8 per cent in 1984, an improvement over an average 2.1 per cent in 1982 and 1983, but significantly less than 6.1 per cent in 1960–73 and 5.5 per cent in 1973–80. The spread of growth was also highly uneven amongst them. Growth rates for low-income countries declined from 7.3 per cent in 1983 to 5.8 per cent in 1984; growth for middle-income

---

[1] This description draws heavily on the documentation in the *Annual Reports* for 1985 of the World Bank and of the IMF, the *Trade and Development Report 1985* of UNCTAD, and the World Bank's *World Development Report 1985*.

TABLE 7.1: GDP Growth Rates, 1960–84

(per cent)

Country Groups	1960–73	1973–80	1981	1982	1983	1984
Industrial market economies	4.9	2.8	1.6	-0.3	2.6	4.5
Developing countries of which:	6.1	5.5	3.1	2.1	2.1	3.8
Low-income countries	5.6	4.8	3.9	5.0	7.3	5.8
Middle-income oil importers	6.4	5.8	1.7	1.0	1.1	3.8
Middle-income oil exporters	6.1	5.6	4.5	1.2	-1.6	1.7
Asia and Pacific	6.4	6.2	5.3	4.8	7.3	6.3
Middle East and North Africa	5.0	7.8	5.0	5.2	5.3	0.4
Sub-Saharan Africa	4.9	2.6	-0.4	-0.1	-2.8	-0.6
Southern Europe	6.7	4.9	2.0	2.2	0.9	2.1
Latin America and the Caribbean	6.1	5.4	1.6	-0.9	-3.2	2.8

Source: The World Bank Annual Report 1985, pp. 35 and 38.

oil exporters at 1.7 per cent in 1984 merely offset a decline of that order in 1983; it was middle-income oil importers who registered a relative improvement from 1.1 per cent in 1983 to 3.8 per cent in 1984. The Asian region, led by reasonable growth rates in China and India, did not do badly in 1984. Latin America registered a growth of 2.8 per cent in 1984, not enough to offset a decline of 3.2 per cent in 1983. Growth rates continued to be negative in sub-Saharan Africa for the fourth year in succession.

The current account deficit of developing countries dropped sharply from $ 71 billion in 1983 to $ 44 billion in 1984. Despite improved exports, imports had to be severely reduced on account of the large interest burden. In this sense, the 'improvement' essentially reflected the shortage in external finance, particularly from commercial lenders and the IMF (see Table 7.2).

Inflation in DCs continued at widely varying rates. While the median rate of inflation among them was contained at around 10 per cent, very high rates in certain countries accelerated the weighted average rate to 38 per cent in 1984 from 33 per cent in 1993 and 25 to 27 per cent in 1980-2.

Amongst the ICs the strongest stimulus to world recovery in 1984 was provided by the US rate of growth of 6.8 per cent, the highest registered in that country in nearly twenty years. Inflation in the US was reduced to 3.7 per cent and the unemployment rate declined from 9.6 to 7.5 per cent in 1983-4. A large budget deficit resulting from an expansionary fiscal policy was primarily responsible for high real interest rates and a rising dollar. The US current account deficit rose to $ 102 billion (nearly a quadrupling from $ 28 billion in 1982). It was financed largely through capital transfers from the rest of the world induced by the US interest rate which continued to be high despite some softening since late 1984. US import demand in 1984 was oriented more towards investment than towards consumption and benefited exporters of manufactures rather than of primary commodities. Its first and second round effects stimulated exports mainly from Western Europe, the newly industrializing countries of Latin America and East Asia, and Japan which recorded a growth rate of 5.8 per cent based mainly on export demand and reflected in a large current account surplus of $ 35 billion.

In contrast, growth in Western Europe at 2.3 per cent has been sluggish. Both monetary and fiscal policies in Western Europe have been restrictive. Inflation was contained at 5.4 per cent in 1984 but

TABLE 7.2: Developing Countries: External Financing, 1980–4[a]

(in US $ billion)

Item	1980	1981	1982	1983	1984
Requirements	103	128	102	77	66
Current account deficit	77	113	103	59	38
Increase to reserves	18	–2	–14	10	22
Capital outflows (net)	8	17	13	8	6
Sources	121	147	125	90	71
Non-debt-creating flows[b]	24	28	29	23	23
Long-term borrowing from official creditors	24	27	30	29	30
Borrowing from private sources[c]	70	84	48	19	14
Use of Fund credit	2	6	7	11	5
Arrears	1	2	11	8	–1
Errors and Omissions	–18	–19	–23	–13	–5

[a] Excluding eight major oil exporters in the Middle East.
[b] Official transfers, direct investment, SDR allocations, gold monetization and valuation adjustments.
[c] Long-term and short-term mainly from banks and other private creditors.

Source: IMF: Annual Report 1985, p. 22.

a stiff price has been paid in terms of unemployment which increased by a one half percentage point to 9.9 per cent and in absolute numbers by one million to 18 million persons. Low growth in Western Europe has provided little stimulus to its traditional primary commodity exporting partners, notably in Africa, and has kept commodity prices depressed.

The world energy market has remained stagnant and the earnings of the major petroleum exporting countries were about $ 100 billion less in 1984 as compared to 1980. As already noted, middle-income oil exporters had stagnant growth, taking 1983 and 1984 together. This has affected the export of goods, services and manpower to them from DCs and has resulted in declining remittances to the latter.

The pace, pattern and spread of the recovery in the ICs and oil exporters have had diverse transmission effects on different regions and categories of the DCs. These effects have been superimposed on longer-term structural factors in respect of commodity prices and terms of trade, protectionism, debt, and capital flows which have affected growth and welfare in the DCs in the late seventies and early eighties. We shall briefly annotate them before returning to a discussion of the specific impact of the current world economic environment on the DCs which are most seriously affected.

Primary Commodities

Since 1973, there has been a series of swings in commodity prices. Large increases occurred in 1973–4, 1976–7 and 1979–80 accompanied by smaller decreases of shorter duration in 1975 and 1978. There was a severe recession in 1981–2 which was followed by a weak recovery in 1983–4 (see Table 7.3). Apart from demand and supply factors specific to individual commodities, monetary factors in major markets such as inflation, exchange rates, and interest rates have played a significant causal role in influencing commodity prices. UNCTAD has estimated the cumulative loss of export earnings due to the 1980–3 commodity price collapse at $ 28 billion for forty-eight commodity exporting countries. Weak commodity prices in combination with increases in import prices have considerably worsened the terms of trade for developing countries in 1982 and 1983, with DCs in Latin America, Africa and West Asia being most affected (see Table 7.4).

TABLE 7.3: Commodity Price Changes, 1973-4 to 1983-4
(cumulative per cent)

Period	In US $	In Real Terms[a]
1973-4	90	42
1975	-20	-9
1976-7	35	2
1978	-7	-19
1979-80	30	5
1981-2	-31	-25
1983-4	6	15

[a] UNCTAD index in US $ divided by the United Nations index of manufactured goods exported by developed-market economies.
Source: UNCTAD, Trade and Development Report 1985, p. 30.

TABLE 7.4: Terms of Trade: Annual Rates of Change, 1975-84
(per cent)

Country group	1975-80	1982	1983	1984
All developing countries	4.8	-3.3	-3.8	0.4
Western Hemisphere	-1.3	-5.1	1.9	-0.8
North Africa	8.7	-5.4	-8.2	1.0
Other Africa	5.4	-5.9	-2.5	2.0
West Asia	11.1	0.1	-10.9	0.9
South Asia	-6.9	-2.2	5.2	5.0
East Asia	-6.9	-2.9	2.9	1.2

Source: UNCTAD, *Trade and Development Report 1985*, p. 188.

Protectionism

The trend towards protectionism continued in 1984, spurred by the large trade deficit and high unemployment in the US and weak growth and increased unemployment in Western Europe. The situation was aggravated by import contraction in the DCs, which meant lesser jobs in exporting ICs: Western Europe was particularly affected in this respect by falling exports to Africa. UNCTAD estimates that over one-third of developing-country exports (by value) are now subject to one or more kinds of protectionist measures in developed countries. There has been a growth and tightening of non-tariff barriers (NTBs): their extent more than doubled in the US between 1980 and 1983 and increased by about 40 per cent in the European Community.

An especially pernicious aspect of NTBs is that they are particularly loaded against imports from DCs (for example, footwear and apparel) and, within them, against imports from major debtor countries (for example, steel, sugar, beef).

Debt and Debt Service

Total debt outstanding and disbursed (medium and long term) for DCs has grown more than ten-fold, from $ 68 billion in 1970 to $ 686 billion in 1984. In the same period, the proportion of private debt has increased from 50.9 to 65 per cent. For developing countries as a whole, key ratios such as debt to GNP, debt to exports, the debt-service ratio and interest to GNP have all increased significantly (see Table 7.5). With the growth in private lending, average maturity of total public debt of DCs has significantly shortened from 20.4 years in 1970 to 14.2 years in 1982. Between 1974 and 1983, the proportion of floating interest rate loans in the public debt of DCs has increased from 16.2 to 42.7 per cent, and along with the increase in interest rates since 1980, this has meant a steep escalation in debt-servicing costs, reflected in the ratio of interest service to GNP, which has moved from 0.8 per cent in 1974 to 2.8 per cent in 1984 (see Table 7.5). Another measure is the proportion of interest payments to medium- and long-term floating interest debt, which within two years has risen from 12.3 per cent in 1979 to 17.4 per cent in 1981.

In 1981–4, there has been a dramatic decline in DCs net borrowing from market sources. New commitments to borrowing countries from commercial sources has virtually dried up. Excluding the major oil exporters, the net external borrowing of developing countries (long term and short term) from private creditors dropped from a peak of $ 84 billion in 1981 to $ 14 billion in 1984 (see Table 7.2). 'Market borrowers' in the IMF classification, namely, countries that obtained two-thirds or more of their external borrowings in 1978–82 from commercial sources, borrowed $ 120 billion (net) from private creditors in 1981–2 but only $ 20 billion in 1983–4 and this too as a result of obtaining some $ 23–4 billion as 'involuntary lending' involved in debt restructuring arrangements. The contraction in new lending has meant an increase in negative net transfers (that is, excess of debt service over new lending) from DCs since 1982. UNCTAD estimates the negative net transfer to be of the order of $ 7 billion in 1984.

TABLE 7.5: Debt Indicators for Developing Countries, 1970-84

(per cent)

	Debt to gNP 1970	Debt to gNP 1984	Debt to exports 1970	Debt to exports 1984	Debt-service ratio 1970	Debt-service ratio 1984	Interest service to gNP 1970	Interest service to gNP 1984
All Developing Countries	14.1	33.8	108.9	135.4	14.7	19.7	0.5	2.8
Low-income Asia	7.0	9.7	183.6	100.0	12.4	8.4	0.2	0.3
Low-income Africa	17.5	54.5	75.2	278.1	6.1	19.9	0.5	2.1
Major exporters of manufactures	16.2	37.6	91.5	109.1	15.1	16.0	0.7	3.6
Other middle-income oil importers	21.4	53.0	111.0	183.9	13.6	24.9	0.8	3.9
Middle-income oil exporters	18.4	43.8	115.3	164.2	18.1	28.1	0.7	4.0

Source: World Bank Development Report 1985, p. 24.

180 □ *India's Development Experience*

The contraction in new lending, shorter maturities, depressed export earnings, and high interest rates acting on a large portfolio of floating interest loans have together contributed to a spate of debt reschedulings. Thirty-two developing countries either signed or reached agreement in principle to reschedule their debt service payments in 1983 and/or 1984, of whom thirteen countries were involved in debt rescheduling in both years. From January 1984 to April 1985, twenty-one developing-country members of IMF reached agreements to restructure debt totalling about $ 105 billion, postponing debt service payments for about $ 21 billion. In the same period, $ 36 billion of short-term debt had to be rolled over or converted into medium-term debt. Payment arrears had mounted to $ 8–11 billion in 1982–3.[2]

Official and Institutional Flows

There has been no relief to this situation from official flows from governments or from international financial institutions. The seventies witnessed a rapid growth in official development assistance (ODA) from $ 8 billion in 1970 to $ 37.5 billion in 1980, in which OPEC flows increased from $ 400 million to $ 9.6 billion. In 1980–3, ODA has steadily declined (see Table 7.6), DAC bilateral aid has stagnated, and there has been a decline of over 40 per cent in ODA from OPEC countries. The UN Conference on the Least Developed Countries (LDCs) held in 1981, had proposed a target of 0.15 of GNP from ODA donors to LDCs. From DAC countries, the ODA/GNP ratio to LDCs has stagnated at 0.07 per cent and to all recipients it has decreased from 0.38 per cent in 1980 to 0.36 per cent in 1983. Official capital flows, concessional and non-concessional, provided 50 per cent of inflows to all DCs in 1970 and 78 per cent for low-income DCs. By 1983, these figures had fallen to 46 per cent and 45 per cent.

Along with this, there has been a retrogression from multilateral to bilateral assistance. DAC contributions to multilateral financial institutions have fallen from 32 per cent in 1977–8 to 28 per cent in 1982–3. This has an important implication because political and commercial rather than developmental considerations play a major

[2] It is noteworthy that overdue obligations from its members to the IMF (that is, repayments overdue for six months or more) amounted to SDR 176.3 million on 30 April 1985 (*IMF Annual Report 1985*, p. 74).

TABLE 7.6: Net Resource Receipts of Developing Countries
from all Sources, 1970–83

(US $ billion, current prices)

Source	1970	1980	1981	1982	1983
Official Development Assistance	8.08	37.50	37.28	34.74	33.65
Bilateral	7.01	29.71	29.35	27.23	26.12
Multilateral	1.07	7.79	7.93	7.51	7.50
Grants by private voluntary agencies	0.86	2.31	2.02	2.31	2.20
Non-concessional flows	10.95	59.34	70.46	60.36	63.90
Multilateral	0.71	4.85	5.72	6.61	7.00
Bilateral: Official or officially supported	3.25	19.57	16.42	15.38	12.60
Private	6.99	34.92	48.32	38.37	44.30
Total	*19.89*	*99.15*	*109.76*	*97.41*	*99.75*

Source: OECD, *1984 Review of Development Cooperation*, p. 64.

part in the allocation of bilateral assistance: 39 per cent of US bilateral aid goes to Egypt and Israel; 38 per cent of French ODA to four of its overseas departments and territories; and 42 per cent of OPEC aid to Jordan and Syria. During 1980–2, only 40 per cent of DAC bilateral aid and less than 20 per cent of ODA from OPEC went to low-income countries whereas two-thirds of all multilateral aid was directed to them. The stagnation in multilateral aid is reflected in lower lending commitments from IBRD and IDA. In fiscal year 1985 (July 1984 to June 1985), IBRD commitments were 4.9 per cent less than in FY 1984. The decline in IDA commitments, of special interest to low-income countries, was much steeper, being 15.3 per cent less than in FY 1984.

There has also been a striking decline in the use of IMF credit by DCs, whose net drawings from the Fund dropped to $ 4.4 billion in 1984 from the peak of $ 10.7 billion in 1983. This was accompanied by an acceleration in the trend towards high-conditionality borrowing. Net low-conditionality flows to developing countries declined to almost zero in 1984 from $ 3.2 billion in 1983.

THE CONTINENTS IN CRISIS

We may turn to a closer examination of the situation in the two regions which have been affected to crisis proportions by the current international economic environment, namely, Latin America and sub-Saharan Africa. GDP in Latin America after a slow growth of 1.6 per cent in 1981 declined by 0.9 per cent in 1982 and a further 3.2 per cent in 1983. The growth of 2.8 per cent in 1984 has provided a break but barely exceeded the increase in population. In over two-thirds of the countries in the region, per capita real incomes declined and were at the level of the early seventies. Growth being inadequate to keep pace with the expansion in the labour force, there was a rise in open unemployment. Inflation in terms of the weighted average rate increased from a high of 100 per cent in 1984 by a further 20 per cent points. Among the larger countries, consumer prices rose by almost 680 per cent in Argentina and by nearly 200 per cent in Brazil. The increase was still as high as 60 per cent in Mexico despite a relative decline.

Latin America's current account deficits have shown a significant decline in the last two years; from around $ 42-3 billion in 1981-2 they dropped to about $ 12 billion in 1983 and to $ 5.5 billion in 1984. With exports rising at 9.3 per cent and import growth limited to 4.4 per cent, there was a sharp turn-around in 1984 in the trade balance which turned to surplus. Little consolation could however be derived from this development since virtually all of the trade surplus was absorbed by interest payments on outstanding debt. For Latin America as a whole, negative net transfers amounted to $ 27-30 billion in 1983-4, equivalent to more than a quarter of the region's export of goods and services. Net transfers from Mexico were as high as 47 per cent of the country's export of goods and non-factor services. By themselves, interest payments in the region absorbed 35 per cent of exports of goods and services in 1984, with Argentina recording a proportion as high as 52 per cent. Added to this have been large outflows of capital triggered by inflation, exchange instability, and speculation. UNCTAD estimates that such outflows may have amounted to as much as 40 per cent of the increase in debt of five major Latin American countries in 1974-82. With a sizable drain of resources in all these ways, imports had to be severely cut back with consequences for inflation and unemployment in the immediate present and affecting future growth, incomes, consumption and employment via the retardation of investment.

The harshness of the international environment has been compounded in sub-Saharan Africa by widespread and prolonged drought, which has led to food shortages of famine proportions in a number of countries—Ethiopia, Mali, Niger Mozambique, Sudan, Tanzania— and to a lesser extent Kenya, Somalia, and Zimbabwe. 1984 was the fourth successive year of negative growth in this region, bringing a decline in GDP of 0.6 per cent on top of a 2.8 per cent decline in 1983. The very low per capita incomes in the region fell between 5 and 10 per cent in 1980–4. The decline in real per capita absorption was even larger since terms-of-trade losses, debt-service payments, and food imports drained out an increasing proportion of the region's output. It is also noteworthy that although the absolute size of Africa's debt is small, DCs in the region have experienced the highest rates of increase in debt in relation to income and exports. The ratio of debt to GNP for African DCs increased in 1970–84 from 17.5 to 54.5 per cent and the debt-service ratio more than tripled from 6.1 to 19.9 per cent (see Table 7.5). Sixteen African countries some of them among the poorest in the world, have had to enter into debt rescheduling arrangments.[3]

In the face of poor export earnings, food deficits, declining availability of official and commercial flows, and high debt-service payments, there was inevitably a strong contraction in industrial imports—to the point of 'import strangulation'—in a number of major countries in sub-Saharan Africa such as Kenya, Sudan, Tanzania, Zambia, Ghana, and Nigeria. In Nigeria, reduced availability of raw materials and spare parts led to widespread plant closures, extensive lay-offs and a substantial drop in capacity utilization in the manufacturing sector. In Ghana, chronic infrastructural constraints and a continuing shortage of foreign exchange deprived the manufacturing sector of essential raw materials and spare parts. In 1984, Kenya's exports declined for a fourth consecutive year and its GDP declined for the first time in the current decade. Somalia suffered a major setback in 1984 with an inflation rate of 92 per cent. Zambia was perhaps the worst hit. Starting with the copper price collapse in 1975, per capita incomes have fallen by 44 per cent in 1974–5 and real imports in 1984 were only 40 per cent of the level in the early seventies. The investment rate has dropped from 41 per cent to

---

[3] Moreover, despite numerous debt reschedulings in recent years, arrears owed by twelve major developing countries in eastern and southern Africa had accumulated to $ 2.4 billion at the end of 1984 (*World Bank Annual Report 1985*, p. 86).

12 per cent in 1975–84. External payment arrears amounted to $ 600 million in 1984.[4]

We have not referred to the third continent of Asia only because the near-term experience there is much more mixed and not because Asia can be considered to be out of the woods in any lasting sense. The Philippines is in deep trouble and Bangladesh, the largest of the least developed countries, is facing a severe import crisis, with floods and cyclones in 1984–5 adding to its long-term difficulties. The NICs in East Asia have shown a great deal of resilience but recession and protectionism in the ICs and contraction of commercial credit have already affected them deeply. India and China have been helped by a run of good agricultural years but face declining official flows— concessional and non-concessional—on an already very low base of per capita aid. In the coming years they too—India sooner than China—will be forced into sharply increased commercial borrowing and 'debt-led growth' with the familiar consequences that can be expected in its wake.

No Silver Lining

The prospects for 1985 are not particularly promising. According to the World Bank's assessment, GDP growth in industrial countries is expected to slow down in 1985, notably in the United States and by a smaller extent in Japan. Growth in Western Europe is expected to continue more or less at the low level of 1984. Average growth in industrial countries may be no more than 3 per cent. The slowing down of growth in the developed countries does not augur well for manufactured exports, and much less for primary commodities, where, ironically, better agricultural prospects in the poor commodity exporting countries may only tend to depress prices further by increasing supplies. Projected debt-service payments from developing countries in 1985–7 are of the order of $ 100 billion in each year as compared to $ 88 billion in 1984. With lower export earnings and

[4] On Zambia, 'Zambia's "Magic Elevator" Evidence of Decline' in the *Guardian Weekly*, 6 October 1985 (p. 16) provides a vivid account:
...the country has almost no foreign exchange to import wheat for bread, to buy diesel fuel, to fix farm tractors (62 per cent of which don't work), to upgrade factories (which operate at less than 32 per cent capacity), or to pay off an ever-growing foreign debt. 'What is happening is that Zambia is being strangled, and not so slowly any more' said an International Monetary Fund official who is a specialist on Zambia.

continuing high debt-service burdens, the present crisis is likely to get further exacerbated in the medium term.

The World Bank's 'high case' projection for 1985–95 postulates a growth rate of 4.3 per cent for industrial countries and 5.5 per cent for developing countries during the coming decade. At present sight, these indicative targets seem out of reach. And what is truly depressing is that even in the World Bank's 'high case', already dismally low per capita incomes in low-income Africa are projected to decline by 0.1 per cent annually in the decade ahead.

In sum, the crisis is spread over a wide spectrum of middle-income, low-income and least developed countries comprising also a variety of categories: exporters of oil, manufacturers and primary commodities as well as oil importers. The generic features are sluggish export growth, low commodity prices, terms-of-trade losses, a large drain on debt service payments, and a severe contraction of essential imports. A tangled skein of domestic policies in DCs, exogenous developments in ICs, and climatic factors have contributed to the crisis but the consequences, in terms of declining production, inflation, unemployment, and worsening income distribution are the harsh immediate reality. What is involved is economic disarray which can trigger political and social upheaval.[5] In the longer run, insufficient investment over a span of several years will reduce future growth and accentuate the downward spiral. In these circumstances it is clear that survival, reconstruction, maintenance, and stabilization are matters of the highest immediate priority to a number of developing countries. Essentially, the prime requirement is blood transfusion in terms of flexible and quick-disbursing flows of foreign exchange for essential imports of food, fuel, and industrial raw materials, which have had to be severely cut back owing to export earning shortfalls and high debt-service payments. Finance to meet such needs will have to be provided, effectively and urgently, in a combination of ways: directly, and along with debt relief and compensatory financing facilities which would release freely usable foreign exchange.

Role of Bank-Fund

This being the context, it should be clear that the World Bank group and the IMF will have a central role to play in defusing the crisis.

[5] Peru's President Alan Garcia told the UN General Assembly in October 1985: 'We are faced with a dramatic choice. It is either debt or democracy.'

For one thing, the debt crisis and the contraction of both commercial and bilateral flows entail a compulsive involvement of developing countries with these two 'public' financial and monetary intermediaries which are the only ones operating at the global level. Major borrowers, who have hitherto mainly relied on the market, will have to turn to the World Bank for external finance. The poorest countries, with little or no access to commercial finance and inadequately favoured with bilateral aid, have similarly to look to the IDA as their mainstay. For a wide spectrum of countries, debt restructuring arrangements have already involved the Fund's brokerage between creditors and debtors in terms of stand-by arrangements, creditor coordination, and policing of borrowers' policies. Closer collaboration between the Bank and the Fund,[6] and the large number of consultative groups of bilateral and multilateral aid agencies under the aegis of the Bank, have greatly increased the power and the potential of the Bank and the Fund to 'coordinate policies' at all stages of the transfer process.

In principle, a greater role for the Bank and the Fund in dealing with the emergent needs of developing countries need not be unwelcome since the developing countries are not merely borrowers but shareholders in them with some say and much stake in their policies and functioning. But a number of conditions will have to be met before one can be sure that the Bank and the Fund will act up to the role of friends-in-need. Otherwise, there is the danger of their becoming a counter-productive stranglehold. First, the Bank and the Fund will have to be equipped with adequate resources. Types of finance which are non-debt-creating (namely, IDA), unconditional (namely, SDRs) and automatic-compensatory (namely, CFF) will be especially important. Increased IMF quotas can provide larger low-conditionality funds, and with improved access formulae, enable a larger resort to IMF resources under different facilities. Of crucial importance will be non-project or programme lending from the Bank and IDA which can finance industrial raw materials, spare parts, and other maintenance requirements for improved capacity utilization.

Current developments on all these fronts are uniformly discouraging. The seventh replenishment of IDA at $ 9 billion was 25 per cent less than the projected demand and has meant significant reductions

---

[6] On increasing collaboration between the Bank and the Fund, see *World Bank Annual Report 1985*, p. 56.

in IDA commitments to low-income countries. The enlarged access policy adopted by the Fund in 1981 has been progressively whittled down in 1984 and again in 1985. As Table 7.7 will show, non-project lending from the Bank and IDA which was less than 5 per cent of their total lending in fiscal years 1975-80 went up to 9.9 per cent in 1983—still a small proportion—and has precipitously dropped to 4.4 per cent in 1985. The strong case made out by DCs for a general capital increase to the Bank and for a further issue of SDRs has not been accepted at the 1985 Fund-Bank meeting in Seoul by the ICs, who are their major shareholders. The only encouraging development has been the establishment of a Special Facility for sub-Saharan Africa in May 1985 under the aegis of IDA with expected contributions for $ 1.2 billion. The Special Facility however raised several questions: is it too little, too late? Will it be fully additional to what sub-Saharan Africa could otherwise hope to receive? And, most important, what are the conditionalities subject to which finance from this source will be made available?

TABLE 7.7: Non-project Lending from the World Bank and IDA, 1975-85

Fiscal year (July–June)	Non-project lending from Bank and IDA (US $ billion)	Total lending from Bank and IDA (US $ billion)	Per cent of non-project lending
1975-9	0.25	7.58	4.6
1980	0.52	11.48	4.6
1981	1.01	12.29	8.2
1982	1.24	13.02	9.5
1983	1.43	14.48	9.9
1984	1.38	15.52	8.9
1985	0.63	14.39	4.4

Source: World Bank, *Annual Reports 1984 and 1985*.

Conditionality and Policy Reform

The lending conditionalities followed by the Bank in its structural adjustment loans (SALs) and by IMF in its conditional loan operations,[7] which compound inadequate resources and inflexible forms

[7] On the complementarity between the Bank's structural adjustment loans and conditional lending from the IMF see Ernest Stern, 'World Bank Financing of

of lending, are the greatest source of concern. First, we might notice that the Bank-Fund have chosen to squarely lay the blame for the present ills on the domestic policies of borrowers, ignoring the plethora of causes outside the control of DCs which have contributed to the crisis—high interest rates, terms-of-trade losses, exchange instability, contraction in commercial and official flows, natural calamities. Take the following statement in the Bank's *World Development Report*, 1985 (p. 43): 'Economic policies of developing countries are the *fundamental determinant* of the level of capital inflows, the efficiency with which they are used and a country's capacity to service its debts' (emphasis added). Proceeding from this premise, the concentration of the Bank-Fund has been on promoting (pressurizing) domestic policy reforms in DCs which (in the economic ideology of the World Establishment) are expected to rectify balance-of-payments disequilibria in the shortest possible time. Directed at symptoms rather than causes, the policy prescriptions of the Bank-Fund have broadly tended to constitute the same package regardless of the country or the context. Typically, the 'patent cure' includes measures to (a) depreciate the exchange rate; (b) liberalize imports; (c) increase agricultural producer prices; (d) reduce public expenditure by reducing subsidies, retrenching public enterprises, and postponing or curtailing investment programmes; and (e) increase real interest rates and restrain credit expansion, especially net credit to government.

The thrust of this policy reform package is to place overriding emphasis on demand curtailment regardless of implications for growth, equity, and welfare. Administered price increases, reduction of subsidies, and retrenchment constitute the 'policy reform' to be pursued by countries facing import scarcities, declining production, rising unemployment and soaring prices. The harsh and perverse logic of the prescription is so obvious that even the World Bank has not been able to ignore it. Take the following (in relation to southern and eastern Africa) in the Bank's *Annual Report* for 1985 (p. 88):

Structural Adjustment' in John Williamson (ed.) *IMF Conditionality* (Institute for International Economics, Washington DC, 1983). Stern points out:
> Structural adjustment can only take place effectively in the context of actions to limit aggregate demand, and where necessary, external borrowing. Thus, conditions to permit access to Fund resources are usually a prerequisite to a detailed programme of structural change (p. 101).

The initiation of such measures (that is, 'policy reform') has been made more difficult by the impact of untoward events over which governments can exercise little control. The continuing financial crisis has made it especially hard for many countries to pursue those stabilization measures needed to correct financial disequilibria and those structural-adjustment and reform measures needed to reverse trends in declining production and to foster longer-term growth. For example, countries experiencing continuing falls in their export prices have found it particularly difficult to raise producer prices and reduce input subsidies. Countries in which real incomes of consumers are declining are often loathe to remove food and other consumer subsidies. The same difficulty is encountered in reducing government employment in the face of urban unemployment, and in recapitalizing public enterprises when public budgets are under pressure.

Declines in export prices, aid disbursements and production of export crops have reduced revenues at a time when demands on the budget for financing maintenance and critical economic and social services are growing. Countries that are simultaneously experiencing declining or stagnant export earnings and growing debt-service obligations are also hard put to liberalize their import regimes. And government leaders and administrators in countries that are experiencing severe drought can focus only with difficulty on medium-term to longer-term adjustment objectives.

The Fund has not been impervious either to the anomaly. In its words (*IMF Annual Report 1985*, p. 12):

External adjustment typically requires changes in the relative price structure of the economy, changes that are affected in part through the depreciation of the exchange rate and the reduction or elimination of subsidies. Such changes are a source of upward pressure on the domestic price level...

The remedy that the Fund proceeds to advocate is that the 'upward pressure' should be counteracted through 'suitably restrictive financial policies and/or changes in indexation mechanisms', that is, in plain language, by reducing real incomes. The operation must succeed even if it kills the patient.[8]

In criticizing the Bank-Fund approach to policy reform, we do not wish to imply that the external payments and growth problems of developing countries have no relation to their own policies or economic (mis)management. However, situations of dire social distress,

---

[8] Or as another commentator has put it: 'So successful has the IMF been at squeezing developing countries...that (it) is like a doctor treating haemorrhage by taking blood away' ('On the Edge of a Financial Precipice', *Guardian Weekly*, 13 October 1985, p. 10).

such as those which face many developing countries today, raise issues which are more complex than crude one-sided culpability. They relate to the basic causes of disequilibria and hence to the remedy; to the extent to which welfare and growth in the present should be made to pay for lapses in the past; to the sustainable pace of adjustment in a democratic polity; the appropriate mix in the short to medium term between 'adjustment', and 'finance' to enable and ease the process; and the scope and timing of adjustment measures and their phasing. A basic point is whether it is the business at all of the Fund (or of the Bank) to make loans conditional on policies whose connection to the balance of payments in the short or even medium run might be tenuous.[9] In the face of such complex issues, which are essentially related to the political economy of growth, any external

[9] In this connection see the contributions from Dragoslav Avramovic, Sidney Dell, Carlos F. Diaz-Alejandro, Reginald Herbold Green and Samuel Lichtensztejn in John Williamson (ed.), *IMF Conditionality*. Samuel Lichtensztejn draws attention to the ways in which stabilization on the IMF model might encourage authoritarian governments (pp. 220–1):

Why did stabilization programmes become fused with authoritarian political doctrines? In other words, how could authoritarian regimes make anti-inflationary policies a source of their legitimacy? Since an in-depth analysis of these questions is quite complicated, we will deal only with those elements which are most relevant in analyzing IMF policies.

One such element is the theory according to which inflation is progressively caused by the conflict between forces with monopoly control over labour (that is, unions) and capital. The profits-wages struggle tends to increase costs and prices. With growing economic concentration and social contradictions, stabilization programmes following this line will highlight wage and profit (that is, incomes) policies.

Thus the emphasis on increasing wage costs as the cause of inflation also implicit in the IMF interpretation turns anti-labour policies into an equivalent of anti-inflationary efforts (for the benefit of the common interest, by definition). That is then one of the major economic justifications of authoritarianism.

Another element that contributes to make the fight against inflation a part of authoritarian theory is directly related to the conditions stipulated for an efficient implementation of economic policy. In particular, utmost importance was given to formal principles such as 'coherence', 'compatibility', and 'consistency'—between anti-inflationary objectives and instruments. The implementation of stabilization policy became increasingly subordinated to those principles; however, its final success depended upon its maintenance. In fact, political changes or interruptions (due to

intervention will need the skills and patience of a surgeon—supported by sufficient blood for transfusion—while the adjustment packages being imposed on developing countries are rather like a barber's knife.

We must also note that 'adjustment' is more than a technical-neutral word. Social scientists have recognized the important role that 'labelling', that is, the use of certain 'code words', plays in public policy discourse.[10] 'Adjustment' provides an excellent example of labelling. The word legitimizes the unwillingness of the rich, and of institutions accountable to them, to respond to the suffering and needs of the poor. It helps to rationalize the situation by demanding instead that the poor live with (that is, adjust to) their misery by arguing that what has caused it are the economic policies of the poor themselves. This is a version of the 'culture of poverty' argument: the poor are poor because they are feckless.

At another level, the emphasis of the Bank-Fund on 'adjustment' reflects their own adjustment to reality. They are powerless to effectively advise either the deficit or the surplus industrialized countries to adjust: the ICs are providers of resources to the Bank-Fund, not borrowers from them. The Bank and the Fund are

---

elections, etc.) were pointed out as the source of a lack of continuity in anti-inflationary policy.

In our view, the IMF approach—and more recently that of Friedman and the Chicago School—had such a strong influence on the military regimes precisely because, besides 'scientifically' supporting a specific stabilization policy and admitting all its negative effects as necessary, they make its success depend almost exclusively on a rigid discipline and on the continuity of implementation of their recommendations. Thus politics needed to be exempted from demagogical and populist practices, which are constantly invoked and criticized to justify and defend the need for an iron hand and a prolonged regime.

As time went by, stabilization experiences proved that rather than being an improvement on preceding policies, they represented a link in a transformation and reorganization process undergone by the state and its functions. That is why it can be said, that conditionality has contributed so much to destabilizing certain governments. In addition to the recent classical examples in the Southern Cone (especially Chile) we should also point out as examples the cases of Portugal, Peru, Turkey, Jamaica and Tanzania.

[10] 'Labelling in Development Policy: Essays in Honour of Bernard Schaffer', *Development and Change*, 16(3), July 1985.

especially impotent vis-à-vis the most powerful industrialized country which sucks in capital from the rest of the world to finance its fiscal and trade deficits and is the epicenter with respect to which others have to adjust. Resources available to these institutions are scarce and will have to be somehow rationed. In such circumstances, it is not unnatural that adjustment (or the advocacy of the poor having to lift themselves by the bootstraps) should be adopted as a theory of convenience.

TOWARDS A SOUTHERN RESPONSE

The South will surely have to unite to fight the theory and practice of adjustment. The spread of the crisis, affecting as it does a variety of countries in different regions, provides the need and opportunity for a united response. Since the Cancun summit in 1981, the North has made it clear that in any global negotiations 'the competence of the specialized institutions (namely, Bank and Fund) should not be affected'.[11] Mrs Thatcher has elaborated this position by stating:

>...the independence of specialized bodies like the IMF and the World Bank must be respected. It would certainly not be in the interests of developing countries if those institutions lost the confidence of their major subscribers and of the financial markets... The IMF and World Bank must always be excluded from receiving instructions from the UN...[12]

Negotiation has thus been ruled out by the North leaving appeal and/or agitation as the only options open to the South.

The route of 'appeal', that is, of 'reasoning together' is now being taken in the discussions being held in the Development Committee (Joint Ministerial Committee of the Board of Governors of the Bank and the Fund) which in its meetings in April and October 1985 has taken up an 'extended agenda' of financial and monetary issues for consideration. Neither in these meetings of the Development Committee nor in the Annual Bank-Fund Meeting in October 1985 (Seoul) could agreement be reached on augmenting resources for the Bank or for IDA or on SDR issues in the IMF. Conditionality has not explicitly figured as a topic. The only tangible 'progress' is in the fomulation of a scheme for a Multilateral Investment Guarantee

---

[11] Co-Chairmen's summary on monetary and financial issues, Cancun 1981.
[12] Mrs Thatcher in the debate in the House of Commons on the Cancun Summit reported in *The Times*, London, 27 October 1981.

Agency (MIGA) to protect direct investment against commercial and non-commercial risks, that is, the strong from the weak.

What form can 'agitation' take? It could take the form of a Southern Conference on International Monetary and Financial Issues aimed at formulating an agenda for: (a) the scaling down and reorganization of debt; (b) increasing non-debt, creating unconditional, compensatory, and non-project forms of lending in the Bank and the Fund; and (c) the reform of conditionalities so that adjustment, which is inevitable, can be without jeopardy to welfare, equity, and growth, and for this purpose, supported by finance that is adequate, timely, and provided on appropriate terms. A process of coercive persuasion, which the North has so far adopted towards the South, will then have to be pursued to make the agenda acceptable to the international financial institutions and their major shareholders. Numbers and unity can give the political strength—and indebtedness the economic clout—for the South to pursue such a strategy. In the interests of both the North and the South the opportunity should not be missed to work out, in the Brandt Commission's words, a programme for 'joint survival' that can reconcile adjustment with global growth and welfare.

In a world which is informed by such a mutuality of both interest and goodwill, it should be possible to work out the modalities of ensuring a reasonably predictable and continuous flow of funds to alleviate the constraints on development faced by the South: some prescriptions towards such a practical agendum of 'automatic resource transfers for development' are spelt out in the annex to this paper. (Ed)

ANNEX

SOME NOTES ON 'AUTOMATIC RESOURCES'

The observations of the Brandt Commission on the subject of 'Automatic Revenues' in its report *North–South: A Programme for Survival* (pp. 244–7) were based on a detailed paper on 'International Automatic Revenues for Development' which was considered by the Commission. This paper might also be of interest.

Some General Points

Although the Working Group's concern is with 'proposals for automatic or autonomous sources of aid', it will be desirable to situate the discussion in an overall context of facilitating all forms of non-discretionary resource transfers to developing countries such as export earnings, market borrowings and remittances.

The rationale or motivation for seeking automatic transfers is many-sided. The qualitative and quantitative improvements they can bring about are worth spelling out:

(i) Development planning requires that resource flows should be 'predictable, continuous and assured', but as pointed out by the Brandt Commission, 'at present, the amount of aid depends on the uncertain political will of the countries giving it, and to the shifting priorities of annual appropriations, and the vagaries of legislatures.'[13] Ways need to be found to resolve this contradiction.

(ii) The political will for aid is fluctuating and should be steadied. As Dr Wiesebach points out:[14]

The aid budget seems to be one of the politically weakest parts of the budget in general, feeling the impact of cuts very severely and getting little benefit from additional public spending. This is just another way of saying that the political will to help the poor countries, which undoubtedly exists in most DAC member countries, does not assert itself well in daily political life. It needs, therefore, to be supported by long-term decisions bearing on the budget, giving aid figures a very firm basis, preferably with strong parliamentary backing or legal devices which oblige the treasury to turn to Parliament if it wishes to cut aid.

Automatic forms would not, of course, evade or avoid the political process; but once there is the initial will to set up the required arrangements, annual reiterations of it would be unnecessary.

(iii) Automatic arrangements can lead to more equitable burden-sharing among donors.

(iv) The disposition of automatic transfers can be more closely related to needs in developing countries. This is an important consideration as automaticity is desirable not only in regard to the source of revenue but also in respect of the direction of its use.

(v) The search for automatic resources is also a quest for additional resources which could preferably be raised in an 'automatic' form.

(vi) International taxation as an analogue to the progressive domestic income tax and as a move toward global welfare.

It may be mentioned that the subject by now has had a long history: in the early days of the United Nations a coordinating committee under Secretary-General Trgve Lie is reported to have considered the feasibility

---

[13] *North–South: A Programme for Survival*, Pan Books, 1980, p. 244.

[14] Horst Paul Wiesebach, 'Mobilization of Development Finance: Promises and Problems of Automaticity', *Development Dialogue 1980: 1*, p. 24.

of international taxes.[15] It might be interesting to trace the historical progress of the idea.

'Automaticity' has to be sought in many ways: not only in terms of *measures* such as taxes, enterprise revenues and the like but also through *means* such as target-linked forward aid planning and larger support to multilateral institutions which function on multi-year replenishments and capitalization, thereby enabling predictable flows.

The Trade Tax

The Brandt Commission came to the view that a tax related to international trade offered the best possibility. Earlier, it was also viewed favourably in the Brookings Study on 'New Means of Financing International Needs' and by the Bellagio conference which discussed its findings.[16]

The main problems involved in a tax on imports are well known. Imports as a proportion of GDP vary widely: among DAC countries from 61.1 per cent for Belgium to 8.8 per cent for the US (see Table 7.A1). A uniform tax rate will mean differential burdens in terms of GNP. If set-off against the ODA-GDP target of 0.7 per cent, the overall burden-sharing can be controlled but the *degree of automaticity* in meeting the burden will still be different amongst donors.

Adjustments can however be thought of to keep the GNP burden the same. Essentially, they will entail bringing everybody else's share to that of the USA which has the lowest imports-GDP ratio. In effect, this will mean that differential *rates* of import taxes will be indicated; if such differentials are too wide, the principle of reciprocity in tariffs will be impaired.

These difficulties can be mitigated if we can think of a tax on imports that leaves out imports arising from intra-trade within common markets such as the EEC and EFTA and also imports from non-OPEC developing countries. On policy considerations, these exemptions can be justified. Table 7.1A1 will indicate that for DAC countries the range in the import-GDP ratio can be narrowed from 0.61–0.09 to 0.23–0.07 by introducing these exemptions. For want of data, it has not been possible to do the exercise country-wise but the fact that more than 50 per cent of imports of EEC-DAC members are intra-trade suggests that the exclusion of such imports will provide a significant means of moderating the differential burden.

The yield from the tax will have to be set off against the 0.7 per cent target. It will therefore produce additional revenues only in the case of countries who have under-fulfilled the target to the extent of the estimated yield or by more. Again a country-wise exercise will be necessary to estimate the

---

[15] E. B. Steinberg and J. A. Yager with G. M. Brannon, *New Means of Financing International Needs* (The Brookings Institution, 1978), p. 243.

[16] Ibid.

TABLE 7.A1: Imports and GDP: DAC Countries, 1981–2

Country	Imports (cif) 1982 (US $ billion)	GDP 1981 (US $ billion)	Imports ÷ GDP (%)	Intra-trade 1982 (US $ billion)	Imports from non-OPEC LDCs 1982 (US $ billion)	Residual imports ÷ GDP (%)
(1)	(2)	(3)	(4)	(5)	(6)	(7)
EEC	*596*	*2397*	*24.9*	*303*	*50*	*10.1*
Belgium	58	95	61.1			
Denmark	17	58	29.3			
France	116	569	20.4			
FRG	156	683	22.8			
Italy	86	350	24.6			
Netherlands	63	140	45.0			
United Kingdom	100	502	19.9			
EFTA	*105*	*378*	*27.8*	*12*	*5*	*23.3*
Austria	20	66	30.3			
Finland	13	49	26.5			
Norway	15	57	26.3			
Sweden	28	112	25.0			
Switzerland	29	94	30.9			
USA	255	2906	8.8		66	6.5
Japan	132	1130	11.7		24	9.6

(Contd.)

Table 7.A1 contd.

(1)	(2)	(3)	(4)	(5)	(6)	(7)
Other	85	479	17.8		8	*16.1*
Canada	55	284	19.4			
Australia	24	170	14.1			
New Zealand	6	25	24.0			

Source: UNCTAD, *Handbook of International Trade and Development Statistics 1984 Supplement*.
Tables 1.1 for col. 2; 6.1 for col. 3; 3.1 for cols 5 and 6.
Note: Col. 7 = Col. (2−5−6) ÷ Col. 3.

additional revenue. A one per cent levy on residual imports will mean $ 2.6 billion from the USA and $ 1.3 billion from Japan. These sums are not inconsiderable. Another $ 1.2 billion may come from the FRG and the United Kingdom which are two laggards in meeting the 0.7 per cent target with large GDPs. Altogether, we can expect *additional* revenues of the order of $ 5 billion from the measure, namely, a one per cent tax on 'residual imports' (that is, imports net of intra-trade and of imports from non-OPEC LDCs).

For what it is worth, attempts to bring in the eastern countries into the scheme may be pursued. However, such attempts are not likely to succeed and it would be a pity if they were to hinder a possible agreement among DAC countries.

The Brandt Commission's recommendation that the developing countries should also share the burden of aid is a wholesome one. Their willingness to participate, in an appropriately graduated manner, in automatic arrangements may make it easier for OECD countries to do so; and, in the longer term, induce the eastern countries also to fall in line.

Other Possible Measures

Some other measures to which support may be given are:

- the SDR-link;
- IMF gold sales linked to interest-subsidization from the return on profits;
- the brain drain tax: an example of LDC self-effort on the basis of 'cooperation from developed host countries';
- recycling of loan repayments and interest payments; and
- tax relief for donations to approved NGOs.

The Aid Target

An orderly movement towards the time-bound fulfilment of the 0.7 per cent target will, of course, be a major contribution to automaticity. Planned aid programming, as has been done by the Netherlands and the Scandinavian countries, is to be highly commended.

It may be necessary to suggest some milestones in this process. Table 7.A2 gives the present position. Of the five countries which have met the target, two did so in the mid-seventies (the Netherlands and Sweden) and three in the late seventies or early eighties (Norway, Denmark and France). Any postponement of the deadline, in these circumstances, beyond the eighties, would be inequitable from the burden sharing aspect.

We are in 1985. If 3 per cent of an expected 3 per cent annual growth is set apart for increases to ODA, countries such as Japan, USA and Italy who

TABLE 7.A2: ODA Target Performance, 1982: DAC Countries

Country	Net ODA to GDP (%)	Date of reaching target	Per capita GDP 1981 (US $)
Netherlands	1.07	1975	9924[a]
Norway	0.98	1978 or earlier	13977
Sweden	0.95	1975	13595
Denmark	0.75	1979	11394
France	0.74	1981	10624[a]
Belgium[b]	0.59		9558[a]
Australia[b]	0.57		11630
Austria[c]	0.52		8890[a]
FRG[b]	0.45		11256
Canada[c]	0.42		11673
UK[b]	0.37		8997[a]
DAC average	0.36		10874
Finland[c]	0.28		10157[a]
New Zealand[b]	0.28		7592[a]
Switzerland[d]	0.25		15007
Japan[b]	0.25		9644[a]
USA[d]	0.24		12965
Italy[c]	0.23		6126[a]

[a] Below DAC average per capita GDP.
[b] Have accepted target without date.
[c] Intend to reach target by end 1980s or earlier.
[d] Have not accepted target.

Source: UNCTAD, *Handbook of International Trade and Development Statistics 1984 Supplement*, Table 5.9B II, p. 351 and Table 6.1, p. 380.

are now in the 0.25 per cent level can reach 0.70 in five years, that is, by 1990. It does not seem necessary or logical to suggest a reduced rate of progress for countries whose per capita GDP is less than the DAC average: notice that two of the 'below-average' countries have already met the target and three more have gone beyond the DAC average ratio of 0.36.

Operationally, it might be useful to relate incremental ODA targets to total government expenditures rather than to growth rates. Table 7.A3 will be of interest. If government expenditures to GDP ratios can be assumed to be constant, it shows that annual increments to ODA to the extent of 0.5 per cent or less of *total* expenditures can enable the target to be reached by 1990.

TABLE 7.A3: Incremental Proportions of Government Expenditure Required to Reach ODA Target by 1990: DAC Countries

(per cent)

Country	1982 ODA GDP	1981 government expenditure to GDP	ODA to government expenditure	ODA Target to government expenditure	Annual increments to ODA to government expenditure
(1)	(2)	(3)	(4)	(5)	(6)
Belgium	0.59	55.8	1.06	1.25	0.04
Australia	0.57	24.6	2.32	2.85	0.11
Austria	0.52	39.4	1.32	1.78	0.09
FRG	0.45	31.0	1.45	2.26	0.16
Canada	0.42	23.3	1.80	3.00	0.24
United Kingdom	0.37	40.8	0.91	1.72	0.16
Finland	0.28	29.9	0.94	2.34	0.28
New Zealand	0.28	39.6	0.71	1.77	0.21
Switzerland	0.25	18.3	1.37	3.83	0.49
Japan	0.25	19.0	1.32	3.68	0.47
USA	0.24	23.4	1.03	2.99	0.39
Italy	0.23	47.3	0.49	1.48	0.20

(Contd.)

Table 7.A3 contd.

(1)	(2)	(3)	(4)	(5)	(6)
Memo					
Netherlands	1.07	55.5	1.93		
Norway	0.98	38.9	2.52		
Sweden	0.95	43.7	2.17		
Denmark	0.75	43.8	1.71		
France	0.74	42.1	1.76		

Note: Col. 5 = Col. 2 ÷ Col. 3.
Col. 6 = (Col. 5 − Col. 4) ÷ Col. 5.
Source: Same as for Table 2 for Col. 2.
World Bank, *World Development Report 1984*, Table 26, p. 269 for Col. 3.

It is well known that bilateral ODA is much more skewed in favour of middle income ($ 500 to $ 1500 per capita) and higher income ($ 1500 and above) countries then multilateral concessional aid. Table 7.A4 clearly brings this out. It is encouraging that the multilateral proportion in DAC-ODA has gone up from under 17 per cent in 1970 to over 29 per cent in 1982. Is it possible to suggest a separate target—50 per cent or 40 per cent—for multilateral ODA? More multilateral aid, particularly through IDA, will introduce greater automaticity by making flows more 'predictable, continuous and assured', particularly to the poorest countries. This objective should certainly have high priority.

TABLE 7.A4: Distribution of Multilateral and Bilateral Aid: DAC Countries, 1982

Country group (in Per capita GDP)	DAC net ODA 1982 (US $ billion)	%	Concessional net flows from multilateral agencies largely financed by DAC 1982 (US $ billion)	%
$ 1500 and above	2489.5	17.0	280.9	4.6
$ 500–1500	4429.9	30.2	1278.6	21.1
$ 500 or less	7732.3	52.8	4505.8	74.3
	14651.7	100.0	6065.3	100.0
Least developed	3448.6	26.5	1962.2	32.5

Source: UNCTAD, Handbook of International Trade and Development Statistics 1984 Supplement. Table 5.6B, p. 332 and Table 5.8A, p. 344.

8

Social Discrimination and Caste Reservations*

In the last four months, the anti-reservationist agitation has rocked the country. The self-immolations, the campaigns against the Mandal report that have been orchestrated by most newspapers and magazines, and finally the marriage of casteism and communalism that resulted in the fall of the V. P. Singh Government have injected much drama and intensity to this episode. Despite the high passion generated, or probably because of it, there has been very little reasoned debate on the issue of reservations. The Government of India itself must share a large part of the blame for the failure to educate the public in the matter. The tragedy is that this failing, instead of getting compensated by the press and the academic community, has been compounded by the dissemination of prejudice, propaganda and misinformation.

Essentially, the case for caste-based reservations, whether in educational or employment opportunities, rests on the need, justification, and desirability of redressing historically accumulated inequalities—social, educational and economic—arising from the caste system. Indians do not need any elaborate introduction to the caste system or to its toxic effects on society.

In the Hindu social order, caste contributed to a stratified and compartmentalized society based on status, hierarchy, and ritual purity or pollution. Endogamy, occupational rigidities, and constraints on upward mobility and migration strengthened and perpetuated

---

* Originally appeared under the title 'Social Discrimination has to be Corrected' in *The Hindu*, Madras, 11 December 1990.

caste-based inequalities. Such inequalities had wide ramifications in terms of the significant overlay between dominant caste status on the one hand and, on the other, economic power and educational advancement. As far as the forward communities were concerned this was reflected in ownership of land and assets and access to educational opportunities, particularly professional education and 'English' education; arising from this, access to employment in government, private sector and the learned professions such as law and medicine, representation in elected bodies ranging all the way from panchayats to Parliament, and so on. The list is indeed long. These inequalities have persisted. They are not only 'historical', but in a large measure current. They have been pervasive over time and space in India. They have permeated various sectors of activity: politics, administration and the private, sector. Caste also has been tenacious and self-perpetuating given its ramifications in nepotism, caste fraternity and marriage (vide matrimonial columns in the newspapers).

By way of substantiation, let us consider a few facts relating to the historical as well as current status of caste-related inequalities. Taking Tamilnadu first, the literacy rate among Brahmins in 1901 was 73.6 per cent and English literacy was 17.9 per cent compared to only 6.9 per cent and 0.2 per cent for Vellalas or upper caste non-Brahmins. From 1870 to 1918, 67 per cent of Madras University graduates were Brahmins. Jobs followed education. Brahmins, who were about 3 per cent of the population, had a share in 1912–17 of 55 per cent in deputy collectorships, 83 per cent in posts of subjudges, 73 per cent in district munsifs, and 65 per cent in higher ministerial posts in the revenue and judicial departments.

In the neighbouring state of Karnataka, reservation for castes other than brahmins was introduced as far back as 1918. Even so, more than thirty years later in 1952, they claimed 39 per cent of government posts while being about 4 per cent of the population. In Andhra Pradesh, the forward castes (mainly brahmins, Kapu, and Kamma) who are about 30 per cent of the population, together enjoyed a 55 per cent share in government jobs and a 76 per cent share in gazetted employment in 1982. Moving to the central government, one finds that as late as 1980, the share of the other backward classes—about 50 per cent in population—was only 12.6 per cent in jobs under the government and public sector and only 4.7 per cent in class I posts. Of Hindu IAS officers in 1985, 37.7 per cent were brahmins and 32.2 per cent belonged to other forward castes.

As might be expected, the position in the private sector was much worse. A study of the caste background of top executives of 1100 large companies in 1979–80 undertaken by the Corporate Studies Group of the Indian Institute of Public Administration showed that the forward castes (brahmins, vaisyas, khatris, kayasthas and marwaris) accounted for 94.7 per cent of top positions such as chairman, managing director, general manager, and director with brahmins alone claiming a 43.5 per cent share.

At the most simple and human level, the case for compensatory discrimination rests on the need to reasonably correct these age-long inequalities. In the great race for opportunities, those who have been handicapped by the caste system should be allowed to start the race a few paces ahead in relation to others not so handicapped. This is necessary in the interests both of justice and fraternity which, along with equality and liberty, share the pride of place in the preamble to the Constitution. The Supreme Court has also, on more than one occasion, articulated this central rationale for reservations. In the Balaji case, for instance, the Supreme Court pointed out that 'the claims of the backward classes are not necessarily in derogation of the interests of the wider public; they may be the instrument for forwarding the public interest in an egalitarian society.' Reservations should thus be seen as being not just in the interests of the backward classes, but of society as a whole.

The problem really arises because providing a social handicap to the disadvantaged involves an unavoidable element of reverse discrimination against the socially privileged. This is so because for any fixed number of seats or jobs a quota for the backward group necessarily entails to the same extent a reduction in open competition seats or jobs in which the forward group hopes to gain the major share. This they view as 'injustice'. Some others will recognize it as an unavoidable element of 'injustice' in the present to correct 'injustice' in the past. The dilemma inherent in any effort to combine formal equality (that is, equality of opportunity) with substantive equality was the one expressed by Jawaharlal Nehru when he remarked that 'we arrive at a peculiar tangle. We cannot have equality because in trying to attain equality we come up against some principles of equality.' In other words, if equality is practised among unequals, it will only perpetuate inequality. *Per contra*, in order to treat them equitably one has to accept a reasonable measure of unequal treatment.

A dimension of 'unfairness' which is felt as arising at an individual level, is voiced in the following type of question: 'Is it not "unfair" that the son or daughter of a poor brahmin cook or purohit should yield his seat or post in favour of the less meritorious son or daughter of a high official belonging to a backward caste?.' Such a displacement is certainly unfortunate. However, one has to reconcile oneself to the fact that group injustice, which has operated age-long through the unequal and exploitative caste system can be remedied only in the form of group justice provided through caste-based preferences. In the process, the present generation of forward communities, rich and poor, has perforce to bear a cost in part as redress for past inequalities which have continued into the present and in part as a price for social cohesion in the future. One cannot ignore or dismiss this cost but one should not exaggerate or dramatize it. One should also set it off against the need for, and benefits of reservations.

Another contention, related to the issue of 'fairness', is that reservations tend to benefit only the elite of the backward classes and do not reach out to the most backward among them. There is some truth in this but there are also ways to reasonably take care of the problem. They consist in (a) being careful in including the uppermost groups in lists of backward classes; (b) periodical graduation of certain castes from out of the list; and (c) providing separate reservations, as has been done in Tamilnadu, for the 'most backward classes'. Those among the forward groups who bemoan that reservations reach only the backward class elite not only overstate the problem, but also ignore the point that elites fulfil a useful function in groups that have, over centuries, remained backward. This point was tellingly clarified by Dr Ambedkar while answering certain questions put to him by the Kalelkar Commission. To quote what he said:

Our problem is not so much to distribute wealth in order to make everybody happy. Our problem is that differences in status should disappear. If there are 10 barristers, 20 doctors, 30 engineers etc. in a community, I regard that community as rich, although everyone of them is not educated. Take, for instance, Chamars, you look upon this community with hatred, but if there are some lawyers, doctors and educated persons among them, you cannot put your hand upon them and you will not do that, although everyone of them is not so highly educated. You will say he is a Bhangi but suppose there are educated persons among them, you will respect them.

The other major argument against reservations has been advanced on the grounds of its social cost in impairing efficiency. For a number of reasons, this concern, to my mind, is vastly exaggerated besides being misplaced in large measure. First and foremost, efficiency in government depends on a number of factors such as systems, training, trust, and motivation; only to a very limited extent is it a function of 'merit' at the stage of entry. Second, minimum qualifications at entry are mentioned in seats and jobs and minimum performance at exit is enforced in educational institutions. It is not, therefore, as if that beneficiaries of reservations are 'unqualified'; only that they may be 'less qualified' than those selected through open competition. Third, as the Tamilnadu experience has shown, given two or three generations for reservations to work themselves out, 'merit' ceases to be the monopoly of the 'forwards' and the 'backwards' tend to catch up fairly fast. For instance, in the 1990 admissions to the MBBS course, the distance in terms of the cut-off marks between the lowest performer in open competition and the one among backward classes was only 2.04 per cent points while it was not more than 5.6 per cent points even *vis-à-vis* the lowest performer among the most backward classes. If there were not reservations, the lowest performer in open competition would be closer still to the cut-off levels of the beneficiaries of reservations. Fourth, reservations improve the morale of the services in terms of caste cohesion and social orientation. Consequently, the internal and external functioning of the administration is improved making it 'more efficient' in the broadest sense of that term. I would suggest that this is what has happened in Tamilnadu.

Finally, one must realize that 'merit' can also be legitimately viewed in a relative sense. Mr Justice O. Chinnappa Reddy gives eloquent expression to this point. Referring to a backward class child 'who has no books and magazines to read at home, no radio to listen to, no TV to watch, no one to help him with his home work; whose parents are either illiterate or so ignorant and ill-informed that he cannot even hope to seek their advice on any matter of importance', Mr Chinnappa Reddy asks: 'Has not this child got merit if he with all his disadvantages is able to secure the qualifying 40 per cent or 50 per cent of the marks at a competitive examination where the children of the upper-classes who go to St Paul's High School and St Stephen's College and who have perhaps been specially coached for the examination may secure 70, 80 or even 90 per cent of the marks?' He concludes that 'surely a child who has been able to jump so many hurdles may be expected to do better and better as he progresses in life' (K. C. V. Kumar vs. Karnataka, 1985 SCR 394).

At the risk of being extremely selective and somewhat abstract in dealing with this complex and emotional issue, I have confined myself to the essential principle of reservation—its rationale and benefits. In doing so, I have tried to meet the concerns of those who are opposed to reservations on the two major grounds of 'justice' and 'efficiency'. There is much to discuss about the modalities of schemes of reservation such as the one in the Mandal report—the criteria of backwardness, the quantum of reservations, the domain of reservations, the periodical review of lists of backward classes, the supplementation of reservations with other measures for preferential treatment, and so on. There can be constructive debate on these practical matters but what is of prior importance is to agree that philosophically and politically social discrimination in India has to be corrected through concrete measures for social justice. The process is bound to be painful, but we should accept the pain as the necessary concomitant of the maturation of our society and nation.

9

Comprehending Equalities*

Galanter's has been a basic source book to all those interested in preferential policies. First published in 1984, it covers developments up to 1980, that is, until the report of the Mandal Commission in 1981. Its reissue in an easily accessible paperback edition is timely and useful for a number of reasons. The jurisprudence of compensatory discrimination, which is Galanter's theme, had its formative period between the mid-sixties and the beginning of the eighties and has not undergone any major changes since then. Galanter's discussion of it continues, therefore, to be quite up-to-date. Secondly, as the author himself notes in the preface, 'the Mandal Report revives for replay on the larger national stage all of the questions and perplexities traced in this book'. We have by now witnessed this replay in the intensely emotional debate in 1990 that followed the decisions of the V. P. Singh Government on the Mandal Report. Galanter's careful and objective discussion of the whole gamut of issues involved in compensatory discrimination should be most useful in replacing heat with light. Thirdly, the Narasimha Rao Government's decisions on the Mandal Report are now before the Supreme Court and the book will be of great value for situating the court's judgment, as and when it is available, in an historical framework. For all these reasons, the reissue of the book is to be greatly welcomed. It is highly recommended to all those who are, or ought to be, interested in preferential policies, especially to the critics of Mandal and to every one of the honourable judges who constitute the Supreme Court bench.

* Reprinted from *Economic and Political Weekly*, XXVII (31-2), 1-8 August 1992, (pp. 1657–62).
Competing Equalities: Law and the Backward Classes in India by Marc Galanter; Oxford University Press (paperback), 1991, pp. xxviii+625.

The principle of 'formal equality' is laid down in various provisions of the Constitution—articles 14, 15(1), 16(2) and 29(2)—which prohibit the state from discriminating against any citizen in employment under the state or in the matter of admission into educational institutions maintained or aided from state funds on grounds such as religion, race, caste, descent, and language. At the same time, the Constitution recognizes that formal equality (or equal treatment of unequals) needs to be qualified if 'substantive equality' is to be ensured: equality of opportunity is not the same as the opportunity to be equal. In the Indian context, the inequalities in initial position which have been considered to require a 'social handicap', if they are to be overcome for promoting equality in outcomes and not just in opportunities, are entrenched and cumulative inequalities arising from the age-old caste system. Accordingly, the Constitution also contains a number of provisions to ensure, what Galanter calls, the 'competing equality' of compensatory discrimination. Article 46 requires the state 'to promote with special care the educational and economic interests of the weaker sections of the people, and, in particular of the Scheduled Castes and Scheduled Tribes and protect them from social injustice and all forms of exploitation.' Article 15(4) enables the state to make *any* special provision for the advancement of *any* socially and educationally backward classes of citizens or for the Scheduled Castes and Scheduled Tribes. Article 16(4) permits the state to make '*any* provision for the reservation of appointments or posts in favour of *any* backward class of citizens which, in the opinion of the state, is not adequately represented in the services of the state.' To effectuate these provisions, the Constitution (Article 340) envisages a Commission 'to investigate the conditions of socially and educationally backward classes...and the difficulties under which they labour' and to recommend the steps necessary 'to remove such difficulties and to improve their condition.'

The broad theme of Galanter's book is to explore how the competing equalities—formal and substantive—have interacted in terms of the implementation and interpretation of these provisions by governments and by the courts at the all-India and state levels. The first part of the book (Chapters 1 to 4) describes the caste-based 'compartmental society' of India and the impact on it of British rule and nationalist politics. This is followed by an evaluation of the performance of compensatory discrimination programmes addressed to Scheduled Castes and Scheduled Tribes (SCs and STs) with particular reference to reservations in government employment. The six chapters in the second part deal with various problems encountered in the identification of beneficiaries among SCs, STs and other backward classes and how they have been attempted to be resolved. The five chapters that follow in the third part relate to the judicial process. After setting out the scope of constitutional provisions relating to compensatory discrimination policies, Galanter discusses the views that courts have taken on various issues related to the scope, extent, design, and operation of policies and programmes for compensatory discrimination. He then provides a critique of the judicial system and processes ending up with a balanced assessment of their achievements and shortcomings. The final chapter of the book ('The Little Done, the Vast Undone') reflects on the costs and benefits of the policies.

Throughout, Galanter's position is that of a scholarly external observer who is sympathetic to compensatory discrimination. He believes that persistent and cumulative caste-related inequalities need to be corrected through compensatory (or reverse) discrimination in the interests of securing substantive equality. At the same time, he is sensitive to the fact that compensatory discrimination is 'akin to the old discrimination' and is not just 'a benign process of inclusion'. Admittedly, it carries with it its own costs of 'arbitrariness and unfairness'. An objective view has to be taken about how these costs arise, their nature and extent, and how they can be mitigated so that the competing equalities can be accommodated in a larger framework. Galanter believes that the Indian effort has been to secure such an accommodation and although the reality might have disappointed 'many fond hopes, the turn away from the older hierarchic model to a pluralistic participatory society has proved vigorous and enduring'. This standpoint—sympathetic to compensatory discrimination while sensitive to formal equality—distinguishes Galanter from many Indian critics of the Mandal Report who have underplayed caste-related inequalities, wilfully exaggerated the costs of compensatory discrimination, misunderstood or misrepresented how compensatory discrimination has worked, and have adopted a destructive animus to the whole issue of promoting substantive equality in a deeply inegalitarian society. It is not surprising, therefore, that so few of them have referred to, or taken note of, Galanter's book in their tirades against the Mandal Report. By the same token, Galanter's careful discussion provides a most useful text for correcting the several errors of fact and judgment that abound in the anti-Mandal literature of the past few years.

Backward classes (BCs) comprise SCs, STs and other backward classes (OBCs). Preferences for SCs and STs are constitutionally guaranteed or permitted and include: (a) reservations in Parliament, state legislatures and other bodies such as Panchayati Raj institutions and cooperatives, (b) reservations in educational institutions, in government employment, and in benefits from government schemes (such as IRDP, housing allotments), (c) special welfare programmes (for example, scholarships, hostels, house-sites, loans for economic advancement), and (d) protection against exploitation and victimization (for example, legislation against offences related to 'untouchability'). On the face of it, this wide array of measures might suggest that a great deal has been, or is being, done for SCs and STs as spontaneous reparation for their exploitation by 'caste' Hindus. The facts as brought out by Galanter are less comforting. Historically, although 'untouchability' and all the disabilities that went with it, were recognized by social reformers as the scourge of Hinduism, preferential treatment for SCs was realized only after prolonged political struggle, under the leadership of B. R. Ambedkar. In its initial years, the Indian National Congress tended to evade social issues, as evidenced by Dadabhai Naoroji's presidential statement (1886) that 'a National Congress must confine itself to questions in which the entire nation has a direct participation, and it must leave the adjustment of social reforms and other class questions, to class Congresses'. After separate electorates were provided to Muslims in the Minto-Morley reforms of 1909, there arose the danger that the 'untouchables' (then known as the depressed classes) might want political recognition as a group distinct from the Hindus, eroding the vote base of the Congress. It was only in 1917 that the Congress was to pass its first anti-disabilities resolution, that too 'a mild and hesitant' one. The Poona Pact of 1932, which first accepted the principle of reserved seats for SCs, was reached only after overcoming Gandhi's stubborn opposition. Thus, efforts to remove untouchability and to help its victims basically originated from 'a real crisis in the *political* life of the Hindu community' rather than from the 'evangelical' impulses espoused by the Mahatma for Harijan uplift.

Galanter's appraisal of the benefits that had actually accrued to SCs and STs up to the beginning of the eighties, that is, during nearly three decades after independence, indicates that reality has been far behind the rhetoric. Very few of SCs and STs have got elected to general seats in the legislative bodies, confirming the necessity for reservations. (Recall the experience in the recent elections to the Congress Working Committee in the Tirupati session of the Congress.) Further, inasmuch as the reserved seat legislator is dependent upon a constituency made up overwhelmingly of non-members of his group, the interests of the SCs and STs are 'filtered and muffled' insofar as they diverge from the interests of other groups. Schemes for educational and economic advancement present a general picture of poor implementation. Allocations for them have not significantly risen in real terms and tend to be under-spent from year to year. Enrolment at higher levels of schooling and in professional courses continues to be low and dropout rates in elementary education are still very high.

The central government has provided reservations in government employment for SCs since 1943 and for STs since 1950. The quotas were originally 12.5 per cent and 5 per cent and were increased to 15 per cent and 7.5 per cent in 1970. Yet, SCs and STs, accounting for 15 and 7 per cent of total population, claimed 5 per cent or less of class I and II jobs as late as 1975. Inasmuch as reservations apply only to current recruitments and not to the entire complement of posts, they can in any case be expected to result in the full quota only over a long period of time following their enforcement. To allow for this factor, Galanter has estimated what proportion of total posts that could have been expected to be filled, if reservations had been fully implemented, were actually filled. His finding for 1953–75 is that while this proportion was fairly high (70 to 80 per cent) at the top and bottom ends of the spectrum, namely, the IAS and class III posts, there was great under-representation in the middle layers (class I and II posts). The main reason for this was not lack of qualified candidates. At the lowest echelons, reservations had been underfilled because of 'indifference or hostility on the part of appointing authorities, insufficient publicization of vacancies, and the sheer expense of application.' At higher or promotion levels, formal and informal procedures had operated to keep out SCs such as *ad hoc* and temporary promotions, elimination through personal evaluation procedures like interviews and personality tests, and unfair adverse entries in confidential records. Altogether, the slow but steady progress in the matter of government employment for SCs has taken place in the face of 'resistance that is seldom articulated but nevertheless dogged. It is resistance compounded of ignorance, apathy, prejudice and resentment.'

Galanter's evaluation of the effective reach of preferential programmes for SCs is somewhat dated and has had to contend with inadequacies of data, which is itself a reflection on the seriousness with which these programmes have been taken. Nevertheless, it brings out forcefully the lack of political and administrative commitment which has characterized ameliorative programmes for the SCs in the three decades after independence. Many critics of the Mandal Report have argued that similar special programmes for OBCs could be relied upon to promote their educational and economic status obviating the need for reservations. The SCs have all along been recognized as the most disadvantaged of the backward classes; preferential policies in their favour have been comprehensive and in existence for a long period; they have been supplemented with electoral, employment, and educational reservations; SCs are only one-third or one-half in number compared to OBCs; and, politically, they are much better mobilized. If, despite all these factors, ameliorative efforts, even in their case, have fallen so far short of expectations, surely too much cannot be expected from such measures for remedying the backwardness of the OBCs.

We can now turn to the more complex set of issues relating to OBCs to which the bulk of Galanter's book is devoted. The caste system in India represents a wide spectrum of graded inequalities, extending from the lowliest 'untouchable' at one end to the brahmin at the other and it is erroneous to view it as a sharp dichotomy between the SCs and all other Hindus. The substantial backwardness, relative to the 'forward' castes, of the other backward castes has been recognized since the late nineteenth century in official documents and in the provision of educational concessions in the old Madras presidency and in the old Mysore state. It is also reflected in the Objectives Resolution of the Constituent Assembly, moved by Nehru on 13 December 1946, which resolved to provide adequate safeguards for 'minorities, backward and tribal areas, depressed *and* other backward classes'. Although, as Galanter points out, there had been no attempt to define or employ it at a national level, the term 'other backward classes' had definite meanings in local contexts. In a number of states, educational concessions were provided to OBCs and in some major ones, such as Bombay, Madras and Mysore, preferential treatment for OBCs included reservations and welfare schemes as well. It is also the state lists of OBCs, wherever available, that the Centre has relied upon for extending post-matriculation scholarships, a benefit initiated as far back as 1949-50. It is in this background that the Constitution included the provisions, namely, Articles 46, 16(4) and 340, which refer to backward classes in a connotation not limited to SCs and this was also the purpose of the First Amendment which included Article 15(4) in the Constitution. Thus, there has never been any question about the existence of OBCs and of the need for preferential treatment in their case. This needs to be explained at some length because the anti-Mandal lobby has sought, in dubious and devious ways, to promote the impression that OBCs have been, as it were, invented for the first time by Mandal and V. P. Singh.

The Constitution left the OBCs to be identified at the national level by the Commission envisaged in Article 340 and the centre did appoint such a Commission in 1953. The Commission listed 2,399 communities as belonging to OBCs with an estimated total population of 116 million or 32 per cent of India's then population. It proposed reservations for OBCs in government service of at least 25 per cent in class I, 33⅓ per cent in class II, and 40 per cent in class III and IV. In the matter of educational reservations, it proposed a 70 per cent quota in medical, scientific, and technical colleges. The report of the Commission was, however, sabotaged by Kalelkar, its chairman, who while forwarding the report to government questioned the very basis of caste as a criterion for backwardness. Galanter's summary of Kalelkar's volte-face brings out how, apart from being thoroughly unprincipled, his belated second thoughts were utterly confused and full of internal contradictions. However, the central government was only too happy to exploit the last-minute desertion of its chairman to delay and debunk the entire report. The report, presented in 1955, was released to Parliament in late 1956 accompanied by a 'withering critique' from the Minister of Home Affairs (none other than Pandit Govind Ballabh Pant, the venerable brahmin from Uttar Pradesh) condemning wholesale its criteria and conclusions. Five years later in 1961 the central cabinet decided not to draw up any national list of OBCs and to leave the matter to the states with the observation that in the view of the Government of India, 'it was better to go by economic tests than to go by caste'. The report was finally buried with the Parliament discussions on it in 1965 (a decade after its submission) with the government spokesman reiterating opposition to the caste basis and endorsing vague economic criteria. With this, at an operational level, the issue was shuttled to the states. These are the footsteps on the sands of time of the then Congress government at the Centre that the current one is apparently trying to follow. *Plus ça change, plus cest la même chose*!

Thereafter, since 1965, commissions were established in a number of states to identify OBCs and to recommend reservations and other preferential measures in their favour. Some of the states such as Kerala, Karnataka, and Tamilnadu have had more than one Commission reporting on the issue. Jammu and Kashmir, Andhra Pradesh, Gujarat, Punjab, and Uttar Pradesh are examples of other states which have had commissions or committees on OBCs. Quite a few of them have been headed by distinguished jurists or administrators (for example, P. B. Gajendragadkar in J&K, J. G. Havanur and O. Chinnappa Reddy in Karnataka, A. N. Sattanathan and I. A. Ambhashankar in Tamilnadu). As Galanter observes, although state governments have not always been receptive to their critical assessments, the best of the more recent commissions have displayed admirable industry and sophistication in gathering and analysing data. In large part, this has happened in response to the courts because actual litigation, or the threat of it, has required of the states to ensure that preferential schemes are well reasoned and grounded on the best available data. However, in the absence of caste enumeration since the Census of 1931, the state commissions (as well as the Kalelkar and Mandal Commissions) have had to rely necessarily on extrapolations and sample surveys to estimate the numbers and the social and educational backwardness of the OBCs. Although the Kalelkar Commission and a number of state commissions had recommended collection of caste-based data in the census, the Centre has stuck to its view that caste enumeration would aggravate caste consciousness and impede the 'disestablishment of caste'. Clearly, this stand is both dubious and hypocritical. We have a no-win situation here: preferential schemes cannot be accepted unless they are based on reliable data and reliable data cannot be collected for fear of exacerbating caste feelings. As Justice Havanur has pointed out, the central government has not found it necessary to cease recording data on the basis of other divisive criteria such as religion and language (not to speak of sex!). His devastating rejoinder to the argument that omission of caste enumeration lessens caste consciousness is that it is 'as amusing and absurd as a merchant omitting to label grain bags in order to prevent bandicoots from eating the grains.'

The Centre, in a spirit of malign neglect, having opted out of the scene, the jurisprudence of compensatory discrimination in India has evolved in a process of interaction between the states, the commissions, and the judiciary. The inadequacies in data and analysis of commission reports, caste politics which has resulted in state governments modifying the recommendations of the commissions, contests by affected parties, and the limitations of the judicial process are all factors which have determined the evolution of compensatory discrimination policies over the years. In Part Two of his book, Galanter documents and discusses this evolution, or rather 'meandering', which has been characterized by ambiguity and vacillation. Basically, his finding is that the 'gross effect of litigation on compensatory discrimination policy has been to curtail and confine it' and that, in general, courts have been 'a brake and a baffle rather than a stimulant and energizer' of the policy. This is to be traced to various limitations of the higher judiciary and the Indian judicial process which Galanter brings out in two very insightful chapters at the end of the second part. Given the fact that most judges are elevated to the Supreme Court by promotion from the High Courts and retire from there at age 65, they are subject to rapid turnover and a very limited tenure. This, combined with the system of sitting in benches, has allowed few judges to be exposed to a sufficient number and continuity of litigation so as to be able to articulate 'an explicit and comprehensive point of view on compensatory discrimination' in their judgements. Added to this is the fact that judges tend to be conservative on social issues, given to formal legalisms, and inadequately exposed either to empirical social enquiry or to 'theoretical nourishment'.

Courts selectively encounter compensatory discrimination policy 'in its incidence on aggrieved individuals'. Their stance is 'passive or reactive' and what they do depends very much on 'the cases the parties bring to the courts and the arguments that lawyers make to them'. In this process, 'the beneficiaries of compensatory discrimination have been at a disadvantage in the development of the law; the competitors have occupied the strategic heights in the litigation battle.' In its turn, the legal profession has provided 'an agency for addressing the sins of commission—the "wrong thing" and "too much" criticism—but has had less to offer to those who are aggrieved by the sins of omission.' Consequently, in many cases, litigation has transformed a settled policy into an open issue. Typically, features of particular schemes are struck down, commissions are appointed to take up a fresh investigation, infirmities in their reports generate another round of litigation, a different court comes out with a new set of dicta, and so on.

Despite all these problems, Galanter is judicious enough to point out that

it would be wrong to visualize the courts as enemies or even as inadvertent wreckers of compensatory discrimination policy, somehow responsible for its deficiencies and shortcomings. If courts have in a few instances played a restrictive role, this has been far outweighed by their positive contributions. Probably the greatest of these is to give compensatory discrimination legitimacy... the courts have made crucial publics feel, if not enthusiasm, that at least it is not out of control and is somehow compatible with the welfare of all. By containing and curtailing the system, the courts have helped to maintain and preserve it, although at a level of performance below that of paper commitments.

The judicial doctrine that has actually evolved from the mid-sixties on various issues relating to the scope and extent of preferences and the design and operation of compensatory discrimination programmes can now be summarized. The major issue that arises at the outset is the basis on which the 'backward classes' referred to in various articles of the Constitution should be identified. Are 'classes' the same as castes? If not, is it necessary or permissible to use caste as a criterion at all? What criteria, other than caste, are appropriate to classify classes as backward? How is backwardness to be reasonably determined in relation to castes or to other classes? As might be expected, these issues were debated at the stage of Constitution-making itself and, more specifically, when Article 15(4) was included in the first amendment in 1951. As Galanter sums up: 'examination of the debate leaves it abundantly clear that the backward classes, by whomever designated and according to whatever tests they were chosen, were expected to be a list of castes or communities.' Ambedkar forthrightly observed that 'what are called backward classes are...nothing else but a collection of certain castes.' The purposes for which and the ways in which the caste criterion could be reasonably used came up thereafter in a number of cases before the high courts and the Supreme Court. Analytically, the two central issues were whether caste could be used as 'a unit of measurement' (that is, to define a target group) and/or whether caste could be used as 'a measuring rod', in terms of its rank, standing, or prestige. After reviewing the zigzag course of judicial pronouncements on these issues, Galanter summarizes the doctrine that has crytallized as follows: (1) caste or communal units may be used as classes whose backwardness is to be established'; (2) caste or communal rank or status may be one of the tests or measures of backwardness by which these groups are selected; and (3) caste or communal rank or status may not be the sole or exclusive measure of backwardness. In one sentence: castes, being also classes, can be legitimately treated as target groups for preferential policies so long as their 'backwardness' is established, that is, the test of backwardness could be applied to a caste as a whole and need not be confined to individuals within it, with the rank or status of the caste being one among other relevant indicators of backwardness. Essentially, thus, the courts have taken the line that 'whether to use caste units or not is a matter of policy, not of Constitutional prohibition or command'. But policy itself, Galanter points out, cannot ignore that the central purpose of the inclusion of Articles 15(4) and 16(4) was the reduction of caste disparities by adopting measures along caste lines. Thus, the contention of the anti-Mandal lobby that reservations and other preferential policies should not be related to caste would amount to a travesty of the Constitution and to a revisionist view of India's history, sociology, and politics that is totally illegitimate.

On 'backwardness', the questions that have arisen relate to the nature (what kind of backwardness?), extent (how backward is backward?), and the determination of backwardness (the kinds of criteria to be used). Article 15(4) refers to 'socially and educationally backward classes of citizens' while Article 16(4), which relates to reservations in employment, refers to 'any backward class of citizens, which in the opinion of the state, is not adequately represented in the services of the state'. In construing Article 15(4), courts have tended to favour the conjunctive use of 'social' and 'educational', that is, to require that backwardness must be established in relation to both social and educational criteria. They have expressed the view that social backwardness should not be just relative but 'comparable' to that of SCs and STs. Similarly, that educational backwardness, according to criteria such as literacy or schooling levels, should be assessed at levels 'well below' the state average. In dealing with Article 16(4), they have taken the view that it is not enough if the target beneficiary group is 'not adequately represented' in public services but that it should also be 'backward', with backwardness being understood in the same sense as in Article 15(4); 'adequately represented' has also given room for views on how (in)adequate is (in)adequate. Thus all the key words, namely, 'backward', 'socially', 'educationally', and 'adequately' have provided play for restrictive positions being taken. This is to be expected given the scope for expansive intervention by a judiciary with a narrow sense of social justice. The consolation is that more liberal views are also capable of being accommodated in qualitative judgements of what is 'reasonable'. Over the years, on one hand, courts have tended to be less restrictive and, on the other, commissions and states, in response to courts, have tended to be more judicious and restrained in listing communities eligible for reservations under Articles 15(4) and 16(4).

Anti-Mandal critics have strongly favoured so-called 'economic criteria' in preference to community-based preferential treatment. Various judgments of the courts, especially if exploited selectively and out of context, have been perceived as favouring the use of economic criteria. And, politically, the forward castes have recognized that economic criteria provide scope for rearguard action to fight caste-related reservations confined to OBCs. In this context, Galanter's careful discussion of this issue (section G in Chapter 8 and section G in Chapter 9) is most useful in sorting out its conceptual and practical implications. To start with, it is important to distinguish different approaches to economic criteria. The first, and the most radical, is to use such criteria for selecting individuals, across all castes, and to group the 'economically disadvantaged' in this sense into a 'backward class'. Such a view would be clearly in contravention of the spirit and letter of the Constitution. The Constitutional provisions themselves speak only of social and educational backwardness and of inadequate representation in services of classes of citizens and do not refer to the current economic disabilities of individuals. On the face of it, these provisions were not designed as an anti-poverty measure or to remedy 'incidents of individual life history but the accumulated disadvantages of palpable social groups'. Actually, the option of including economic backwardness as a criterion was considered by Parliament in 1951 during the debate on the First Amendment and was explicitly rejected. On that occasion, K. T. Shah moved an amendment to Article 15(4) which would have done away with the word 'classes' and would have added 'economically' to qualify the criterion of backwardness. Nehru opposed the proposed amendment and insisted on confining preferential treatment to socially and educationally backward classes. He also observed that if he added 'economically' he would 'at the same time not make it a kind of a cumulative thing but would say that a person who is lacking in any of these three things should be helped', the 'three things' here being social or educational or economic advancement. Thus, even the concession that Nehru—who was least disposed to the use of an exclusive caste criterion—was willing to contemplate would not have extended to the rejection of caste-related group justice. In a number of judgments, the courts have also taken the view that a classification based solely on poverty 'will not be logical' and the chief concern must be 'to determine whether the class or group is socially and educationally backward'.

In the face of these difficulties, a second approach to the economic test might consist in arguing that income and/or occupation might be used as criteria for selecting backward communities. Unlike the more radical view, the test in this alternative is to be applied to groups, not individuals, but what is to be assessed is economic, and not social or educational, backwardness of the group as a whole. This view too has no sanction in the Constitution except to the extent that economic deprivation is a cause, correlate, or consequence of social and educational backwardness. On a practical level, Galanter points out that the application of economic criteria to castes would be exceedingly difficult in the absence of caste-wise census data. He also explains that assessments of the income and occupational distribution of communities have all along played a prominent role in the work of the state commissions and, in practice, economic disadvantage, insofar as it is congruent with social and educational backwardness, has not been ignored.

The third approach—which is the one that is now being widely canvassed—is to qualify or supplement caste-related criteria with an economic criterion. This approach forks off into three versions: (a) to apply the economic criterion only to OBCs; (b) to extend preferential treatment to the economically disadvantaged in all communities, classified as backward or otherwise, in addition to caste-related reservations for OBCs, SCs and STs; and (c) to extend reservations, based on the economic criterion, only to the castes not classified as backward. The motivation for version (a) is to confine benefits to the economically worse off among OBCs. The experience of Kerala, which has attempted this version, shows that in practice the cut-off limit tends to get pushed so high that very few of the economically better-off get weeded out, especially since they are also in a better position to get themselves certified as falling within the cut-off limit (wherever set). Also, among those who are deemed to fall below the economic cut-off level, it is the relatively socially and educationally advanced who are likely to benefit. Thus, version

(a) is not an effective measure to tackle the 'creaming-off' effect. In version (b) the OBC poor have to compete with the poor from forward communities within the quota reserved under the economic criterion. This, as Galanter points out, 'broadens the field against which the most backward and deprived... communities have to compete; it substitutes for their more prosperous caste fellows a much larger array of poor (or allegedly poor) families among the more prosperous and powerful groups.' By definition, the separate quota in version (c) will be available only for the poor of the forward castes and, for the same reasons as in version (a) may not also succeed in keeping out the relatively better-off among them. Moreover, the separate quotas (additional to the one for OBCs) under the economic criterion in versions (b) and (c) will entail an increase in the overall reserved quota (reducing the space for open competition) or cut into the quota that might have been otherwise available for OBCs (at the cost of social justice) or may have to be marginal (5 per cent or so) having only a tokenistic impact.

The practical problems in the application of the economic criterion are important because they can substantively thwart what is sought to be achieved. The economic criterion will have to be defined in terms of a family income limit and/or a list of family occupations. As is well known, there are a number of serious problems in assessing incomes, and especially family incomes, in the Indian context. Incomes widely tend to be understated, particularly when benefits are involved (the moral hazard problem). Regular salary earners are confined to the organized sector, which is pretty small in India, and they are smaller in numbers in the low-income groups. By and large, incomes arise from self-employment and casual labour, especially in the dominant agricultural sector and, being highly variable over time, have an inherent element of indeterminacy about them. Such incomes are not capable of being objectively verified and can at best be certified by village officials, elected members of panchayats, legislators, etc. This has obvious implications in terms of corruption, manipulation, patronage, and influence, all of which will have free play and in all of which the 'forward' sections with local-level clout have a comparative advantage. Another set of problems arise from the concept and definition of 'family income': what kind of family, nuclear or joint, or any unit in which expenses are shared? Whatever it is, the assessment of the family income involves assessing incomes from diverse sources of a number of persons, compounding the problem of income verification. Also, inequity is inherent in the family income concept because family size is not taken into account. Similar, in fact more serious, problems are involved in the occupational criteria. Is a landlord who supervises his labour an 'actual cultivator'? Is a 'mechanic' an artisan? Why is not a 'poojari' who uses his hands for 'archana' not a 'manual labourer'? Does a 'coolie' who is without work because of illness have an occupation at all? Are all thirteen co-parceners of a joint family to be disqualified just because one of them earns some money from a higher-status occupation? What about composite occupations, some included in the criterion and some not? What if occupation changes over time, for example, a recently retired school teacher who is now an agriculturist? These examples are not figments of the imagination: Galanter's account shows that they have all been actually agitated before the courts.

In sum, as I have argued elsewhere (*Economic Times*, 25 and 26 December 1991), the motivation for the economic criterion is largely to provide psychological consolation to the advanced communities and its impact will be two-edged: the blunt side might promote some economic justice but the sharper edge will chip off at social justice. On the other hand, as Galanter points out, it is easier to target benefits on the basis of the caste criterion. Also, 'distribution of benefits to members of a caste group may mobilize ties of kinship, loyalty, and mutual support to multiply the effect of the benefits more than does distribution to isolated individuals.'

On the extent of reservation, the Supreme Court had held in the Balaji case (1962) that 'speaking generally and in a broad way, a special provision should be less than 50 per cent; how much less than 50 per cent would depend upon the relevant prevailing circumstances in each case.' While the 50 per cent limit for all reservations (including those for SCs and STs) has come to be perceived in popular discussion as an absolute maximum, the court itself has indicated the possibility of a more liberal view and has lived with a higher quantum of total reservations in many state schemes (for example, 68 per cent in Tamilnadu). A related issue is whether reservations should be available over and above seats gained by beneficiary groups in open competition or whether they should be viewed as 'guaranteed minimums' including such seats. The 'advantage' claimed for the guaranteed minimum approach is that it is self-liquidating: the effect of the reservation declines *pari passu* with the better performance of the OBCs in merit competition. However, this is likely to be at the expense of the most backward groups who are not likely to do well in open competition and depend on a larger reservation quota to be able to obtain a fairer share. Although courts have favoured the (more restrictive) minimum guarantee alternative, 'over and above schemes have come up before them on several occasions without exciting judicial condemnation.' The Constitution itself has opted for the 'over and above' principle in the case of reservations of legislative seats: a seat won by a SC/ST candidate in an unreserved constituency does not entail a reduction in the number of reserved seats.

There has been a tendency to extend the scope of reservations beyond the traditionally understood backward classes to groups such as families of ex-servicemen, political sufferers, handicapped, women and, most importantly, the economically disadvantaged. Galanter's cautionary argument against this trend is:

The broader the categories for which reservation is made, the more likely they are to pick up students who would be selected on merit... The more the categories cut across one another, the less will a simple addition of percentages reveal the effective extent of reservations. The Constitution and a quarter-century of attendant policy-making embody a sustained commitment to offset a specific historic constellation of inequalities implicated with the traditional social hierarchy in India. To generalize from this commitment may diffuse rather than strengthen it.

Galanter's review brings the story up to the beginning of the eighties when the Mandal Commission was set up. There has been ambivalence, inconsistency, and formalism in judicial pronouncements but, over the years, some sort of a conservative 'bottom-line' has emerged in the judicial doctrine on compensatory discrimination in terms of what the courts would be prepared to accept as regards the scope and extent of reservations. Seen against this perspective, any objective examination of the Mandal Report will reveal that its methodology and recommendations are on lines that should strike even establishmentarians—so long as they are literate—as eminently 'sound'. In the classification of OBCs, the Mandal Commission has utilized 11 criteria, four of them economic, and has adopted well-below-the average cut-off limits for determining backwardness. Within the couple of years available to them, the commission's surveys and use of available data were about the most that could be reasonably expected although falling short of indefinitely perfectible academic standards. The commission's estimate of the proportion of OBCs (52 per cent) in total population has been much criticized by its detractors. But, it is only a broad indicative figure to justify the 27 per cent reservation that has been recommended and it is not in itself an operational parameter. This quantum, along with 22.5 per cent available for SCs and STs, is within the overall 50 per cent limit favoured by the courts. The extent of reservation recommended by Mandal, namely, 27 per cent, is generally less than the quotas favoured by the Kalelkar Commission for job reservations and much less than the 70 per cent recommended by it for educational reservations. Furthermore, the actual decision of the V. P. Singh Government considerably diluted the recommendations of the Report: reservations were confined to services; the armed forces and promotion posts were excluded; no reservations were announced for seats in educational institutions. All along, it should also have been clear that reservations would apply only to incremental recruitment from year to year and not to the entirety of posts. We can estimate the current OBC share in central government employment to be 15 per cent on the basis of available data; if staff strength grows at 1 per cent per annum, a prospective 27 per cent reservation will improve it, at a snail's pace, only to 18 per cent in thirty years from now.

After such knowledge, there can be little forgiveness. Leaving aside the forward caste induced self-immolations in the streets, how is the sound and fury in the media and in academic writings on the Mandal decision to be explained when it should have been clear that all that was being proposed was a modest, all too modest, measure of preferential treatment? Indeed, it is the OBCs who had every reason to be thoroughly dissatisfied that so little was being grudgingly yielded after so long. What the academic critics of the Mandal decision did was to simply ignore the Constitution—our basic social contract—and the quarter century of judicial interaction with policy and practice at the state level, the 'what' and 'how' of reservation, and to reopen the 'why' of reservation in terms of its social costs and benefits as perceived by them. While Galanter's main preoccupation in this volume has been with the legal process, he has also devoted some space to the discussion of costs and benefits, in the earlier part of the book with reference to SCs and STs and towards the end in a section entitled 'Fairness and History'. His own approach can be described as that of a pragmatic liberal. He recognizes that compensatory discrimination is not without its costs at both the societal and individual levels but believes that such costs could be reasonably controlled and need not be used as arguments to deter society from proceeding on this path. His response to this set of issues, compared to his detailed treatment of legal aspects, is, however, limited. This is perhaps because of two main reasons. First, the so-called costs of compensatory discrimination have been laboured by its critics in terms of general arguments regarding 'efficiency', 'creaming-off', 'intergenerational unfairness', and so on. While such critics have quibbled at data deficiencies when it comes to schemes for reservations, they have themselves offered no data to substantiate their abstract misgivings. As Galanter points out:

> Considering the readiness with which many Indian intellectuals, including some eminent social scientists, have passed severe judgements on compensatory discrimination, it is surprising how little systematic study of its presumed effects we have... Courts have required that in designating backward classes, government act on the basis of adequate data rather than mere assertion or casual opinion. No comparable standards have yet developed for the kind of factual basis that must serve as the foundation for assertions about efficiency, morale, effective use of talent, etc.

In these circumstances, *a priori* argument can only be met by counter arguments on a similar plane and this Galanter has succinctly done in two tables (Tables 4 and 10) on 'Alleged Benefits and Costs' of compensatory discrimination and of preferences in government employment. Secondly, Galanter's position on these issues, while leaving no doubt on where he stands, is articulated with a certain restraint presumably because being an external observer, and a modest one, he does not consider it appropriate to overly prescribe what Indian society should do to correct its heritage of deprivation. The tragedy is that, as far as the backward classes are concerned, contemporary India is yet to produce Gramscian 'organic intellectuals' with Galanter's endowments of head and heart.

10
Dark Forebodings*

I welcome this opportunity to speak at the series of meetings which the Centre for Policy Studies is organizing on Ayodhya and the Future India. The first reason why I very readily agreed to speak is that I think this is one of the most important issues that the country has faced in its history. And, therefore, each of us—to whatever inclinations and persuasions we might belong—should take every opportunity to come together and interact with each other and share our perceptions. We may not always agree with each other, but all thinking people should give an opportunity for others to convince them, and to be convinced. And even if we are not convinced, we should at least try to understand why somebody is arguing what he is arguing, and what is behind it. I think such interactions are always useful.

Secondly, I was told that my good friend, Arun Shourie, had spoken here earlier. And my views are diametrically opposite to his views. I know his views both from personal conversations with him and his public writings. And, I can say with certainty that my views are 180 degrees away from Sri Shourie's. So I thought you might have an opportunity to evaluate these diametrically opposite views, and come to your own conclusions.

Thirdly, it is the timing of these meetings which seemed very appropriate to me. I think it is very good that we are talking about Ayodhya almost nine weeks after the event. During this time we have had some time to reflect on the issue. Passions are a little less strong. And in the meanwhile, a lot of literature has come out on the subject. People of different persuasions and colours have written about it.

---
* Reprinted from Jitendra Bajaj (ed.), *Ayodhya and the Future India*, Centre for Policy Studies, Madras, 1993, pp. 71–92.

And, most importantly, we have also witnessed and heard a number of actions and utterances of the leaders of the *sangha parivar*.

The 'sangha parivar' is a term I shall keep using throughout my talk. The parivar I define as the Rashtriya Swayamsevak Sangha (RSS), the Vishwa Hindu Parishad (VHP), the Bajrang Dal and a number of front organizations going under different names. The parivar also includes various people who are, in some sense or the other, of the same persuasion or under the same control, openly or secretly.

There is no necessary continuity in the utterances and writings of the leaders of these groups. They say one thing today, something else two weeks later. One organization strikes a moderate pose, another strikes a militant pose. And, like an adept musician playing a piano, they've been orchestrating these views, very strategically, very cleverly. This is what makes them a parivar, an entourage, an assemblage, or as you say in Tamil, *parivaram*.

I would not like to say 'A' said this or 'B' said this, because I am not an expert on who said what on which day, and who denied himself on any other day. Or, on who contradicted each other, and who corroborated each other. So instead of referring to specific individuals and their statements, I shall refer to the parivar. That is why I am taking a little trouble to explain my use of the term 'sangha parivar', or simply the 'parivar'.

In the last nine weeks we have had various utterances from the parivar. Sri Vamadeva Maharaj has spoken, Swami Muktananda has spoken and, most important, Bal Thackeray, who is one of the allies of the parivar, though at one remove from it, has had his say. Then, what is more important from my point of view as an academic, we have had two very cogent—cogent in the sense of being carefully structured—articles from two outstanding theoreticians of the parivar. One is Jaswant Singh, who is a very articulate, very learned Oxford graduate, and has written on the subject at length in a recent special issue of the *Seminar* on Ayodhya (number 402, February 1993). And in the same special issue of the *Seminar*, we also have Arun Shourie. Here are two theoreticians of the parivar who, after the Ayodhya event, have spelled out their views on how it happened, what it means to the country, and what lessons are to be learnt. So, we have the raw material before us for a comprehensive analysis.

On my own part, I would like to cover four main topics this evening. First, the demolition of the mosque itself: What does it represent? What led to it? And how did it happen? This analysis, it seems to me, is very important. Because, I do not think we can look at the future of India, forgetting what happened at Ayodhya on 6 December 1992. We cannot say: 'Whatever happened has happened, let's look at what is going to happen.' We cannot strike that stance. Because, if we sow the whirlwind, we shall reap the whirlwind. We cannot sow the whirlwind and then hope that we shall reap a lush green crop.

Second, I shall speak on secularism: What is understood by secularism? What has been the practice of secularism in this country? What does secularism mean in theory? And what has it meant in practice?

Third, I shall speak on an issue which is really a side issue, but a very important one: Federalism. It is an issue in which I am very interested. What effects do the events of the recent past have on federalism?

And fourth, of course, I shall conclude with saying something about what the Ayodhya events, in my mind, augur for the future of India, because that is the subject of these discussions.

To start with the first issue, that of analysing what happened at Ayodhya: We can, I think, straightaway dismiss that Ayodhya was an aberration, or a small accident. It is not as if some cat jumped over a table and upset a glass of water, though even a person like Jayendra Saraswati, Sankaracharya of Kanchi Kamakoti Peetham, has said that 'by chance' the mosque was demolished. There was nothing 'by chance' about it. There is evidence that it was carefully planned, that people were trained, that they were equipped with implements to demolish the mosque. You cannot demolish an old, strong structure, covering an area of 6000 square feet, in six hours without planning and without being equipped to do so. We have all seen demolitions of buildings in our neighbourhoods. It cannot happen without careful planning.

But let us for a moment leave aside the physical planning that went before the demolition of the mosque. Let us look at what really led to it in a longer span. And, the best way to do it is to look at the analysis offered by the leaders of the parivar. They have given an account of why it happened. In fact, some of them had justified the demolition even before it happened. They had been appealing for the demolition on the basis of spurious and dubious facts. They had been spreading misinformation about many things. And now, many others, like Arun Shourie and Jaswant Singh, have rationalized the demolition after the event.

The parivar utilizes three types of arguments. One type is for the gullible people. For them the parivar uses factual arguments: 'This was the Janmasthana of Srirama, this precise spot. On that precise spot there was a temple. That particular temple was demolished. On that a mosque was built.' This story has been broadcast. It has been propagated to a certain kind of audience, who will believe that kind of argument, to the kind of people who would not go into history or archaeology, and be taken in by this kind of wrong facts, wrong archaeology, wrong history and wrong logic.

But the parivar has a different argument for persons like me. For example, when Arun Shourie talks to me, he would not use these arguments. He knows the argument is hollow—I would laugh at him. Therefore, with persons like me he uses another argument. And, that is also the argument Jaswant Singh has used in the Ayodhya issue of the *Seminar*. This argument makes the Janmabhoomi a matter of faith. Just as Christians have believed for 2000 years that Bethlehem—that stable in Bethlehem—was the birthplace of Christ, just as Muslims believe that Karbala in Mecca is the birthplace of Prophet Mohammed, so the Hindus believe that that precise spot in Ayodhya is the birthplace of Srirama. It is a matter of faith. Any number of trivial factual arguments are meaningless. And, since people hold this faith, since millions of people for hundreds of years have held this faith, let us not go into the facts. The facts do not matter.

I am willing to take this argument at its face value. I would accept it if indeed it were the case. I do not discount faith. Faith does not always rest on facts, but faith itself is a fact. If the faith has been strong, if it has been continuous, if it has been held by a very large number of people, we have to respect it, even if we do not share it. But is that faith itself a matter of fact? That is the issue we have to face. And we shall come to it.

The third level of arguments advanced by the sangha parivar is built around the concept of 'reaction'. That is the level at which Arun Shourie argues in the *Seminar* issue. The argument goes like this: 'Hindus in this country have been provoked so much by appeasement of the minorities by pseudo-secularists, that they have reacted sharply by demolishing the mosque. It is merely a reaction to the events of the last few decades, and in the face of this reaction facts and faith about the birthplace do not matter.' That, of course, is a *post-facto* argument, but we will evaluate that too.

Let us begin with the argument about the facts first. But before beginning, I should make it clear that I do not believe the temple should be reconstructed even if there were factual evidence to prove that there was a temple there under the mosque. I do not believe the temple should be reconstructed. One could, of course, say that if in any case we are not going to rebuild the temple, why go into the facts at all? If there was a temple that we are not going to rebuild, why should we go into the fact of whether there was a temple or not? One can logically take that stand.

But we shall look at whether there was a temple, because on this rest some of the beliefs and the faith that are being so talked about. I shall, therefore, look into the argument regarding the facts, without however yielding to the argument that if there was a temple it should be rebuilt.

What does this factual argument imply? First, that Srirama was a historical person, because only historical persons can actually be born in this world. Second, he was born at a place which can be identified as the present-day Ayodhya in Faizabad district of Uttar Pradesh. Third, in Ayodhya he was born at the precise spot where the idols are placed: that precise spot is the *Janmasthana*. Fourth, there was a temple at that spot. Fifth, the temple was demolished and the Babri Masjid was built on it around 1528. These are the five propositions required to establish the factual argument. The factual argument will follow, if and only if all five of these propositions are proved to be true.

But, none of the propositions stands to reason. First, there is absolutely no evidence that Srirama was a historical person. Although the epic and the myth might have grown around a historical king, of some dim past, certainly there is no evidence that Srirama of the epic was a historical person. Internal evidence of the *Ramayana* itself is against the possibility of the hero being a historical character. The various exploits of Srirama described in the epic—the various miracles he performed and the way he fought with an army of monkeys and squirrels and so on—are not facts that might pertain to a real historical being.

Second, there has always been considerable doubt about the exact location of Ayodhya. Vikramaditya Skandagupta, the historians tell us, went around trying to locate Ayodhya. And then Saketa of the old days, on the banks of the Sarayu, was renamed as Ayodhya. That is the historical fact. That was why our grandmothers used to say, 'Don't ask where is Ayodhya. Wherever there is Srirama, there is Ayodhya.' The sangha parivar has put the wisdom of our grandmothers upside down. They say, 'Where Ayodhya is, there Srirama was'!

It is because traditionally the physical location of Ayodhya, the precise geographical spot, was in doubt, that we had this saying among our grandmothers. Even I have heard it from my grandmother, 'Where Srirama resides, there is Ayodhya.' Then what is the controversy about?

Archaeological evidence suggests that prior to the fifth century BC there was no habitation at the site of the present-day town of Ayodhya, while Srirama is dated to the Tretayuga, in 3100 BC, or something like that. So if this be so, we cannot be sure that the Ayodhya of Srirama is the Ayodhya of Faizabad district.

The third proposition in need of evidence is that the exact spot where the Babri Masjid stood is the birthplace of Srirama, that exact spot is the Janmasthana. Where is the Janmasthana first mentioned? The Vishwa Hindu Parishad, during its discussions with the Babri Masjid Action Committee (BMAC) held in 1990-1 at the initiative of the then Prime Minister Chandrashekhar, gave a memorandum arguing the facts. In the memorandum the only evidence the VHP adduced in favour of the spot being the Janmasthana is a reference to a text called 'Ayodhyamahatmya', which is attached to *Skandapurana*. And the *Skandapurana* is dated to somewhere between the fourteenth and the sixteenth century.

Experts have looked into this document, and they have arrived at the exact compass readings for the Janmasthana as described in this text. The Janmasthana, according to this reckoning, is nowhere near the Babri Masjid, it is much closer to the river Sarayu. So the one document produced by the VHP does not prove their claim about the Janmasthana, and in any case this document is of as late a date as the sixteenth century. Srirama was born in the Tretayuga, around 3000 BC, and the first document mentioning the place of his birth, the Janmasthana, that the VHP can produce is of the fourteenth to sixteenth century. And the precise compass readings deduced from that document do not place the Janmasthana anywhere near the mosque.

The next proposition that we need to establish is regarding the existence of a temple at the site before the Babri Masjid was put up there. What is the evidence for this? Absolutely none. None that would stand the test of any kind of history or archaeology. Mir Baqi, who is said to have built the mosque, would have been the first person to claim that he demolished a temple and built a mosque, because by doing so he would be praising Babar for his Islamic piety. As a *mujahid*, as a person engaged in waging war against Hinduism for the greater glory of Islam and Allah, he would have been the first to say. 'I destroyed this Temple'. But he does not say so in his inscription of 1528.

No mention of the demolition is available in *Babarnama*, the memoirs of Babar. The pages corresponding to the period of his visit to Ayodhya are missing from the memoirs. Nothing at all is said about the destruction of this temple in *Ain-e-Akbari*, which was written a little later, in the seventeenth century. Most importantly, there is no mention of the temple and its destruction in the *Ramacharitamanas* of Goswami Tulsidas. Swami Tulsidas wrote the *Manas* around 1575–6, less than fifty years after the Babri Masjid was built. Is it conceivable that Swami Tulsidas would not have mentioned the demolition of the temple at Ayodhya, if any such demolition had indeed taken place?

The first mention that there was a temple at all in Ayodhya begins to appear in the works of western historians, like Carnegy, Neville, Beveridge, and Hans Bakker, around 1850, near the time of the first Indian War of Independence. And all of them attribute the existence of the temple to local belief. Beveridge attributes it to speculation. She only says, 'There would have been a temple'. Bakker says that there is belief that there was a Janmasthana temple, but that it was outside the mosque, not inside.

Most pertinent in the series of historical evidence about the existence of a temple at the alleged Janmasthana is the well-recorded incident of an armed conflict between Sunni Muslims and Vaishnava Bairagis around 1855. The conflict took place over Hanumangarhi, and not the Janmasthana. Hanumangarhi is an old temple in Ayodhya, dedicated to Hanuman. And this temple has been the principal site of pilgrimage in Ayodhya. If you look at the *Divyaprabandham*, where all the 108 *divyasthalams* of India are listed, you will find an entry corresponding to 'Thiru Ayodhya', and Thiru Ayodhya is there described as the Hanumangarhi Kovil.

But let us return to the incident of the armed conflict of 1855. The story is that there was a Hindu Mahant in Hanumangarhi, who was chased out. He converted to Islam. Then he went and told the Maulavi that there was a mosque on Hanumangarhi, which was demolished, and on that site the Hanumangarhi temple was built. Thereupon, the Sunni Muslims, about 500–600 of them, gathered and they tried to invade Hanumangarhi and demolish the temple. In response, the Hindus mobilized in large numbers, about five to six thousand gathered there, leading to an armed conflict. The Muslims were chased back to the Babri Masjid. Nearly a hundred Muslims were killed in the encounter and in fact the ground where they were buried is still remembered.

Even after this encounter the Hindus involved in the incident, the Vaishnava Bairagis of the Ramanandi sect of Hanumangarhi, did not claim that the Babri Masjid was the Janmasthana. Is it conceivable that if the site of the Babri Masjid had been believed to be the Janmasthana of Srirama, the Hindus would have kept quiet and not claimed the mosque, even after a bloody riot in which many people had been killed? And, especially when the Muslims were laying claim to their own temple, the Hanumangarhi, as the site of a mosque! The Hindus, however, did not put up any claim to the site of the Babri Masjid then, not even as a counter to the Muslim claims.

It is only in 1857, the time of the first war of independence or a little later, that the Mahant of Hanumangarhi built the Chabutara, a 17 foot by 21 foot raised platform, outside the Babri Masjid. That was clearly a counter response to the Muslim claims on Hanumangarhi, because by that time the British had set up a Committee to go into the Hanumangarhi incidents and to determine whether there had been a mosque at the site of the temple. It was only at this stage that the Hanumangarhi Mahant claimed the Janmasthana, and the claimed spot was still not inside the Babri Masjid, but on the Chabutara outside, which was built in or around 1857.

The British allowed the Chabutara to be built for their own reasons. During the war of independence, the Muslims of that region had fought the British, while the Hindu landlords and the Mahants had extended them their support. Therefore the British turned a Nelson's eye on what the Hindus did, and thus the Chabutara was constructed. But the British insisted on putting up a fence between the mosque and the Chabutara, and decreed that no Hindu would enter the mosque, and no Muslim would enter the Chabutara.

This position was contested only in 1885. It was then that Mahant Raghubardas made a plea before the sub-judge of Faizabad for permission to build a temple on the Chabutara outside the Babri Masjid. Notice that the Mahant was not pressing any claim over the site of the mosque, but only over the Chabutara outside. The sub-judge was one Pandit Harkishan Prasad, a Hindu. He gave an excellent judgment, which remains relevant even today. Delivering the judgment on 24 December 1885, he said that if 'permission is given to Hindus for constructing a temple on the Chabutara, then one day or the other a criminal case will be started and thousands of people will be killed'. Therefore, in the interest of expediency, the sub-judge refused to permit a temple on the Chabutara. The order was upheld by the district judge, and the judicial commission.

Incidentally, all this litigation took less than one year. Mahant Raghubardas had moved the sub-judge of Faizabad in late 1885 and by November 1886 he had exhausted all appeals. He had nowhere else to go. This is in stark contrast to what is happening in the Allahabad high court and in the Supreme Court today. Three appeals were disposed of by the British in one single year, and they took a sensible pragmatic position that if a temple came up there it would lead to violence and bloodshed.

This happened in 1885. Once again there is a tremendous lull of sixty four years between 1885 and 1949, when the idols were installed on the night between 22 and 23 December. It was claimed that the idols had miraculously appeared inside the mosque. Before the event there was a nine-day non-stop recitation of *Ramacharitmanas* organized by the Akhil Bharatiya Ramayana Mahasabha. The descriptions of the scene at Ayodhya at that time remind us of what the sangha parivar has been doing in the recent past. Like now, so in 1949, people were going about mobilizing and collecting great multitudes, recitations were being held, loudspeakers were blaring. There is an eyewitness account of the events of 1949 by a local Congressman, Akshay Brahmachari.

It should be remembered that in 1949 only two years had passed since partition. Also, the RSS was banned in 1948 and the ban was lifted in 1949. So, they had to assert themselves and show their strength. The installation of idols in the Babri Masjid in 1949 was thus purely a show of strength by the RSS in the relatively tense atmosphere of post-partition north India. The gullible were of course told that those idols had appeared miraculously on the site. And, this happened fully sixty-four years after 1885, when the Hindus had last raked up the issue.

The events following 1949 are recent history, and many of you must be familiar with these. So, I shall just rush with this part. But I shall take time to mention every milestone in this snowballing movement, because each of the milestones is important in itself.

The installation of the idols was protested to by the Muslims. The judiciary ordered the doors of the mosque to be locked, the Hindus were restricted to performing puja of the idols from the outside, and at the same time the Muslims were also restrained from entering the mosque and offering prayers there. So the Muslims could not pray in the mosque, and the Hindus also could not perform puja inside, but they could offer worship from the outside.

This position was confirmed by the Allahabad high court in 1955. Thereafter another twenty-five years passed and nothing happened in Ayodhya. These intervals are very important. The VHP was formed in August 1964, but even the VHP did not take up the Ayodhya issue for almost twenty years. It was only in 1984, thirty-five years after the appearance of the idols in Ayodhya and twenty years after the VHP itself was formed, that a call for the 'liberation' of the Janmabhoomi was given in the VHP-sponsored gathering of sadhus and Hindu religious leaders, in the so-called Dharma Samsad, that met at the Vigyan Bhavan in Delhi in April 1984. It was then that Mathura and Varanasi were also mentioned along with Ayodhya. And then the first rathayatra started from Sitamarhi in Bihar, which took place in September 1984, when Indira Gandhi was still alive. This then is the exact time when this whirlwind was formally sown by the VHP.

In 1986 a tacit understanding was reached between the then Prime Minister, Rajiv Gandhi, and the VHP. The judiciary was certainly influenced. And on an application by an unknown lawyer, Umesh Chandra Pande, the sub-judge of Faizabad ordered the locks to be opened and the Hindus to be allowed to perform puja there. The sub-judge did not even allow an opportunity to the Sunni Wakf Board to be heard. He disposed of the application in forty minutes and summarily passed orders directing unlocking of the gate and allowing Hindu puja there. Appeals on that are still pending.

The next major event took place in 1989. The then Home Minister in the Union government, Buta Singh, reached an accord with the VHP permitting a limited performance of *silanyasa*, the ceremonial laying of the foundation stone, on 10 November 1989.

At that time Ashok Singhal, secretary of the VHP, had clearly said that the proposed temple would subsume the mosque, that the temple would extend into the mosque. He said it openly. Also the VHP had given its plan for the temple, and that incorporated the place where the idols were kept inside the mosque as the *garbhagriha*, the sanctum sanctorum, of the proposed temple. Knowing all this the government of Rajiv Gandhi allowed limited silanyasa in November 1989.

The events following the silanyasa are too recent to need recounting: The rathayatra of Lal Krishna Advani in 1990, the fall of the government headed by V. P. Singh, discussions between the VHP and the BMAC at the initiative of Chandrashekhar, and later at the initiative of the present Prime Minister, P. V. Narasimha Rao, and finally the demolition of the mosque at Ayodhya.

What I would like to bring out from this somewhat long recounting of the history of Ayodhya events is the hollowness of the claims of the protagonists of the temple. Their claims are hollow on the factual basis. There is no evidence to prove that there was Srirama, that he was born in Ayodhya, that he was born at the precise spot occupied by the Babri Masjid, that there was a temple at that site, that the temple was demolished and the mosque was built upon its ruins. There is no evidence to prove any one of these propositions. The whole set of arguments blared out to the gullible people by trained propagandists is factually wrong. But today if you ask an ordinary person in India, he would say, 'What do you mean? Can we not even build a temple to Srirama in India? Don't we have the right to do this?' That is what has been put in the minds of the people. The minds have been vitiated.

Not only is there no evidence to prove the existence of a temple at the site, there is also no evidence to show that there has been any widespread belief in the existence of the temple there. Jaswant Singh refers to the belief that Jesus Christ was born in Bethlehem which has moved Christendom for twenty centuries, and he compares that belief with the belief of the people of India in the birthplace of Srirama. He is asking us to believe that the Hindu belief in the Janmasthana at Ayodhya is of the same validity as the Christian belief in Bethlehem! Just as that belief has moved Christendom, the whole of Christendom, for twenty centuries, similarly this belief has moved all Hindus!

I think this is utter rubbish. If there was such a belief, what happened to that belief between the Tretayuga and 1885, when the first claim on the Janmasthana was made and the Chabutara was built? What happened to that belief between 1885 and 1949? What happened to it between 1949 and 1984? This is mere rubbish. I cannot give up my common sense. If there was such a strong belief held by millions of Hindus, just as the Christians have held the belief in Bethlehem for twenty centuries, then does it stand to reason that this off-on, off-on approach to reclaiming the supposed Janmasthana would have gone on in this desultory fashion?

I have not yet come to the arguments advanced by Arun Shourie, which are a little more sophisticated. The parivar has gradations of sophistication within it. Jaswant Singh is a little more sophisticated than Ashok Singhal, and Arun Shourie is more sophisticated than Jaswant Singh. Sri Shourie does not touch the argument about Hindus having faith in the Janmasthana. He only puts forward the argument about the Hindu reaction to the alleged Muslim appeasement. He says, 'Forget about faith. This is only a Hindu reaction against appeasement of the Muslims over many decades.' But what is this appeasement? Muslims, according to all available statistical evidence, are far behind the majority in terms of their economic standing, their representation in the bureaucracy and the armed forces, their levels of education, and so on. Then where is the appeasement? And what are the Hindus reacting to?

The claims of the sangha parivar have no validity. There is no evidence to establish any one of the arguments advanced by them. Nothing can be proved, neither the argument about the facts, nor about the faith, nor the one about appeasement and the consequent reaction.

If you look at the sequence of the Ayodhya events, you find nothing more than the incremental political strategy of the parivar. They are adopting a strategy of building up incremental pressure to gain political power. For this strategy to work they have to mobilize crowds around a physical issue or a target that is extremely vivid to the people. They know that if they talk about issues, about policies, about programmes, or about constitutional changes, then people will not understand all this. The people must be mobilized around a physical object. So they say, 'That mosque there, that is our enemy. Demolish it!' It is easy to whip up crowds around a physical object. This is exactly what they have done.

The other part of this incremental strategy is that you should gain some ground, and then withdraw, only to move up again to gain further ground. This is very important in politics. You demonstrate to the people that you have gained ground, that you have made some advance. Then you withdraw, in order to keep the issue alive. You take up an impossible task, a task that cannot be completed. If you complete the task, the game is over, the balloon is punctured. So you must make an advance to show your strength to your enemies and your friends, and then you withdraw a bit to threaten the enemies again, and keep the game going, keep the issue alive.

This is exactly what the members of the sangha parivar have done from time to time. They have done it at the time of every election. They did it in 1984. They did it at the mid-point of a government in 1986. They prepared for it till 1989 and activated it again on the eve of the elections. And then in 1990, utilizing the issue of reservations in government jobs for the backward castes according to the Mandal Commission report, an issue that was given to them on a platter by V. P. Singh, they raised the pressure again. They thought it was an excellent time for action, so that they could whip up sentiments against the reservations and also utilize the resulting atmosphere for building support for the Ayodhya movement.

If you are a student of politics—as I have been, sometimes even a close student of politics, having moved very freely with politicians—this is a very good strategy so far as it goes. But it cannot go on forever. I hope it does not. But so far as it goes, this strategy of advance and retreat, off and on, hot and cold, pays well. It has paid rich dividends to the parivar, as is clear from the results of successive elections. The BJP won two seats and 7 per cent of the popular vote in the 1984 elections to the Lok Sabha, their share went up to 85 seats and 11 per cent of the popular vote in 1989, and in 1991 their representation in the Lok Sabha went up to 119 seats. They were obviously on to a good political strategy, but it was no more than a political strategy. It had absolutely nothing to do with faith or fact.

A transcript of the discussion that followed Guhan's talk is provided below. (Ed)

Discussion

Radha Rajan: Sir, academics in India seem to have a rather derogatory attitude towards most things. In the same vein you too are crying down everything. You are dismissing all arguments that do not suit you. You are belittling all opinions that do not happen to be in consonance with yours. You do not give any weight to the feelings of others. You have very clever arguments, you have very learned arguments. But, do you ever give consideration to what other people feel? They might not be as learned as you are. But their views and opinions are about as valid as yours.

Guhan: Do you have consideration for my feelings? Do you have any idea how I feel about this stupid movement that has been unleashed upon this country? In spite of my strong feelings about it, I have not used a single unparliamentary word. Please challenge me if I have done that.

Radha Rajan: You don't have to use unparliamentary words in order to hurt the feelings of others. I am very perturbed by your way of arguing, of belittling and dismissing everyone, and of sarcastically laughing at the faith and feelings of the people.

But, sir, let me turn to a more specific question. You came down rather heavily on Arun Shourie and Jaswant Singh. You have interpreted them according to your reasons and your convictions. In the same way I take the liberty of interpreting what you and the 'secular club' have been saying. The club asks, 'Why is the sangha parivar worried about issues like Shah Bano and Salman Rushdie? Is the sangha parivar shedding tears for Shah Bano or for Salman Rushdie?'

Of course, there are always intellectuals who are clever at raising arguments and diverting attention. But the questions you and the 'secular club' raise are irrelevant. One need not shed tears for Salman Rushdie, but can still question the ban. One does not have to be a sympathizer of Mr Rushdie in order to ask, 'Why are we being denied the right to read a book? Why this ban on religious grounds? Why this eagerness to spare the sentiments of one particular religious community, while a vast body of literature inimical to and abusive of the Hindu religion is not only tolerated, but also is often positively encouraged? Why doesn't anyone think of banning that?' One can ask all these questions, without at the same time having to shed tears for Salman Rushdie.

Similarly, shedding or not shedding tears for Shah Bano is also not the issue. Without being sentimental about that courageous lady, one can still ask, 'Why is it that when a person comes to our courts of justice, and when religious fundamentalists protest against the relief provided by the courts, we make it into a major political issue and bring in legislation to overrule the Supreme Court'? This weak-kneed response to fundamentalist pressures is the issue. The question of shedding tears or not shedding tears for Shah Bano or anyone else does not come into the picture.

Guhan: Let me first respond to your question about the banning of that book by Salman Rushdie. You say that you have been denied the opportunity to read the book, just because the Muslims said that it contains heretical reflections on the Prophet. You say that this is not fair. I on the other hand would defend the banning of that book for this simple reason: Just as the parivar says, and Jaswant Singh has said it very clearly, that there has been a monumental faith among the Hindus about the Janmasthana of Srirama, similarly, whether you like it or not, the 80 million Muslims of India have a certain feeling for their Prophet. And if the introduction of this book were going to lead to large-scale riots and a breakdown of law and order, then it was perfectly legitimate to ban the book. You know what happened in Iran over this book.

I have been in the government for thirty-five years. And I know that any civil servant or politician or anyone else entrusted with the task of running this country, would have to weigh the availability of this book for some people to read, on one pan of the scale, and the fact that there may be extensive rioting, widespread breakdown of law and order, and tension between the communities, on the other. What judgment will a sensible person come to? I shall leave it to you to form your own judgment. I don't want to say anything more.

Radha Rajan: But, sir, when there is so much literature condemning Hinduism, how is it that only this book gets banned?

Guhan: By all means let people protest against the books that condemn Hinduism. Is there any example involving a text which brought Hindu religion or gods into disrepute, and the people protested against it, and the government refused to ban it? Periyar was banned. If you find a book that hurts the Hindu sensibilities, make a demand for banning it!

Ambadi: Sir, the suggestion you are making has very serious implications. What you are saying is that if a certain group is capable of concerted militancy on an issue concerning freedom of expression, freedom of speech, freedom to criticize religion—if the group is capable of unleashing national and international violence on such an issue—then you will concede to its demands. You will concede to national and international violence. You will ban a book here if somebody issues a *fatwa* in Iran to kill somebody in England. You will ban the book here because there is a possibility of organized, mindless violence by some groups. I know I am using strong words. But your argument calls for strong words. If violence is the benchmark, if this is the criterion for allowing or not allowing something, then how can we blame anyone for the demolition at Ayodhya? Sir, your argument shall please Bal Thackeray the most. What you are suggesting is: Demand what you want, demand vociferously, threaten violence, indulge in violence, and what you demand shall be conceded.

Guhan: He seems to have a point, but he does not have a point. I did not say that the state must concede to the threat of violence. What I said was that on an issue like this we have to take the possibility of violence into account and come to a practical decision. You and I might differ. There are many who have looked upon the ban as another instance of appeasement, some have even characterized the ban as communal. The parivar can add this to its long list of examples of minority appeasement. I have no problems with that.

And I agree that in the matter of Shah Bano, the government failed totally. I make no bones about it. Even S. Gopal says that this was an instance of the government buckling under communal pressure and deviating from the path of secularism.

Ravi: Sir, in your presentation you mentioned that Swami Tulsidas does not mention the demolition of the temple at Ayodhya in the *Ramacharitamanas*, and this you said is one of the most important proofs that there was no temple there. All of us in Tamilnadu know that Malik Kafur entered and desecrated the Madurai Meenakshi Temple and the Srirangam Temple. But I have not heard of any Tamil saints, savants or poets having written songs about those events. We also know that Belur and Halebeedu were ravaged around the same time. To my knowledge there are no songs in Kannada about that. Have you, sir, heard of any songs or of any great poetry in Tamil or Kannada literature describing the desecrations and ravages of that period?

Guhan: All I am saying is that if somebody claims that something was there, he has to produce evidence. Logically it is impossible to prove the negative. If somebody says that there was a temple in Ayodhya, he has to produce the evidence for its existence. He cannot say, 'I cannot produce any evidence, but you produce evidence to show that there was no temple.' I refuse to take the onus of proving the non-existence of the temple. Logically it is impossible to prove the negative. One cannot function according to such demands and rules.

Govindacharya: Sir, much reasoning, intellectualizing, and championing for the cause of secularism has gone on in this country for decades. How is it that in spite of it the sangha parivar is able to get away with all that you are accusing it of? And what do you think of the future of our 'secular' forces? Do you think that the secular forces and secular minds will be able to come together? Will they be able to put up a good fight for what they believe in and tilt the scales in favour of their ideas? And what is the way that our country is going to take? What is your assessment of the future in the light of our experiences of the past forty years? Viewing dispassionately the political forces active in the country, what do you feel about the future polity of India?

Guhan: I am extremely touched that Govindacharya wants to know the way out! I have heard a lot about you, and I speak with respect. I do not say that I have a definite and clear answer. But as a dispassionate analyst my suspicion is that the sangha parivar is not 'super-life size'. It is not 10 foot tall. It talks and acts and bluffs as if it has done a great and wonderful thing. It believes that it has launched this country in this tremendous crisis, and now it is for others to tackle it. To me all this is less than convincing. I think that the parivar has in a sense exhausted itself. Let us take the claims of the parivar with a pinch of salt.

If the members of the parivar themselves realize their limitations, which I hope a very good, a very enlightened person like our questioner will realize some day, then they should not have their sessions with 'academics' like me. They should do some introspection amongst themselves.

I shall request them to kindly withdraw from this, to kindly sit down and talk brasstacks. Talk about the Shah Bano affair, by all means. I shall welcome it. Talk about article 356, talk about article 370, talk about any other relevant articles of the Constitution. Talk about all these and about a hundred other things which in your opinion are important for this country. By all means talk about them. But do not talk about mosques and temples.

Do not talk about one more silanyasa, about one more Ayodhya. Because if you do this you would be beaten up, somewhere or the other. I am not going to beat you up. But there are enough Hindus who will do the beating. This is in fact a debate between Hindus. What is going on is not a fight between Hindus and Muslims. It is between the Hindus themselves. This is a fundamental thing I want to say. Please do not pretend that you have aggregated the Hindus behind Srirama. Not even 10 per cent of them are worried about this. So, do not make a balloon out of yourself and get pricked.

Jhunjhunwala: Sir, when the Ayodhya movement began I was very happy that we have begun to take Maryada Purushottama Sirirama as our ideal, and probably I was hoping that something great would come out of this. But I believe that the name of Maryada Purushottama Srirama has nothing to do with the talk of anti-Islam, and if we keep mixing the two we are taking the name of Srirama in vain.

I am very worried about the way ordinary Hindus have begun to hate ordinary Muslims. I wouldn't be bothered if they were to hate some leaders of the Muslims. But, I am very worried when the ordinary man in the street is filled with hate for his fellow Muslim. And I wonder why and how it has happened?

Guhan: I endorse every word of what you say.

Chamundeswari: I think you are wrong. I do not believe that Hindus have started hating Muslims. Many Hindus still go to the *dargahs* of Muslims Pirs and the churches of mother Velankanni and others, as they, with their expansive understanding of the divine, have always been doing.

I think the point the Ayodhya movement has emphasized is that the faith of a majority of the people cannot be denied or ignored. The movement has shown that the faith of the people can supersede the designs of the state, that the nation is in any case bigger than the state. And Maryada Purushottama Srirama is the symbol of that assertive faith of the Indian in themselves and in their nation.

Vaidyanathan: Sir, if we are serious about discussing the future of India, there are two issues we need to pay attention to. The first is: Are we going to create a situation where we justify all manner of aggression and violence on innocent people on the ground that their leadership or parts of their clergy happens to mouth some kind of extremist nonsense? After all, that extremist nonsense is not confined to any one community. There are fringes in every community, which pursue one kind of extremism or the other.

The other issue, which is a much more serious cause for worry and reflection, is this tendency to imagine that somehow we can create a new, resurgent, dynamic India under the banner of Hindutva. We should recognize that the reality of Indian society is caste. This society is riven with caste-based fragmentation, regional fragmentation, linguistic fragmentation. Hindu society is seething with these tensions.

By talking about Hindutva we are skirting the issue of confronting modernity. We are living at a time when the world is being flooded with technologies. We are being flooded with things which we all use shamelessly. We are not like the East Asians, who have tried to meet this technological invasion on their own terms, who have recognized the inevitability of technology, and have gone about wresting control over it, and using it to good purpose. Instead, we are creating this myth of Hindutva, of the great Hindu ethos which has answers for everything, the great Hindu society which will arise again as a homogeneous entity and make India into a great nation. And, we are creating these myths in ways that are going to tear the fabric of this society.

Neelakanthan: I endorse what Professor Vaidyanathan has said. We must all look into the future with all seriousness.

Guhan: Allow me to conclude this discussion. My grandfather and my mother were both great scholars of *Ramayana*. I have read *Kambaramayanam* in my younger days. I know Maryada Purushottama Srirama and his *Ramayana* limb by limb, word by word, verse by verse. It is because of my acquaintance with Srirama that I feel total revulsion for what has happened at Ayodhya. I feel this revulsion not merely as a citizen, not as a non-Hindu, not also as a practising Hindu, but as someone who knows about the ideal of Srirama. I am not a practising Hindu, but I know my *Ramayana* very well. I have read it in Sanskrit. I have had it told to me in Hindi. I have read it in Tamil. I have a right to talk about Maryada Purushottama.

Recently my friend Girish Karnad gave me this verse, and I would like to end the evening by reading this beautiful verse of Basavanna. He says:

The rich will make temples for Siva,
What shall I, a poor man, do?
My legs are pillars, the body the shrine,
the head a cupola of gold.
Listen O Lord of the meeting rivers,
things standing shall fall,
but the moving ever shall stay.[1]

[1] Translation by A. K. Ramanujan: *Speaking of Siva*, Penguin, 1985, p. 88.

11

Corruption in India*

CORRUPTION: DEFINITIONS, CHARACTERISTICS, CAUSES, AND CONSEQUENCES

All those who are likely to read this volume can be assumed to be familiar with the phenomenon of corruption in India from their own personal experience or based on what they have heard and read. However, it is not easy to propose a compact and comprehensive formal definition of corruption. *The Oxford English Dictionary* offers as many as nine meanings of corruption which can be grouped into four main categories. Corruption may apply to an object (physical decomposition, putrefaction, spoiling of quality, adulteration); to the perversion of language or taste; to morals (to destroy moral purity, to debase, to defile); or to public office (to destroy or prevent the integrity or fidelity of a person in his discharge of duty, to induce to act dishonestly or unfaithfully, to make venal; to bribe). The last two aspects are captured in the etymology of the word, based on the Latin verb to break, *rumpere*, which implies that something is broken, such as a moral or social code of conduct or, more narrowly, a law or an administrative rule (Tanzi 1994).

Corruption can straddle both the public and private sectors. However, given our focus on corruption in the public services, it might be useful to start with the narrow definition that corruption is the 'misuse of public power for private gain' (Senturia 1931). Other definitions have been offered citing the misuse of public office, violation of public interest, disapproval of public opinion, and the illegal use of public office for private gain. These and similar

---

* Reprinted from S. Guhan and Samuel Paul (eds), *Corruption in India: Agenda for Action*, New Delhi: Vision Books, 1997, pp. 9–28, 305–8.

definitions have been critiqued on the ground that they tend to be too broad and indeterminate since there could be much debate on what constitutes 'misuse' or 'public power' or 'public interest'. On the other hand, definition, which link corruption narrowly to bribery have been faulted on the ground that they leave out forms of misconduct which can lead to or result from corruption, such as nepotism, patronage, and a variety of white collar offences which may or may not involve direct or immediate financial considerations.[1]

Faced with this dilemma, it might be useful to look for an operational, rather than an abstract, definition. In India, the Prevention of Corruption Act, 1988, which applies to public servants, deals with corruption basically in terms of 'taking gratification other than legal remuneration in respect of an official act'. The word 'gratification' is not restricted to pecuniary gratifications or to gratifications estimable in money. The offence consists of accepting, or agreeing to accept, or obtaining, or attempting to obtain, any such illegal gratification 'as a motive or reward for doing or forbearing to do any official act or showing or forbearing to show, in the exercise of his official functions, favour or disfavour to any person or for rendering or attempting to render any service or disservice to any person' (Section 7). Other offences under the Act include related misconduct, such as taking gratification in order to influence a public servant in the exercise of his official duties, acceptance of gifts by public servants, and possession of wealth disproportionate to known sources of income (Sections 8, 9, 11, and 13). Thus, the various provisions of the Prevention of Corruption Act, 1988 add up to a reasonable working definition of corruption.

Corruption can assume many forms, cover a wide variety of transactions, and operate at many levels. It can relate to acts of commission, omission or delay; involve the exercise of discretion; or the violation of rules, but not necessarily since illegal gratification can be taken even whilst technically conforming to rules.

The *quid pro quo* in corruption could relate to the past, present or future. Bribery can be in the form of cash, kind, services or other favours. At lower bureaucratic levels, it could take the form of 'speed money' to facilitate or expedite the issue of approvals or the delivery of public services or the fulfilment of rightful entitlements. Corruption may involve a voluntary or collusive relationship between the bribe-giver and the bribe-taker or it may be extortionate for

[1] For a discussion of definitions see Theobald, 1990, Ch. 1.

rendering an entitlement, doing an undue favour or desisting from a harmful action.

Corruption can also reside in general policy decisions explicitly or implicitly aimed at benefiting special interest groups for a *quid pro quo* as well as in a wide gamut of specific transactions: public sector contracts for the purchase of goods and services; allocations of scarce materials; permits, licences, exemptions, and waivers; levy and collection of taxes; implementation of projects and programmes; delivery of public services; appointments, postings, transfers and promotions of public servants; different stages of the electoral process; conduct of legislators; and *so on*, for no list of this kind can be exhaustive.

In the public sphere, corruption operates at various levels of the political and bureaucratic hierarchies. It can do so independently among politicians and bureaucrats but, more commonly, there is a nexus between corrupt politicians and bureaucrats who are themselves corrupt or who passively collude with their political masters. In such a relationship of complicity, both gain and each protects the other. There is also a 'vertical integration' between different layers of the political and bureaucratic echelons: for example, minister-legislator-party functionary and minister-higher bureaucracy-middle and lower bureaucracy. The lower levels operate as agents of the higher levels passing up to them shares in the bribes received at the operating level. Alternatively, the corrupt official may make an up-front lumpsum payment 'commuting' recurring payments of a share in the bribes. In such cases, government posts with lucrative potential for money-making are informally auctioned to the highest bidder from time to time. In this process of collusive corruption, appointments, postings and transfers play a prime role providing the bridge between corruption and political interference in administration.[2]

Several characteristics of corruption make it difficult to track its course, expose it and effectively punish the culprits. Corrupt transactions take place in secret. In collusive corruption, the mutual interest between the recipient and the source of bribery make it difficult to unearth the evidence. In extortionate corruption, the victims are intimidated. Above all, corrupt politicians and officials who occupy high positions in government are in a position to suppress evidence or resort to threat or inducement because of their privileged access to government records. Furthermore, legal processes involved in tackling corruption—as is generally the case with the

[2] On the role of transfers, see Wade 1985 and 1989; Zwart 1994.

Indian legal system as a whole—are cumbersome, expensive, and time consuming.

The extensive literature on the subject of corruption draws attention to political systems and practices, economic development, economic policies, sociological characteristics and the cultural milieu as the main factors which are relevant for a causal explanation of corruption.[3] For example, it has been argued that democracies and the costly electoral cycles associated with them are fertile grounds for political corruption. While in office, the political leadership and legislators, dependent on external sources of funding for their re-election campaigns, tend to be influenced by pressure groups. In poor developing countries, there is acute competition for the sharing of benefits. At the same time, inequality and expectations are both high. Such a situation provides an in-built impetus for corruption. Furthermore, economic policies based on administrative regulations—using devices like permits and licences for the allocation of investment approvals, scarce resources, welfare benefits and subsidies—create powerful incentives for bribery.[4] In terms of sociological factors, it has been argued that caste, kinship and patron–client relationships, especially in predominantly rural societies, generate and reproduce corruption through networks of nepotism, patronage and dependency. Cultural factors that have been relied upon to explain corruption include the custom of 'gift-giving' in traditional societies with the expectation of reciprocal rewards, something which tends to spill over into institutionalized administration as well, especially in Africa.[5]

While there may be *prima facie* explanatory rationale in all these factors, none of them can be taken to be definitive or deterministic in explaining corruption in different societies at various times in their histories. Corruption, for instance, has been recorded at very high levels not just in democracies, but also in authoritarian regimes in Latin America, Africa and Asia.[6] Advanced economies, both socialist

[3] On causes of corruption, see Clarke 1983; Heidenheimer 1970; Myrdal 1968; Scott 1972; Theobald 1990.

[4] See in this connection, GOI 1978.

[5] For critical assessments of the sociology of corruption, see Alatas 1980; Mauss 1990; Onoge 1982; Theobald 1990; TI 1996.

[6] For accounts of corruption in the developing countries of Africa, Asia and Latin America, see Andreski 1966, 1968; Carino 1986; Ekpo 1979; Harriss-White and Gordon White 1996; Klitgaard 1983, 1990; Le Vine 1975; Palmier 1985; Williams 1987; Wraith and Simkins 1963.

and market oriented, are also prone to corruption (for example, USA, the former USSR, Japan and countries in Western and Eastern Europe).[7] Even sociological and cultural factors cannot be relied upon to systematically account for differential levels or trends in corruption. Accordingly, the conclusion that emerges on the basis of available empirical evidence is that it would be untenable to characterize democracies, developing countries or traditional societies as immutably condemned to a state of corruption. Within each such category there are less corrupt and more corrupt societies and also those which, over time, have been able to move to a lower level of corruption. In some societies, pervasive corruption has yielded to corruption which is more or less confined to certain sectors or types of activities. All that can be said is that while the various causal factors referred to have a bearing on the incidence of corruption, they cannot be taken—singly or jointly—to adequately account for it always and everywhere.

There is considerable agreement about the adverse effects of corruption on society, polity and the economy. Corruption corrodes the moral fibre of society. It undermines the legitimacy of governments because of the widespread cynicism bred on a mixture of facts and perceptions concerning the level of corruption. It has been pointed out that general impressions about corruption, circulated in public discussion and gossip, might be 'unfair and exaggerated but the very fact that such impressions are there causes damage to the social fabric' (GOI 1964).[8] One result of such deterioration is political instability when one democratic regime after another is outvoted from office on the issue of corruption. More serious is the replacement of democratic governments with authoritarian or military rule. In a number of countries, such governments have come to power on the slogan of providing a clean administration but have themselves become highly corrupt in due course.[9]

The adverse effects of corruption on the economy and on public administration are manifold. Government expenditure is inflated and wasteful projects and programmes are taken up in order to obtain

---

[7] For corruption in developed countries, see Benson 1978; Doig 1984; Gardiner and Olson 1968; Levi and Nelken 1996; Tanzi 1982; Theobald 1990, Ch. 3. For interesting historical accounts, see Hurstfield 1973; MacMullen 1988; Noonan 1984.

[8] On the 'folklore' of corruption see Baxi 1989; Myrdal 1968.

[9] Notable examples are to be found in Brazil, Mexico, Ghana, Nigeria, Pakistan, Bangladesh, and Indonesia.

kickbacks. Standards get diluted in investments (for example, dams, roads, bridges and buildings), goods (for example, drugs), and services (for example, quality of doctors, engineers, teachers) causing hazards to safety, life and health. Government revenues get reduced on account of tax evasion. Subsidies and incentives are abused. The poor are the worst affected since they cannot pay bribes in order to obtain benefits to which they are legitimately entitled. Worse, they are denied basic justice in the hands of corrupt officials, such as the police and village officials. Corruption thus aggravates inequality in an already unequal society.

At the other end of the spectrum, it places a premium on directly unproductive rent-seeking activities on the part of officials and businessmen who seek to profit from, or utilize, opportunities for corruption in regulatory or tax administration.[10] The costs of bribery ultimately get loaded on to the consumer resulting in domestic inflation and non-competitive export prices. The rewarding of corrupt officials and penalization of honest ones undermines morale and efficiency. In course of time, corruption tends to cascade, deepen and spread and thus acquire a self-propelling momentum. It is clear that corruption can gravely undermine the public interest in terms of morality, economic development, equity, and welfare.

While the foregoing is a summary of the mainstream view on corruption, there is also a revisionist standpoint that holds that corruption may be justified or actually be beneficial under certain circumstances. A bribe offered to escape from an unjust law or a repressive act, for instance, may not be morally reprehensible. If economic regulations are dysfunctional, corruption, by evading them, can result in greater efficiency. Speed money can expedite decisions. Corruption may provide an opportunity for disadvantaged or minority groups to obtain benefits from which they might otherwise get excluded. Should the gains from corruption accrue to those who are able to invest them efficiently, the economy can benefit.[11]

A number of reasons can be advanced for not acquiescing in these arguments related to such purported 'benefits' of corruption. The first is the normative position that corruption is morally unacceptable regardless of any instrumental advantages it might bring.

[10] For discussions of rent-seeking, see Bhagwati 1982; Buchanan *et al.* 1980; Krueger 1974; Rose-Ackerman 1978; Tanzi 1994; Tullock 1987.

[11] On this issue, see Leff 1964; Nye 1967; Rose-Ackerman 1978, 1987; Scott 1972; Theobald 1990, Ch. 5; Tullock 1987.

The second is the practical argument that it is not feasible to confine corruption to those areas or activities in which it might be marginally beneficial. And the third, the 'benefits' from corruption are argued on the assumption that corruption provides a safety valve from repressive regimes, over-regulated economies, administrative delays, and discriminatory practices. There is no reason for taking this set of evils for granted. They also need to be tackled as part of the overall reforms for curbing corruption. Altogether, therefore, one should conclude that the costs of corruption are bound to overwhelm the benefits which might be associated with it on a superficial reckoning.

CORRUPTION IN INDIA: CURRENT CONTEXT

In the background of the characteristics, causes and costs of corruption, we could move on to the specificities of corruption in the contemporary Indian context. It would appear that most of the political, economic, sociological, and cultural factors that generally account for corruption operate in India to a greater rather than a lesser degree. India is a low-income developing country in which there is intense competition among both the affluent and the poor for scarce resources in an environment of rising expectations. It is an active democracy in which the high cost of electoral politics has been a major factor in fuelling corruption in the electoral process and, subsequently, governance. In recent decades, there has been a great deal of political instability, as reflected in frequent elections and changes of government, especially in the states, which has accelerated corruption.[12] Divisions based on region, caste and language are the other factors that have promoted corruption, nepotism, and patronage.

India has not been free of corruption, whether in ancient times (at least as far back as the *Arthasastra*), the immediate pre-colonial period, British rule or the decades following Independence. Gandhiji was concerned with corruption in the provincial Congress ministries formed after the 1935 Act. A number of cases of corruption in the states have been documented during the critical decades after Independence when Nehru was Prime Minister; nor were cases of

[12] The frequent and mostly improper use of article 356 of the Constitution to dismiss state governments has exacerbated instability at the state level. Shortlived governments at the Centre (for example, the Chandrashekhar government in 1990–1) and in some of the states (for example, the Mayawati government in Uttar Pradesh in 1995) have been associated with a high degree of corruption.

corruption absent in the Centre itself.[13] It was in response to the concern expressed in Parliament on 'the growing menace of corruption in public administration' that the Government of India set up a Committee of MPs and officials, under the chairmanship of K. Santhanam in the closing years of the Nehru period, to undertake a comprehensive inquiry into the problem (GOI 1964).

Neither the incidence of corruption in India nor the concern with it is, thus, new. However, the current state of corruption in the country is not just a linear continuation of the experience in the fifties and sixties. Beginning with the seventies, changes in the level, trend, nature and spread of corruption in the eighties and nineties have been such as to suggest that corruption has assumed critical proportions. In other words, it might not be an exaggeration today to talk about corruption in terms of a crisis or a cancer endangering India's society, polity and economy.

Consider the following:

1. There has been a distinct increase—in terms of the number and amounts—in transactions in which the presence of corruption has been substantiated. At the Centre, these have included, but have not been confined to, defence contracts (for example, Bofors, HDW submarines), civil contracts (for example, railways), telecommunication contracts, commodity imports (for example, fertilizer and sugar), privatization (for example, Bailadilla mine), housing allotments, the financial sector (for example, the Bank scam) and violations of the Foreign Exchange Regulation and Income Tax Acts (*Hawala* cases).

2. A number of ministers and governors of states have had to resign on account of being legally charged with corrupt transactions.[14] Leading politicians belonging to different political parties have been charged in the *Hawala* proceedings related to violations of the Foreign Exchange Regulation and Income Tax Acts.[15] In more than

[13] For an informative account of post-Independence corruption at the centre and in the states, see Noorani 1973.

[14] During the P. V. Narasimha Rao government at the centre (1991–6), as many as fourteen ministers in the Union Cabinet and three governors of states had to resign on account of their alleged involvement in irregular financial transactions. See Noorani 1996.

[15] Apart from politicians belonging to the then ruling Congress party, those belonging to major opposition parties such as the BJP (L. K. Advani), Janata Dal (Sharad Yadav), INC (T) (Arjun Singh, N. D. Tiwari) were involved in the *Hawala* proceedings.

one instance Prime Ministers have been tainted with suspicion though investigations against them do not seem to have been expeditiously or effectively pursued.[16] In any event, it is not credible that widespread ministerial corruption would have been possible without the acquiescence if not the involvement of the head of the government.

3. India has acquired the unenviable reputation of being among the most corrupt countries in the world. A careful poll taken among business interests and financial journalists by Transparency International (TI), the anti-corruption non-governmental organization of repute, placed India ninth from the bottom in its 1996 list of fifty-four countries. India scored 2.63 on a scale with a maximum of 10 for the totally corrupt-free country.[17]

4. In a number of states, Chief Ministers and ministers have been implicated in major corrupt transactions relating to liquor regulations, real estate approvals, large government contracts, allocation of scarce materials, transfers of public servants and so on. Similarly, on the basis of proven cases, well-substantiated allegations and reliable internal information, it would appear that corruption among ministers in the states is widespread. This again cannot be the case unless it is countenanced by the heads of government in the states (Noorani 1973).[18]

5. At both the Centre and in the states, evidence points to an increase of corruption in the higher bureaucracy. A sizable proportion of higher-level civil servants are believed to be either corrupt on their own and/or to be acting as accomplices, conduits or agents for corrupt ministers. A larger proportion, while keeping themselves clean, have had to be silent witnesses to corruption among ministers and their peers in the civil services. Some of them have been induced or intimidated into going along with financially irregular decisions and corrupt administrative practices. Yet others have eased themselves out by taking early retirement. Many have paid the price for

---

[16] For cases involving Indira Gandhi and Rajiv Gandhi see Singh 1996. P. V. Narasimha Rao has been alleged to be involved in the St. Kitts, *Hawala* and Jharkhand Mukti Morcha (JMM) bribery cases.

[17] 1996 TI Corruption Index released in June 1996 by TI. India's score in the 1995 index was 2.78, higher than in 1996.

[18] An updated version of this valuable book is forthcoming. See also Padhy and Muni 1987.

maintaining integrity by being exiled to posts which are not commensurate with their seniority or experience. Only very few have taken a principled stand in resigning from the civil service in a protest against corruption. Correspondingly, the transfer of civil servants in many states has been aimed at positioning pliable officials in posts with a high potential for corruption, moving out honest officials to innocuous posts and frequently transferring those who have refused to oblige their political masters in corrupt transactions. The result of all this has been immense damage to morale, motivation and efficiency in the public services.

6. Concerning the lower levels of the bureaucracy, corruption mostly takes the form of speed money for expediting approvals and the demand for bribes for providing (or not withholding) legitimate services (for example, in utilities such as telephones, electricity boards and civic services) (Paul 1995). Corruption is also rampant in the administration of welfare schemes, the public distribution system, the police, revenue, and irrigation departments and several other sectors in which the people come into daily contact with the administration. The higher bureaucracy seems to be unwilling or unable to tackle corruption at its subordinate levels.

7. Of grave concern is the interlocking or 'vertical integration' of corruption at various levels of the governmental hierarchy—elected politicians, higher bureaucracy and lower bureaucracy. The normal assumption is that the 'principals' at each of the higher levels would be committed to ensure that their 'agents' at respective lower levels would act according to standards and norms of probity.[19] In a situation in which the principals and agents collude with each other in corruption, the problem of tackling it becomes much more intractable.

8. In the public domain, corruption is not confined to the executive government. It has spread to legislatures, the judiciary, media and the independent professions (such as lawyers, doctors, chartered accountants and contractors)[20] Through mutual interaction, such a horizontal spread of corruption has entrenched it further in

[19] For a lucid discussion of corruption in the principal-agent framework, see Klitgaard 1988, Ch. 3. For theoretical contributions, Banfield 1979; Montias and Rose-Ackerman 1981; Rose-Ackerman 1978.

[20] Numerous cases of the 'buying' and 'selling' of legislators have been reported, the JMM bribery case in Parliament being a glaring recent example.

government and made its prevention and control much more difficult.

9. Mechanisms to prevent, monitor, and punish corruption are not adequate nor have they proved to be effective to the extent that they exist. At the national level, India still does not have an Ombudsman-type, Lok Pal legislation and machinery to deal with corruption among ministers and the higher bureaucracy. In general, governments at the Centre and in the states have been tardy, at best, and insincere, at worst, in investigating and pursuing corruption. Commissions of Inquiry established for the purpose over the years have not been able to effectively prove or punish corruption. Corruption has been politicized—just as politics has been corrupted—in the sense that cases of corruption have been used for partisan political purposes rather than with any serious intent to objectively tackle the problem. As is to be expected, opposition parties in Parliament and state legislatures have played a role in agitating issues relating to corruption but, by and large, their efforts have not been effective.[21] Judicial processes under normal anti-corruption laws are dilatory although in recent times the Supreme Court, in response to public interest litigation, has intervened to enforce the law.[22] Investigative journalism has helped to expose corruption but, given its nature, media coverage has been episodic rather than sustained. A number of activist groups have taken up local issues of corruption.[23] However, their contributions have varied widely over different parts of the country and have not assumed the critical mass required to generate a popular movement against corruption.

THE RESPONSE TO CORRUPTION

Despite the fact that corruption is pervasive and has gone largely unchecked and, indeed, perhaps because of it, there is now a strong

---

[21] This is borne out by the experience with the Joint Parliamentary Committees on the Bofors contract and the Bank scandal.

[22] The Antulay case, for instance, lasted for nearly seven years. In his study of it, Upendra Baxi (1989) comments: 'The temporality of the adjudication is inherently and irredeemably circular; the case against Antulay moves round and round in various forums with vertiginous speed and pace in a way which makes the calendar time virtually meaningless'.

[23] For an impressive example, see Bunker Roy 1996.

demand by the public for effective punitive and corrective measures to tackle the problem. That corruption is a national concern in the consciousness of the people has been demonstrated by the fact that it was the most important issue in the general elections to Parliament in 1989, 1996 and in several elections to state legislatures.[24] Essentially, the challenge that concerned citizens face is to translate the widespread public sentiment against corruption into effective public action.

What needs to be taken into account at the outset is that the very scale and spread of corruption has generated helplessness, at best, and apathy, at worst. These, in turn, tend to be rationalized in terms of cynicism or in arguments that tend to acquiesce in corruption. The first task is to generate the confidence that India is not doomed to live with corruption forever and that in India—as has happened in many other countries—it is possible to mobilize public pressure for reforms aimed at containing and rolling it back. As corruption intensifies and spreads its tentacles, it tends to reproduce and perpetuate itself on an increasing scale. No time should, therefore, be lost in undertaking all possible efforts to put a brake on the process. At the same time, there is a need for the sober recognition that it would not be feasible to eliminate corruption altogether. Tackling corruption is not achieved in one stroke but through a continuous and cumulative endeavour. In addition, it carries its own costs. All that can be aimed at is to progressively move toward a state of affairs in which corruption is the exception rather than the rule.

It is possible and legitimate to approach the problem of tackling corruption from different angles. Generally speaking, four approaches can be distinguished. One consists of fundamental changes in the Constitution which would, like a Presidential system, insulate executive authority from legislatures and include appropriate checks and balances against the abuse of political power.[25] The second would emphasize thorough deregulation and privatization of governmental activities so as to reduce the role of the state as much as possible along with reforms aimed at enhancing efficiency. The third would argue

[24] A nationwide poll conducted by *Times of India* in April 1996 prior to the general elections to Parliament indicated that corruption was considered to be the single most important failure of the government with 33 per cent of the respondents citing it. In Tamilnadu, the incumbent Jayalalitha (AIADMK) government suffered a massive defeat on account of its corrupt record.

[25] For a cogent articulation of this thesis, see '*The Roots of Corruption*' and '*A Proposal for Constitutional Reform*' in Nehru 1986.

for an extensive decentralization of governance so as to promote accountability and transparency at local levels in order to check corruption. The fourth would rely on an increased development of moral values among the people at large beginning with youth and focused on politicians and officials in particular.

Each of these approaches is doubtless germane to be problem of tackling corruption; they are necessary but not sufficient. They cannot be relied upon singly for each has its limitations. There can be much debate about the pros and cons of fundamental constitutional changes and, in any event, they would not appear to be readily feasible. Nor can there be the assurance that the replacement of parliamentary democracy with an executive government, notwithstanding the checks and balances that might be introduced, will not prove to be a remedy worse than the disease. Similarly, deregulation and decentralization, for which there is already a wide consensus, cannot be a panacea. The state cannot be wished away, nor can it be expected to wither away. Corruption can continue under different forms in a largely privatized economy,[26] likewise, it can itself get decentralized, persisting in less visible ways under local authorities. The upgrading of moral values is of fundamental importance but a moral revolution cannot be expedited on the basis of rhetorical appeals that urge its necessity. It can be promoted and sustained only around a series of concrete incremental measures which demonstrate that reform is possible and can cumulate. This is the surest way to strengthen and channel the moral impetus for a more honest polity.

NEED FOR PUBLIC ACTION

No set of proposals, however well conceived, will themselves be able to bring about the necessary changes. They can only provide a basis for action. They will remain a dead letter unless public action is forthcoming at several levels for winning acceptance for the proposed reforms.

A very encouraging development is that the major Indian political parties—Bharatiya Janata Party, Indian National Congress, Janata Dal, Communist Party of India (Marxist) and the Communist Party of India—included a number of proposals for tackling corruption in their manifestos for the 1996 general elections to Parliament. Undoubtedly, this came about in response to the strong revulsion

---

[26] See Harriss-White and Gordon White 1996.

against corruption on the part of the electorate. The extracts reproduced in the Annexure from the party manifestos on (a) the Lok Pal, (b) electoral reforms relating to probity of legislators and political parties, and (c) other aspects, such as vigilance machinery, accountability, transparency, and preventing abuse of political power would indicate that there is a great deal of convergence as well as a high degree of specificity in the electoral promises relating to the control of corruption. This opens up an excellent opportunity for public action in the form of a sustained and orchestrated campaign against corruption based on a concrete but evolving agenda. Such a campaign will have to be pursued by a wide alliance against corruption forged among politicians, administrators, legislators, jurists, academics, journalists, industrialists and other sections of the concerned public. Meanwhile, citizen groups should be encouraged to tackle corruption at local levels on specific issues. Citizens should be made to feel that, as taxpayers and consumers of public services, they can demand administrative accountability as a matter of right and entitlement.

ANNEX

Extracts from the 1996 Election Manifestos of National Parties Relating to Controlling Corruption

Lok Pal

BJP: Appoint a Lok Pal to entertain complaints of corruption against anybody holding public office, including the Prime Minister.

INC(I): Establish Lok Pal with jurisdiction over all political offices, including that of the Prime Minister and Chief Ministers.

JD: Lok Pal Bill will be adopted to enquire into complaints of corruption against Union Minister, including Chief Minister and Prime Minister and others holding high public office. Multi-member Lok Pal will be appointed by the President in consultation with the Chief Justice of India, Speaker of the Lok Sabha and Chairman of the Rajya Sabha, and leaders of government and the opposition in the two Houses of Parliament.

CPI(M): The immediate setting up of Lok Pal, bringing in its purview the Prime Minister; to be appointed by an authority consisting of the executive, legislature and judiciary.

CPI: Lok Pal Bill, which includes within its scope legislators and also the Prime Minister, should be adopted. Lok Pal institutions should be set up at the Centre and in the states to investigate charges against ministers and bureaucrats.

Electoral Reforms Relating to Probity of Legislators and Political Parties

BJP: Update and adopt the Goswami Committee report. Make it obligatory on every elected representative to make public his entire income and wealth within ninety days of election. Amend the anti-defection law whereby a member of any legislature who changes parties will lose his or her membership of the House. Grant statutory status to the code of conduct drawn up by the Election Commission and give it teeth. Take steps to curb expenditure on elections by imposing a ban on advertisements, cut-outs, etc. Introduce electronic voting machines. Introduce a scheme of state funding of candidates to all legislatures. Provide suitable incentives for open, official corporate funding to all recognized political parties. Make it mandatory for political parties to submit audited accounts for public scrutiny annually.

INC(I): All members of Parliament, legislatures and local bodies to declare their assets when assuming office and leaving office.

JD: Legislative initiatives will be taken to organize wide-ranging reforms based on Dinesh Goswami Committee Report. Statutory provision will be made so that all those holding public offices and offices of political parties declare their assets annually, which shall be scrutinized by an independent commission. Janata Dal favours state funding of elections and legitimate activity of recognized political parties. Public auditing of the accounts of political parties will be made a statutory requirement.

CPI(M): Comprehensive electoral reforms to ensure the elimination of money and muscle power from elections on the basis of the Dinesh Goswami Report. Amend Section 77 of the Representation of People Act to plug loopholes in enforcing ceiling on election expenditure of candidates. Strict action against all manifestations of the criminalization of politics.

CPI: The Representation of the People Act should be amended to (i) curb money and muscle power, (ii) ensure state funding specially in the form of necessary election material. Persons with known criminal records should not be put up nor allowed to contest as candidates in elections.

Vigilance Machinery, Accountability, Transparency, and Preventing Abuse of Political Power

BJP: The BJP will address itself to this challenge and task (of curbing corruption) by adopting measures that are mentioned hereunder.

We do not claim that this is either the ultimate blueprint for the reduction of corruption or the last word on it. It is an expression of our commitment; a first step to setting right a very great wrong of many years' malignancy; a beginning and that, too, with ourselves. A government that intrudes the least, we hold, governs the best. We will endeavour to combine this with open and transparent governance. Introduce extensive regulations and requirements upon those who hold public office so that no conflict of interest is ever permitted to influence a proper discharge of their duties. Take measures to modify and reform the methodology of government approval for contracts, schemes and large money value agreements so as to make them more transparent. The powers of patronage, the right to say 'Yes' or 'No' to simple daily requirements of the citizens will be reduced drastically. Expeditiously deal with cases of corruption unresolved and in which no action has been taken in the past ten years.

INC(I): Appoint a high-powered commission consisting of eminent jurists, parliamentarians and administrators to recommend legal, administrative, and enforcement measures to control and contain corruption and implement these measures within six months.

Reduce the amount of discretion obtaining in administrative decision-making, including at minister's level, so as to render them public, transparent and accountable.

Review the work of the enforcement agencies at the Centre and in the states with a view to accord adequate autonomy and insulation from interferences in discharging their duties.

Strengthening of internal vigilance and anti-corruption mechanisms for preventive and punitive vigilance in all government, quasi-government and public agencies/organizations.

Involvement of the public in vigilance and control of corruption through public hearings, access to information and promotion of voluntary organizations in this area.

JD: Honest civil servants at all levels will be protected from harassment and high-handedness.

Rules of business governing administrative work will be reviewed and role of people's representatives at all levels will be strengthened in relation to administrative processes.

Official Secrets Act will be drastically revised. Right of Information will be included in the list of Fundamental Rights of the Constitution.

Transparency will be introduced in all business dealings of government with foreigners and Indians, including contracts of sale and purchase and granting of credit by public financial institutions.

The CBI will be freed from the control of the Department of Personnel and made autonomous. For investigation of white-collar offences, a separate autonomous organization on the lines of the CBI will be set up.

CPI(M): Streamline functioning of investigating agencies; protect them from political interference; ensure speedy disposal and appropriate action.

CPI: Transfers and postings which are a fertile source of corruption should be done by a committee of senior officials.

Citizens' committees composed of personalities of well-known integrity to be set up at different levels for rousing public opinion and with right to initiate proceedings before Lok Pal institutions.

There should be more transparency in government, in all deals of contract and supply.

The Right to Information must be established so as to make administration more accountable to the people and their elected bodies.

REFERENCES

Alatas, S. H. (1980), *The Sociology of Corruption: The Nature, Functions, Causes, and Prevention of Corruption*, Singapore: Times Books.

Andreski, S. (1966), *Parasitism and Subversion: The Case of Latin America*, London: Weidenfeld and Nicolson.

——— (1968), *The African Predicament*, New York: Atherton Press.

Banfield, E. C. (1979), 'Corruption as a Feature of Government' in Ekpo.

Baxi, Upendra (1989), *Liberty and Corruption, The Antulay Case and Beyond*, Lucknow: Eastern Book Company.

Benson, G. C. S. (1978), *Political Corruption in America*, Lexington: D. C. Heath and Co.

Bhagwati, Jagdish N. (1982), 'Directly Unproductive, Profit-Seeking (DUP) Activities', *Journal of Political Economy*; 90.

Buchanan, J., R. Tollison and G. Tullock (eds), (1980), *Toward a Theory of the Rent-Seeking Society*, Texas: Texas A and M University Press.

Carino (ed.), (1986), *Bureaucratic Corruption in Asia: Causes, Consequences and Controls*, Quezon City: JMC Press.

Clarke, M. (ed.), (1983), *Corruption: Causes, Consequences and Control*, New York: St. Martins Press.

Doig, A. (1984), *Corruption and Misconduct in Contemporary British Politics*, Hammondsworth: Penguin Books.

Ekpo, Monday U. (ed.) (1979), *Bureaucratic Corruption in Sub-Saharan Africa: Toward a Search for Causes and Consequences*, Washington, DC: University Press of America.

Gardiner, J. A. and D. J. Olson (eds), (1968), *Theft of the City: Readings on Corruption in America*, Bloomington: Indiana University Press.

GOI (Government of India), Ministry of Home Affairs (1964), *Report of the Committee on the Prevention of Corruption (Santhanam Committee)*, New Delhi.

GOI (Government of India), Ministry of Finance (1978), *Report of the Committee on Controls and Subsidies*, New Delhi.

GOI (Government of India), Ministry of Law (1988), *Prevention of Corruption Act, 1988*, New Delhi.

Harriss-White, B. and Gordon White (1996), *Liberalization and Corruption*, Institute of Development Studies Bulletin, 27 (2), Sussex.

Heidenheimer, A. J. (ed.), (1970), *Political Corruption: Readings in Comparative Analysis*, New York: Holt, Rinehart and Wilson.

Hurstfield, Joel (1973), *Freedom, Corruption and Government in Elizabethan England*, Cambridge: Harvard University Press.

Klitgaard, Robert (1983), *Corruption in Mexico*, Cambridge: Harvard University Press.

———— (1988), *Controlling Corruption*, Berkeley: University of California Press.

———— (1990), *Tropical Gangsters*, New York: Basic Books.

Krueger, A. O. (1974), 'The Political Economy of the Rent-seeking Society', *American Economic Review*, 64 (3).

Leff, Nathaniel H. (1964), 'Economic Development through Bureaucratic Corruption', *American Behavioural Scientist*, 8.

Levi, Michael and David Nelken (ed.), (1996), *The Corruption of Politics and the Politics of Corruption, Journal of Law and Society*, (Special Issue), March, Oxford: Blackwell.

Le Vine, V. T. (1975), *Political Corruption: The Ghana Case*, Stanford: Hoover Institution Press.

MacMullen, Ramsay (1988), *Corruption and the Decline of Rome*, New Haven: Yale University Press.

Mauss, Marcel (1990), *The Form and Reason for Exchange in Archaic Societies*, London: Routledge.

Montias, J. M. and Susan Rose-Ackerman (1981), 'Corruption in a Soviet-type Economy: Theoretical Considerations', in Steven Rosefielde (ed.), *Economic Welfare and the Economics of Soviet Socialism: Essays in Honour of Abram Bergson*, Cambridge: Cambridge University Press.

Myrdal, Gunnar (1968), 'Corruption: Its Causes and Effects', *Asian Drama: An Inquiry into the Poverty of Nations*, vol. II, Hammondsworth: Penguin.

Nehru, B. K. (1986), *Thoughts on Our Present Discontents*, New Delhi: Allied Publishers.

Noonan, J. (1984), *Bribes*, New York: Macmillan.

Noorani, A. G. (1973), *Ministers' Misdeeds*, Delhi: Vikas Publishers.

———— (1996), 'Rao & Scam', I, II and III, *The Statesman*, New Delhi, 10, 11 and 12, March.

Nye, Joseph S. (1967), 'Corruption and Political Development: A Cost-Benefit Analysis', *American Political Science Review*, 61.

Onoge, O. F. (1982), 'Corruption in Development', Zaria, Nigeria: Ahmada Bello University.
Padhy, K. S. and P. K. Muni (1987), *Corruption in Indian Politics: A Case Study of an Indian State*, Delhi: Discovery Publishing House.
Palmier, Leslie H. (1985), *The Control of Bureaucratic Corruption*, New Delhi: Allied Publishers.
Paul, Samuel (1995), *A Report Card on Public Services in Indian Cities: A View from Below*, Bangalore: Public Affairs Centre.
Rose-Ackerman, Susan (1978), *Corruption: A Study in Political Economy*, New York: Academic Press.
―――― (1987), 'Bribery', in John Eatwell, Murray Millgate and Peter Newman (eds), *The New Palgrave, The World of Economics*, London: Macmillan.
Roy, Bunker (1996), 'Right to Information: Profile of a Grass Roots Struggle', *Economic and Political Weekly*, 11 May.
Scott, James C. (1972), *Comparative Political Corruption*, Englewood Cliffs, NJ: Prentice-Hall.
Senturia, J. J. (1931), 'Corruption, Political'. *Encyclopaedia of the Social Sciences*, vol. IV.
Singh, N. K. (1996), *The Plain Truth*, Delhi: Konark Publishers.
Tanzi, Vito (ed.) (1982), *The Underground Economy in the United States and Abroad*, Lexington: D. C. Heath and Company.
―――― (1994), *Corruption, Governmental Activities and Markets*, Washington DC: International Monetary Fund.
Theobald, Robin (1990), *Corruption, Development and Underdevelopment*, Durham, North Carolina: Duke University Press.
TI (Transparency International) (1996), *National Integrity Systems: The TI Source Book*, Berlin: Transparency International.
Tullock, Gordon (1987), 'Rent Seeking', in John Eatwell, Murray Millgate and Peter Newman (eds), *The New Palgrave, The World of Economics*, London: Macmillan.
Wade, Robert (1985), 'The Market for Public Office: Why the Indian State is not Better at Development', *World Development*, 13 (4).
―――― (1989), 'Politics and Graft: Recruitment, Appointment, and Promotion to Public Office in India' in Peter M. Ward, *Corruption, Development and Inequality, Soft Touch or Hard Craft?* London: Routledge.
Williams, R. (1987), *Political Corruption in Africa*, Aldershot: Gower.
Wraith, R. and E. Simkins (1963), *Corruption in Developing Countries*, London: George Allen and Unwin.
de Zwart, Frank (1994), *The Bureaucratic Merry-go-round, Manipulating the Transfer of Indian Civil Servants*, Amsterdam: University Press.

12

Thinking about Governance*

Issues relating to politics, the state and government have attracted some of the best minds, over space and time, throughout history. Separated by centuries and continents, Aristotle, Confucius, and Kautilya have theorized on them. Ancient Indian epics, like the *Mahabharata* and the *Ramayana*, while describing a variety of actual kingdoms, have thrown light on the relationship between society and polity on which they rested.[1] The modern western tradition has witnessed an unbroken continuity of outstanding political philosophers from Thomas Hobbes in the sixteenth century to John Rawls in the twentieth.

The term 'governance' is, however, a new-fangled one.[2] Nevertheless, it does not lack a basis in the current objective situation. In the

---

* This is a revised and self-contained version of (principally) the second section of a paper titled 'Three Pieces on Governance' presented at the Workshop on Governance Issues in South Asia held at the Economic Growth Center, Yale University, on 19 November 1997, and submitted to the Working Papers series of the Harvard Center for Population and Development Studies.

[1] Of particular interest is the account of Ramrajya or the rule of Rama (Adigalar 1994). According to Kambar, the author of the epic's Tamil version, Rama was not just a constitutional monarch but a thoroughly democratic one; the people were the 'breath' of the body politic while the ruler represented only its organs and limbs; Rama was the 'loyal' king of his 'royal' citizens. The society on which such a polity was based was one where virtues and excellences were conspicuous by their absence: there was no charity because no one was poor; no role for power because of the absence of conflict; no notion of truth because falsehood was unknown; and with enquiring minds all around, no primacy for knowledge. More generally, on theories of government in ancient India, see Altekar 1997 and Coomaraswamy 1993.

[2] There is, for instance, no entry on 'governance' in *The Encyclopedia of Social Sciences* or in *The Oxford Companion to Politics of The World, 1993*.

eighties, a number of factors—worldwide—have drawn sharp attention to various aspects of governance: replacement of authoritarian governments in the Soviet Union and Eastern Europe, their collapse altogether in parts of Africa on account of external or civil conflicts, the proliferation of ethnic strife, the movements for democracy and human rights in China and South East Asia and for competitive democracy in Latin America and Africa.[3] Concurrently, other issues, more specifically related to the economic aspects of governance, have come to the fore: the superior performance of pro-market economies in contrast to command systems, widespread inefficiencies in state-owned enterprises, fiscal crises provoked by unsustainable levels of public expenditure, and endemic corruption in low-income developing countries which can ill afford to countenance it. These streams have converged to form a triad of issues with governance at the apex. On the one hand, they relate governance to pluralist democracy (i.e. the values and form of political governance) and, on the other, to pro-market approaches to economic development (or the objectives and content of economic governance).

It is also the case that, in the current context, the World Bank has been the principal protagonist in the debate on governance with its initiative being paralleled or followed by other multilateral financing institutions (IMF, the African, Inter-American and European Development Banks), OECD, and bilateral donor agencies (for example, ODA in the UK).[4] Given its role and functions as the leading international development finance institution, it is not unnatural that the Bank's concern should be directed to those aspects of governance that relate to economic policy and management in developing countries. These are, no doubt, important. In particular, the emphasis on controlling corruption as a central issue in good governance is to be unreservedly welcomed. On the other hand, the overall substantive content of the Bank's notions of governance is open to serious questioning. Most important, it is necessary to be alert that the

[3] Besides, external conflict and/or extended civil strife have resulted in 'humanitarian crises' in recent years in a number of countries: Afghanistan, Cambodia, Mozambique, Rwanda, Somalia, Sudan, Zaire. In 1995 alone, thirty-two ethnic wars or conflicts were reported in as many countries; see Bardhan 1997a.

[4] For a review of definitions of governance adopted by various agencies, see Box 1 in World Bank 1994. At their last joint meeting (Hong Kong, September 1997), IBRD and IMF issued formal statements on governance.

essentially political concept of governance is not diluted or distorted by the narrow techno-economic, ideological connotation given to it in the Bank's official documents.[5] I have discussed these issues elsewhere in some detail (Guhan 1997). As a sequel, this paper attempts to explore wider and deeper aspects of governance relevant to any comprehensive understanding of the concept. It concludes with some thoughts on the possible application of the principles of good governance to actual conditions in developing countries.

THEORIES OF THE STATE

The astonishing aspect of the current debate on governance—as promoted by the World Bank—is that it proceeds independently of a political theory of the state, being content, as it were, to define the state in relation to the market, as the residual of the latter in social organization. In the background of its frustrations with implementation problems during the eighties in a number of African countries—involving project loans and, more particularly, adjustment lending—the World Bank first raised the issues of governance, rather laconically, as 'the exercise of political power to manage a nation's affairs' (World Bank 1989). Clearly, this debut of the Bank into the discourse on governance does not take us far since its definition is not only neutral between forms of government of fundamental importance to the nature of governance (namely, democratic or authoritarian) but even between 'good' and 'bad' governance since both would, in their own ways, qualify as the exercise of political power to manage a nation's affairs. The World Bank has itself, therefore, been compelled, in course of time, to elaborate on its definition. On the latest occasion, this has been done in its *World Development Report 1997* (*WDR*) on 'The State in a Changing World', while other and earlier pronouncements, in its official documents and by its authoritative spokesmen, are also germane for understanding what the World Bank wishes to convey through its notions of governance.

First, it is clear that essentially the World Bank is not concerned with the *form* of government. The political components in its concept of governance—such as participation, transparency, accountability, human rights and so on—feature in its literature as 'tag-ons' which are desirable in so far as they could contribute to economic efficiency but not strictly necessary as integral components of the notion.

[5] See World Bank 1997, 1994, 1991 and 1989.

Liberal democracy, in this view, could be of instrumental value but need not be of foundational or intrinsic importance.

The second issue relevant to the topic for forms of government is the relationship between democracy and development: is an initial measure of development necessary for the establishment of democracy? Does democracy promote or inhibit economic development or is it neutral in its effect? In recent years, an extensive literature has been generated on these issues.

One important finding which emerges from this literature is that, apart from democracy being an intrinsic value, it could have a mutually reinforcing interaction with human development; it has not proved to be an obstacle to growth, fair income distribution, or prudent fiscal management; nor have authoritarian governments necessarily scored better on any of these counts. Besides, an important fact of history should be taken into account, namely, that while authoritarian regimes have coexisted with market economies, democracy has not been able to go along with command systems—which suggests that sustaining democracy could be a good way to ensure the stability of market economies as well.[6] Coming back to the World Bank, the criticism of it is not that it has been in disfavour of democracy—but that on such central issues as the constitutive form of governance, it has not chosen, in clear and ringing tones, to take a stand against authoritarian regimes and squarely in favour of democratic ones. While the World Bank's support for an open economy has been loud and long, its endorsement of an open polity has been muted at best and ambiguous at worst.[7] It is, therefore, the conception of the state and politics, conspicuous by its absence in the current Bank discourse on governance, that must be our initial concern.

---

[6] Clarke Lindblom (1997) points out (p. 5) that 'Liberal democracy has arisen only in nations that are market-oriented, not in all of them but only in them. The tie between market and democracy is on many counts an astonishing historical fact'.

[7] Deepak Lal (1994) attempts to provide what might be called a meta-instrumental justification for the World Bank's instrumental approach to democracy by arguing: 'To avoid drowning in the "treacherous waters" of slippery concepts like "participation" and "democracy", it may be best for the World Bank to concentrate not on the forms of government but the *characteristics* of good government—on policies. As the World Bank is charged with advising on the latter and, forbidden to deal with the former, it should find this congenial.'

The necessity for the state arises in the Hobbesian version because it is intolerable to contemplate its alternative: 'the state of nature' characterized by the war of all against all resulting in continual fear and danger of violent death. The nightmarish conditions under which it is given makes the consent to the Hobbesian state unconditional, rendering it an absolutist one. For Locke as well, the state was necessary in order to avoid the natural anarchy that would otherwise prevail but it had to be based on consent, not fear and contingent on safeguarding the primary rights of 'life, liberty, and estate'.

The earlier and Christian view, shared by both St Augustine and Martin Luther, was that the state was not (necessarily) a necessary evil but a duality of evil and good. While being a consequence of the sinfulness of human nature, it was also a divine institution which God had created to enable men to live in peace. Temporal authority was a 'divine ordinance' and rulers were God's 'agents and instruments' (Cargill Thompson 1969).

Ancient Indian (Vedic) theories of government were based on the legitimation of temporal power (the *regnum*) through the ritualistic seal of approval of the spiritual authority (the sacerdotium) (Coomaraswamy 1993). The two were to be 'married' like the earth to the sky', the king being the bridegroom and the priest performing the ceremony. One of its important sociological consequences was the forging of a 'natural alliance' between the two upper castes—the priestly brahmin and the ruling kshatriya.

In the illustrations we have cited, the state is a secular institution (with its authority being absolute or qualified), or it is a combination of secular and sacred elements, or it is based on the sacralization of the secular. There are, of course, other versions of the origins of the state or of 'state formation'. Related to them, or independently, there are theories of the political economy and sociology of the state (absolutist, constitutional, bourgeois, Marxist, developmental, predatory, etc.).[8] Also available are descriptive analyses of individual states during specific historical periods and normative accounts of what the state ought to be.

THE ARISTOTELIAN PARADIGM

It is, however, to Aristotle that one must turn for a vision of the state that is both entirely secular and a necessary good, rather than an

[8] For a useful survey, see Vincent 1987.

inescapable evil, or a mixed blessing, or one entailing transcendental involvement.[9] In his view, the *polis* existed by nature and did not have to be invented through fear, consent, contract, or divine dispensation. Its role was to enable the individual to achieve the full potential of his or her own good, which was not possible except in the context of the state. In this reflexive relationship between the state and the individual, the aim of political organization was to promote the good life of the citizen; while, at the same time, the good of the state was itself defined via that of the individual. In other words, the state was 'well organized' when it was so organized as to fulfil its aim, namely, the promotion of the good life of the individual.

Entirely consistent with this concept are Aristotle's notions of politics as the 'master skill' and of man as a 'political animal'.[10] Politics both serves and subsumes the skills required for creating wealth and the pursuit of practical wisdom at the level of the individual. Neither are ends in themselves but only means to the good of the polity without which again it is not possible to pursue either. This also is the reason why man is a political animal for the exercise of practical wisdom (*phronesis*)—the highest human virtue—which is possible to its fullest degree only in the context of life in the *polis* and not otherwise. A person who is incapable of participating in the *polis* is a mere animal while one who feels no need for the *polis*, being so self-sufficient as to be above it, qualifies to be a god. Between the two, to be human entails being a 'political animal', the nature of such an animal being defined through participation in the *polis*.

At its core, the Aristotelian paradigm has three essential aspects.[11] First, as between the two constituents in the relationship of governance, it is not—unlike other and modern theories—divisive in

[9] I have relied on Sinclair and Sanders (1981) and Everson (1988) for translations of Aristotle, *The Politics*. For the paraphrase of his conceptions, I have drawn heavily (and in places literally) from the excellent articles by D. S. Hutchinson on 'Ethics' and by C. C. W. Taylor on 'Politics' in Barnes 1995.

[10] In the *Eudemian Ethics*, Aristotle referred to the combination of 'politics', 'economics', and 'wisdom' as the 'master skill'. He changed his mind in the *Nicomachean Ethics* and chose to regard only political wisdom as the master skill consistent with the treatment in his *Politics*.

[11] 'Aristotelian paradigm' is used as a convenient shorthand. It has been abstracted from its context of the city-state. It does not claim to represent a full account of Aristotle's ideas on the subject, nor is there an implication that it represents notions that entirely originated from, or were confined to, Aristotle.

juxtaposing the individual against the state (or vice versa) but integrative in viewing governance as a process that continually takes place in the inclusive, interactive, mutually reinforcing social space between the two. Secondly, it is founded on the primacy of politics over the atomistic pursuit of wisdom at the level of the individual as also over truncated forms of social interaction as in the market economy. Thirdly, the Aristotelian model is that of a genuinely pluralistic state. In Aristotle's words: 'Is it not obvious that a state may at length attain such a degree of unity as to be no longer a state? Since the nature of the state is to be a plurality, and in tending to greater unity, from being a state, it becomes a family, and from being a family, an individual. So that we ought not to attain this greatest unity even if we could, for it could be the destruction of the state.'[12]

In sum, the great appeal of the paradigm lies in that it holds together—morally and conceptually—the state, the good society, participatory politics, and the free and fullest development of the individual: in this sense, it is truly 'comprehensive'.[13] Accordingly, it is not surprising that the spirit and substance of such an ethos of governance should have inspired a whole range of thinkers down to present times. Without attempting to trace its lineage—which space and, much more so, my limited erudition will not permit—I shall refer to four philosophers, with different perspectives, but all belonging to the moral-political and political-economy traditions whose writings could be readily seen as resonating with the Aristotelian conception.

For John Stuart Mill (1806–73), belonging to the utilitarian tradition, 'the principal element of the idea of good government is the improvement of the people themselves... A government is to be judged by its action upon men, and by its action upon what it makes of the citizens, and with them; its tendency to improve or deteriorate the people themselves; and the goodness or badness of the work it performs for them, and by means of them' (Mill 1910: 210).

[12] Aristotle, *The Politics*, Book II (ii), Everson (1988: 21). According to Aristotle, the 'self-sufficiency' of the state was based on 'reciprocal equivalence' (or the mutually supporting diversity of functions), the management of which required that the state be a plurality: 'Since, then, a greater degree of self-sufficiency is to be preferred to a lesser, the lesser degree of unity is to be preferred to the greater' (Sinclair and Sanders 1981: 104–6).

[13] Etymologically, 'comprehend' is 'hold together'.

T. H. Green (1836–82), who had a remarkable influence on a whole generation of ethical socialists in Britain, approached the issues of state and society from the standpoint of evangelical humanitarianism. To him, individual freedom and fulfilment were attainable only through society. And by 'society', he meant not only the state but also:

[T]he other forms of community which precede and are independent of the formation of the state, do not continue to exist outside it, nor yet are they superseded by it. They are carried on into it. They become its organic members, supporting its life and in turn maintained by it in a new harmony with each other (T. H. Green, 1931: 146, quoted in Thompson 1969: 198).

The Marxist intellectual Antonio Gramsci (1891–1937) asked:

Is it the intention that there should always be rulers and ruled, or is the objective to cerate the conditions in which this division is no longer necessary? In other words, is the initial premise the perpetual division of the human race, or the belief that the division is only an historical fact, corresponding to certain conditions? (Gramsci 1996: 144).

Gramsci's view of the state alternated between an amalgam of political society and civil society, a balance between the two, and an identity of the two but 'his constant preoccupation was to avoid any undialectical separation of 'the ethical–political aspect of politics or theory of hegemony and consent' from 'the aspect of force and economics' (Gramsci: 1996: 207, Editors' introduction to section on 'State and Civil Society').

Among twentieth-century contemporaries, Amartya Sen, economist and philosopher, introduces his lectures *On Ethics and Economics* by pointing out that in economics, 'the ethics related tradition goes back at least to Aristotle. At the very beginning of *The Nicomachean Ethics*, Aristotle relates the subject of economics to human ends. Economics relates ultimately to the study of ethics and that of politics, and this point of view is further developed in Aristotle's *Politics*.' He proceeds to explain that 'while Aristotle discusses the role of the state in economic matters, it is also firmly kept in view that "the end of the state" is the "common promotion of good quality life"', (Sen 1987).

Our last example, John Rawls, the most outstanding moral-political philosopher of our times, is a source on which we shall heavily rely at a subsequent stage for explicating the Aristotelian conception.

Altogether, given its intrinsic appeal and historical hold, it is not possible to stop short—or for that matter proceed much beyond—the Aristotelian paradigm in any search for the most enlightened form of 'governance'. Having arrived at it, it is important, however, not to read too little or too much into it: the model is much more than a mere Utopian fantasy but much less than a blueprint for good governance in any detail. More importantly, it should not be read wrongly either. It would be erroneous to think that what it implies is a subrogation of the economy and society to politics. While, no doubt, for Aristotle, politics has primacy as the 'master skill', it is not apotheosized in and for itself: its purpose is the fullest development of the individual within a state that is genuinely pluralist.

In fact, while politics may have primacy, the primordial field of focus is society. It is as part of society that individuals, in themselves or in association with one another (linked together on the basis of affinity or interest), enter into interactions that are political and/or economic, giving rise to the 'polity' and the 'economy'. In this sense, the latter are epiphenomena of 'society' which provides the foundation for both. Nor are politics and economics autonomous of each other: they overlap, intertwine, intersect and interact in complex and ever-changing ways because of what happens in their common base which is society. In an underlying sense, however, politics has primacy over economics because the economy cannot be insulated from social preferences—notably, for justice, liberty and equality—which have necessarily to be arrived at through the political process in a free society.

'CIVIL SOCIETY' AND ITS LIMITATIONS

Attention must, therefore, turn to the kind of society that would be consistent with Aristotelian notions of polity and governance. In the discourse on the democratic basis for governance, the term that has come to the forefront is 'Civil Society'. As Ernest Gellner tells it:

> A new ideal was born or reborn in recent decades: Civil Society. Previously, a person interested in the notion of Civil Society could be assumed to be a historian of ideas, concerned perhaps with Locke or Hegel. But the phrase itself had no living resonance or evocativeness. Rather, it seemed distinctly covered with dust. And now, all of a sudden, it has been taken out and thoroughly dusted, and has become a shining emblem (Gellner 1996: 1).

The main reason for this, as Gellner points out, is the collapse of communism in the Soviet Union and Eastern Europe and the democratic challenges to authoritarian rule that have surfaced in China and elsewhere in the world.

Civil society, 'Yes, but of what kind?' We find it useful to explore this in terms of Gellner's own stimulating account of it. He defines Civil Society as 'that set of diverse non-governmental institutions which is strong enough to counterbalance the state and, while not preventing the state from fulfilling its role of the keeper of the peace and arbitrator between major interests, can nevertheless prevent it from dominating and atomizing the rest of society' (ibid.: 5). He prefers the term Civil Society to democracy for denoting an open, liberal, pluralistic social order. However, Civil Society is not to be confused with any and every plural society. Pre-modern 'segmentary communities' based on class and tribe would not qualify as civil society. We may add—although Gellner himself does not touch on this—that, by the same token, post-modern 'anarcho-communitarian' local communities should be equally unacceptable as rivals to Civil Society.[14] Secondly, according to Gellner, Civil Society 'is an a-moral order'. Unlike as in the secular ideocratic Umma of Marxism, or in the religious unitarian Umma of Islam, virtue is not imposed on Civil Society as the aim of public policy. This is not to say that 'virtue, freely practised between consenting adults, may be a great boon to Civil Society, or even its essential precondition' (Gellner 1996: 77). Thirdly, the source of pluralism in Civil Society is located in the economic rather than in the political sphere, for in the modern world, political pluralism in terms of independent or autonomous coercive units is not feasible while economic decentralization is necessary and desirable for securing both liberty and economic efficiency. In fact, Gellner goes further to assert that in his Civil Society, 'the economy is not merely independent but actually dominant, treating the polity as its accountable servant.'[15] Fourthly, Civil Society is culture dependent: for Gellner, preaching it across cultural boundaries and in conditions which do not permit it would 'seem to be a pointless exercise'.

[14] For an incisive critique of 'anarcho-communitarians', see Bardhan 1997b.
[15] Even more provocatively, in Gellner's view (p. 205), 'Marxism made it a taunt that the bourgeois state was merely a kind of executive committee of the bourgeoisie: that this should even have become possible is mankind's greatest social achievement ever.'

Admittedly, Gellner's Civil Society is a specialized, custom-tailored concept to fit the transitional polities of the erstwhile Marxist states in Eastern Europe and the European parts of the former Soviet Union which, having embraced the market economy, are struggling to clone themselves to models of society consistent with democratic capitalism, as available in Western Europe and North America. His 'Civil Society' will seem to best fit 'advanced', 'mature', or 'welfare' capitalist societies in which a broad ideological consensus comprising democracy, capitalism and welfare has, over history, crystallized and largely stabilized. Even in such societies—as the eighties and nineties have shown—the consensual pendulum does continue to swing between right and left (although, perhaps, the amplitude of the oscillation is getting progressively narrower). Furthermore, as Gellner himself acknowledges, his model has no application to 'cultures' to which (tautologically) it cannot apply: presumably to the developing countries whose populations are culturally too rude to absorb the mores of civil society as they obtain in the western world. The 'lesser breeds without the law' are condemned to be 'lesser' because the law is not able to reach out to them!

The problems with Gellner's portrayal of Civil Society lie not merely at the level of application but, more basically, stem from its theoretical inadequacy. As Rawls has rightly reminded us, a society, properly conceived, is neither a community—strongly held together by a set of shared beliefs—nor an association that is open-ended and voluntaristic (Rawls 1993: 40). Rawls, therefore, feels the need for a 'political conception of justice' in order to bridge the gap between freedom and consensus in a free society. Aristotle does the same:

> Those of noble birth or who are free or have wealth are quite right to lay claim to honours...and must have taxable property... But obviously something more is needed besides: I mean justice, and the virtue that is proper to citizens. For without these additions it is not possible for the state to be managed. More exactly, whereas without free population and wealth there cannot be a state at all, without justice and virtue it cannot be managed well. (Aristotle, *The Politics*, Book III (ii), Sinclair and Sanders 1981: 206-8)

Gellner's Civil Society cannot, therefore, provide the basis for the Aristotelian polity—in as much as its social fabric is badly woven, lacking as it does a horizontal weft of justice to give binding strength to the vertical warp of pluralisms.

In fact, Gellner is not correct in claiming that Civil Society in his paradigmatic bourgeois states is amoral. No doubt, virtue has not been imposed from above on their societies; this does not mean that it has been left to be practised among consenting adults (on par with adultery). Rather, the broad social consensus on economic justice, which has evolved in welfare-capitalist societies, has become, to a large degree, implicit and internalized. In the process, that the consensus has become relatively invisible testifies to its strength and stability which should not be taken to mean that it is non-existent or that, in these societies, only reward is its own virtue.

RAWLS ON THE WELL-ORDERED SOCIETY

We then have to continue the search for the characteristics of a society that will supply the soil on which the tree of Aristotelian good governance can strike roots, grow, spread and yield fruit. The candidate I propose to meet this need is John Rawls's 'well-ordered society' as outlined in his *Political Liberalism*[16] which extends his classic contribution *A Theory of Justice* (Rawls 1972). In summary, and paraphrasing it mostly in his own words, the desiderata that Rawls sets forth for the well-ordered society are the following:

- First, an overlapping consensus on a political conception of justice will have to provide the basis for social cooperation among free and equal citizens in a well-ordered society.[17]

[16] See Rawls 1993, Lecture I: Fundamental Ideas, pp. 3–46.
[17] To annotate the key words: The consensus is overlapping in the sense that it is attained, and sustained, despite reasonable pluralism—in religious, philosophical and moral doctrines—which is to be expected in a free society. It is political in the sense that it is limited to the domain of the political; it does not claim a 'metaphysical' or 'epistemological' basis and is a 'free standing' political conception in itself. Cooperation is freely entered into and is not just social activity coordinated by a central authority. Fair terms of cooperation involve, besides equality of opportunity, reciprocity on the basis of each participant's rational advantage, not just strict mutual advantage. On justice, Rawls's two principles of justice are well known. As presented in Rawls 1993, they are as follows: (a) Each person has an equal claim to a fully adequate scheme of equal basic rights and liberties, which scheme is compatible with the same scheme for all; and in this scheme the equal political liberties, and only those liberties, are to be guaranteed their fair value. (b) Social and economic inequalities are to satisfy two conditions: first, they are to be attached to positions and offices open to all under conditions of fair equality of opportunity; and second, they are to be to the greatest benefit to the least advantaged members of society. Regardless of

- Second, the political conception of justice has to be articulated through a framework of basic institutions—political, social and economic—which fit together into a unified system of social cooperation.

- Third, equally important, are the principles, standards, and precepts that apply to it and how the norms relating to them are expressed in the character and attitudes of the members of society.

- Fourth, accordingly, the society's main institutions and their accepted forms of interpretation are a fund of implicitly shared ideas and principles which are familiar and intelligible to the educated common sense of citizens generally. Such a 'public political culture of a democratic society' is grounded in the social culture of its civil society; the culture of daily life and of its many associations as well as that of its comprehensive doctrines of all kinds—religious, moral, and philosophical.

Principles of Good Governance: A Summing Up

The elements that go into Aristotelian governance, of which the infrastructure could appropriately be the Rawlsian well-ordered society, can now be summed up:

- Governance is a moral conception which knits together the individual, the citizen, and the state in the sense that the 'good' of each of these entities entails and enables the 'good' of the others.

- Politics has primacy over all other forms of social interaction, with participation being of its essence.

- The management of pluralism is a primary responsibility of the state and centralization (unity) is its nemesis.

- An adequate conception of justice based on liberty and equality, arrived at through a political consensus, is essential for achieving solidarity within a pluralistic social framework.

---

whether one is prepared to precisely subscribe to them or share the priority that Rawls himself would appear to give to the first principle, the essential elements of justice implied in the principles should be unexceptionable: the entitlement for all citizens of the same basic rights and liberties and the attempt to realize the values of both liberty and equality.

- Such a conception is also the basis for social cooperation among free and equal citizens in the well-ordered society.
- Social cooperation has to be articulated as a unified system through basic political, social, and economic institutions.
- Equally important are the normative principles, standards, and precepts that apply to the functioning of the basic institutions.
- To make this possible, the attitudes of members of the well-ordered society to its basic institutions should be implicitly shared; such a political culture of a democratic society will have to be grounded in the social culture of its civil society.

Of these eight elements, the first five relate to the principles of good governance, the sixth to institutional structures, and the last two to the value-based culture that will have to underpin the basic institutions through which the principles of good governance will have to find their articulation in practice.

Exploring the Practical Relevance of the Principles of Good Governance

Good governance is an intensely practical matter and a crying need in the real world. We ought, therefore, to explore how the principles, institutions and values—discussed so far—which are so general and, in part axiomatic, help in any practical way. In particular, what might be the relevance of these principles of good governance for countries in the Third World, each with its history, sociology and culture along with its specific stage of political evolution and economic development?

While one cannot expect to obtain definitive answers to these questions it would be irresponsible to refuse to explore them from practical and operational perspectives. The beginning of wisdom in any such enterprise will be to recognize that the reform of governance cannot be approached—as it often tends to be—in terms of sociopolitical or economistic engineering: nations and societies are not 'greenfield' locations in which installations are put up on the basis of feasibility, detailed engineering and cost-benefit studies.

In contrast, the promotion of good governance in real space and time in most countries—especially in the post-colonial Third World—is bound to be fraught with uncertainties, fluctuations and frustrations. The political process involved is likely to resemble putting together various pieces of a jigsaw, over an extended period of time, being reconciled to the pieces not always fitting well with one another, and sometimes even coming apart. What is important, however, is to be able to see the picture as a whole, to know what the pieces are, to be alert to opportunities to put them in the right places and to be skilful in honing them to make them fit. Only in such ways can theories of good governance help in its promotion and praxis.

Fundamentally, good governance can be promoted only through political and other forms of public action helped by favourable conjunctures and opportunities—importantly, enlightened leadership over extended periods and at crucial phases. At the same time, academic analysis can be important and useful in two main respects: (a) to help in envisioning the principles of good governance steadily and as a whole; and (b) thereby to provide the framework for understanding, interpretation, evaluation, and appropriate prescription that might be relevant for the political process whether in constructive or critical ways as circumstances might call for.

The academic contribution to this process, I suggest, could concretely consist of three elements. First, an elaboration—or 'shaking loose' as it were—of the Aristotle-Rawls principles into sets of interrelated issues which can help in the analytical understanding of what is involved in the promotion of good governance. Secondly, using such issues as a broad frame of reference, the evaluation of the 'state of governance' in given countries, having regard to their relevant specificities. Thirdly, the exploration of feasible ways and directions in which institutional structures and the values that will have to underpin them can be reciprocally strengthened, once again taking into account country-specific circumstances.

On the sets of issues—consistent with our analysis of the principles of good governance—the indicative list could be the following:

(1) Is the form of governance one that is based on (a) competitive electoral democracy, and (b) the assurance of an open polity which guarantees basic rights of life, liberty, religion, language, speech, association, rule of law and the like? Are these rights and entitlements effectively assured?

(2) Is democracy merely nominal or does it function on the basis of local participation and accountability?

(3) Is there a 'political conception' of social and economic justice? How and to what extent is it formally articulated in the Constitution, laws and settled policies of the state? To what extent has the conception been maintained, eroded, or developed over regime changes?

(4) How adequate and effective are political, social and economic institutions? In particular, are due separation and balance maintained between the basic institutional triad: the legislature, the executive and the judiciary?

(5) How satisfactory and sustained have been the observance in practice of 'the normative principles, standards and precepts that apply to the functioning of the basic institutions'?

(6) How have been pluralities—territorial, religious, ethnic, linguistic and other—handled without jeopardy to both freedom and cohesion? Positively, how has cohesion been sought to be promoted amidst such pluralities?

(7) Are non-governmental associations in civil society fostered or discouraged?

(8) Is the governance of the economy decentralized, technically efficient, socially just and morally acceptable in terms of relations between the state and the market and in the handling of corruption and of special interest groups?

(9) Lastly, does governance seek to promote these and such objectives, in practical action, through an optimal combination of the reform of institutional structures, the legal framework and the values and virtues essential for sustaining them?

I shall conclude by suggesting that the decolonized larger countries of South Asia (India, Pakistan, Bangladesh and Sri Lanka) offer—in themselves and on a comparative basis—rich clinical material for research and analysis on these issues. They have experienced five decades of freedom for autonomous nation-building; undergone changes from one form of government to another; represent different types of political economy; have had varying successes and failures in the management of pluralities; reflect different levels of nominal and participatory democracy; have had varying policies and experience with economic growth and social justice; are currently going through a shift from relatively dirigiste to open economies; and have many commonalities and differences in their political and social cultures. And, above all, the common people of South Asia deserve much better governance than it has been their lot to endure during nearly two centuries of colonial rule or the last five decades of self-government.

REFERENCES

Adigalar, Kunrakudi (1994), *Kamban Kanda Achiyil Arasiyal Samukam* (in Tamil), Madras: Vanathi Pathipakam.

Altekar, A. S. (1997 reprint), *State and Government in Ancient India*. Delhi: Motilal Banarsidass.

Bardhan, Pranab (1997a), *The Role of Governance in Economic Development, A Political Economy Approach*, Paris: OECD Development Centre.

——— (1997b), 'The State Against Society: The Great Divide in Indian Social Science Discourse' in Bose and Jalal.

Barnes, Jonathan (ed.) (1995), *The Cambridge Companion to Aristotle*, Cambridge.

Bose, Sugata and Ayesha Jalal (eds) (1997), *Nationalism, Democracy and Development*, New Delhi: Oxford University Press.

Cargill Thompson, W. D. J. (1969), 'Martin Luther and the "Two Kingdoms"' in Thompson 1969.

Coomaraswamy, Ananda K. (1993 reprint), *Spiritual Authority and Temporal Power in the Indian Theory of Government*. New Delhi: Oxford University Press.

Everson, Stephen (ed.) (1988), *Aristotle, The Politics*, Cambridge.

Gellner, Ernest (1996), *The Conditions of Liberty: Civil Society and its Rivals*, London: Penguin Books.

Gramsci, Antonio, (Ed. Quinton Hoare and Geoffrey Nowell Smith) (1996 reprint), *Selections from the Prison Notebooks*, Madras: Orient Longman.

Green, T. H. (1931 edition), *Lectures on the Principles of Political Obligation*, London.

Guhan. S. (1997), 'Three Pieces on Governance', paper presented at the Workshop on Governance Issues in South Asia, Economic Growth Centre, Yale University, 19 November.

Hutchinson, D. S. (1995), 'Ethics' in Barnes.

Lal, Deepak (1994), *Participation, Markets and Democracy*, Washington, DC: World Bank.

Lindblom, Charles E. (1991), *Politics and Markets: The World's Political-Economic Systems*, New York: Barn Books.

Mill, John Stuart (1910), *Utilitarianism, On Liberty, Considerations on Representative Government*, edited by H. B. Acton, London: Everymans Library.

Rawls, John (1972), *A Theory of Justice*, Oxford: Oxford University Press.

——— (1993), *Political Liberalism*. New York: Columbia University Press.
Sen, Amartya (1987), *On Ethics and Economics*, Oxford: Basil Blackwell.
Sinclair, T. A. and Trevor J. Sanders (Trans.) (1981), *Aristotle, The Politics*, London: Penguin Books.
Taylor, C. C. W. (1995), 'Politics' in Barnes.
Thomson, David (ed.) (1969), *Political Ideas*, London: Pelican Books.
Vincent, Andrew (1987), *Theories of the State*, Oxford: Basil Blackwell.
World Bank (1989), *Sub-Saharan Africa: From Crisis to Sustainable Growth*, Washington, DC: World Bank.
——— (1991), *Proceedings of the Annual Conference on Development Economics*, Washington, DC: World Bank.
——— (1994), *Governance—The World Bank's Experience*, Washington, DC: World Bank.
——— (1997), *The State in a Changing World—World Development Report 1997*. Washington, DC: World Bank.

Outside the Curriculum

13

Bala's Sringara*

The *bhava* or the attitude of sringara was for Bala the soul of Bharatanatyam. 'Sringara', she said, 'stands supreme in the range of emotions. No other emotion is capable of better reflecting the mystic union of the human with the divine. I say this with deep personal experience of dancing to many great devotional songs which have had no element of sringara in them. Devotional songs are, of course, necessary. However, sringara is the cardinal emotion.'

The supremacy that Bala gave to sringara has been the subject of some controversy. Her own reactions were sharp and unremitting towards those who could not grant it the same status as she did or who, she thought, misunderstood what sringara really was. The word has no exact translation in the English language. Bala's Bharatanatyam was, of course, the best means available to those who witnessed it to *know* what she meant and what sringara could do for her and for them. She has helped us to experience sringara but still what is the concept of it to which we can hold?

Sringara is one of those 'perennial' concepts that one encounters in space and time. It was the 'Eros' of Plato. The English novelist and philosopher Iris Murdoch explains it as follows:

In his conception of the beautiful, Plato gives to sexual love and transformed sexual energy a central place in his philosophy. Plato's Eros is a principle which connects the commonest human desire to the highest morality and to the pattern of divine creativity in the universe...it is the whole Eros that concerns him, and not just some passionless distillation. This Eros, who is lover not beloved, is the ambiguous spiritual mediator and moving spirit of mankind...Carnal love teaches us that what we want is always 'beyond' and it gives us energy which can be transformed into creative virtue.

* Reprinted from *Sruti* Magazine, Madras, 1 March 1981.

It has been said that the best commentary on the Eros of Plato's *Symposium* is to be found in Dante's *Divine Comedy*. To Dante, the figure of Beatrice was the image of Romantic Love, of 'a deep and undetermined sense, of unknown modes of being.' Charles Williams, a great scholar on Dante, explains this 'unknown mode' on 'Romantic Love' by saying that 'there is no other word so convenient for describing that particular kind of sexual love... It includes other loves beside the sexual... It defines an attitude, a manner of receiving experience.'

Bala's sringara was no other than Plato's Eros or Dante's figure of Beatrice. While they celebrated it in philosophy and in poetry, she practised it—for us and for herself—in the living dialectic of dance. To her, sringara and bhakti were synonyms. Bhakti comes from the root *bhaj*, to participate or relate. It is the same as the *'Uravu'* of the *Tevaram* through which Beauty Hidden is made Beauty Manifest. Sringara is nothing but the rod and the rope through which fire could be kindled from wood or butter won from milk.

Bala was therefore angry and annoyed with those who tried to 'purify' sringara with so-called bhakti. She felt completely at a loss to understand what there was in sringara that needed to be sanitized. Being totally free of cant and hypocrisy, she refused to take the easy way out by arguing that sringara was a sublimation of the erotic impulse or a reflection of the *jivatman* in search of the *paramatman*, which are the usual cliches of 'respectable' discourse on this theme. She had the courage of her conviction, like Plato and Dante, not to speak of Siva himself (who has been described as the Erotic Ascetic), that the energy and creativity of sexual love deserved the central place. The emotions it inspired could branch off continually into the portrayal of innumerable moods full of newness and nuance. It was the way of affirmation whereby the dancer could relate to 'the Other', to Krishna. If this was not bhakti, what else could it be?

Through her, we too could relate to Krishna. Wherever she danced, on the most prestigious platform of the world or in a marriage pandal, whether the audience was Indian or American or British or Japanese, she led us into her own experience and ecstasy. Is not sringara the Beatrice who led Dante to Paradise? As Bala said: 'In their shared involvement, the dancer and the spectator are both released from the weight of wordly life and experience the divine joy of the art in total freedom.'

Bala has now finally escaped the 'weight of worldly life'. We can only remember the great joy we were able to share with this lovely and lovable philosopher-dancer of sringara-bhakti.

14

Eight Poems of Thayumanavar*

Kallada Perhala

Indeed those without learning are the truly good.
A scholar but stupid, there isn't much to be said
  for my thoughts or deeds.

With those who expound *jnana*, the path of knowledge,
I shall debate the importance of *karma*, the path of action.
If someone emphasizes the path of action,
The primacy of knowledge is what I shall argue.

If a Sanskrit scholar comes along,
'It is all there in Tamil', I will hold forth.
At the appearance of a Tamil scholar,
I shall smatter a few phrases in Sanskrit.

Will salvation come from such debating tricks
That browbeat people but carry no conviction?

My lord, you are the *summum bonum*,
Which is the common ground of Vedanta and Siddhanta.

Asaikor Alavuillai

For avarice, there is no limit.
Not content with holding sway over the earth entire,
They would want to rule the sea and the islands.

---

* Thayumanavar was an eighteenth-century Tamil mystic poet, and author of the *Paraparakkanni*. These eight verses were translated from the Tamil by Guhan for use in concert presentations by T. Visvanathan, Professor of Music at the Wesleyan University, Connecticut, USA.

Despite owning as much gold as the God of riches,
They will wander, here and there, to learn alchemy's tricks.
A full and healthy life doesn't prevent them
From hankering after the elixir of immortality.
Think! all told, what we end up doing
Is only to eat well and sleep.

What I am and what I own is enough,
Let not my ego, clutching one thing or another,
Drown in the sea of greed.

Oh absolute Joy, seamless and whole,
Bless me with the flawless state, devoid of mind.

KAGAMANNADU

A single stone suffices to scare away the assembly of
    a million crows.
A millions sins cannot afflict one who has thirsted after
The gracious flood of your compassion.

It is apparent that I don't have the slightest yearning
    for your grace,
My body is tormented much by the accumulation of sins,
Elusive is the path of yoga which could rid me of my sufferings,
The gap is huge between my restless mind and inner peace.

When can I hope to become whole and one with you?
Will that day come in this life?
You are the life of all beings, in this world and
    in the one beyond,
The fulfilling Presence that is everywhere.

ETHANAI VIDANGALTHAN

The myriad things and many ways in which
I have learnt, through study and discourse,
    have not my heart subdued.
My ego, the I-in-me, has not diminished
    even by the size of a sesame seed.
Swayed by love of material things, I utterly
    lack charity or compassion.

Good conduct, austerity, self-control—these
 I haven't glimpsed even in a dream.
Only falsehood I speak, never truth
 even in a medicinal dose.
Fool that I am, instead of receiving
 your grace, quietly and in silence,
I give advice to all who will listen.

Have you seen or heard anyone in this
 world so low in wisdom and virtue?
Wholesome Joy, that encloses the
 inner and outer universe.

Pannen Unakkaga

By whatever means I try, to worship you seems impossible.

I thought of worshipping you with flowers,
But seeing you, cool and fresh, in the flower,
My heart couldn't bear to pluck it.
It was not right either to worship you with folded hands:
You being yourself within me, that will be only half a salutation.

My lord, you are the firmament
And its origin—the Spirit,
Music, the Vedas and the Vedanta,
The awesome question of questions,
The seed within the earth, the
 sprout of that seed,
Sight and insight, my thoughts and words.

You are the silent path to salvation
The god of grace who dances joyfully
In the chit-sabha, the theatre of consciousness.

Kanduga Madakariai

One can control a rogue elephant,
Muzzle a bear or tiger,
Climb upon a lion's back,
Make the cobra dance,
Transmute the five base metals into gold,

Become invisible and roam the world,
Order about the heavenly beings,
Retain one's youth forever,
Enter another's body,
Walk on water, sit on fire,
Acquire all such supernormal powers.

What is difficult though is to control the mind
By practising the skill to be silent

My lord, you dwell in my consciousness,
 as joy and goodness:
You alone are the true knowledge.

Kallarkum Kattravarkum

Scholars as well as those without lore
 in you find happiness,
You are the one giving vision to those that can see
 and to the blind.

You bless alike the able and the skilful
As well as those who are not.

You are the intelligence of the intellectual
And also that of those who only respect you.

Resting in the middle of good and bad people,
You are their Common Ground.

You are the well-being of both celestials and humans.

You who dance in the space, central and common to all,
My lord, bestow your grace, allow me to reach you

Yengu Niraikinrai Porul

The great seer Appar taught us
Without His willing nothing can move,
Not even an atom.
This being the truth,

What is knowledge? What is ignorance?
Those who understand the two, those who do not,

Those who are silent and the wide-mouthed ones
Like me, who prattle forever.

The illusion called the mind, whence does it come?
What is strength, what is compassion?
Why was the universe created? Where did it take place?
What explains the five elements of nature?
What is falsehood, what is truth?
What is soothing, what is not?
Tolerance or impatience with good and evil
   —how are they begotten?
Who is young, who is old?
Who is your near and dear and who your enemy?

All these, my lord, on you depend,
You are the life of the living
On this earth and in the one beyond.
The substance—here, there, and everywhere.

15

The Cat and the Mahatma*

We should know our national heroes, Gandhi and Nehru, not just as distant historical figures but as persons with qualities which are appealing at the simple human level. One such was their involvement in everything around them, including animals. Their busy political lives gave little time for enjoying the company of animals except during the long periods of imprisonment they suffered in the cause of India's freedom from British rule.

In his autobiography, Nehru has a whole chapter on 'Animals in Prison' in which he describes the birds, insects, reptiles and animals that kept him company in the Dehra Dun jail where he was locked up during all of 1932. He avidly watched the eagles, kites and wild duck in flight and was charmed by pigeons, parrots and mynahs. He felt the 'plaintiveness' of the *kuyil's* call and was troubled by the persistent cry of the 'brain-fever' bird during 'daytime and at night, in sunshine and in pouring rain'.

Above all, Nehru was tormented in his small prison cell by a variety of insects and reptiles—bed-bugs, mosquitoes, flies, ants, wasps, hornets, lizards, bats, centipedes and, on occasion, even snakes and scorpions. He admired an angry monkey which chased away a whole lot of prison warders to rescue her young child. For pets he could have only squirrels and mongooses since dogs were not allowed in jails. Cats, however, were permitted but Nehru's acquaintance with a kitten was a passing one for it belonged to a jail official who took it away when he got transferred.

At the same time that Nehru was imprisoned in Dehra Dun, Gandhiji was lodged in the Yeravda jail in Maharashtra along with

* Reprinted from *The Hindu* (*Young World* supplement), 9 March 1996.

Sardar Patel and Mahadev Desai. For Gandhiji, this detention gave him the much-needed rest after a year of strenuous political activity ending with the journey to London for attending the Round Table Conference. He took the opportunity to relax completely for a few months and it has been said that in Yeravda he 'passed his time in peace such as he was not destined to enjoy ever again in his life'.

Gandhiji's animal friends in prison consisted of a cat and her two kittens. Their doings absorbed him greatly; and he describes them in loving detail in a number of letters. The first of these is a letter of May 1932 in which he says that the cat gave birth to kittens about a month and half earlier. He then says:

Their ways are wonderful. The three are rarely found separated. The mother-cat lets the kittens suck whenever they indicate their desire. The two cling to her and suck at the same time. It is a sublime sight. The mother has no feeling of false shame about the matter. As soon as the kittens could walk and play, she taught them the procedure to be followed for defecation. She withdrew to a quiet spot where the earth was soft and dug out a small hollow. She put the kittens in position over the hollow, afterwards covered the excreta with earth and made the spot as clean as it was before. The kittens now follow that procedure every day. They are a brother and a sister. Four days ago, one of them was trying to dig a hollow in the earth, but the ground was rather hard. The other one went to its help and the two together dug out a hollow of the required size. After defecation, they covered up the excreta with earth and left the place. Why should we not willingly do what these creatures—even the little ones—do?

Later in the same month, Gandhiji informs Nan and Tangai, two children he knew, how he has made friends with a cat and her kittens. 'I call her sister. It is delightful to watch her love for her young ones. She teaches them all sorts of things by simply doing them.' In another letter written on the same day, Gandhiji develops the theme of the cat as a teacher-through-example, not only to her kittens but also to grown-up human beings. This is what, he says, we can all learn from cats:

I have already written about our cat's love of cleanliness. Observing her and her kittens' ways, I feel that she is an ideal teacher, Whatever they have to be taught, she teaches quietly and without any fuss. The method is quite easy. She demonstrates to them by her own example what she wishes to teach, and the kittens learn the thing very quickly. In this manner they learnt to run, climb trees and come down again carefully to eat, to kill a prey and to lick their bodies and clean them. In a very short time they have learnt to do all that their mother can do.

The cat does not leave the kittens alone for long. Her love for them is just like that of a woman's for her children. She sleeps with the kittens clinging to her. When they indicate a desire to suck, she lies down and lets them do it. If she has killed a prey, she brings it to them. Vallabhbhai gives them some milk every day. All three of them lick it from a saucer. Sometimes the mother only looks on without sharing the milk. She plays with them as if she were their own age, and even engages in a sort of wrestling with them.

Gandhiji continues with some advice for parents:

I have drawn a lesson from all this, namely, that if we wish to educate children properly we should ourselves do what we want to teach them to do. Children have a great capacity for imitating others. They do not easily understand what is explained to them orally. If we wish to teach them truthfulness, we ourselves should be scrupulously truthful. If we wish to teach them not to keep with them more things than they need, we too, should not do that.

Later that year, in a letter to Manibehn Patel, Gandhiji draws yet another lesson from his cat family. He writes:

Our cat family has three members. They present themselves daily without fail at both the meal times, without a bell being rung for them or without being called. If we all become as punctual as these dear creatures, we would save millions of hours of time. And we have doubtless been taught how time is money. This is perfectly true, and so money saved is money earned. Who can compute the loss of wealth to this world through people who do not value time?

It is a mistake to think that cats, unlike dogs, do not display their affection for humans. In October 1932, for some reason, Gandhiji seems to have been separated from the cats. This is how he describes the reunion. 'Our cat was really mad with joy when she saw us. She simply would not leave us. She must have keenly felt the separation from us. She is contented now.'

Gandhiji's only regret was that his cat family 'won't attend the prayers' and that 'their recognition of kinship is confined to the common board.' This does not seem to have been always the case for Mahadev Desai, who was in prison with Gandhiji at that time, notes in his diary: 'The kittens now enjoy our company. They sit in Bapu's lap at prayer time, play with us and kick up a row at dinner time. The Sardar teases them.' Mahadev Desai also quotes Gandhiji as saying 'the gods should shower flowers upon these kittens from the sky,' indicating how fond the Mahatma had become of his feline companions.

The last in this series of letters, addressed in December 1932 to Mirabehn, has a sad story to tell. Gandhiji reported:

> Our cats have suffered disgrace. The mother has been found helping herself to food without permission and during nights dirtying our carpets and papers. Vallabhbhai has therefore cut off the food supply. Thus interdining has stopped. What other ordinances Vallabhbhai will promulgate I do not know. Ordinance rule is the order of the day even for poor kitty!

We see from this letter that Sardar Patel was as much a disciplinarian with cats as he was later to prove with the princes of India when he became the country's iron Home Minister.

In our mythology, various birds and animals—the eagle, the peacock, the vulture, the bull, the dog, the rat, monkeys and squirrels—have provided transportation, support and companionship to Vishnu, Siva, Ganesa, Murugan, Rama and Yudhishtira. The cat has not been recognized in this fashion. Cat lovers can feel happy that Gandhiji has righted this wrong.

16

Policy, as it has been laid down in the Mundaka Upanishad*

Then Yagnavalkya said to Nachiketas:

Now that I have instructed you on the nature of the Brahman, it is time to go into a deeper mystery, one that has baffled many of the rishis and pandits in our country.

N: What can that be, Master?

Y: Industrial deceleration in India.

N: In what period, Master? In which industries? Why? Please enlighten me.

Y: Nachiketas, if you had understood my lesson on *nasti asti vada* you would not ask the first two questions. Time is relative; classification is subjective. Do you not know this?

N: Forgive me, Master but why did this deceleration take place?

Y: Think for yourself. How could it have happened?

N: Could it have been the wage goods constraint?

Y: No. Think again.

N: Income distribution?

Y: Many have misguided themselves that that might be the reason including the great Shastratna Sukhomoy but it is not that.

N: I see a glimmer. Could it be worsening income distribution?

Y: Have I not told you, my son, that what cannot improve cannot worsen either? Try again.

* Rescued from S. Guhan's personal files.

N: Could it be deceleration in public investment?

Y: You are beginning to see some light now.

N: I shall try harder, Master. Is it poor agricultural growth?

Y: Yes, that too is a cause but the truth lies deeper still.

N: Master, I have come to the end of my meagre intellectual powers. You, and you alone, can lead me to the final truth. Please have compassion.

Y: My son, it is policy. In Bharatakanda, everything is policy. From policy, policy arises and into policy it returns. Take away policy from policy and policy remains. Do you not know that ancient sages like Bhagwati Bhagwan, Ma Padma, and Srinivasan Acharya have told us this?

(Begins chanting):

This lesson you must surely learn.
If you cannot locate causes elsewhere,
It is to policy that you must turn.

N: Sir, endless is your power to enlighten me.

17

Memories of an Uncle
K. Swaminathan*

This memoir is primarily based on the papers left behind by KS. It has not been possible to supplement them with archival research or oral history. Nevertheless, inasmuch as KS seems to have retained all that appeared to him of interest and importance, it has been possible to provide a reasonable account of the main events in his life, as also of his personality and preoccupations. KS's life, spanning nearly a century, intersected with a particularly eventful period in India's spiritual, social, and political history in which—according to his own measure—he involved himself fully, both as participant and observer. He had three careers as college teacher, newspaper editor, and editor of Gandhi's collected works. He was an active bhakta *of Sri Ramana as also an enthusiastic* rasika *of Tamil and English literature. His personality was not only rich but complex. Given all this, KS merits a full biography which relates the man to his times while also being psychologically insightful.*

In the preparation of this memoir, my first debt is to Sri La. Su. Rengarajan. For useful information, correction of errors, and improvements to an earlier version, I am grateful to Professor S. Ramaswami, Fr Lawrence Sundaram, and members of the family—Mahalakshmi and P. R. Suryanandan, Santa Ramachandran, Gita and N. Gopalakrishnan, and Shanta Guhan. (Guhan)

☆

P. S. Krishnaswami Iyer and his wife Dharmambal were blessed with four children, of whom the first born was daughter Veda, followed by three sons—Swaminathan, Venkataraman, and Srinivasa Sanjivi.

---

* Originally appeared as 'K. S.: A Memoir', in S. Guhan (ed.) *K. S.: Tributes to Commemorate his Birth Centenary* (printed for private circulation by the family of K. Swaminathan).

Like KS, his brothers enjoyed long lives marked by activity and achievement. Dr K. Venkataraman (1901–81) retired as the Director of the National Chemical Laboratory, Pune and continued with his scientific researches in chemistry for many years thereafter. Dr K. S. Sanjivi (1903–94), after his retirement as Professor of Medicine in the Madras Medical College, founded the Voluntary Health Services, Madras. Till the end of his active days, he was involved in medical relief for the poor and the promotion of community health. All three brothers were honoured with Padma Bhushan, a rare event to occur in a single family. Veda was remembered by her brothers for her exceptionally gentle disposition. She suffered from pleurisy for more than two decades and died in her early forties leaving behind her husband Subbaier and three daughters. Throughout, the brothers, their wives and children, and the sister's family have remained close to one another.

☆

Despite the digression involved, it is worth summarizing at this stage all that can be gathered about P. S. Krishnaswami (PSK), for he was an exceptional person who left a deep imprint on all his children. Born in 1870, PSK completed his high school in Pudukkotai and, after a brief foray into accountancy, moved to Madras at the age of eighteen for taking the two-year diploma course in the Engineering College, Guindy. The diploma qualified him to become an 'Upper Subordinate' in the Public Works Department (PWD) and he was recruited straightaway by the then Sanitary Engineer, J. A. Jones, to work as a draughtsman in his office. In the Sanitary Engineer's establishment, PSK worked throughout on designs, rising to positions such as Head Draughtsman, Technical Superintendent and Personal Assistant to the Sanitary Engineer.

In 1916, PSK was superseded in promotions to the gazetted post of Sub-Engineer on the ground that he had not had executive experience in a field division of the PWD, which was clearly unjust since it was successive Sanitary Engineers who would not part with his services in the draughtsman's office. PSK repeatedly and vigorously petitioned the Governor against the supersession but to no avail despite the consistent support he received from successive heads of his department. All that he could do, at the conclusion of these proceedings, was to compile a 'Personal File' and get it printed and firmly bound. This document, carefully preserved by KS among his papers, reveals the very high esteem in which PSK was held. He was considered to be 'an exceptionally capable and intelligent man'; one who 'does not spare himself and works both hard and fast' and with 'unabated zeal', a 'first class draughtsman and estimator', and 'an excellent mathematician'. To cap it all, J. A. Jones, with whom PSK had worked for thirteen years, wrote: 'As I am leaving Madras, I desire to place on record that all through my 30 years' service in India, I have never had a more conscientious, a more able, or a more energetic Assistant'—high praise which was endorsed by Jones's successors as well.

PSK's connection with the Madras PWD came to an end in 1922, some three years before he would have retired in the normal course. It is believed that his name was included in the 'retrenchment list' by the then ruling Justice Party because he was a brahmin. The loss of the Madras government proved to be the gain of the Government of Bombay under whom PSK took employment between 1923 and 1925. On his retirement from that government, PSK worked for a short while with a private sanitary engineering firm before moving back to Madras. In 1926, his wife Dharmambal passed away at age 46, having been afflicted with asthma all her life. Too self-reliant to move in with any one of his sons, PSK live in a basically one-room house he had built in the Alwarpet area of Madras ('Dharmalayam', which KS was to occupy later), doing his own cooking for which and for other domestic help he employed a Harijan boy. He improved his Sanskrit and was engaged from 1927 in translating Valmiki's *Ramayana* word-for-word into Tamil, a task that was completed before his death in 1935.[1]

While the 'Personal File' gives an idea of PSK's professional excellence and dedication to work, we have to turn to other sources to learn about the kind of man he was. PSK lived simply and believed in regular savings. KS recalls that, when his father's monthly salary was Rs 150, he would, at the beginning of the month, bring home Rs 135 in cash and a sovereign of gold. The savings mostly went into the education of his sons, with what remained being spent on the construction of 'Dharmalayam'. PSK's pension, a part of which had been commuted for house-building, being meagre, the

---

[1] The translation was first brought out in the late thirties by M. N. Ramaswamy Iyer of the Ramayana Publishing House, Alathur (Palghat) in several volumes as the 'Dharmalaya Edition'. It has been reprinted three times since then.

expenses involved in translating the *Ramayana* had to be met from a 10 per cent levy on the salaries of his sons, all of whom were by then employed.[2] It is not surprising, therefore, that PSK was to record on the eve of his retirement that 'he had no local interests anywhere, no cash or jewellery worth caring for or mentioning'.

Although by no means affluent, PSK's solid investment was in the education and upbringing of his sons and his real treasure was his own rock-like integrity. In his Madras Service as a draughtsman, there was, perhaps, not much occasion for his honesty to be tested or demonstrated, but the years in Bombay were another matter. His tenure there overlapped with one of the Backbay Reclamation scandals (perhaps the first) followed by a judicial inquiry into charges of corruption. The Judge is reported to have observed in his findings that one of the few honest officials among those involved in the transaction was a 'South Indian engineer called Krishnaswami'.

K. S. Sanjivi recollects a telling incident in the same connection:

During one of my summer vacations, I went to Bombay to stay with my parents. An incident which happened at that time is still vivid in my memory. At 9 p.m. one evening, a gentleman came up to the third floor flat in Tardeo Road where we were living and told my father that he had come to invite him with some traditional gifts of fruits for his daughter's birthday on the following day. My father took the tray and noticed a small cloth bag hidden amongst the fruits. Immediately, he threw that bag over the parapet and the horrified visitor ran down fast. Later, my father told us the reason for his throwing the bag out. The next day, a contract of several lakhs of rupees was to be finalized and the man who brought these gifts was resorting to this foul method to compromise him. The bag had been full of currency notes.[3]

Yet another incident from the Bombay days brings out PSK's steadfastness in sticking to his values, a trait which was very much a part of KS's inheritance.

In 1923, when Congress activity was at its peak, my father was in Government service in Bombay. At that time, a political meeting in Chowpatty was addressed by two Congress leaders, Shri A. Rangaswami Iyengar and Shri S. Satyamurthi. My father took a risk by bringing them in the car to

---

[2] A slight delay on the part of one of them in making the monthly remittance invited the threat of legal action for breach of promise from a father who expected the same standards of financial rectitude which he himself practised.

[3] The source for the other two recollections that follow is the same.

our house and giving them dinner. Sure enough, he was asked for an explanation by the Bombay government as to how he could entertain Congress leaders. His answer was that his hospitality had nothing to do with politics or politicians since Satyamurthi hailed from his native town, Pudukottai, and Rangaswami Iyengar was his neighbour in Madras.

A third incident is also well worth recounting for it illustrates a combination of humour and humanity as remarkable as it is moving:

I must tell you the story of Bommaiya. Bommaiya was a young boy working for my parents when they were in Bombay. I was a medical student in Madras then. Every evening, my parents would drive up to the gardens at Malabar Hill and Bommaiya went with them, sitting in the front seat, next to the driver. When I went to Bombay for a holiday, my father, understandably, made me sit in the front next to the driver, leaving Bommaiya at home. After a couple of days of this, Bommaiya couldn't take it any more and suddenly one evening slapped my face. Instead of getting angry with him, my father understood his feelings of jealousy. He explained patiently to Bommaiya that my visit was only temporary and he would get back his privileged seat after I returned to Madras.

PSK was clearly not a joyless specimen of strait-laced virtue. By all accounts, he was the democratic head of a cheerful and relaxed family in which the children felt no need to rebel. To anyone acquainted with KS, PSK's formative influence on his eldest son should be self-evident. It was also a lasting influence: right up to his death, KS used to repeat that there was nobody like 'Anna' (as he used to call his father). Above all, it was his father who led him to the figure of Rama which, later in life, provided KS the key to the understanding of Gandhi: the Mahatma's *Ram Nam* and *Ram Rajya*. As KS was fond of saying, 'the Gandhi legacy is the rediscovery of the Rama legend.'[4]

☆

When KS was born in 1896—on 3 December, in his maternal grandfather's place in Pudukottai—the family had been settled for some years in the Purasawalkam area of Madras. KS went through his primary classes in the Lutheran Mission School, the best-known school in that part of the city. KS has not left behind any recollections

---

[4] In an article on 'Gandhiji and Ramanama', KS quotes Gandhi as saying: 'I cannot adore God as God. To me that name makes no appeal, but when I think of Him as Rama, He thrills me. There is all the poetry in it.'

of the LMS—except that he hated going to school! However, LMS was the same school to which R. K. Narayan was admitted about a decade later and which is vividly described in his autobiography, *My Days*. Going by Narayan's account, LMS must have given KS an early grounding in the Bible and, at the same time, an aversion to the cruder forms of proselytization in a missionary school of those days.

KS has, however, provided a description of Madras at the turn of the century. It was a string of villages with paddy fields, stretched all the way between Purasawalkam and Mylapore. Trams had not come into operation yet and transport depended on the rickshaw, *jutka*, and the bullock cart. There was no electricity. 'On return from school, we used to clean the kerosene lamps, fill them up with oil and replace the wicks. The street lights used to be lit every day by the Corporation staff. I saw electric lights and fans for the first time in Bangalore during a vacation and was astonished how a switch could make light and air.'

In 1908, the family moved to Pelathope (literally, orchard of jackfruit trees) in Mylapore, a street off the road that connects Luz Corner with the square around the Kapaleeswarar temple and tank. The house into which they moved, and were to live in for the next eighteen years, was reported to be haunted; not being superstitious, PSK took advantage of its reputation to secure the tenancy at a low rent and on a long-term basis.

With the move to Mylapore, KS was enrolled in the P. S. High School where, between 1909 and 1912, he completed his schooling. KS has recorded vivid and interesting reminiscences relating to his teachers and fellow students. He was fortunate in both. The formative influence on KS of three of his teachers is discernible. One was P. N. Srinivasachari, scholar and authority on Vaishnavism, whose regular lessons on Sanatana Dharma sowed 'the seed which has yielded the flower and fruit of many long years' happiness.' Also, 'PNS was an affectionate friend and an inspiring philosopher who told me in confidence—in my early teens—about William James's *Varieties of Religious Experience* and saw to it that I read it.' The second was his Tamil teacher, B. V. Anantarama Iyer, who introduced his students to Sangam poetry. He was the student of the Grand Old Man of Tamil U. V. Swaminatha Iyer whom he succeeded years later on the staff of Presidency College. The third, also a student of UVS, was the Judge and playwright, P. Sambanda Mudaliar, who inducted the boys into amateur dramatics and personally supervised their rehearsals.

Among his memorable contemporaries, KS counted M. Bhaktavatsalam, future Chief Minister of Madras, his junior by a year in the school and later in Presidency College. Nityananda, younger brother of Jiddu Krishnamurthi was a classmate: 'a shy, sensitive, inward-looking boy'. KS admired M. Balasubramaniam for his scholarship in Tamil and Saiva Siddanta; V. C. Gopalaratnam for his fluency in English and talent in theatricals; and Jawad Hussain for his prowess in football. P. S. Chandrasekharan was his fellow-secretary of the Literary Society. Together they organized meetings in the school which brought them into contact with a galaxy of Mylapore luminaries: P. S. Sivasamy Iyer, C. P. Ramaswamy Iyer, T. Sadasiva Iyer, V. S. Srinivasa Sastri, V. Krishnaswami Iyer, and S. Radhakrishnan.

His younger brothers—both in the same school with KS—were beneficiaries and victims of their 'big brother' as the following extracts from Sanjivi's recollections will show:

My eldest brother, Swaminathan, was a voracious, even a fanatical reader. What he was given as pocket money was spent on buying books, so that in a few years he had built up a very good library... He introduced us to the best in prose, poetry and drama and taught us the finer points of grammar and pronunciation... Because of our respect and affection for him, we used to carry out his instructions implicitly. Sometimes, he used to give us funny orders; on 12th December 1912, he told me and my other brother that we would not be able to write 12-12-12 for the next hundred years, although after ten years 2-2-22, eleven years later 3-3-33 and so on could be written. Taken up by the novelty of this idea, we sat down to write 12-12-12 a hundred times. After a few minutes, my father saw what we were doing and stopped us!... Harindranath Chattopadhyaya, brother of the famous poet and patriot Sarojini Naidu, had published a book of poems called *Feast of Youth*. Swaminathan wrote a sort of reply to that in verse and made me sign it as 'Sanjivi, a boy of 14'. Harindranath was so interested in this reply that he called at our house to make my personal acquaintance. Naturally, I was embarrassed and told him the truth that my brother, not I, had authored it. After that, Harindranath became a good friend of our family.

☆

In June 1912, KS entered the prestigious Presidency College, established in 1840, about two decades earlier than the University of

Madras. He was to be there as a student for five years, two in the Intermediate class followed by three more in the B.A. Honours course in English Literature. In the Intermediate examination of 1914, he stood third in the entire old Madras Presidency and first in English. (His competitive instinct made him note, as late as 1984, that he might have secured an even higher rank if his second language in the examination had been Sanskrit instead of Tamil, a poorer scorer.) His contemporaries included several who distinguished themselves in future life: K. Santhanam, N. S. Varadachari, K. V. Rajagopalan, S. Ramanathan, and Sengodayan.[5]

S. Radhakrishnan and U. V. Swaminatha Iyer were on the staff of the college. KS was privileged to have had Iyer for his Tamil teacher in the Intermediate class. He was impressed as much with Iyer's knowledge of families, persons, places all over Tamilnadu as with his deep scholarship. In a tribute paid to him years later, KS has said that no one, anywhere in the world, at any time in history, has rendered to any language the kind of service that UVS had done to Tamil.[6]

In the Honours course, KS came under the tutelage and profound influence of Mark Hunter. After serving as Principal in the Government Colleges in Mangalore and Rajahmundry, this legendary Professor of English had moved to Presidency College in 1910 with the mandate of organizing the Honours course in English. KS was thus among the earliest batches of students in the course. In a tribute to Sir Mark Hunter on his death in 1932, KS noted:

It was an excellent thing for the English Honours School in Madras that it was conceived and inaugurated by the great man in his prime... Alike in extent and intensiveness, in the quantity and thoroughness of the work demanded of the student and tested by the examiners, the English Honours course of Madras, with its ten papers and its compulsory Gothic and Germanic Philology, was not only much heavier than any other Honours course in any Indian University, it was apparently heavier than the English Honours course of any English University.

KS graduated in 1917 and, a year later, Mark Hunter was to move out to Burma as Director of Public Instruction. Coming from him,

[5] K. Santhanam and N. S. Varadachari were Congress leaders, Santhanam also held many high positions under the central government; K. V. Rajagopalan was Law Secretary to the Madras government; S. Ramanathan was a Minister in the Rajaji cabinet; and Sengodayan was one of the earliest entrants to the ICS.

[6] KS was also instrumental in getting the statue of U. V. Swaminatha Iyer erected in the compound of Presidency College, facing the Marina.

the following certificate to his student was indeed worth retaining and we are fortunate that it was:

Mr K. Swaminathan was my pupil for five years, two in the Intermediate and three in the Honours English Language and Literature classes. Throughout his courses he showed himself to be a young man of quite exceptional ability and he distinguished himself for the invariable excellence of his work. He is one of the most gifted and promising pupils I have ever had and those who could compete with him are very few indeed... In the Honours course and examination he carried everything before him in the College and the University. He secured a fine first class, again with an easy lead, and took the two University prizes awarded for distinguished merit in English Language and English Literature respectively... No record could be more satisfactory... Mr Swaminathan's success has not been due to narrow concentration on those matters only which appeared to have a direct and immediate bearing on the books and subjects of the prescribed University courses. He has, for his years, read widely in English Literature with keen and at the same time critical appreciation... his pleasant, frank, and gentlemanly manners render the relationship of teacher and taught in his case peculiarly agreeable.

The summer of 1915, when KS was still an undergraduate, saw two important milestones in his life. On 26 May, he was married to Visalakshi who was to be his steadying hand and staunch support for the next seventy-nine years.[7] Her father, also K. Swaminathan, was a well-known figure in the legal profession and public life of Pudukottai: State Vakil and Public Prosecutor, an elected member of the Legislative Council, Municipal Councillor and President of the Cooperative Bank. His services were free for poor clients to whom justice had been denied. An ardent nationalist, he associated himself with the Congress and the States' People's Conference on numerous occasions. One of the obituary tributes to him speaks of his remarkable qualities of 'plain speaking, sturdy independence and moral stamina'. Further, he was 'a man of strong likes and dislikes who hated sham, cant and corruption wherever they were'.

Through marriage, KS also acquired Dr M. K. Sambasivan for his brother-in-law. Based in Kumbakonam, Dr Sambasivan was a medical practitioner, Congressman, and Municipal Chairman at a very young age. In all these capacities, he was much loved by a wide circle of

---

[7] They had four children, a son (who died early) and three daughters: Mahalakshmi (m. P. R. Suryanandan), Santa (m. R. S. Ramachandran) and Dharma (m. Tarun Chatterji).

friends and admirers. He died suddenly, when only 37 years old, leaving behind his wife (Thangammal, Visalakshi's sister) and four children, one of whom is the renowned agricultural scientist, Dr M. S. Swaminathan, a contributor to this volume. KS was very close to Sambasivan and guide and guardian to his children during their higher education in Madras.

The other event that made 1915 a memorable year for KS was his first encounter with Gandhi. Having finally returned to India from South Africa in January, Gandhiji spent nearly three weeks in Madras in April–May of that year, as a guest of G. A. Natesan, editor of the *Indian Review*, staying on the first floor of the journal's office in George Town. As one of the young volunteers assigned to attend to Gandhiji's needs, KS sharpened his quill pens (Gandhi would not use nibs which were then all imported) and filled his ink-pot with 'swadeshi' ink. He also escorted him by tram to the Catholic Archbishop's place in San Thome and to the Anglican Bishop's house next to St George's Cathedral; with them Gandhiji was canvassing the support of the Christian community for the Indian struggle in South Africa. KS seems to have tried to persuade Gandhiji to use the *jutka* (horse-drawn carriage) for these trips, but was turned down on the ground that that would have cost two rupees while the tram fare was just a few paise.

KS's substantive meeting with the (by then) Mahatma had to wait until 1920, when Gandhi was involved in seeking and accepting lifetime recruits to the Non-cooperation movement. In Madras, K. Santhanam and N. S. Varadachari were among the young men chosen by Gandhiji 'after carefully examining their abilities, aptitude, and family obligations'. KS too was interviewed, but was told by the Master, 'You may not join me now, but I shall call you when I need you and you are ready.' It would appear that, at that stage, KS himself was not too eager to make a lifelong commitment to the national movement because of the precedence he gave to his family responsibilities. As far as Gandhiji was concerned, the call was given posthumously, forty years later, when KS was appointed Chief Editor of the Mahatma's *Collected Works*.

It was also around the early twenties that KS began engaging himself in 'social service' in the slums of Madras city—Harijan welfare, adult literacy, and other educational and welfare activities. In the company of fellow Congress volunteers (who included K. Kamaraj) he used to cycle around a number of slums in this connection. He continued with his involvement in social service as a teacher in Presidency College, interesting his students also in it. In a later phase, he attempted to combine social service with the activities of the Ramana Kendra in Delhi in the seventies and eighties; this is described in Kala Rani Rengaswamy's contribution to this collection.

☆

When KS graduated from Presidency College, Madras, in 1917, he could have hardly imagined that thirteen years later he would, as a member of its staff, return to Alma Mater; for, the intervening period veered off widely for a while from the main course of his career. There was some talk, as was usual in the case of promising young men, of his going to England to sit for the ICS examination but, despite the likely availability of a scholarship, his mother firmly ruled out a sea voyage during war time. Law was a ready option and, after taking his law degree (1917–19), KS was apprenticed to the formidable S. Srinivasa Iyengar, a leading lawyer and future President of the Congress. KS was to describe him as 'a fine blend of Birkenhead the legal genius and Churchill the patriot' besides being a 'Vaishnava with a warm, compassionate heart'.

On completing the apprenticeship, KS moved to Pudukottai for law practice under the aegis of his father-in-law, but life as a 'mofussil' lawyer was mercifully short. KS not only participated in a public agitation against the Maharaja led by S. Satyamurthi, the mentor of Kamaraj and an old family friend, but also invited him to address the Bar Association. This led to the British government threatening to withdraw KS's *sanad* (licence to practise law). The government was prepared to relent if the delinquent apologized, but—fully supported by his equally stiff-necked father-in-law—KS refused to do so. At this point, Raja Sir Annamalai Chettiar, friend and client of K. Swaminathan Senior, came to the rescue and gave KS an appointment as lecturer in the English department of Sri Minakshi College which he had founded in Chidambaram. From thereon, it was also the 'Raja Sir' who advanced the money for KS to go to Oxford for further studies.

☆

Unfortunately, not much is known of the two years (1922–4) that KS spent in Christ Church College, Oxford studying for his BA in English Language and Literature. As always, he involved himself in extra-curricular activities and served for a term as President of the Indian Majlis, forming a good friendship with his predecessor, S. W. R. D. Bandaranaike, future Prime Minister of Ceylon. This also gave him the opportunity to meet notables like John Woodroffe, Gilbert Murray, Bertrand Russell, Hilaire Belloc and G. K. Chesterton. Nothing is known of these encounters, except that Russell is reported to have remarked that the trouble with Hinduism was that 'it lacked guts. It tolerated all things including intolerance', a remark that was to stay with KS as far as the mid-eighties when he became much exercised over conversions to Islam in south India. Contemporaries among Indian students included Ali Yavar Jung and Vishnu Sahay, but closest to KS were C. R. Ranganathan, V. S. Kuppuswamy, and T. S. Ramachandran, all from native Madras.[8] All of them were non-smokers, teetotallers, and vegetarians; after a boat race, being among the few sober ones, they were much in demand for 'taking charge of things'.

Eventually, despite his outstanding performance under Mark Hunter's tough curriculum in Madras, KS scored only a high second at Oxford in the Honours degree. Perhaps, his extra-mural activities proved to be too much of a diversion. All that we know is that Dr A. J. Carlyle, his tutor, thought it fit and necessary to record that 'Mr Swaminathan is a most accomplished scholar, and the excellent second class which he obtained is not in my opinion at all adequate to his real merits.' Dr Carlyle's certificate went on to say: 'His (KS's) work for me was consistently of very high quality, and his knowledge of English literature is wide, but also precise and exact, and his critical judgement is excellent, independent and individual, but also sane and free from mere eccentricity.' Dr Carlyle referred to KS's 'very pleasant and unassuming manners' and expressed the confidence that 'he will prove himself a first-rate scholar and a most interesting and stimulating teacher.'

☆

On his return from Oxford, KS rejoined Sri Minakshi College, which had by then become a part of the Annamalai University, as the Head of its department of English. The Rt. Hon. V. S. Srinivasa Sastri was

[8] Ali Yavar Jung had a diplomatic career; Vishnu Sahay was Cabinet Secretary and Governor of Assam; C. R. Ranganathan and V. S. Kuppuswamy had distinguished careers in the Indian Forest Service, while T. S. Ramachandran was a respected member of the ICS in Madras state.

the Vice-Chancellor of the University, to be followed by S. E. Runganadhan. His students included R. Venkataraman, who would become President of India, T. N. Jagadisan, who dedicated himself to the relief of leprosy, and K. Subrahmanyam. The latter, apart from being one of KS's oldest students, was one who remained closest to him. He liked to call himself KS (Junior) and was indeed so to younger generations of students in the Loyola and Vivekananda Colleges where he taught English.

KS threw himself not only into the organization of English studies in Annamalai but was also active in the Madras University through his membership of its Board of Studies for English and the Board of Examiners for the Honours course. He also delivered university lectures in Presidency College, Madras which, in the words of Prof. D. S. Sarma, were 'characterized by great learning, sound judgement and unerring taste.' Once again, KS did not confine himself narrowly to the role of the English teacher. K. A. Nilakanta Sastri, the noted historian and then Principal of Sri Minakshi College, had this to say:

I know that his administrative capacity is equal to his eminence in scholarship. There is practically no department of College life which has not been galvanized into brisker activity and taken to a higher level by his versatile talent and ubiquitous energy. The Hostel, the Union and the Magazine could have hardly become what they are today but for his great enthusiasm and initiative.[9]

The best thing that was to happen to KS at Chidambaram was, however, something quite outside the realm of English studies. It was his getting to know T. K. Chidambaranatha Mudaliar (TKC), scholar, host, critic, and connoisseur of all that was best in Tamil literature, music, and dance. It was TKC who brought out KS's latent creativity in Tamil. KS recollects (1968):

Originally, I used to write only in English—I was afraid to write in Tamil. It was actually in Oxford that I heard many Professors praise the antiquity

[9] S. Ramabhadran (age 76), retired Tahsildar, after reading an article about KS in *The Hindu*, wrote to him in 1986 as follows: 'I was studying in the Intermediate between '27 and '29 in Sri Meenakshi College, Chidambaram, when you were the Vice-Principal there—You were the warden of the hostel and you used to come on rounds in the night to see the students engaged in reading. You were so good and kind-hearted that you earned the admiration and respect of one and all. Your simplicity and easy approachability will ever be remembered.'

and greatness of Tamil... Later in Chidambaram I came to know TKC. It was he who gave me the enthusiasm and confidence to study Tamil and to write in it... He was not only a friend but a great inspiration. I learnt so many poems from him. He wanted me to write them down but instead I got them by heart for which I am grateful. These days, when I am not able to read much because of poor eyesight, it gives me great joy to keep repeating the poems I had memorized in my younger days.

It was again TKC who introduced KS to the verses of Guhai Namasivayam on Annamalai, the holy hill, while one of KS's students, M. G. Shanmukham (son of a Police Inspector) was the first to speak to him about Sri Ramana Maharshi. However, despite the proximity of Tiruvannamalai and Sri Ramanasramam to Chidambaram, KS did not respond. Much later, writing about his first *darshan* of the Maharshi (which took place in 1940), KS frankly noted that, in 1927, 'when Shanmukham spoke enthusiastically to me about Sri Ramana, I was not interested in someone sitting still and doing nothing when so much needed to be done to change this mad, bad world and Mahatma Gandhi strode the land doing so many things "socially relevant".'

The contradiction that KS perceived between the Maharshi and the Mahatma, between the pursuit of individual salvation and socio-political public action was to be a continuing concern. It was not something which could be put aside or passively contemplated; it had to be wrestled with and resolved. This process, as we shall see', was to underlie much of KS's activities and writings in later years.

☆

The beginning of the academic year 1930 was home-coming for KS, true to his college motto 'Unde Orte Recurrit' (Whence risen, it returns).[10] The circumstances under which he left Chidambaram and was intercepted en route to Trivandrum by Professor Erlam Smith for being appointed as Additional Professor in Presidency College, Madras are recounted in S. Ramaswami's contribution to this collection. The vacancy itself was obligingly created by Professor W. C. Douglas extending his furlough. The whole episode, which

---

[10] Inscribed over a picture of the rising sun, the motto is intended to convey that learning which rose from the East returns from the West in the form of English education.

marked a watershed in KS's life, is a remarkable illustration of the lengths to which the best of the British went to recognize and reward competence.

The two decades that followed were to be the most crowded and lively in KS's career. The contributions to this collection from students of different vintages during the thirties and forties express the affection and admiration he inspired in them. And, the spontaneity and freshness of their tributes—despite the passage of more than half a century—indicate the intense impact he must have had. While it is not necessary to summarize or supplement this testimony, the common threads are worth setting out. As a teacher, KS developed a personal relationship with his students, attending to their individual academic advancement in the best tradition of the Oxford tutor; as S. Ramaswami says, 'Few of us regretted Madras was not Oxford in name. It was Oxford in fact.'

The enduring effect that KS had is also attributed by many of his students to his mode of teaching which related the values of literature to the values of life, taking every opportunity to contextualize the texts within specific Indian terms, whether it was the praxis of Gandhi or, in later years, the philosophy of Sri Ramana. As N. S. Jagannathan points out, such was KS's use of political parallels that the teaching of English literature in his hands became 'an instrument of Gandhian subversion'. Equally, and at a deeper level, it could lead to an appreciation of basic concepts in Hindu philosophy. Wordsworth's nature mysticism, for instance,

had none of the certainty, the steady strength and serene brilliance of the vision of our *rishis* ancient and modern. And yet, since his poems are accurate records of his real experience of *kshana samadhi*... poetry with him was not an art or a trade; it was a *sadhana*, a means of attaining *jnana*, the knowledge of that truth which alone can make us free.

Similarly, there was 'Upanishadic wisdom' in Keats's notion of 'negative capability'; so also, the immortality of his nightingale was the same as that of the twin birds in the Mundaka Upanishad. And, because Shakespeare was 'as unique and yet as natural as one's own mother, he was as universal as motherhood... (and) the name that suits him best is the sweet name of our poet, Thayumannavar, "He who is mother also".'

KS thus opened many vistas in the minds of his students by making connections—often unexpected, sometimes far-fetched, but always stimulating. In the words of a character in one of Umberto Eco's novels, 'Genius, and therefore Learning, consists in connecting remote Notions and finding Similitude in things dissimilar.'[11]

KS's involvement with his students went far beyond the academic environment. While he did not interfere with their decisions, he was not indifferent to major problems in their lives: he ventured to offer his reaction or advice, whether it was on Lawrence Sundaram joining the Society of Jesus or G. N. S. Raghavan, the Communist Party of India. He and his wife took his students in as members of their own family; 'Dharmalayam' was open house to them at all hours and in all seasons; if discussions lasted too late in the evening, they just ate and slept there; some of them moved in for longer periods; they became friends of his wife, children, nephews, nieces, and even grandchildren; and lifelong, KS kept in touch with them, promptly responding to their letters or to something he had heard or read about them. The spontaneous respect of his students, the parental solicitude on his part, and the natural and easy informality that characterized their mutual interaction were as remarkable as they were heart-warming.

Two extracts from letters that KS had carefully preserved give a feel for the kind of bond that existed between him and his *chelas*. K. Subrahmanyam writes in 1964 from Nagapattinam, his home town, where he had settled:

Herewith two more of my spiritual outpourings. I am ashamed of being intense, profound, etc. I have been re-reading during the last 10 days or so all of P. G. Wodehouse I can lay hands on in this illiterate region. I see into his philosophy of the frivolous. His butts are those who are incapable of taking their ease in the inn of this world, the would-be world-transformers, the efficiency-fanatics, the go-getters, the soulful, the blazing idealists, etc. If you are not relaxed you are not stable. The apostles of earnestness are in a febrile or delirious state—not in good health.... Is not a sense of humour the same as a sense of detachment, freedom from involvement or pet intensities, 'mission in life', etc.? Unless we can be good and wise with the flippancy of Bertie Wooster and his ilk, our self-conscious goodness and wisdom do not really belong to us. We are strutting and not walking with our normal gait. Emotionally we should be able to saunter through life—a piece of wisdom that has come to me in my sixtieth year.

The other letter, which is from Father Lawrence Sundaram (in 1990),

---

[11] Padre Emanuele in Umberto Eco, *The Island of the Day Before*, Secker and Warburg, 1995.

is equally friendly although polemical and serious. He vigorously picks a theological bone with KS:

You often compare the O.T. to Dwaitam and the N.T. you identify with Advaita...I submit that in Christianity God is neither only transcendant nor only immanent. He is both; neither, therefore, Dwaitam nor Advaitam can explain Him. The main problem for Advaita...is the love of the Atman in a manifestly wicked and wrong-doing person, if this Atman is to be identified with the internal Brahman, the Self. I love my enemy because he, like me, is a child of God, my brother or sister and like me is destined for ultimate happiness. His wickedness or sinfulness cannot be merely part of a world of avidya—cosmic ignorance. He is a reality to be reckoned with as we see everyday to our cost all over the world and in our country. I humbly submit to you that the Christian solution of the problem—not simply of 'evil'—but of sin meets the case: the redemptive suffering of Christ to which I unite myself and by which with Him I expiate the sins of the world. Did not Gandhiji accept and live by the truth? What else is Satyagraha?

These extracts should not suggest that KS's affinities were confined to an inner core for, in many ways, he succeeded in reaching out to wider circles of the student community. He had 'an extraordinary knack' for spotting and encouraging promising students who, but for his material or moral support, might have remained disadvantaged on account of economic status or religion or caste. He quietly assisted many poor students and used every opportunity to promote their welfare. He encouraged his students to write, and helped them to get published. In college, he was formal or informal adviser in respect of all student activities, whether it was the Union, the hostel, the Magazine or dramatics.

In the last analysis, the appeal that KS had for a wide circle of students in Presidency College and the influence he was able to exercise over them are to be explained by the fact that he represented a form of Gandhian nationalism that was at once principled and practical. During the thirties and forties, when the national movement had entered a heightened phase, the tension in the minds of most sensitive students was between some degree of participation in the freedom movement on the one hand and the pursuit of their studies, career interests, and family obligations on the other. KS himself made no secret of his loyalties. All along he wore only khaddar—suit, shirt, tie and socks; what is more, his sartorial elegance was often remarked upon. He was openly friendly with a number of leading Congressmen; and had made Gandhi and his struggles a part of the classroom. At the same time, he was serving a government under an anti-national colonial rule. He did not recognize any contradiction in doing so because the good citizens that free India would need would have to come from good students taught by good teachers. By the same token, he conveyed to his students that they too need not feel any contradiction between nation building and the pursuit of their studies; indeed, the latter was a necessary element in the former.

It should be said, however, that such a reconciliation between what KS—quoting A. D. Lindsay—used to call the 'two moralities' (namely, the lower morality pertaining to 'my station and its duties' and the higher morality of obligations to God or country) could endure largely because of a particularly enlightened and liberal-minded constellation of British administrators in the Madras educational system of those days—Erlam Smith, W. C. Douglas, H. C. Papworth, R. M. Statham, and A. F. Dixon. KS himself fully acknowledged this fortunate conjuncture.[12] Matters, however, came to a head on 9 August 1942, 'when the British government suddenly let loose its leonine violence and deprived Gandhiji of his freedom and the country of its natural leadership.' The outbreak of the 'Quit India' movement found the staff and students of Presidency College deeply divided: the pro-Congress majority did not know how to give expression to its nationalist sentiments, a few were for violent demonstrations and many were dead against 'quarrelling with their bread and butter'. However, the student body, as a whole, went on a strike that was near-total until it ended five weeks later in mid-September.

For KS, these events were a crisis that was 'personal, institutional and national'. Indeed, KS was in an especially difficult position: he was not only the informal adviser to the students, but also happened to be the Additional Professor nominated to assist the Principal. His agenda—based on much consultation with Rajaji—was twofold. One was to ensure that the students' protest remained peaceful and that they were united in deciding how long the strike should continue.

---

[12] A. D. Lindsay, *The Two Moralities*. KS discusses the two moralities in relation to Gandhi in his 'The Third Ashrama', *Swatantra*, Madras, Deepavali Number 1951. Erlam Smith and W. C. Douglas were Professors in Presidency College; H. C. Papworth was the Principal; R. M. Statham was Director of Public Instruction; and A. F. Dixon was Education Secretary.

The other was to ensure that the authorities did not attempt to repress the agitation or to divide the ranks of the students, but could be persuaded to respect their sentiments, at least tacitly. In both these aims, he succeeded admirably. Many 'thoughtful observers'—officials and nationalists alike—were impressed with the 'genuine democracy, autonomy and solidarity' demonstrated by the Principal, staff, and students of Presidency College. The British blimps, however, exacted their price by demoting Principal Papworth but he was more than rehabilitated by C. P. Ramaswamy Iyer, who invited him to become the Vice-Chancellor of the Travancore University.

☆

It was during his days in Presidency College that KS emerged as a versatile, original, and lively writer in Tamil. Inspired with self-confidence by TKC, he contributed extensively to journals such as *Ananda Vikatan, Kalaimagal, Kalki, Hanuman, Manikkodi,* and later in *Kanaiyazhi.* For several years, the special Deepavali issues of some of them used to carry an article by him.

What brought KS to wider public attention was the Tamil opera *Kattai Vandi* based on Gilbert and Sullivan's *Gondoliers.* Published in 1934, it used much in the political and social setting of those times as grist for its satirical mill. Its numerous songs, taking off from popular tunes, parodied the verse forms of Valluvar, *Nandanar Charitram,* and Bharati while in content they lampooned party politics, electoral democracy, dyarchy, socialist rhetoric, casteism, communalism, westernization, and so on. On all these, the songs hit the nail on the head—in rollicking humour and lilting language. In an appreciation, S. Satyamurthi pointed out that the 'drama deals in a kindly cynical spirit with all the contemporary evils in our political, social, and religious life. Those who witness this drama...will be challenged to think strenuously of several contemporary problems.' Since 'thought leads to action', Satyamurthi also expressed the hope that 'this drama may do a great deal towards elevating us in all spheres.'

KS dedicated *Kattai Vandi* to TKC with the inscription 'For TKC who told me "Why teach swimming to the fish and Tamil to the Tamilian, just write, my fellow"'. In a foreword, he warned that the play was meant for acting and not reading. 'It can be enjoyed only in the pleasant stupor created by a crowded hall, music, lighting, colours, the appearance, voices and acting of the cast, and so on. These are the hot water, milk and sugar; the text is mere coffee decoction, bitter if tasted by itself.' Acted the opera was several times in Madras, starting with Presidency College, and before appreciative Tamil audiences elsewhere including Delhi, Calcutta, and Simla, in the process raising funds for good causes such as the Bihar Earthquake Relief Fund. Despite KS's cautionary foreword, *Kattai Vandi* is very enjoyable reading and, if revived, could be as topical today as it was in the mid thirties.[13]

A little known fact, but one of some historical and biographical interest, is that KS was one of the earliest to recognize the genius of Bharatidasan (Suppuratnam) who was to become, and remains, the Poet Laureate of the Dravidian movement. This happened in 1938 when, in a talk broadcast over All India Radio on recent developments in Tamil literature, KS hailed Bharatidasan as the Tamil poet in contemporary times who was 'most active and most likely to endure'. KS noted that his poetry was not without its faults: inconsistencies, a tendency to be propagandist, a certain parochialism, caste consciousness, irreverence that can be an irritant, and so on. But none of this did matter: 'they were like the rough kicks of a cow while being milked, or the bees' stings when golden honey was being collected.' KS then proceeded to give rich praise to the power, passion, pace, beauty, social awareness, realism, directness, simplicity, and humour in Bharatidasan's poetry with copious quotations from it.

The broadcast had an important practical fallout besides being a reflection of KS's critical acumen, objectivity, and generosity. Bharatidasan, a primary school teacher under the Pondicherry administration, was being tossed from one village to another as punishment for his nationalist views; at the time of the broadcast, he was posted to a particularly god-forsaken village called Nettapakkam. Fortunately, one of the higher officials, who happened to listen to KS, was impelled to seek out Bharatidasan, apologize for the treatment meted out to him, and arrange for his transfer to Pondicherry. These events are recorded, with a handsome acknowledgment to KS, by Mannarmannan, the poet's son, in his biography of his father (*Karuppu Kuyilin Nerrupu Kural*).

---

[13] KS also authored a few short plays and skits in Tamil: *Padaviye Udavi; Varam*; and *Daridranarayanan*.

KS felt that the best in Tamil poetry were the hymns of the Alwars and Nayanmars:

They are incredibly beautiful...Vaishnavite poetry is like painting. It has to be experienced slowly and at leisure. It is not easy to set these poems to music. In contrast, Saivite sacred poems have beat and music. They tend to come at a continuous pace; they run rapidly without interruption like the lively flow of a river. They should be read fast and enjoyed.

KS's involvement in Tamil was recognized and utilized by the government. He served as the Secretary of the Technical Terms Committee (1940–6), as a member of the Script Reform Committee (1949–50), and succeeded 'Kalki' R. Krishnamurthi in 1954 as Secretary of the Tamil Development Committee which brought out the Tamil Encyclopaedia.

KS's association with Presidency College came to an end with his promotion and transfer as Principal of, what was then known as, the Government Muhamadan College, where he spent the last five years prior to his retirement from the State Education service (1948–53). His period there was marked by a number of improvements and reforms testifying once again to his involvement in practical administration. During these years, the Intermediate classes were fully shifted from Presidency College; a system of tutorials was established; attendance was left to be monitored by student representatives; and, there was tangible improvement in the percentage of passes. Moreover, what pleased KS was that 'he quietly changed the name of the institution to Government Arts College'—to attempt and achieve which must have demanded a lot of daring and diplomacy from its first non-Muslim Principal. There has been a subsequent change in its name and gender to the present Qaid-e-Milleth College for Women.

☆

KS began a second career when, soon after retirement, he accepted Ramnath Goenka's invitation to become the Associate Editor of the *Indian Express* at Madras. To him, the move was not only 'from one side of the Mount Road to the other' but also to a proximate vocation, for Rajaji had told him 'You are not changing your profession. The journalist, like the teacher and the preacher, tries to communicate something useful.' Goenka gave him complete freedom and Frank Moraes, the Chief Editor, warned him against wasting too much time or energy in the pursuit of perfection for it was 'not attainable within a deadline'. Copies of editorials in the *Indian Express* which KS had preserved are mostly on standard topics, while some are 'third edits' in a lighter vein. Of the latter, a fine example is one on the jibbah titled 'Jibber-ish'. The editorial takes issue with the Commissioner of Police, Madras, who had warned 'gentlemen in jibbahs' that they were relatively easy prey to pickpockets. 'The tall order', it points out,

> to discard it will only evoke resentment... The jibbah is an indispensable symbol of our personal, political and social ethos. The emblem of civilian status, the foamy essence of mufti, it is to a uniform what the gentle moon is to the fiery sun... The police should think of other and more feasible methods of putting down crime. It is their job to nab the thief, not jib at the jibbah.

The years at the *Express* (1953-9) were not confined to routine journalism. It was during this time that KS undertook two major translations into English, one of Vinoba's *Talks on the Gita* and the other of Rajaji's *Ramayana*. Both were serialized in the *Express* over two years. Also, during this period, Vinoba was on his Bhoodan *padayatra* in Tamilnadu and southern Andhra; KS took the opportunity to drive down over the weekends to where he was and have long discussions with him on the *Gita* and on the translation. So also, he spent many hours with Rajaji on the *Ramayana*.

KS found time to prepare a memorandum on 'Roman Script for Official Hindi' and submitted it in 1955 to the Official Language Commission, with the endorsement of several others, for 'careful study and vigorous support in appropriate quarters'. The memorandum made out a concise and cogent case for the replacement of English with Hindi in Roman script as the official language of the Union. Among the several arguments in favour of the proposal, KS pointed out that it would equalize the burden of learning two scripts (their own and Roman) among all language groups and, in particular, extend equality of opportunity to south Indians who were not familiar with Devanagari.

At the end of 1958, the Government of India's Ministry of Education invited KS to lead a delegation of 'Workers of Indian Art' to the Soviet Union, Poland, Czechoslovakia, and Yugoslavia. The delegation undertook an intensive tour between the first week of December 1958 and the third week of January 1959. It was KS's first and last trip abroad since his Oxford days. He kept a diary of the hectic schedule consisting of visits to museums, libraries, educational institutions at various levels, participation in cultural events, and meetings with officials, academics, orientalists, journalists, and Indian residents in these countries.

In his recommendations to the government, at the end of the tour, KS made a vigorous plea for strengthening cultural and educational relations between India and the East European countries through the exchange of books, teachers and students, and a systematic programme of translations. He also made a number of concrete suggestions for policy: (a) From Russia, we ought to learn the importance of language and mathematics in the school curriculum; they are 'tool subjects, not memory loads'; (b) India must also emulate Russia in following 'a strictly impersonal and scientific approach to pedagogical and organizational problems'; (c) Following Yugoslavia, the medium of instruction and the language of administration should be the regional language, and all regional languages should be given 'a status of complete equality with the language of the dominant majority; (d) Yugoslavia also offered a good model in the treatment of scripts by giving equal recognition to the Roman and Cyrillic scripts and enabling flexible use between them; (e) The lesson to be learnt from Poland and Czechoslovakia was flexibility in the choice of medium; students were not only free to choose them according to their convenience but also to change their choice from time to time. In our case, all major languages should be university media with English being insisted upon as an alternative.

KS also took the occasion to point out that 'to insist on south Indian children learning Hindi in the Nagari script (in addition to English in the Roman script) is educationally unsound, as it is burdensome and wasteful, and politically undesirable as it would cause needless friction. Thus, he was not only against the official three-language formula, but did not hesitate to make his views known in an official report.

☆

In 1960, with nearly two-thirds of his life behind him, KS began his third career, which was to be the longest and most impressive. The collection, editing, and publication of all that Gandhiji wrote and every authentic account of what he had said was conceived as a project by the Government of India in 1956. The work was to be supervised by an Advisory Board, chaired by Morarji Desai, and implemented under the full-time direction of a Chief Editor. The first Chief Editor, Bharatan Kumarappa, died in 1957 and was succeeded by Jairamdas Daulatram who resigned in 1959. By then, only three volumes of the *Collected Works of Mahatma Gandhi* (CWMG) had been brought out. KS was neither an obvious nor a logical choice for the post of Chief Editor. He was not a member of the Gandhian establishment, either as an activist or as a Gandhian scholar; he did not know Hindi or Gujarati; and he lived in the obscurity of Madras. It is not known how he first came to be considered for the post, but KS was given to understand that it was Vinoba Bhave who had recommended his name to Nehru.[14] In October 1959, Dr B. V. Keskar, the then Minister of Information and Broadcasting, invited KS to become the Chief Editor, CWMG. This was, however, subject to the concurrence of Morarji Desai, the Chairman of the Advisory Board, to meet whom KS was summoned to Delhi.

KS's recollection of the rather rough meeting with Morarji was as follows:

Morarji could realize that not only do I not know Hindi or Gujarati, but also that I did not know much of Gandhi himself. Morarji asked me rather sternly, 'you have strong recommendations.... But are you competent to organize research and publish Gandhi's utterances with proper explanatory notes?' I shot back: 'May be I am not very familiar with Gandhi's writings. But I am well-read about the Alwars, the Tamil Vaishnavite Saint poets. Gandhiji belongs to the same category, does he not?'

It is not known whether Morarji was convinced by the reply, but KS's interpretation of Gandhi—consistently brought out in his prefaces to the CWMG volumes—was fundamentally in terms of a seeker of personal salvation in and through politics, in the Vaishnavite tradition of surrender and enquiry. For KS, 'Gandhi was first, last and all the time a Vaishnava, a *Vishishtadvaitan*, a believer in *Ramrajya.*' With Morarji himself, KS forged a strong relationship that endured through thick and thin for the rest of his life.

KS was also fond of drawing attention to Gandhi's Tamil connection. 'Gandhi's greatest support in South Africa, not only in numbers but in solid moral strength,' he pointed out,

---

[14] According to H. Y. Sharada Prasad, U. S. Mohan Rao, Gandhian and Director of Publications Division (Ministry of Information and Broadcasting), played a crucial role in conceiving the CWMG project and in the choice of KS as Chief Editor in 1959.

came from the Tamil coolies—the Nagappans, Narayanaswamis and Valliammas. The minds and hearts of these poor, helpless Indians had been moulded by a long cultural tradition whose latest embodiment was Ramalingaswami, and they were ready to recognize, and willing to obey, the call of *dharma* when it came to them from a man of God.[15]

By the mid-eighties, when KS returned to Madras, all ninety of the main volumes had been brought out. KS was naturally proud of the achievement. He pointed out: 'In these 90 volumes, we have the *ipsissima verba*, the very words of Gandhi, faithfully recorded with notes, appendices, and critical apparatus, helping the common reader to know the facts and leaving him free to form his own judgement.' Also, that 'while similar volumes on the works of Karl Marx, Lenin and Abraham Lincoln have been published so far, the collected works of Gandhi was the largest.' Even after his return to Madras, KS provided continuous and detailed editorial advice to CWMG right until 1990. Along with supplementary volumes, index volumes, and a volume of the prefaces, a full 100 volumes had been released by 1994 when KS passed away.

The contributions by La. Su. Rengarajan, Lalitha Zackariah and Madan Gopal, supplemented by that of H. Y. Sharada Prasad, give a vivid idea of KS's functioning as Chief Editor, CWMG—the team spirit (indeed, family bonds) that he fostered among his staff; his capacity to make solid and sustained personal contributions without inhibiting their initiative; the meticulous attention to detail in research and editing;[16] and the principled way—combining fortitude and firmness—in which he faced the extreme stress, including near-dismissal, he was subjected to during the Emergency years. Of the latter, a full and detailed account can be found in the articles by La. Su. Rengarajan and Madan Gopal in this collection.

KS's contribution was recognized with honours and praise. He was awarded the Padma Bhushan in 1972. Releasing the 89th and 90th volumes in 1980, Prime Minister Indira Gandhi (who had decided in 1977 to dispense with his services!), said:

Shri Swaminathan is with us. He has personally looked after this series, except for the first few... for all of you, it was a love of labour as well as perhaps a labour of love. A major project has been completed. Only

---

[15] 'Gandhiji in South Africa', *Vivekananda Patrika*, February 1973.
[16] KS warned his staff: 'The lawyer's mistakes are hanged or jailed, the doctor's mistakes are buried or burnt, but the editor's mistakes are printed and published.'

those who know how very difficult it is to edit historical documents will appreciate the magnitude of this work... Above all, our thanks are due to Prof Swaminathan who has worked with the dedication expected of a follower of Ramana Maharshi and Mahatma Gandhi.

KS was conferred an honorary doctorate by the Gandhigram Rural University in 1987 on which occasion, its Chancellor, Vice-President R. Venkataraman said:

Prof Swaminathan is a rare person. Combining in himself western education in Oxford with the eastern devotion of a *Madbhakta*, Prof Swaminathan symbolizes the best of Indian culture.... Prof Swaminathan's monumental work in the *Collected Works of Mahatma Gandhi* is, of course, a service of which there are few parallels. The meticulousness with which the writings of Gandhiji have been collected, translated and published would have been impossible but for Prof Swaminathan's labours.

H. Y. Sharada Prasad points out in his contribution that, although KS became easily 'the most outstanding book editor of the land', his name did not appear in any of the CWMG volumes he edited. 'It was printed only in the final volume of the series along with the names of all those who have worked on the project. This kind of self-abnegation, absence of *aham*, is rare to come across. It would have been approved by his own Guru.' KS's sense of anonymity was also apparently approved by the Government of India for, when the hundredth and final volume was released in October 1994, just a few months after KS passed away, neither the Prime Minister (P. V. Narasimha Rao) nor the Minister for Information and Broadcasting nor the Secretary of that Ministry even referred to KS by name in their speeches, much less his contribution to the project over thirty years and 88 volumes.[17] This was an unforgivable lapse, although KS himself might have brushed it aside as an inverted and ironic form of poetic justice.

☆

The considerable demands that the CWMG made on him, apart from his advancing years, did not discourage KS from throwing himself into a whole host of cultural, literary, and other activities during his days in Delhi. He took an active part in the activities of the Delhi

[17] H. Y. Sharada Prasad, 'Two Who Were Forgotten', *National Herald*, 9 October 1994.

Tamil Sangam. His strong sense of 'Tamil cultural nationalism' made him look for every opportunity to familiarize the north Indian capital of the nation with the best from Tamilnadu, whether it was the music of M. S. Subbulakshmi, the poetry of Subramania Bharati, or the teachings of Ramana Maharshi. In a tribute to MS on her sixtieth birthday (1976), KS said:

Gifted with a voice that is a perfect amalgam of the melodious, the meditative, and the devotional, Subbulakshmi holds her audiences spell-bound by a natural charm more powerful than mere technique. Truly has she opened the portals of Karnatak music to a vast appreciative audience, both at home and abroad. Hers is the first voice from the south to have been so widely heard and so intensely enjoyed.

Some years later, releasing a record of Bharati's songs sung by MS, he declaimed: 'May I, as a born Tamilian and a born Indian, remind the great Moghuls who rule this land from Delhi that India is most Indian in south India?'

KS was a natural choice to head the Publications Sub-Committee when the Government of India decided in 1982 to celebrate the birth centenary of Mahakavi Subramania Bharati. Moreover, he edited a substantial volume, *Subramania Bharathi—Chosen Poems and Prose*, himself translating a large number of the poems included in it. In his introduction to this volume, KS pointed out:

With its steady, regular oscillation between *Aham* and *Puram*, love and war, inner and outer, the Tamil genius has been through the ages centroverted, never unduly extroverted or introverted... in Tamil land the voice of poetry had never been neglected or suppressed in the conversation of the people. In singing of the ideals of social equality, individual freedom and human unity, Bharati was only reviving an ancient Tamil tradition.

☆

In KS's own life, the 'steady and regular oscillation', particularly during his days in Delhi, was between Gandhi and Ramana. A more appropriate metaphor might be that Gandhi and Ramana were like the chains at the two ends which made KS pleasantly swing like the traditional Tamil *oonjal*. KS's first darshan of Sri Ramana Bhagavan was in 1940 in the company of his wife and his students, K. Subrahmanyam[18] and M. M. Ismail. Until the Bhagavan's

---

[18] K. Subrahmanyam's article in this collection describes this first visit.

mahanirvana in 1950, KS spent many weekends and vacations in Sri Ramanasramam, each time taking with him friends, students, and family members. The same enthusiasm—almost compulsion—for making others share the Ramana experience was responsible for his organizing weekly meetings of the Ramana Bhakta Sabha in 'Dharmalayam' in the mid-fifties. From the early sixties, he organized a similar *satsang* in Delhi in his small flat in Netaji Nagar on Sunday evenings. Usually, it would begin with the recitation of the Bhagavan's teachings, followed by some music and concluding with a short talk by KS or by someone else in the group. In course of time, KS gathered around him a fairly large Ramana family which overlapped somewhat with the CWMG family. His relationship with them was sustained lifelong through personal contact and correspondence.

In the early seventies, the time had come to put the activity on a permanent basis. KS took great efforts to raise finance and get land allotted for establishing a Ramana Kendra in the capital. The Kendra, inaugurated on 1 September 1974 in the Lodi Institutional Complex, has proved to be a vibrant centre for the sharing and transmission of the Maharshi's message. An equally solid contribution was his biography of Ramana in the National Book Trust series, which came out a couple of years later. The original in English was subsequently translated into Hindi, Tamil, and some other Indian languages. Through many reprints, it has provided a simple and succinct introduction to the Bhagavan's life and teachings to thousands of readers. In other ways as well, KS busied himself with popularizing the form, name, and message of Ramana: he lobbied successfully for the issue of a Ramana Maharshi commemorative postage stamp (1971); recorded an introductory talk to a special Ramananjali music programme of MS over All India Radio (1979); helped to organize the Ramana Maharshi centenary celebrations and seminar in New Delhi (1980); and, in the same year, managed to have an important arterial road in the Lodi Estate area renamed as Maharshi Ramana Marg.

Throughout his years in Delhi, KS had continued his association with Sri Ramanasramam as informal adviser on their publications, including the *Mountain Path* (MP), the Asram's quarterly journal. Around the mid-eighties, he functioned for some years as the Chief Editor of MP. A monumental contribution to Ramana literature was his translations of Sri Muruganar's verses on the Bhagavan—all 1253 of them. They were serialized in the MP and subsequently brought out in book form: *Garland of Guru's Teachings* (*Guru Vachaka Kovai*).

KS has also translated from Tamil into English Sri Muruganar's *Ramana Sannidhi Murai* (1851 verses), of which a selection has been published, and other writings by and on Sri Ramana Maharshi. Ramana and Gandhi, the two stars by which KS regulated his course, he also saw as two aspects of a single unity. Using an array of metaphors, he enjoyed expressing (and repeating) this insight in language that compares with Sangam Tamil poetry in its 'leanness of expression and richness of implication.'[19]

Witness the following quotations:[20]

Gandhiji represents *Satya*, applied religion, Ramana represents *Sat*, pure religion.

The transcendental or vertical dimension of moksha, the reciprocal, complementary or horizontal dimension of *dharma*, and the blend of both in normal living are symbolized by the Holy Cross and the Living Tree.

The Mahatma exemplifies the tree's *dharma* of rootedness and the Maharshi embodies its openness to light. They both knew... that the earth that holds the tree that holds the branch that holds the leaf is in its turn held by the Sun.

The sunward-facing side or *moksha* and the earthward-facing side or *dharma* represent a tension necessary for growth... the growth of the tree is the result of the tension between the pull of the earth and the light and warmth of the sun.

Since means and ends are inter-changeable it is open for us to choose *moksha* or *dharma*—the two values from the two sides of one coin.

In a *chakki*, the upper stone moving fast depends for its steadiness and its grinding efficiency on the firm stillness of the lower stone. Shanti, awareness and Shakti, power of action, are two aspects—the being and becoming—of the same reality.

Given his personality, it was natural and logical for KS to draw inspiration from both the gurus in the pursuit of his own *sadhana* (striving) as a *mumukshu* (seeker after liberation). Not only did he feel the imperative to relate each to the other, but himself to both, singly and jointly. As an intellectual, he was drawn to abstract Advaita, austere Saivism, the motionless mountain, and the terse teachings of Ramana, while in his active life—whether as lover of

---

[19] A. K. Ramanujan, *Interior Landscapes*, Afterword.

[20] The quotations are from the following articles by KS: 'Living Dharma'; 'For Integral Growth' (Jayanthi issue of *Mountain Path*, 1989); 'Ramana Maharshi—His Dynamic Peace' (*Swarajya*, 5 June 1971); 'Gandhi and Ramana'; 'Gandhi and the Future World Order' (GOI, Publications Division, 2 October 1983); 'Gandhi and Ramana'.

poetry, teacher, editor, patriot, man-of-this-world—he was equally drawn to Visistadvaita, Sri Rama, the happy warrior, the excitement of the freedom struggle, and Vaisnavite Gandhi's empirical approach to truth. Nor was KS content to treat the two paths, *jnana* and *karma*, as parallel tracks on which the journey could progress: in his own way, he felt impelled to establish their 'interchangeability and interpenetration'. His efforts to make Ramana's *jnana marga* accessible to the many through writings, talks, translations, and the *satsangs* was itself a form of *karma yoga*. At the same time, through the CWMG prefaces and other writings relating to the Mahatma, he sought to show that Gandhi's political and social praxis was anchored in the *jnana* of ego-less action.

☆

Despite a considerable written output in the form of CWMG prefaces, translations, articles, edited volumes, reviews, and so on, KS did not author any books, except for the biography of Ramana. Accepting an award from the Publishers and Booksellers' Association in Madras (1989), he said: 'I am no original or creative writer... I am content to popularize and propagate and do not aspire to "create"... I have walked with humble pride in the shadow of giants... They also serve who only spread the light.'

KS exchanged letters from time to time with Morarji Desai, R. R. Diwakar, and R. Venkataraman, but most of his correspondence was with his students and friends in the Ramana circle. During the final years of his life, his letters to the editor of the *Indian Express*, Madras were also a steady flow. They were mostly on issues and events that considerably agitated him at that time—conversions to Islam, the Mandal Commission, and the conflict in Sri Lanka. Epistles to his brothers, nephews, nieces, and grandchildren were often in verse and on a postcard. He sent them off sometimes on their birthdays, or when some achievement of theirs or something that they had written came to his notice. Thus, when I resigned in 1990 as Adviser to the Chief Minister of Tamilnadu to return to academic life, a postcard from him promptly arrived to say: 'We are glad that you are free of tension/ but who will now increase my pension?/ Do I rejoice or am I sorry/ that I shine no more in borrowed glory?'

KS once said that he was paying a 'stiff price for longevity' in the sense that he had had to go through the experience of losing so many of his contemporaries. It also meant that we have from his hands a number of sensitive obituarial tributes to a variety of friends such as P. N. Appuswamy, M. A. Candeth, K. Chandrasekharan, Ku Pa Ra, V. Narayanan, K. Santhanam, V. Saranathan, Periaswami Thooran, N. S. Varadachari, and K. S. Venkataramani.[21] Referring to Varadachari throwing away, at Gandhi's call, not only the legal profession but 'every shred of luxury and symbol of status', KS refers to him as 'a patriot of purest ray serene who lived a long, austere and noble life, shirtless, shoeless and selfless.' V. Saranathan 'was a flame, a stream, a draught, a phenomenon, a process, he was not (like so many of us) a vegetable or an institution'. These words could well apply to KS himself.

Towards the end of 1985, KS was back in Madras after having been away for more than a quarter of a century at Delhi. In the next few years, the Muruganar translations, continuing editorial labours for CWMG, a second edition of Vinoba's *Talks on the Gita*, and the weekly sessions of the Ramana Bhakta Sabha kept him busy. Some of his Madras-based old students began visiting him and renewed their conversations. This was also the period when KS was much exercised by the conflict in Sri Lanka. Apart from a spate of letters to the press, he joined other leading citizens in issuing periodical appeals for peace between the Tamil and the Sinhalese.

At the end of 1991, he moved from 'Dharmalayam' to the home of his daughter, Dr Santa Ramachandran, where he and his wife had more care and company. He enjoyed reasonable health until the end except for age-related debility and a slight hearing problem. Throughout, his mind was lucid, his hand was steady, his speech was clear, and his tongue was sharp. His son-in-law Suryanandan was with him, when around noon on 19 May 1994, after having had a sip of coconut water, he very quietly passed away: there was no struggle or warning of any kind, the breath just stopped. The chanting of 'Arunachala Siva, Arunachala Siva, Arunachala' of the mourners who gathered made one feel that it was Annamalai, the Siva-Arunachala, that had finally claimed him at the end of a full and wonderful life.

[21] P. N. Appuswamy was a distinguished science writer in Tamil; M. A. Candeth was Professor of History; K. Chandrasekharan, Ku Pa Ra, Periaswami Thooran, and K. S. Venkataramani were literary figures; V. Narayanan was a scholar in Sanskrit and Tamil; K. Santhanam and N. S. Varadachari were Congressmen; and V. Saranathan was Professor of English and Principal, National College, Trichy.

Sources

Autobiographical and biographical material relied upon for preparing the memoir is listed below. Publication details have been given only where available. Other references can be found in the text or in the footnotes.

Personal File of Rao Sahib P. S. Krishnaswami Ayyar, Avl: Sub-Engineer, VI Grade, PWD and Personal Assistant to Sanitary Engineer to Government, Madras (14 May 1917).

K. S. Sanjivi, *Reflections*, 1990. M. A. Chidambaram Institute of Community Health, Voluntary Health Services, Madras 600 113.

Certificates (MSS) from: (i) Mark Hunter; (ii) A. J. Carlyle; (iii) S. E. Runganadhan; (iv) K. A. Nilakanta Sastri; (v) D. S. Sarma.

Newspaper cuttings relating to: (i) Late K. Swaminatha Aiyar, Pudukottai; (ii) Late Dr M. K. Sambasivan; (iii) *Kattai Vandi*; (iv) Government Arts College, Madras; (v) Late N. S. Varadachari.

Interviews given by K. Swaminathan to: (i) *Deepam*, July 1968; (ii) *The Indian Express*, 8 May 1984; (iii) *Dinamani Kadir*, 2 February 1986; (iv) *Oru Santhippu*, 1987; (v) *Sunday Mail*, 29 July 1990.

Copies of articles, talks, memoranda, reports authored by K. Swaminathan: (i) 'Sir Mark Hunter', Presidency College Magazine, December 1932; (ii) 'Engal Tamil Pandithar', *Kalaimagal*, 14 March 1935; (iii) 'Greatness of Bharati', *The Hindu*, 15 August 1947; (iv) 'Roman Script for Official Hindi', Memorandum to the Official Language Commission, 24 September 1955; (v) 'Ever Fresh Faces' (Recollections of PS High School), 1959; (vi) Report of Delegation of Workers of Indian Art (December 1958–January 1959), 1959; (vii) 'Golden Voice in Golden Cause', 1976; (viii) 'Gandhi, The Man and the Myths', K. Santhanam Memorial Lecture, 23 August 1984; (ix) Address to Publishers and Booksellers Association, Madras, 6 January 1989; (x) 'Principal V. Saranathan—A Tribute'; (xi) 'Rajaji—A Tribute'; (xii) 'First Darshan', *The Mountain Path*, January 1988.

GOI Press Release: Prime Minister's Observations while releasing volumes 89 and 90 of the CWMG, 30 April 1984.

Presidential Address by R. Venkataraman, Vice-President of India, Ninth Annual Convocation, Gandhigram Rural Institute, 28 March 1987.

La. Su. Rengarajan, A Comprehensive Write-up on Professor K. Swaminathan, 1995.

Recollections of Guhan

I CALLED HIM GUHAN-SAHIB

Granville (Red) Austin[1]

S. Guhan was one of the most engaging individuals I have ever known, so I am pleased and honoured to have been invited to contribute a reminiscence of him to this collection of his writings on economic development, about which I know all too little. His death is not only a great loss to Shanta Guhan and to his friends but also, I dare say, to India and the world at large—the loss of the man and the authority on development.

We met in Philadelphia in 1993 at a conference at the University of Pennsylvania hosted by Delhi's Centre for Policy Research and the University's Centre for the Advanced Study of India. Each of us had an eye out for the other. I knew of his writing on development, and a mutual friend, whom I didn't know he knew, told him that I would be present. We met after the first session and went to dinner in a nearby Indian restaurant. I was immediately taken by him: the white hair, the penetrating eyes behind the dark-rimmed spectatcles, the lively face, the ready grin, and the gentleness that accompanied the sharp-quick wit.

So began a relationship in which he was the teacher and I the learner. My expertise in financial matters falls short of 'balancing' my own cheque book; like many foreigners, I know more about north India than about the south; and my interest in economic development far exceeds my understanding of its many facets. Guhan set about

---

[1] Granville Austin is an independent historian living in Washington, DC.

educating me, as best anyone could, on these and other subjects. Over these sadly-brief years, we met in Madras, at the India International Centre in Delhi, and elsewhere.

In addition to broadening my understanding of many things, he was especially helpful on the book I was then researching about the working of the Indian Constitution from 1950 to 1985. To resume, Guhan taught me from his experiences with international finance and development institutions in Washington, from his working for C. Subramaniam when he was a cabinet minister in Delhi, from his time as adviser to M. Karunanidhi in Tamilnadu, and from his research and writing at the Madras Institute of Development Studies.

He taught me much about processes in the state and central government; about Tamilnadu politics; about the Tamilnadu-Karnataka water dispute—he gave me a copy of his clear and incisive monograph about it, *The Cauvery River Dispute: Toward Conciliation*; about the great 'devaluation' of 1966, the players involved and its consequences; and about the true extent of poverty in India and accurate ways to measure it. Guhan helped me when I was examining the evidence of centralization–overcentralization of government that began even during the Nehru years. I had found one evidence of this in the rapid turnover of governors and chief ministers, especially in certain states. Guhan checked my facts and arithmetic and did his own calculations. He presented me with a clear tabulation of the years in office of these officials, which demonstrated how overcentralization in the form of truncated terms for governors and chief ministers had accelerated under Indira Gandhi.

Prime Minister Indira Gandhi's bank nationalization was primarily a political act, as we all know. But among some of her staff it did have the economic justification of making credit more available in rural areas and for small business. I was curious about whether or not nationalization achieved any of its proclaimed goals, and I was dissatisfied with the results of my own research. So I wrote to Guhan. He soon replied with figures and the comment that 'Bank nationalization has been responsible for a massive increase in the banking network enabling mobilization of rural savings and lending for rural economic activities.' I had my answer. He added the 'con' comment that nationalization had also politicized banking to some extent. Guhan also critiqued portions of the book draft that I sent to him and he should be credited with what I hope are improvements in the text.

Guhan's assistance did not end with 'learned' matters. His anecdotes about political figures and officialdom were endlessly entertaining and pulled no punches. He recalled how, when he was C. Subramaniam's special assistant in 1973, Mohan Kumaramangalam dashed into Subramaniam's office to announce that he was writing a pamphlet about judicial appointments to justify the 'supercession of Judges' and to ask if they had ideas for a title. Guhan responded, 'How about Chamcha CJ?' Kumaramangalm was not amused. (The published pamphlet's title was *Judicial Appointments*.) Guhan sent me a copy of his review of President Venkataraman's memoirs, which in his accompanying letter he called a 'non-book'. When I responded that I thought the review 'good', he shot back a letter with his customary salutation, 'Red-ji', saying that this was 'faint praise and is unacceptable.'

In his approach to affairs Indian, Guhan, it seems to me, had a particular sort of balance. His clear and critical eye for the politics and economics of the poverty stricken and his justifiable scepticism of government's customarily optimistic reporting upon conditions in the country never led him to believe that his own analysis was infallible. His long-simmering, although usually well-concealed, anger over government's laxness or indifference toward the plight of the poor made him their protagonist. But he was not an ideologue. He was a practical thinker even when proposing apparently novel remedies. Somehow, he could both examine the national or local scene from ground level and then look down upon it as from a pinnacle, weighing all its elements. He could both play the game and be the referee.

Thinking of Guhan makes me yearn for his company and homesick for India.

S. GUHAN—AN APPRECIATION

Robert Cassen[2]

I met SG—as I always called him—in the sixties through his cousin, Dharma Kumar. But I really got to know him when we worked

[2] Robert Cassen is Visiting Professor at the London School of Economics, London, where he is doing research on population and development in India. Prior to this he taught development economics in Oxford (Queen Elizabeth House and St. Anthony's College) and Sussex (Institute of Development Studies). He has worked with Professor Guhan on the staff of the Brandt Commission on North–South issues.

together on the staff of the Brandt Commission Secretariat in 1978-9. This was an arduous job, with few breaks even for weekends over two years in Geneva, and frequent travel to the far-flung places where the Commission met. But SG made light of it, or seemed to, and was a constant source of reason and sense throughout. Our main job was to write background papers and prepare drafts of the Commission's Report. SG's contributions were always immaculate, skilfully argued, well-documented—and finished so far ahead of the deadlines that he would help the rest of us complete ours. He also just got things right; hardly anyone ever wanted to change what he wrote.

The staff was quite divided on a number of issues, often on pretty clear 'North' and 'South' lines. SG would prick the bubbles on both sides, appealing to your conscience if you said the North would never buy some proposal or other, or holding you back if you pushed too hard in some cause dear to Third World hearts. His famous sharp tongue and lack of veneer were often in evidence. I remember an occasion when Willy Brandt handed us his introduction to the Report, asking us for our comments. We all wrote some. But I happened to be standing there when Brandt asked SG what he thought of the introduction. (You have to appreciate that Brandt was a commanding figure; the Commission included other notables such as Olof Palme and Edward Heath—L. K. Jha was the Indian member—but Brandt seemed to tower over them all in stature and presence.) SG replied, 'I think it's rambling and rather confused, but if you leave it with me, I'll try to knock it into shape.' Which he did. No one ever spoke to Brandt like that. But he was used to SG by then, and just laughed.

There was another SG moment that I recall. Towards the end of our work, it was becoming clear that we were unlikely to finish on time, mainly because the Commission members were unable to agree on some of the key recommendations to be made in their report. The head of the secretariat, the late Goran Ohlin, felt responsible. There was a meeting at which he argued at length that we could do it; all the rest of us were ranged against him, convinced that we couldn't—an uncomfortable situation, given the history of rancour that had often pervaded our work, during which Ohlin most of the time preserved an almost saintly patience. The atmosphere in the room got worse and worse. Finally there was a silence, broken at last by SG, who till then had said nothing. 'You know, Goran', he said 'there is an old Tamil proverb: when the train is going slowly, you don't reach your destination faster by running inside the train.' It was perfect. Goran knew the argument was lost, but in the most charming way. We all enjoyed the joke, and went out and had a drink.

SG's asperities were fired at friend and foe alike. I remember a book of mine that he wrote an unkind review of—he often seemed unable to resist a witticism even when it was uncalled for. But on another occasion I saw glad of his style. James Cameron had written an unfavourable review of another book of mine, on India. I was wondering whether to reply, which is not usually a good idea, when the editor of the journal told me he had received two rejoinders from India: one by SG, penetrating as usual, and greatly to my comfort.

SG was a contradictory being. He could be both kind and harsh, and however close you felt to him, you didn't know which to expect. There was a deep vein of humour in much that he did and said, as if he saw the foolishness of human endeavour with peculiar clarity. He could be quite cynical; and yet he was an idealist, and a highly practical one. His savings from the Geneva years helped to enable him to resign from the Finance Ministry; but I believe one of the things that made him resign—perhaps Mrs Gandhi's Emergency was the chief one—was his inability to get the bureaucracy to approve the release of food stocks in a bumper harvest year. He argued that people were hungry, while the government was paying good money to store grain that could be sold to keep prices down—no one listened. He also spent time, when he was advising the Tamilnadu government, going to the countryside to convince farmers that paying taxes was in their interest, that they got valuable things in return; this was real political work.

The range of his interests was considerable. One was always discovering new aspects of them. I once sent him a collection of essays by Seamus Heaney, and was rewarded with a long letter describing his quite profound preoccupation with English poetry—about which he had never breathed a word before. His biography of Balasaraswati and collaboration with her over the translation of some of her writings are not the sort of thing many will know about. He did brilliant work on the Cauvery dispute, on corruption, on various aspects of finance: he produced what was arguably the most profound piece in a book on India's economic reforms that Vijay Joshi and I edited; it was about centre-state economic relations, and made a powerful case that the reform were incomplete without a more comprehensive dialogue between the centre and states to make the reforms effective. Perhaps his most lasting monument will be the beginnings of a social security system for the very poor, which he worked out for Tamilnadu, but which eventually became the National Social Assistance Scheme. At the end he was working on a book on governance in India–judging by the pieces of manuscript he had already completed, it would have been a major work, full of his typical insight and trenchancy.

Several of his friends tried to persuade him was to give up smoking the endless cigarettes that eventually killed him. He did give up now and then, never for long. He even made fun of my attempts to stop him. We would have lost him sooner or later. He was a wholly exceptional being, one of the cleverest men I have ever known, who used his gifts to valuable if sometimes self-destructive effect. If you were fortunate enough to be a friend, you saw more of his kindly side than its opposite.

The last time I saw him was in a hotel near Heathrow airport, a few weeks before the end. He had gone to give some lectures in the US, but had been unable to complete them. He stopped overnight with his wife, and I and another English friend came to his bedside. He was like a skeleton, coughing and in pain. But his mind was as lucid as ever, and he talked—when he could—about various intellectual things. His searching gaze still seemed to see through you, to call you to account, as it had ever done. And the twinkle of humour was still there. It was so sad; one could guess that he would not be with us much longer.

He was remarkable, irreplaceable.

S. GUHAN: IN MEMORY

Ashoke Chatterjee[3]

Outrage persists in the knowledge of Sanjivi Guhan's absence. The injustice of his illness and suffering is the more senseless because it could have been, should have been, otherwise. That sharp mind, with

---

[3] Ashoke Chatterjee is Distinguished Fellow at the National Institute of Design (Ahmedabad) where he has served since 1975. NID's Executive between 1975 and 1985, he now teaches communication and management at several institutions. Associated with health and environmental activities in India and elsewhere, he began his career in engineering and later moved to the International Monetary Fund and to the public sector before joining NID.

its sardonic wit, could have better protected the lean body which gave it shelter. It might have been so, if Guhan's own well-being was a stronger factor in his personal priorities.

The well-being of others, and most specially the 'other India' of the deprived, was the hallmark of Guhan's contributions as an economist and citizen. It was a concern directed toward innovating robust alternatives to the development experience of past decades. Well before the global community acknowledged the need to measure the social change behind mere statistics, Guhan's commitments were clear: economics mattered most when it responded to the requirements of the bereft. Early in his career, an ability to articulate this case, with options supported by hard evidence, made Guhan a pioneer in the human development approach that has since won acceptance. It made him a familiar figure in corridors of power at home and overseas, a familiarity he used in order to support good causes and fearlessly express his contempt for arrogance and indifference. Withering scorn and acid wit were used to camouflage a burning conscience and a vulnerable heart. It blossomed in the company of those whose intelligence challenged him or whose purpose he respected. There, Guhan could be equally at home with a craftsman and a minister, with a Willy Brandt and a Rukmani Devi.

I first met Sanjivi Guhan when I joined the International Monetary Fund in the mid-sixties. Guhan and his wife Shanta had moved to Washington some months earlier, where he helped represent India's interests at the World Bank. The turmoil of Vietnam and its aftermath had not yet affected our two multilateral grants, still preoccupied as they were with calculating project loans and balances of payments. Guhan's questioning of basic assumptions of progress and growth was persistent, whether at board meetings or in the warmth of the little India that the Guhan home came to mean for many. It was during these years that he began his seminal contribution to national and international economics, helping to lay the foundations for an economics in which the quality of life is served, and not dictated, by data.

I came to believe that Guhan's compassionate economics was nourished most of all by the depth of his passion and knowledge of Tamil culture. Its literature, music, craft, and dance seemed the sustenance and consolation he needed in an official environment rampant with greed and ignorance. Confident in his own identity, Guhan delighted in cultural expressions of an inclusive humanism.

The entrée which he and Shanta enjoyed with creative spirits personified a quality of embracing universality, as in the poetry A. K. Ramanujan shared with them, or the music and dance of Balasarawati and her lineage which often blessed their home. Integrity and purpose of this calibre were the values Guhan most sought and respected, qualities which he demanded of himself and from the environment around him. They drew him to practitioners of many disciplines and arts, to individuals of worth and to achievements that were visionary, and to everyday evidence of a commitment to quality. It was their relentless concern with quality that first brought me to Guhan and Shanta.

Washington, DC in 1965 was preparing to welcome Nehru and His India, the biographical exhibition that was to set new standards of design and communication. The exhibition was created by the late Charles and Ray Eames, designers from Los Angeles. They had just inspired the founding of India's National Institute of Design (NID) in Ahmedabad, and the Nehru exhibition was its first international achievement. The Indian community had been mobilized to assist a giant task of construction and management at the Smithsonian Institute. Guhan and Shanta were among the volunteers, and so was I. They introduced me to the 'India Report' which the Eameses had authored, and which inspired the idea of NID. Guhan was fascinated by the process through which the West's leading industrial design team had sought to understand the contemporary needs of a civilization as well as the vision of its leader. The Eames' meticulous attention to detail, their skill with artifact and image toward a powerful encounter with a man and his country: all this entranced Guhan. It became part of his lifelong commitment to design as an attitude indispensable to an acceptable and equitable life. He was the first Indian economist to be seriously concerned with design as a force for development.

Our meeting through this Eameses-NID expression was prophetic: years later I would come to NID as its Director, as part of a protective effort that Guhan had powerfully assisted in his capacity as Special Assistant to C. Subramaniam, Minister of Commerce and Industry in the mid-seventies. That was a time of great crisis and turmoil for the fledgling Institute. Guhan's voice was heard among the few that understood and protected NID's experiment in education, with all its risks, as a small band of teachers and students broke with rigid tradition in their search for relevance.

Years later, an established and acclaimed NID sought to acknowledge its debt to Guhan by honouring him as its Convocation Speaker in 1984. He reminded his young audience of the real needs for which their Institute had been founded.

In its economy as well, India is not one but many...India can be viewed as composed of twenty 'average countries'...the fractionalization of India might help us to understand certain distinct differentiations a little better... R-India may stand for rural or the Real India for the Gandhians. More technically, we can take it to mean Retarded India...U (or Uppermost)-India should be quite familiar since most of us here belong to it...The trade market for design is largely confined to U-India and to the upper levels of M-India...In the upper economies of India, incomes are high enough not only for the satisfaction of basic needs but also for being spent on wants...It is in this context that the designer will have to define an identity and integrity for himself in the marketplace. He might be tempted to take a so-called neutral position...Justification might also be sought for catering to luxury, pride, envy, vanity, and fickleness on the ground that these provide employment to the poor...'Neutrality' of this kind will mean that (he) will have to forswear any claim to be in India's life and part of it. He would have to abandon a full citizenship of the country and instead be content with being a mere technician in U-India.

The designer in this context would be catering to 'tawdry idiocies that are continually concocted.' To the designer operating solely or mainly in such a market 'the propensity to silliness is a grave occupational danger...' Guhan called on design graduates to recognize the potential of R-India through enlarging the market for its products, most particularly its crafts, and by reducing drudgery and improving productivity for working men and women through attention to working tools and environments. Design was essential as well to uplift basic goods and services such as educational materials, drinking water 'and above all toilets...Design in its social context cannot be left to institutions alone. It has to become the personal creed of every designer throughout his or her working life. In India as it is today, the practice of such a creed will not be easy...' Sixteen years later, it is more difficult still, with the wave of so-called liberalization sweeping the term designer from noun to adjective. Guhan would have demanded to know who has been 'liberated' and to what purpose, and at what cost to conscience. But that is another story.

Guhan and Shanta returned to New Delhi in 1969, their absence underlining my own distance from home. When I too decided to leave for a future in India, their understanding and welcome helped buffer the shock of re-entry and the disbelief of those for whom abandoning the security of Washington and the IMF was evidence of total insanity. In Delhi, as in Washington and later in Madras, the Guhan home became a special place. Special in its appeal to intellect and compassion. Special as a protective and tranquil retreat, created by Shanta to quietly celebrate the people, ideas and experiences that mattered most to them both. Themselves magnets for creativity, in the Guhan home everyday things assumed a special elegance. Celebrities came and went, basking in its ambience provided they passed the test of Guhan's wry wit or the not-so-gentle sarcasm he used to deflate humbug. Tensions were eased with Shanta's deft ability to deflect or soften the Guhan barbs that could devastate the unwary, just one of her own extraordinary skills and abilities subsumed in the task of facilitating Guhan's life and work. One sensed a certain anger behind the sardonic smile and wink, palpable as Guhan's official career subjected him endlessly to encounters with the corrupt and foolish. Tolerance was a margin that for him was beginning to wear thin, even before the Emergency. He needed the compensation of his roots and soil. Madras could provide these in abundance. Guhan and Shanta moved there, and were soon immersed in its ethos, enriching it with their participation in its activities and discourse. It came as no surprise that Guhan should have sought early retirement from government service. MIDS was a chance to reflect, write and advocate the causes dear to him. This volume is evidence of how creatively Guhan used that opportunity, and of the legacy he has gifted to his profession and to his country. Like his friends Amartya Sen and the late Mahboob ul Haq, Sanjivi Guhan offered alternatives still possible within a subcontinent adrift with cynicism. The approaches he innovated toward resolving the Cauvery dispute and for a social security systems achievable within an Indian reality demonstrated the power and clarity of Guhan's vision. Unafraid of politics and politicians, he associated with them on his own terms, carrying a long spoon. He knew that it was there that solutions would ultimately need acceptance and action.

Then illness came, forewarned over years by the trademark cigarette and punctuating cough. Guhan and Shanta challenged it with characteristic insight and courage. And then he was gone, suddenly it seemed. How now should he be remembered? For those who worked with Guhan, it will be the keenness of intellect and the quality of his economics that will be missed. Those in the arts and crafts that won his esteem and respect have lost a rare *rasika* and counsellor. The many lives he touched and lifted will remember him most as someone who cared, generous to a fault. For me, he is forever 'Guha'—my once and future friend, dear and exasperating, cherished and needed. One of a kind. One who should have stayed.

REMEMBERING GUHAN

Gopal Krishna Gandhi[4]

When Guhan was appointed as Finance Secretary to the Tamilnadu government in 1974, there was a general belief that this very grey but youthful IAS officer had exactly what it takes to mind the state's finances: he was, like his father Dr K. S. Sanjivi, a real 'Don't Care Master'. I have never been sure of the full meaning of that typical Tamil expression but it describes a rather stubborn man who will do exactly as he pleases; a master of the attitude that does not care about what others, especially those in the higher rungs of the power ladder, think of his self-assuredness.

By 1974, Guhan had already worked with two Union Finance Ministers of the first water—T. T. Krishnamachari and C. Subramaniam—and held a key diplomatic position in the Indian Embassy in Washington then headed by the formidable B. K. Nehru. How would he manage the transition? With a flick of mental shutters, he switched from the wood of central and foreign deputations to the trees of a state's administration. To the finest grain, in fact, on the trees' lopped cross-sections. And, as for holding his own in the matter of Tamil—now a 'must' in the state government—he quickly allayed all fears (perhaps to the secret disappointment of some!): he was not only fluent in the language, but something of a stylist in it.

If Delhi and Washington had found that nothing was too big for Guhan, Chennai realized that nothing was too small for him either. He began to engage in policy formulation and go into field situations with the same application, seeing an issue—whether an intellectual proposition or a proposal on file—on the conceptual plane and,

---

[4] Gopal Krishna Gandhi was in the Tamilnadu cadre of the Indian Administrative Service from 1968 to 1992. He has since served as Director of the Nehru Centre, London (1992-6) and High Commissioner for India in South Africa (1996-7), and has been Secretary to the President of India since November 1997.

simultaneously, as a nuts-and-bolts matter. At discussions, he would loop ideas in rings of cigarette smoke and, with equal ease, get down like a mechanic to tighten, unscrew, yank and pat schemes into position on the ground.

It soon became clear that Guhan's working style was not just a personality trait but something deeper. It was rooted in a concept of administration. He was to describe this concept in a Convocation Address at the National Institute of Design, Ahmedabad in 1984 thus:

By definition, no designer can escape translating his concept into detail. This statement should be so obvious that as designers you may tend to take it for granted. Yet, in many other spheres of activity, where concern for detail should be equally paramount, we find that concept and detail are rarely viewed in their integral relationship. Public policy is an important example of this neurosis. At a policy level, there is no lack of schemes, announcements and pronouncements which are meant to tackle the economic and social problems of India. Yet there is, as we all know, a yawning gap between these intentions and what actually happens on the ground. Numerous evaluations have shown that the articulation of policies in terms of programmes, procedures, legislation, implementational instruments and monitoring is rarely, if ever, adequate. The lack of concern for design results in the inability to translate words into deeds. Marx gave an exact description of this deep-seated malady when, referring to the bureaucracy, he said: 'The top entrusts the understanding of detail to the lower levels, whilst the lower levels credit the top with understanding of the general, and so all are mutually deceived.' This dichotomy between the general and the detail is not confined to the bureaucracy. In many academic disciplines as well, notably in the social sciences such as economics and sociology, it is not uncommon to encounter impressive paradigms and overviews with scant attention to the detail on which one would expect them to rest.

As Finance Secretary, Guhan quickly demonstrated this attention to detail and his interest in the *need* and *doability* of a scheme, as opposed to its financial implications alone. He was impatient with airiness in ideas, especially when that airiness was accompanied by the perfume of sanctimoniousness. 'That's all very well, I say', Guhan would cut into unctuous hypotheses, 'but...' and then proceed to dice that idea into jujubes of insubstantiality. The Don't Care Master was not over-awed by anything; not by his return to real-life issues in Tamilnadu, and not by the hero-worshipping cultism practised almost subconsciously in the state.

Not surprisingly, Guhan had more admirers than friends. One of his earliest admirers was, interestingly, the Chief Minister himself.

Used as he was to the dulcet notes of unquestioning acquiescence, the Kalaignar must have found Guhan's directness of speech something of a surprise, but a refreshing one. Guhan acquired, very quickly, an access to the CM which few had enjoyed earlier. He would spell out to the CM his misgivings about any scheme with dry-as-dust candour. It is not as if Guhan's views prevailed always; very often they did not. But when he was overruled it was not for want of respect for his reasoning. *Ponaal pohattum* is a virtually untranslatable Tamil phrase that means, literally, 'if it is going, let it go'. But in its deeper recesses it reflects the knowledge that we can only try and if, after that, success eludes us, well then, have no regrets, let it go. A wry resignation is the *rasa* behind that phrase. And Guhan experienced it, practised it, ever so often.

Chief Minister Karunanidhi and Guhan reached the same wavelength quite effortlessly. Guhan shared the CM's *mega* view on Centre–state relations. Guhan believed that there was a terraced gradient to India's polity and that the state in the lower contours tended, like all lower riparians, to lose out. While I have no specific basis (in terms of conversations or correspondence with Guhan) to say this, I do believe that the Report of the P. V. Rajamannar Committee on Centre–State Relations (1971) found a resonance in Guhan's thinking. In the very month (April 1974) that Guhan took over as Finance Secretary, Chief Minister Karunanidhi moved a resolution in the Tamilnadu Assembly calling upon the central government to accept the views of the Tamilnadu government on state autonomy and the recommendations of the Rajamannar Committee 'and proceed to effect immediate changes in the Constitution of India'. The Chief Minister's written speech in the Assembly, at the time of moving that resolution, was to be quoted *in extenso* in the Report of the Sarkaria Commission which Prime Minister Indira Gandhi appointed in 1983 to go into Centre–state relations. Reading the historical references and the close legal as well as financial reasoning in that speech, I am tempted to surmise that Guhan played a role in its crafting. This was a thoroughgoing political speech and Guhan was an official, not a politician. But he was in sympathy with the thesis that were it not for a major trauma—partition—at the very start of our post-colonial historical evolution, ours would have been a federal polity. Whence arose his sense of the inherent unfairness of the political gradients of modern India.

A little over one year after that speech, Emergency was declared and Chief Minister Karunanidhi went out of office. It remains to Guhan's credit that when the mandarinate seemed eager to discover the faults of the dismissed government and the virtues of the new order, he was one of the few officers in Fort St George who were unafraid enough to pay a courtesy call on the dismissed Chief Minister. He was only respected for doing so by none other than the redoubtable P. K. Dave himself, who had just arrived to take over as Adviser to the Governor of Tamilnadu and to run the state's administration under President's Rule.

The period 1975-7 saw an abatement of all discourse on Centre-state relations, with a self-conscious shift taking place in the direction of micro planning and certain 'radical' programmes. Among these was the 'freeing' of bonded labourers, the majority of whom were tribals. As Director of Rehabilitation I had some responsibilities in regard to the ending of the bonded system in the Nilgiris where *paniya* tribals lived. I recall a meeting to review 'progress' in which I went on a bit on the evils of the bonded system and the steps taken to free the *paniya* from the clutches of the *mudalali*. That was not a period when questions on the 'basics' of the Emergency's programmes were asked. But Guhan was Guhan and he cut in: 'That's all very well, I say, but you are trying to set up a divorce bureau without giving thought to what is to happen to the *paniya* after you have "freed" them. Giving a *paniya* a loan may mean your closing his "case" but how do you know that he will not be worse off than before? You don't have any method of keeping a watch over his fate after finding his "freedom", do you?' Of course, I had no satisfactory answer.

Wheels come full circle. Just as the Kalaignar's departure from office in 1975 was a lonely affair so was P. K. Dave's, after President's Rule ended in Tamilnadu following the general elections of 1977. There were no more than half a dozen officials present at the Madras Central Station to see off the departing Adviser, to whom extreme deference had been shown until only the previous week. Guhan, who had not once cheered the Emergency, and not even tried to bend when others genuflected, was there on the platform as the train carrying the biggest symbol of the Emergency and President's Rule in Tamilnadu steamed off.

Despite his extraordinary record in the service of government, Guhan really came into his own after leaving government. His stint with the Independent Commission for International Development Issues, popularly known as the Brandt Commission and his work at

MIDS unshackled his mind, freed his hand. His thinking, never a prisoner of the civil service, was now totally redeemed from all the obligations that go with being covenanted. This was, essentially, for the good. Seminal work resulted in his studies on the Cauvery, on reservations and economic criteria, the financing of elections, corruption. But occasionally, this freedom led him to dip his pen in acid rather than ink. For instance, he felt 'free' to write in the *Economic and Political Weekly* a scathing critique of president R. Venkataraman's tenure. Objectivity seemed to have been gifted away in that article to antipathy.

He had written, in 1981, a piece on Balasaraswati which showed his 'wider interests' (to use a cliche) that were to be seen ever so often later on, in his occasional pieces on persons like the poet A. K. Ramanujan, the diplomat-thinker K. S. Shelvankar and the volume he edited on his uncle K. Swaminathan for which President K. R. Narayanan (a student of KS) contributed an article.

Guhan's ideological confluence with the political thought processes of the under-endowed region came to the fore again during this period and his appointment as Adviser to Kalaignar Karunanidhi in his resumed Chief Ministership in 1989–90, had a felicity to it. Guhan's intellectual output reached new heights in his reasoned support to the policy of reservation, based on Tamilnadu's experience.

Guhan's affinities were not purblind; they had space for people and ideas as long as they rang true. Guhan was practical enough to see that no one could ring true all the time, and that the days of seamless rectitude were gone. But he knew that people and political parties could find themselves on a good track, almost despite themselves sometimes, and needed to be supported.

In November 1997 while winding my way from Pretoria to Delhi between assignments, I visited Chennai to meet friends and visit the Ramanasrama in Tiruvannamalai. Guhan was already critically ill, but, none the less, was planning to go to the US for a conference. I found him frail and racked by a stubborn cough. But *was* he full of ideas about the country! Shanta, I could see, was consumed by concern for her husband's health, but none the less, she encouraged him in his travel plans if only to make him feel that there was so much he could do. There was an unfamiliar mellowness in Guhan which was disquieting. The magnesium wire emitted no flares this time. I cannot forget his telling me, as if to round out the little 'thing' about his article on the former President, 'You know, R. V. has written to me, enquiring very kindly about my health.'

As I was leaving Guhan came up with me to the *sumaitangi*, the structure of three granite slabs shaped like the Greek Π which can be found alongside pathways in the Tamil countryside, for weight-bearers to rest their loads on. Shanta and he had acquired one and put it up near the gate to their house. A creeper grew on it. I can never forget Guhan standing between the gate and creeper, saying to me: 'It is time I gave you some advice on how to manage your domestic finances.' I told him I did not have very much there to manage. 'That is why you need advice, I say', he cut in. The *sumaitangi*, behind Guhan's white head of hair, seemed to acquire special meaning.

I received a letter, in Delhi, from Guhan, dated 16 January 1998:

I was deeply impressed with the President's interview which came on Zee TV yesterday. His answers, everytime, were substantive, straightforward and succinct. Throughout, he was relaxed and pleasant.

It is a unique opportunity that he is not only the right leader at the right place but also at the right time for the fluid political situation—which is likely to continue even after the elections—is bound to strengthen his ability to influence whichever government comes to power to undertake certain basic reforms. The country has reached a state in which unless something concrete is done on these lines we will be plunged into a terminal crisis. We simply cannot lose this godsend of President KRN being at the helm.

As I mentioned to you when you were in Madras, my suggestion is that we must formulate concrete and unambiguous proposals on a limited, high-priority, feasible set of issues.

My list of issues is:

(1) Amendment to the Anti-Defection law—radical as indicated by the President.

(2) Comprehensive legislation and institutional arrangements relating to corruption—utilizing, and developing on, the recent Supreme Court judgement on the Hawala cases.

(3) Codification of the role of Governors in the formation of Ministries in the States—in appropriate form and manner.

What is your reaction to the idea? Have you yourself started working on some such lines (as a lone wolf from distant Madras I might be presumptuous in advising you)? Can I help in any way—I have divided items (2) and (3) and have useful material on them.

Bharat Ratna for MS was marvellous. Anandi has written an excellent article on MS in *Dinamani* today (16.1.98). Don't miss it.

Within weeks, he was gone, the Don't Care Master. Needless to say, I had done no work during those weeks (nor have since) on the themes he had suggested.

The concluding lines from Vikram Seth's *The Golden Gate* come to me, in a prose adaptation.

That's all right, I say, clear your throat now and get on with it.

THE FERRYMAN

Barbara Harriss-White[5]

While others will celebrate the remarkableness of Guhan's life and personality, this is also the opportunity to celebrate the people whom he once said were those he admired the most, having met them in real life, those who inspired him. They speak more eloquently for Guhan than anything else I could say of this friend: this gregarious and lonely polymath who declared himself content to watch the Game (with delight, despair and wry amusement) not on the field but from the sidelines, who nevertheless also prided himself on his skills as a strategist, adviser and, when needs must, a wily plotter (so who played the Game after all); this nationalist whose interests and friendships spanned the globe; someone who developed teasing into a fine art (because it drew people out into honest engagement or enjoyable swordplay), who never suffered fools (not gladly, not at all, and when few could match his intellectual gifts, we were many...) yet who sustained others with good counsel through testing times; this admirer of Gandhi, this precociously young World Banker and critic of the World Bank, this frugal epicurean, whose generosity, both intellectual and practical, was matched by the intellectual skull-duggery and thuggery described with such tenderness by Subramanian.

It is not a coincidence that although all of these specially admirable people have left influential writings, none on them were 'scholars'. One theme laces its way through these three lives as it does those of others for whom he felt special reverence and whose lives overlapped his—most notably M. K. Gandhi and Guhan's own uncle K. Swaminathan, who edited the works of Gandhi, but also people

[5] Barbara Harriss-White is Professor of Development Studies in Queen Elizabeth House, Oxford University, and founder-director of its M. Phil. in Development Studies. Since 1971 she has worked, by means of primary field research, on three areas of the Indian economy: the political economy of agricultural markets, regional development, and social welfare.

like the writer and philosopher Iris Murdoch. Perhaps to the incredulity of those who dealt with the hard-bitten man of the world, that theme is the self and its transcendence.

The first is Willy Brandt. Guhan had been cherry-picked for the Secretariat of the Brandt Commission, but he had lapped up America, wished to see more of the world and was eager to be sprung from post-Emergency India.

For Guhan, Willy Brandt stood for the power and goodness of a combination of qualities and principles. One set were those of social democracy. Brandt had fled Germany to Norway as a young adult to escape and oppose Hitler. After the war he was a major figure in the development of Germany's social democracy, rising to be Chancellor from 1969 to 1974. After his resignation, because of treachery within his administration, he turned his energies to international distributive justice.

A second kind of quality was Brandt's practical idealism. History has agents as well as big forces and Brandt was the originator of West Germany's Ostpolitik. He embarked on peace talks with Eastern Europe which included East Germany, for which he was awarded a Nobel Peace Prize. Then, in 1977, he rose to the suggestion of Robert McNamara then president of the World Bank, that he head what was to be the eponymous independent commission and multilateralize his political project. It was not entirely independent. The need to recycle OPEC surpluses gave urgency and political visibility to its deliberations. Its terms were set to examine international inequality, to free-think about domestic redistributivist reforms, future flows of aid from the 'international community' and the restructuring and regulation of international trade and finance in order to configure a new international economic order. Guhan and Robert Cassen played a major role in the final writing of 'North–South', the Brandt Commission report. It was a smash hit, selling 250,000 copies in Britain alone and igniting public debate (at least all over Western Europe) in a way few documents had done before or since. But the proposals for global bodies to regulate finance and food met the same fate as did Boyd Orr's proposal for a Grain Stabilization Board in the late forties.

Throughout Guhan's life there ran a creative tension between the political pragmatist and the idealist. The anthropologist John Davis has called policy advisers, not entirely kindly when it came to development consultants, State's men'. The Bard went much further, cartooning them as those who 'do the king best service', those who 'soak up his countenance, his rewards, his authorities' whom he would keep at court 'like the ape an apple in the corner of his jaw' whom he would 'squeeze at will like a sponge'. There was doing all that and keeping one's integrity on the one hand and there was being a committed social democrat not wholly unaffected by the ideas of Gandhi on the other. For Guhan wholly endorsed the vision behind the 1948 Report of the Economic Programme Committee of a society based on social justice and equality with a system of production based on 'an alternative to the acquisitive economy of private capitalism or the regimentation of a totalitarian state' and a system of distribution which assured 'a national minimum standard in respect of all the essentials of physical and social well being'.

Brandt managed the same kind of tension in what for Guhan was an exemplary way.

Brandt's third special quality was a complete absence of hauteur. Guhan also greatly admired this in Karunanidhi. On a long rail journey on one leg of the Commission's work, Brandt had gone missing and Guhan was dispatched to seek him. At some distance away in the third class, Guhan was taken aback to find the great man playing cards, drinking beer and hugely enjoying the exchange of views, street wit and wisdom, completely at ease with 'ordinary people' and from the account, even more astonishingly to Guhan, they with him. This was clearly something uncontrived. It was a normal part of Brandt's life.

The story is not a point about the alienation of a later generation of politicians, it may be somewhat of a point about the intrinsic value of social ease and equality (and consistent with Guhan's convictions about caste). It is mainly a point about a man of action who had reached pre-eminence with ambitions certainly, but without self-regarding ones.

After the Brandt Commission, Guhan famously quit the IAS and became a scholar-activist working out of the Madras Institute of Development Studies. He used his skills as a public finance economist to make significant contributions behind the scenes to the work of the Finance Commissions, the Life Insurance Corporation and the development of embryonic social security systems. Such work was consistent with the Brandt Report's suggestions for domestic redistributivist reform, consistent also with the operational requirements of the distributional aspect of the REPC. He positioned himself with political forces moving, or being moved, to widen access to the modern economy and state and to improve the latter's capacity to tax and distribute, which explains why Guhan had no time for those who argued that corruption was efficient.

The second is Balasaraswati, the great exponent and teacher of classical south Indian yoga through dance and music. Guhan was drawn to her as iron to a magnet, uplifted by the first performance he saw and delighted to be able to have her chauffeured home afterwards and to spark a friendship lasting for the rest of her life.

The forces in the magnet were Bala's capacity to lose herself in a passion of artistic creation expressing sexual love (which *includes* 'other loves besides the sexual... It defines an attitude, a manner of receiving experience...'); to meld herself to her dance, and onwards into a state of spiritual grace and serenity transcending dancer, dance and watcher. They were her disregard for convention other than the liberating structures of bharatanatyam. They were her excellence, discipline, female intelligence and imagination. They were the recognition of the global universality of an experience embedded in the traditions of Tanjavur.

Guhan used one set of skills to translate and spread her ideas and another set to champion the cause by helping with its administration... thereby hanging many other tales. He surely responded by being a conduit, just as this kind of bharatanatyam is. The role also suited the meaning of his name. He was adamant that her ideas needed no interpretation or critical gloss, just a summary: 'The end state of the dance, conceived as a yoking for the artist as well as the audience, is to still the mind and to achieve, at least temporarily, an ego-less, thought-free, sense of complete joy and well-being.'

This compulsive thinker had experienced the end state in another context much earlier, being taken when young to the ashram of Ramana Maharshi at Tiruvannamalai, returning repeatedly both before and after Ramana's death to the temple town under its magnificent hill. He was deeply moved by the bliss and peace expressed on the face and in the body of the great sage, who had achieved (what Guhan's early and eager reading of the western philosophers had not enabled him to figure out) the Objective, a state of transcendental unity in which the ego becomes irrelevant.

Guhan knew as well as anyone else that such a state, if ever attained, is 'clouded over' quite quickly. Being a materialist, atheist and a bit of a feminist, it was inevitable that an argument had to be picked with

Guhan about the maleness of this transcendence, about whether Identity and Liberation were wise or feasible aspirations for those with a responsibility for dependants, about the material base of a society which was generally seeking non-duality. Would't it depend, like Plato's Republic, on the exploitation of an unfortunate, unenlightened underclass of hewers of wood and drawers of water?

Not a bit. The key was to live in the world but without self-interest. He wrote:

The modern world suffers from only one problem namely, the *ego* and the most fundamental solution to all our problems—personal, social, political, institutional etc.—is ego-less living. Western professional philosophers, after centuries of reflection, don't seem to see the truth of this at all or see it off and on, fitfully, through chinks and crevices, while advaita in India, through centuries of thought, action, mythology, fasts, feasts, festivals, music, dance sculpture etc. has *celebrated* ego-less-ness with clarity and coolness—with the clarity of sunlight and the coolness of moonlight.

For the New Year of 1998, he sent us this gift:

Listen! It's simple, the trick of seeking yourself. Darkness will dissolve, obstacles cleared, inbam will brim over (like Pongal at harvest). This is stillness; the sky sole, nothing and supreme, inbam's gift. The abode of grace, the end of the ego; inbam shines forth. Eternal experience, end to all fear; the brimless sea of inbam. Grace we need and added to it to love and be loved; inbam shall be ours.

Guhan was working on all this 'joyfully', as he explained in his very last letter. He had an ambitious reading target for mid-February. And Shanta was there throughout, making possible his contradictions and his enjoyment.

RECOLLECTIONS OF GUHAN

Jonathan Moore[6]

I didn't know Guhan that well. To put it a little differently, there was little apparent reason why, given the limitations imposed by location and vocation over the years between the time when we first met and when he parted company, we comprehended each other so well and felt so close. I neither understood nor questioned this.

[6] Jonathan Moore has worked over a span of almost forty years in government, politics, academia and the United Nations. He is currently a Senor Adviser to the Administrator of the United Nations Development Programme and Associate at the Shorenstein Center for the Press, Politics and Public Policy at Harvard.

Shanta had something to do with it, of course, and so did Katie, my wife: sweet catalysts. It was partly humour, ironic if not sardonic, sharp but not mean, with a glint of recognition of the absurd. I can't cite intellect, since his was so superior to mine. We did seem to have a similar view of life in the world we lived in, a commitment to do something with it but not to take that too seriously or to miss the opportunities for delight that presented themselves or that we could create. There was a great deal of joshing and needling, virtually non-stop. He was extremely talented at this, and it won him pleasure even when my rejoinders weren't up to standard, as long as he had provoked some reaction.

To me we felt like natural allies across a number of differerences and gaps which weren't there. It was just one of those good friendship, I guess, for which I don't claim much credit except being fully ready and willing to be along for the ride. What more there was to us is mysterious enough not to need or want articulation.

Guhan and I first met when he came to Washington as Special Assistant to the Indian Minister for Economic and Defence Coordination, T. T. Krishnamachari, in 1963, at the Pentagon. Their mission was to further a collaboration between the governments of India, the UK and the US who had agreed to build up a defence production programme for India in the aftermath of the 'Indo-Chinese War' in the North-East Frontier Agency the year before. At one point in the deliberations over a couple of days, Secretary Bhoothalingam, also a member of the Indian delegation, jokingly offered to William Bundy, my boss, to swap aides; if this comical deal had gone through, I believe it would've meant somewhat more aggravation for the Americans than the Indians.

And over the following years we managed to get together, not frequently but well, more in the US than in India or Europe, when he was Finance Secretary for Tamilnadu, worked at the World Bank and the Brandt Commission, later becoming a Professor at the Madras Institute of Development Studies; while I scurried around Washington and went back to Harvard and later on to the United Nations. We discussed and shared our work with mutual curiosity, stimulation and respect, providing tasty food for our thoughts and grist, even gristle, for our mills.

Once I asked Guhan what he thought of a colleague of mine in the State Department whom he knew. This person held a position of some responsibility dealing in South Asian Affairs, and was very talented, dedicated and industrious. He was hugely enthusiastic and ingratiating, and one who did not conceal his high moral purpose. Guhan thought for a while, looking away, and then answered: 'I'd rather be stabbed in the back than in the front.' That was good enough for me.

Shanta and Guhan were greatly admired and loved by our four children, and on occasion took them in when Katie and I travelled, which I think was very special for everyone. Two images I have from these times remain vivid and recur frequently in my mind's and soul's eyes. Once Guhan went with us to a local carnival which had set up on Route One in Virginia just south of Washington. Guhan accompanied our daughter Jenny, who was six years old, on the Ferris Wheel, which particular adventure I would not have expected from either one of them, let alone together. But off they went, and the others from our band watched from below. When the ride was over, the wheel had to pause in increments to let the passengers in each seat dismount at the bottom, and when Guhan and Jenny were at the very top the procedure was delayed for some reason which left them for several minutes suspended there in mid-air. They couldn't have looked more different. Jenny was blonde, and so small that she couldn't see over the bar which extended over the laps of the riders to keep them safely in their seat, and with hands gripping it she peered just under it at the scene below. While her companion, tall erect and puffing on a cigarette stared meditatively at the far Appalachian horizon. They never spoke. Yet the companionship was certain.

The second image came from a picnic our two families shared one summer on Cape Cod, in Massachusetts. We had to walk some distance across the sand at Nauset Beach on this occasion, carrying our baskets and various accountrements. Shanta and Guhan had spotted and immediately put to use a long pole, in the middle of which they slung some bundles of food and clothing. Each carrying one end, they moved at length toward the Atlantic surf line. I see them making their way slowly, alone, hitched by their pole, silhouetted against the sand and sky, bathed by sun and breeze, timeless.

Guhan wrote us ('Dear Katie and Jonathan—in that order!') in the spring of 1997 after we had telephoned Madras upon hearing very late of his illness. He said it was 'heart-warming and a joy' to have heard our voices, inquired of all the children, including Joan Brooke's poetry and Joss in Dublin, and provided a very clear and cool recital of the history and present status of his medical condition: post-radiation weakness, moving around, producing written output, good spirits, no pain, Shanta very cheerful and supportive as only she could be. 'Meanwhile, while there is life there is hope or more importantly, where there is hope there is life!' And then: 'However, I feel absolutely wretched that I have brought all this on myself and my friends because of smoking. The humiliation of it all is the worst part of it.'

Another letter in the fall outlined plans for their November–December visit to the States, a Yale, Princeton, Harvard and Columbia academic tour during which he would see his friend Amartya Sen and hopefully us during the Cambridge segment. In this letter he assigned me with barely feigned imperiousness the job of travel agent, scheduler, logistician and virtual valet, in debasing detail, concluding with: 'Please oblige efficiently and fast so as to wipe out the memory of your abysmal performance at the bus in Orleans where you failed to identify a brown, Asian wayfarer of three decades acquaintance among all of three passengers!' Needless to say, I was really looking forward to seeing him, loaded for bear.

The visit would not be implemented as planned, and Katie and I and Charley high-tailed it down to the Yale-New Haven Hospital shortly after they had landed, as soon as we got word what was going on. That was the last time I saw him. He would return home and rally, but now he was dying, and the five of us made a party out of our reunion. We scribbled notes when he wasn't croaking hoarsely, frolicked about his room, imitated the doctors, exchanged small gifts, insulted one another, wept and laughed. It was a spiritual feast. Charley wrote in a poem which he sent to Guhan:

> Sanjivi Guhan wore a clear oxygen mask
> To get more oxygen to his cells
> Because he was short of breath
> Though his first name wasn't Sanjivi
> His wife gave the Yale-New Haven people that
> To placate them when she insisted
> His name was simply Guhan
> Plus he let it fall away from his face
> More nearly
> He took it off
> To speak
> No matter if it tired him out
> Mostly he said

His wife was his audio
The phlegm over his vocal chords
Made his voice faint
He growled with that Madras clip
His caustic wit characteristic
Yet even more defeating
With his whisper...

Later, I read the paper he had brought with him for the Workshop at Yale, 'Three Pieces on Governance'. I wish that I had been able to talk with him about it. The pieces are erudite, incisive, stimulating and useful. It is a privilege to think about what governance should be in concrete terms with the help of Aristotle, Locke, Berlin Rawls—and Guhan, a pleasure to develop governance as a moral conception. Moreover, the paper is great fun to read (and not just during the exposition of the World Bank's lack of moral innards); he is very alive in it, you can feel him going at it intellectually and psychically. He wrote that 'Our concern is with the promotion of good governance in the real world. How can the conceptions relating to principles, institutions and structures...help in any practical way?' He pursues this in discussing avoidance of both pessimism and complacency, tracking pluralities, accommodating passions and interests in a competetive democracy, channelling an underlying tolerance into practical actions.

Taken together, these essays are extraordinarily useful to me, for one, in ongoing activity for the UN, including dealing with governance issues in post-conflict societies. They press me to keep thinking, keep searching. The paper now travels with me, something of his which helps me carry on. In this and other ways he's still around—needling, futilely suppressing a grin, challenging, encouraging.

MY LIFE AND CRIMES WITH MR S. GUHAN

B. K. Nehru[7]

Though I had met Guhan earlier, my real contact with him started when he came to Washington in 1964.

---

[7] B. K. Nehru joined the Indian Civil Service in 1934. In the course of his career he has been a Member of the Indian Legislative Assembly (1939); Minister Economic, Embassy of India, Washington, DC and Indian Director, International

It is curious that the fact that Guhan was technically a First Secretary in the Indian Embassy of which I was the head, was one which I had completely forgotten though I well remember that he was also the Indian Alternate Director of the World Bank. The explanation however is simple. Guhan's rank in the Embassy being relatively low, I presume he did not have the 'distinction' of attending the weekly meeting of the Ambassador with the senior members of the Embassy, a meeting which was designed to coordinate—and hopefully succeeded in so doing—the activities of the various sections of the Embassy.

Rank cannot, however, conceal ability and Guhan's ability which extended far beyond matters of finance could not be concealed for long. It was soon discovered that his knowledge and his views were of value not only in handling questions in which India was diplomatically interested and concerned, but extended to almost every thing concerning the development of human society throughout the world.

The result was that the influence of this technically junior officer on what His Excellency the Ambassador thought and did was often greater than that of his senior colleagues. The person whose views were almost always sought on everything was Mr S. Guhan, hidden away in his small room in the Embassy building on Massachusetts Avenue.

Guhan's knowledge was so extensive, his reading so wide, his personal contacts with the intelligentsia of Washington so close that roots of the international respect with which he was later listened to had already been laid and had already begun to bear fruit during the relatively short time he had been in Washington.

His ability to express himself with vigour and in the smallest number of words was obvious and his capacity to argue a case and convert his opponents to his own views was already becoming as evident, within a smaller circle, as it became, in a larger circle, in later life. The Indian Ambassador was not slow to take advantage of this. Contrary to the practice in the rest of the world where Ambassadors are not expected to open their mouths in public, they are required in the United States to give public speeches all the time. It was,

---

Bank for Reconstruction and Development (1949–54); India's Ambassador to the USA (1961–8); High Commissioner in London (1973–7); and Governor of Jammu and Kashmir (1981–4) and Gujarat (1984–6). In 1999, he received the Padma Vibhushan.

therefore, not unoften that I gave the drafts of my speeches to Guhan to amend or to criticize, and thereby increased their effectiveness.

My relationship with him grew from a mere official one based on his ability to one of mutual confidence, intimacy, respect, and later, affection. This was born out of the fact that we discovered that we had similar ethical and moral values and our common aims were to serve our country. To me it was obvious that Guhan was no careerist but that every action of his and every piece of advice he gave had nothing whatever to do with his own welfare or advancement but was designed solely for the advancement of our common purpose.

In the growth of this personal friendship, Guhan's gracious wife Shanta was an important factor. Ambassadors' wives in Washington bear a great burden, or at least they did, in Jack Kennedy's Camelot. What with receptions and dinners and visitors from India added to the work my wife did for the Handicrafts Board, help was needed. And she found in the person of Shanta Guhan not only willingness and ability but all the qualities her husband had found in Guhan. It is said—by no means wrongly—that behind every success of man there is a woman. In Guhan's case, the peace, tranquility and competence of his wife were no small factor in the heights he achieved.

Neither Guhan nor I was too happy with all the economic policies which were followed by our government. Though both of us seemed to have started as vigorous supporters of socialism we did not agree to the interpretation that was finally given to it in practice. This had led to governmental control, not only of the 'commanding heights of the economy', as the progenitor of this policy, Jawaharlal Nehru, had desired, but had spread itself to control over every detail and every aspect of the economy, with government taking upon itself every economic activity that might occur to any minister. The result was that the rate of growth of national income had been limited to the 'Hindu rate' of 3 per cent per annum. The potential that had been developed since independence as a result of the governmental emphasis on training in science and technology and management had already created a possibility of growth at a much faster rate. While we defended our policies vigorously against the foreign attacks on it, as we were in duty bound, we did not hesitate to tell our government that it was high time they were changed. This had no effect, our policies did not even begin to be changed until eight years ago.

During my time in Washington we were required to handle two of the major harmful effects of our economic policies. The first was the question of the exchange rate of the rupee. Through a continuous deficit in our balance of payments we had exhausted the substantial 'Sterling Balances' which had been created by our sacrifices during the Second World War. Further, in spite of continuous fiscal deficits which reduced the purchasing power of the rupee, we had refused to apply the natural remedy of devaluing it.

The International Monetary Fund, the World Bank and the American Treasury were insisting that before they gave us the money, which was required to finance our Third Five-Year Plan, we should bring down the value of the rupee to a realistic rate. Every economist in India regarded this as essential; so did our economic representatives in Washington, fully supported by Guhan and myself.

Today, 'adjustments' or devaluations are made by the Reserve Bank every day without any 'comment' by anybody. But in the days of the fixed rate of exchange enforced by the IMF, a demand for devaluation was regarded as interference with our sovereignty. After much and continuous argument with Delhi, rationality prevailed and the rupee was devalued. But Mrs Gandhi had to pay a terrific political price for this sensible action, and we in Washington were cursed for advocating surrender to the neo-colonialists. Naturally, Guhan's name was never mentioned, but I as the big boss was considered fit to be lynched.

The second consequence of our out-of-date economic policy that we had to face was the effect of the droughts of 1965 and 1966. For two whole years we were dependent on the mercy of the United States to keep ourselves alive. We had no foodgrains in stock and no money to buy them with. Once again we had, under foreign pressure, to review our policies, this time relating to our agriculture, to permit the farmer to grow what he wanted, to sell at whatever prices he wanted to sell, all of which he had not earlier been permitted to do. We did our bit by getting the food; the pressure for changes was this time applied directly by Orville Freeman, then Secretary of Agriculture, on our Food and Agriculture Minister at an FAO meeting in Rome.

I left Washington quite some time before Guhan, but our contact continued through correspondence and became easier when he came back home even though he soon had got himself transferred to Tamilnadu instead of remaining at the Centre where his chances of career advancement were much greater. I would suspect that the real reason for this was that he wanted to look after his ageing father, the distinguished Doctor Sanjivi, who had set up a charitable hospital for the continuous betterment of which he lived. The devotion with which Guhan and Shanta attended to him was obvious even to the casual outsider such as ourselves.

Though Guhan had deliberately so isolated himself, his international fame was such that he was hijacked to become Senior Economist to the Brandt Commission. And I daresay that the report of that Commission must have owed a great deal to Guhan's ideas and his drafting.

On his return from Geneva he did come officially—I am not sure in what capacity—to Assam and he took a few days off to stay with me. He also came to Gandhinagar to assure himself that I was discharging my gubernatorial duties properly. Though we were separated geographically, the bonds between us continued to grow till the relation became one of a younger brother and the elder. Not that Guhan showed to me the traditional respect that Indians show for age: he continued to oppose my ideas and sometimes, he did so, merely to enjoy the fun of pulling my leg!

Our understanding of, and affection for, each other did not mean that we agreed on everything. In fact, we disagreed vehemently on some subjects—one of which was the relationship between the Centre and the states. Here I was, and continue to be, of the view that it is not desirable to transfer any further powers from the Centre to the states than listed in the Constitution as it stands today. The usurping of states' powers by the Centre through the mechanism of a planned economy which demands much greater centralization of authority than the Constitution, when it was framed, intended, is swiftly being given up by the Centre through the liberalization of industry and of the market.

Another point of disagreement was my advocacy of our parliamentary system of democracy being replaced with a presidential one. This was also unacceptable to Guhan, primarily, I think, because he felt—and quite wrongly—that it would take away power from the states and transfer them to the President of India.

My disagreement with his views was also in the matter of his relations with the DMK. I did not understand how and why he became a very effective adviser to the DMK: a party based on caste was, for me, one which, by definition, had values which were difficult for me to accept. How and why Guhan did so, and how he had so much faith in the DMK, I cannot still understand.

These differences of opinion and of ideas which kept us so affectionately together can no longer, unfortunately, be enjoyed by me. I can have arguments on these subjects with a whole lot of other people but the pleasure that crossing swords with Guhan gave me is no longer, alas, available. Nor is the pleasure of seeing Guhan and Shanta at the airport in Chennai in the middle of the night, waiting for us to arrive from Delhi and taking charge of us, as dutiful and affectionate children do of their parents.

GUHAN: A CHARMER AND AN ACTIVIST

I. G. Patel[8]

It is said that the end is in the beginning. From what I knew of Guhan in the sixties and the early seventies during our association with the Department of Economic Affairs, I could hardly have guessed that the return to Tamilnadu would transform him into an insightful social scientist driven by a keen sense of social activism. I first knew him as TTK's private secretary—someone whom TTK had marked out, as was his wont, for broad-based training with a view to preparing him for assuming the highest positions in economic ministries. TTK had a genius for spotting talent and he knew the value of learning by doing. But young men marked out for upward mobility are not always popular, and the less so if they sit outside the Finance Minister's office and are privy to all kinds of official secrets, personal and related to policies. When he was sent to Washington at an early age, he could not have added to his circle of friends in Delhi.

But the truth was otherwise. Guhan was a charmer then, and he remained that, gratefully, till the end. It was not just that he had a sharp intellect and a wry sense of humour—qualities not uncommon in civil servants coming from south of the Vindhyas. He had that most

---

[8] I. G. Patel has been Secretary in the Department of Economic Affairs, Government of India; Governor of the Reserve Bank of India; Director of the London School of Economics; and Deputy Administrator at the United Nations Development Programme. He is currently Chairman of the Indian Institute of Management, Ahmedabad and of the Indian Council for Research in International Economic Affairs, New Delhi.

mysterious of smiles, now there and gone the next moment. In fact, there was something elfin, fey and ethereal about his composure and demeanour. His presence and discourse were arresting. But if they held you, it was by gossamer threads. There was nothing heavy or imposing about it. And you discovered soon that his wry humour and even biting sarcasm were thin veneers under which lay a very affectionate and loyal heart. I have to admit that this side of his character became more transparent after Shanta appeared on the scene. We virtually ceased to be colleagues in the office and became instead friends for a lifetime, united in largely unspoken or unexpressed affection and admiration, which extended to our spouses and my daughter.

I remember an evening in New York in March 1966. Pitamber Pant and I, among others, had accompanied Mrs Gandhi on her first visit to the US after becoming the Prime Minister. Our daughter, Rehana, was born just a few days before we left India. The Guhans, who were in Washington then, were most anxious to celebrate the birth of Rehana. But how was this to be done in the midst of all the hectic activity in which the Indian delegation was involved? Guhan planned that at the large dinner in New York, no one would notice our absence if we sneaked out at some stage. He also arranged for some of our American friends from Washington to be around. And sneak out we did, in our Bandhgala national dress and resplendent saris—and retired to a discotheque where we were given free admission, as we were members of Mrs Gandhi's party! This sense of fun and mischief was another aspect of Guhan's endearing character. On their return to Delhi, the Guhans and we were part of a circle of friends interested in Indian classical music and dance and I recall many wonderful evenings together. It was not surprising that on his return to Tamilnadu, Guhan did so much to encourage young artists as well as support old teachers.

Watching all this talent and sociability, one would have safely predicted an end as Finance Secretary and Governor of the Reserve Bank. But suddenly Guhan took the other and more difficult road of a scholar, researcher, reformer and indeed an activist. And what a wonderful success he made of his new incarnation! I am not competent to write about this phase of his life in detail as we got physically separated in 1972 and met only occasionally thereafter. But the testimony is all there. Most of us were surprised when we heard that he was actively associated with the DMK Government. But his association and commitment were not to any particular administration, rather to the people of Tamilnadu in particular, and India in general. And throughout, he retained his interest in the advocacy of an equitable and progressive international economic order.

How do we account for this radical turn in his life? Was it there from the beginning? I doubt it. Although his family background was academic and scholarly, his passion was for academics only as a means. His heart responded to the suffering of the people and the injustice of the system. I suspect the influence of persons like Pitamber Pant had a part to play. There is no doubt that the change was a conscious effort of will and could not have been easy to make and sustain. And it was what he made of himself and not what birth and upbringing had given him that commands our admiration.

We saw little of each other after 1972. But he was always there when needed. Unknown to me, he conspired with Manu Shroff to organize a felicitation volume on my completing sixty years, and the contents of this volume landed on my table as I reached the London School of Economics in 1984. After my return to India in 1990, I visited him in Chennai on at least one occasion when despite my plane coming very late, he came to see me around 10 p.m. to make sure that I spent enough time with him and Shanta during my short stay. Even as he valiantly struggled towards the end against ill-health, he lost none of his charm nor passion. The end, when it came, took a lot of sunshine away from many lives.

S. GUHAN: A MEMOIR[9]

Manu Shroff[10]

In the sad demise of Sanjivi Guhan, the profession of economics has lost one of the most brilliant recruits to it from the civil service. For the past two decades and more since he took premature retirement from the Indian Administrative Service, Guhan has been a widely admired contributor to the thinking on a variety of social

[9] Reprinted from the *Economic Times*, 17 February 1998.
[10] Manu Shroff worked in the central government, mainly in the Ministry of Finance Department of Economic Affairs for the major part of his career. He has been India's Alternate Executive Director on the World Bank and Adviser in the Indian Planning Commission. After leaving government service, he has been a Professor at the Indian Institute of Management, Ahmedabad, and Editor of the *Economic Times*. He is a Member of the Governing Council of the Indian Council of Research in International Economic Relations.

and economic issues, in particular for his characteristic penchant for polemics, which, however, never detracted from his keen analysis of data presented with meticulous care and scholarship. He read widely and had a deep interest in philosophy, the social sciences, history, literature and art. An evening spent with him was greatly rewarding as he entertained his guests with wit and wisdom laced with many an anecdote from his varied experience in civil service and outside.

Guhan's writings spanned a wide range, but the focus was always on problems of development. Centre-state relations was a favourite subject with him; he commented on the terms of reference and the final recommendations of successive Finance Commissions and on the need to decentralize economic power. He railed against the abuse of Article 356 of the Constitution and championed the cause of its abolition. He wanted the states to have a greater command over resources; when the Tenth Finance Commission recommended an alternative scheme for transferring to the states 29 per cent of the tax revenue of the Centre, he asked for 40 per cent, saying that the Finance Commission verdict was no more than the prejudices of five men! Guhan was perhaps the first, if not the only, economist to prepare a comprehensive scheme for social security and could claim a part of the credit for the beginnings made in this field.

Guhan was intolerant of administrative agencies making stupid rules and following outmoded conventions. He was responsible for streamlining industrial licensing procedures and the smooth functioning of the Secretariat for Industrial Approvals which he helped set up. He supported economic reforms but was not bowled over by the notion of market orientation, being for ever conscious of the problems of poverty and inequalities and the role of the state in overcoming them. He agonized over the hijacking of the state by corrupt politicians and tended to lapse into cynicism. But he never tired of dreaming up systemic solutions which would lift the country out of the morass.

Most of the time he spent in Delhi was in the Department of Economic Affairs where he was involved in issues of foreign aid. From his position as India's Alternate Executive Director at the World Bank, he participated in the discussions leading to the devaluation of the rupee in 1966 and the subsequent aid negotiations. At one point, in an effort to tackle the Doubting Thomases in the Indian delegation, he demanded, in an after-dinner discussion, that each member must state his position in one sentence—no more. The wafflers were thus isolated and neutralized. He was an artful negotiator and commanded the respect of his opposite numbers. Bernie Bell (the author of the controversial Bell Mission Report) was known for his evangelical zeal about the ideas he had propounded. He was equally adamant on his projections of aid requirements after the devaluation of the rupee. After a lengthy meeting running into the late evening, during which we presented detailed justification for a minimum of one billion dollars of aid, Bernie did not budge. Guhan then came down heavily on him with the remark: 'Bernie, your refusal to see the point suggests that the greater is your knowledge the less becomes your understanding!' One could go on reciting other instances of Guhan's brilliance in committees or his incisive comments on file. That he won the confidence and admiration of T. T. Krishanamachari, B. K. Nehru and I. G. Patel as also eminent academics like Jagdish Bhagwati, Amartya Sen and T. N. Srinivasan among others is a testimony to his ability and dedication.

After retirement from service (his last post was Finance Secretary, Tamilnadu), Guhan was with the Madras Institute of Development Studies. Earlier, he was with the Brandt Commission where his insights on aid relationship proved valuable. While in MIDS, he kept writing on a variety of issues and even started taking active interest in public affairs in Tamilnadu. Before the disease struck him a couple of years ago, he was Adviser to Mr Karunanidhi and was perhaps getting ready to be drawn into the political fray. His illness slowed him down but till the end he kept reading and writing, the last piece being an Essay on Governance which he presented at a Seminar at Yale last autumn. It is truly tragic that a life so full of further promise fell prey to cancer, caused in all probability by smoking, an addiction common to many intellectuals.

Once during a stopover in London on returning from Washington, we were resting after lunch. I was keen to go out and look at some exhibition or the other and I asked Guhan to get ready to come with me. He sent me a slip of paper containing a quote from W. H. Auden:

> Time for the soul to stretch and spit
> Before the world comes upon it again.

Sadly, the world will not come upon him again.

Requiescat in peace.

A Bibliography of Guhan's Work

Books

Growth, Inequality and Poverty in Tamilnadu, Madras: Cre-A Publications, 1983.
Essays on Economic Progress and Welfare: In Honour of I. G. Patel (ed. with M. R. Shroff), Delhi: Oxford University Press, 1986.
Tamilnadu Economy: Performance and Issues (ed. with C. T. Kurien and A. Vaidyanathan), New Delhi: Oxford IBH, 1988.
Poverty in India: Research and Policy (ed. with Barbara Harriss and R. H. Cassen), Bombay: Oxford University Press, 1992.
The Cauvery River Dispute: Towards Conciliation, Madras: Frontline Publication, 1993.
The World Bank's Lending in South Asia, Washington, DC: The Brookings Institute, 1995.
Adjustment, Employment and Equity in India (with K. Nagaraj), Geneva: International Labour Organization, 1995.
Corruption in India: Agenda for Action (ed. with Samuel Paul), New Delhi: Vision Books, 1997.

Papers

INTERNATIONAL ECONOMIC RELATIONS

'Notes on China, 1979', *MIDS Bulletin*, 1979.
'Need for Economic Diplomany', *Yojana*, 26 January 1980 (also published in *Third World Forum Newsletter*, June 1980).
'The Report of the Brandt Commission', *MIDS Bulletin*, 1980.
The Brandt Commission Papers (as contributor), Independent Bureau for International Development Issues, Geneva—The Hague, 1981.
'International Financial Cooperation: Brandt, Cancun and the 1980s', paper presented at seminar organized by the Bangladesh Institute for Law and International Affairs, 10–11 December 1981.
'The North–South Paradigm', *Seminar*, no. 280, December 1982.
'Notes Towards a General Agreement to Borrow,' paper presented at seminar organized by Indian Council for Research in International Economic Relations and International Economics Research Center, Columbia University, New Delhi, January 1983.

'Global Negotiations: A Pragmatic Approach' (as collaborator), Indian Council for Research in International Economic Relations, New Delhi, February 1983.

'Official and Private Capital Flows: Experience, Agenda for Reform and Way Ahead' (with M. R. Shroff), paper presented at Round Table organized by ICRIER, New Delhi, 17–19 December 1984.

'Some Notes on Automatic Resources for Development', paper presented at seminar organized by the Swedish Ministry of Foreign Affairs, Stockholm, December 1984.

'Adjustment: To What End?', paper presented at Second Conference of the RIS for Non-aligned and Other Developing Countries, New Delhi, 20–2 November 1985.

PUBLIC FINANCE

'The Budget: An Expose', *Aside*, April 1981.

'The Twenty-Point Framework', *Economic and Political Weekly*, 20 March 1982.

'The Finance Commissions: A Critique and a Concept,' Working Paper no. 28, Madras Institute of Development Studies, November 1982.

'Centre–State Fiscal Ties: Some Comments', *Financial Express*, Bombay, March 1983.

'The Union Budget for 1985–86', *MIDS Bulletin*, May 1985.

'Seventh Plan: Hard Targets and Soft Projections', *Economic Times*, Bombay, 11 December 1985.

'Devolution Criteria: From Gamble to Policy', *Economic and Political Weekly*, 1 December 1984 (also published in I. S. Gulati (ed.), *Centre-State Budgetary Transfers*, New Delhi: Oxford University Press, 1987).

'Fiscal Policy, Projections and Performance', *Economic and Political Weekly*, 12 April 1986.

'State Finances in Tamilnadu 1960–85,' Working Paper no. 77, Madras Institute of Development Studies, September 1986.

'Salve Commission Terms: Confusion or Cleverness?', *Economic Times*, Bombay, 28 July 1987.

'Administered Prices: Policies and Principles' in Malcolm S. Adiseshiah (ed.), *Price Policy*, New Delhi: Lancer International, 1987.

'The Budget as Propaganda', *Indian Express*, 17 March 1988.

'Issues before the Ninth Finance Commission: On Closing Pandora's Box', *Economic and Political Weekly*, 6 February 1988.

'The Norm and the Tilt: First Report of the Finance Commission', *Economic and Political Weekly*, 14 January 1989.

'Flawed Devolution Scheme', *Economic and Political Weekly*, 9 June 1990.

'Adjustment in the 1991–92 Budget: Hard-headed or Soft-headed?, *Economic and Political Weekly*, 24 August 1991.

'State Finances in Tamilnadu, 1960-90' in Amaresh Bagchi, J. L. Bajaj and William A. Byrd (eds), *State Finances in India*, Delhi: Vikas Publishing House, 1992.

'Report of the Tenth Finance Commission', *Economic and Political Weekly*, 22 April 1995.

'Social Expenditures in the Union Budget 1991-6', *Economic and Political Weekly*, 6 May 1995.

'Centre-State Fiscal Transfers: Beyond the Tenth Finance Commission' *Economic and Political Weekly*, 15 February 1997.

POVERTY AND POVERTY ALLEVIATION PROGRAMMES

Structure and Intervention: an Evaluation of DPAP, IRDP and Related Programmes in Ramanathapuram and Dharmapuri Districts of Tamilnadu (as project coordinator), Madras Institute of Development Studies, August 1980.

'Rural Poverty: Policy and Play Acting', *Economic and Political Weekly*, 22 November 1980 (also published in K. S. Krishnaswamy (ed.), *Poverty and Income Distribution*, New Delhi: Oxford University Press, 1990).

A Primer on Poverty: India and Tamilnadu, Popular Series no. 2, Madras Institute of Development Studies, April 1981.

Poverty, A Symposium, (as participant), *Financial Express*, Bombay, 20 September 1982.

'Rural Development and the Integral Calculus,' paper presented at the National Workshop on Rural Development and Poverty Alleviation Programmes, National Institute of Rural Development, Hyderbad, 9-11 July 1985.

'Poverty Alleviation: Policy Options', paper presented at seminar organized by the Ministry of Rural Development, Government of India, New Delhi, 26 August 1985.

'Rural Poverty Alleviation in India: Policy, Performance and Possibilities,' paper presented at the Franco-Indian Colloquium on Technological Choices for Rural Development, Montpellier, France, 18-20 March 1986 (also published as *Offprint* no 2, Madras Institute of Development Studies, 1986).

'On Reforming the IRDP', paper presented at seminar on Poverty Alleviation Programmes organized by the Ministry of Programme Implementation, Government of India, New Delhi 1988.

'Aid for the Poor: Lessons and Possibilities from India' in John P. Lewis and contributors, *Strengthening the Poor: What Have we Learned?*, Overseas Development Council, Washington, DC, 1988.

Social Exclusion from a Welfare Rights Perspective: The Case of India (as contributor ILO project), Madras Institute of Development Studies, November 1995.

SOCIAL SECURITY

'Social Security: Lessons and Possibilities from the Tamilnadu Experience', *MIDS Bulletin*, January 1981.

'Against Undeserved Want: Report of the Working Group on Social Security, Economic Administration Reforms Commission', (as Chairman of the Working Group), Government of India, New Delhi, June 1984.

'Reaching Out to the Poor', *Economic Times*, Bombay, December 1986.

'Social Security in India: Looking One Step Ahead', Insurance Institute of India, September 1988 (also published in *MIDS* Reprint Series and in Barbara Hariss, S. Guhan and R. H. Cassen (eds), *Poverty in India: Research and Policy:* Bombay: Oxford University Press, 1992).

Social Security Initiatives in Tamilnadu 1989, WP no. 96, Madras Institute of Development Studies, 1990 (also published in S. Subramanian, *Themes in Development Economics: Essays in Honour of Malcolm S. Adiseshiah*, OUP, Delhi, 1992).

'Social Security for the Poor in the Unorganized Sector: A Feasible Blueprint for India' in Kirit S. Parikh and R. Sudharshan, *Human Development and Structural Adjustment*, Delhi: Macmillan, 1993.

'Safety Nets,' paper presented at seminar organized by Indira Gandhi Institute for Development Research, Bombay, 11–12 January 1993.

'Social Security Options for Developing Countries', paper presented at symposium organized by the International Institute for Labour Studies, Geneva, 22–4 November 1993 (published in *International Labour Review* 133 (1), 1994).

'Towards a Comprehensive Social Security Policy for India,' paper presented at Round Table organized by the International Labour Organization, New Delhi, 16 March 1995.

'Poverty and Social Security' in Shoba Raghuram *et al.* (eds), *Structural Adjustment: Economy, Environment, Social Concerns*, New Delhi: Macmillan, 1995.

'Social Security in India' in Dietmar Rothermund (ed.) *Liberalising India: Progress and Problems*, New Delhi: Manohar, 1996.

'Social Security in India: Recent Research and Policy,' paper presented at symposium held by UNDP and Harvard Center for Population and Development Studies, Cambridge, MA, 23–5 April 1997.

CENTRE–STATE RELATIONS, DECENTRALIZATION

'Administrative Aspects of Centre–State Relations,' paper presented at seminar organized by Karnataka State Planning Council, Bangalore, 5–7 August 1983 (published in *MIDS Bulletin*, October 1983).

'Centre–State Relations: Sarkaria Commission's Questionnaire', *Economic Political Weekly*, 18 February 1984.

'Decentralised Planning and Implementation', paper presented at seminar organized by Rajaji Institute for Public Affairs, Institute for Social and Economic Change and Madras Institute of Development Studies, Bangalore, 29 November 1984.

'A Novel but not New Proposal for Panchayat Elections', paper presented at seminar organized by Rajaji Institute for Public Affairs, 29 November 1984.

'Election Systems for Panchayat', *Indian Express*, 4 March 1987.

'Constitutional Breakdown: In Tamilnadu or New Delhi?' *Frontline*, Madras, 16 February 1991.

'Centre and States in the Reform Process', paper presented at conference at Merton College, Oxford, 27-9 June 1993 (published in Robert Cassen and Vijay Joshi (eds), *India: The Future of Economic Reform*, Delhi: Oxford University Press, 1995).

'Federalism and the New Political Economy in India', paper presented at the workshop organized by the Center for the Advanced Study of India, University of Pennsylvania and Centre for Policy Research, New Delhi, October 1993 (published in Balveer Arora and Dougl as Verney (eds), *Multiple Identities in a Single State*, New Delhi: Konark Press, 1995).

'The Sardar's Long Shadow: The All-India Services, An Issues Paper', paper presented at workshop organized by the Centre for Policy Research, New Delhi, 11-13 January 1995.

RESERVATIONS

'South India and Reservations: A Reply to André Beteille', (with others), *The Hindu*, Madras, 27 October 1990.

'Social Discrimination has to be Corrected', *The Hindu*, Madras, 11 December 1990.

'Reservations: Are Economic Criteria Suitable?', *Economic Times*, Bombay, 25 December 1990.

'Economic Criteria: Problems of Implementation', *Economic Times*, Bombay, 25 December 1990.

'Reservation: The Tamilnadu Experience', *Manushi*, March-June 1991.

'Comprehending Equalities', *EPW*, 1 August 1992.

TAMILNADU ECONOMY AND DEVELOPMENT ISSUES

'Agriculture Aggrieved: Notes and Issues from a Tour in Kinathukadavu, Coimbatore District', Madras Institute of Development Studies, July 1980.

'Madras Urban Development: Towards a Policy Frame', *MIDS Bulletin*, June 1981.

'Tamilnadu—An Overall Assessment', *Economic Times*, Bombay, 14 August 1981.

'Health in Tamilnadu: Facts and Issues,' WP no. 21, Madras Institute of Development Studies, October 1981.

'Irrigation in Tamilnadu: A Survey', WP no. 49, Madras Institute of Development Studies, June 1984.

'Economic Performance of Tamilnadu', *Indian Express*, 29 October 1987.

Tamilnadu Economy: Performance and Issues (as editorial coordinator and contributor), New Delhi: Oxford & IBH, 1988.

'Tamilnadu Economy', *India Today* (Tamil), 21 August 1990.

'A Pragmatic View on Prohibition', *The Hindu*, 6 May 1991.

'The Cauvery Dispute: What Next?', *Frontline*, Madras, 13 August 1993.

'Cauvery Dispute: Seizing an Opportunity', *Frontiline*, 14 January 1995.

'The Unquiet River', *The Hindu*, 8 January 1996.

'Cauvery Dispute: Combine Conciliation and Adjudication', *Frontline*, 9 August 1996.

VILLAGE STUDIES

'Village Studies in Tamilnadu: Availability and Suggestions for Further Work', Digest Series no. 1, Madras Institute of Development Studies, February 1980.

'Iruvelpattu Revisited', (with Joan P. Mencher), WP no. 28, Madras Institute of Development Studies, September 1982 (also published in *EPW*, 4 and 11 June 1983).

'Palakurichi: A Resurvey', WP no. 42, Madras Institute of Development Studies, November 1983.

'Dusi: A Resurvey', (with K. Bharathan), WP no. 52, Madras Institute of Development Studies, December 1984.

'Thirty One Villages of Tamilnadu: The 1961 Census Monographs', Digest Series no. 4, Madras Institute of Development Studies, June 1985.

'Resurvey of Slater Villagers in Tamilnadu', *MIDS Bulletin*, November 1985 (also published in ICSSR Research Abstracts July–December 1991).

'Systematic Elementary Village Studies', paper presented at workshop on Measurement of Rural Economic Change: Differences in Approach and Results of Village Studies and Large-scale Surveys, by Social Science Research Council, New York and Indian Statistical Institute, Banglore, 5–8 August 1985.

OTHERS

'Bharatanatyam by T. Balasarsawati' (translation), *National Centre for the Performing Art Quarterly Journal*, Bombay, December 1976.

'A Note on State-level Industrialisation in the Indian Context', Madras Institute of Development Studies, January 1980.

'Bala's Sringara', *Sruti*, 1 March 1981.

'Planning: A New Approach to State Planning?, *Economic and Political Weekly,* 18 April 1981.
'The Service Society', (as participant), *The Hindu,* 16 June 1981.
'Financing of Education', paper presented at National Seminar on Financing of Education in India, Ministry of Human Resource Development, Government of India, Madras, 23–5 October 1981.
'Towards a Policy for Analysis' in R. S. Ganapathy *et al.* (eds), *Public Policy and Policy Analysis in India,* New Delhi: Sage Publications, 1985.
'State Planning: Some Issues', (with A. Vaidyanathan), paper presented at annual conference of Indian Economic Society, Tirupati, 25–6 October 1995.
'Bureaucracy', (as participant), *Financial Express,* 6 October 1986.
'Bridging the Gap', *The Independent,* 27 October 1990.
'Bala on Bharatnatyam' (translations), *Sruti,* November 1991.
'The Urban Economy in India: Facts, Issues and Policy', paper presented at seminar organized by the governments of Germany and India, Berlin, 4–6 November 1991.
'Designers as Part of India's Life', in *Reflections on Design,* Ahmedabad: National Institute of Design, 1992.
'The Shepherd's Cut', *The Hindu,* 26 July 1992.
'Health in India During a Period of Economic Adjustment', The Fr James S. Tong Memorial Oration, Voluntary Health Association of India, New Delhi, 4 September 1992.
'Sunya is the Solution', *Seminar,* no. 402, February 1993.
'Dark Forebodings', in Jitendra Bajaj (ed.), *Ayodhya and the Future India,* Madras: Centre for Policy Studies, 1993.
'The Business of Business', *Business India* 15th anniversary issue, 1993.
'An Unfulfilled Vision', *IASSI Quarterly,* July–December 1993.
'A. K. Ramanujan, The Man and the Scholar', *Frontline,* Madras, 13 August 1993.
'What then Must We Do?', paper presented at seminar organized by the Rajiv Gandhi Foundation, Vadodara, 13 November 1994.
'Breakthrough in Sri Lanka', *The Hindu,* 8 August 1995.
'The Cat and the Mahatma', *The Hindu,* Young World, 9 March 1996.
'So Far, Very Good', *Frontline,* 27 December 1996.
'Shelvankar Remembered', *The Hindu,* 8 January 1997.

CONSULTANCY REPORTS

Financial Management System of the Lanka Jatika Sarvodaya Shramadana Sangamaya, Ford Foundation, September 1981.
'Thailand Country Study', Asian Development Bank Manila, April 1982.
Marga: An Evaluation (with J. D. B. Miller), Ford Foundation, July 1983.
Review of the Role and Functions of the Development Bank of Western Samoa, Asian Development Bank Manila, August 1984.

The Indian Council for Research on International Economic Relations: An Evaluation Report (with David G. Wall), Ford Foundation, May 1985.

The State Resource Centre, Tamilnadu: An Evaluation, Tamilnadu Board of Continuing Education, January 1986.

'Report of the Group on the IIFT, TDA and TFAI', (as Chairman), Ministry of Commerce, Government of India, September 1986.

Grants-in-Aid to PVOs in Family Welfare and Health: India, Maharashtra and Tamilnadu, World Bank, November 1986.

World Bank's Project Supervision Activities in India (with Ajit Mozoomdar), World Bank, January 1989.

The World Bank's Project Lending in South Asia, The Brookings Institution, Washington, DC, December 1992.

The World Bank in India, World Bank, New Delhi, October 1993.

'Adjustment, Employment and Equity in India', (with K. Nagarai), International Labour Organization, Geneva, December 1993.

The Marga Institute: an Evaluation, International Development Research Center, Canada and Ford Foundation, New Delhi, April 1994.

Oxford
s/4581
27/11/2001